ESSENTIALS OF TORTS

SECOND EDITION

ESSENTIALS OF TORTS

SECOND EDITION

WILLIAM P. STATSKY

WEST

THOMSON LEARNING™

Australia Canada Mexico Singapore Spain United Kingdom United States

WEST LEGAL STUDIES

Essentials of Torts, Second Edition
by William P. Statsky

Business Unit Director:
Susan L. Simpfenderfer

Executive Editor:
Marlene McHugh Pratt

Acquisitions Editor:
Joan M. Gill

Developmental Editor:
Rhonda Dearborn

Editorial Assistant:
Lisa Flatley

Executive Production Manager:
Wendy A. Troeger

Production Editor:
Betty L. Dickson

Cover Design:
John Walker Design

Executive Marketing Manager:
Donna J. Lewis

Channel Manager:
Nigar Hale

For permission to use material from this text or product, contact
us by
Tel: (800) 730-2214
Fax (800) 730-2215
www.thomsonrights.com

Library of Congress Cataloging-in-Publication Data

Statsky, William P.
   Essentials of torts/William P. Statsky.—2nd ed.
     p. cm.
   Includes index.
   ISBN 0-7668-1157-3
     1. Torts—United States. 2. Legal assistants—United States—
Handbooks, manuals, etc. I. Title.

KF1250 .S73 2000
346.7303—dc21   00-049945

NOTICE TO THE READER

Publisher does not warrant or guarantee any of the products described herein or perform any independent analysis in connection with any of the product information contained herein. Publisher does not assume, and expressly disclaims, any obligation to obtain and include information other than that provided to it by the manufacturer.

The reader is notified that this text is an educational tool, not a practice book. Since the law is in constant change, no rule or statement of law in this book should be relied upon for any service to any client. The reader should always refer to standard legal sources for the current rule or law. If legal advice or other expert assistance is required, the services of the appropriate professional should be sought.

The Publisher makes no representation or warranties of any kind, including but not limited to, the warranties of fitness for particular purpose or merchantability, nor are any such representations implied with respect to the material set forth herein, and the publisher takes no responsibility with respect to such material. The publisher shall not be liable for any special, consequential, or exemplary damages resulting, in whole or part, from the readers' use of, or reliance upon, this material.

CONTENTS

Dedication

For Commie and Bob Farrell

Tort law has a profound effect on our way of life. It is the arena of law that is primarily responsible for trying to make citizens "whole" after they have been injured by the wrongs, i.e., by the torts, of others. From a broader perspective, the fear of being a defendant in a tort case has caused substantial change in a number of areas. There are public swimming pools and playgrounds, for example, that have shut down because of the increasing number of lawsuits they have faced due to injuries at these facilities. Some doctors have ceased practicing certain specialities because of the frequency of tort litigation in those specialties and the high cost of purchasing malpractice liability insurance. In 1995, the Girl Scouts were spending $120,000 a year for liability insurance. Some charge that we live in an era of government by tort litigation in the sense that judges and juries in tort cases have brought about change that the political system has been unable or unwilling to achieve. Tobacco is a primary example. Hundreds of thousands of deaths a year result from illnesses caused by tobacco. Yet this staggering reality has not caused legislators and other political leaders to impose more stringent safety and health controls on the tobacco industry. The onslaught of multi-billion dollar tort judgments, however, is about to change this dynamic.

At the Republican National Convention in 1992, Former President George H. Bush made the following observation: "Sharp lawyers are running wild. Doctors are afraid to practice medicine. And some moms and pops won't even coach Little League anymore. We must sue each other less and care for each other more. I'm fighting to reform our legal system, to put an end to crazy lawsuits." *Them Crazy Lawsuits,* 55 Texas Bar Journal 1114 (December, 1992). One of our goals in this book is to help you determine whether such attacks on our tort system are valid as we take a dispassionate look at tort law in the twenty-first century.

The book is based on material in Statsky's *Torts: Personal Injury Litigation,* Fourth edition (2001). This Essentials edition deletes material on general litigation and both condenses and updates coverage of tort law.

CHAPTER FORMAT

Each chapter includes features designed to assist students in understanding the material:

- A chapter outline at the beginning of each chapter provides a preview of the major topics in each chapter.
- Figures and tables are used extensively to clarify concepts and present detailed information in an organized chart form.
- Assignments are included within most chapters that ask students to apply concepts to particular fact situations.
- A chapter summary at the end of each chapter provides a concise review of the main concepts discussed.
- Key terms are printed in bold face type the first time they appear in each chapter. Also, a list of key terms is found at the end of each chapter to help students review important terminology introduced in that chapter.

- Examples are used extensively to highlight critical legal doctrines and practices.
- Prior to the discussion of every major tort in a chapter you will find a comprehensive checklist of definitions, defenses, relationships, paralegal roles, and research references for the tort. The checklist is designed to provide the "big picture" by making connections between the particular tort examined in the chapter and related material on other torts discussed in other chapters. The checklist will also serve as an on-the-job refresher for the individual torts.

CHANGES IN THE SECOND EDITION

- Many new and revised examples and assignments are included.
- The material on medical malpractice has been expanded in Chapter 12.
- The chapters give greater attention to the role of constitutional law and torts, particularly in the areas of civil rights, defamation, invasion of privacy, and intentional infliction of emotional distress.
- A new section on tort law on the Internet has been added to Chapter 1. In addition, the comprehensive checklists on the major torts throughout the book now include online references to the law governing specific torts.
- Expanded coverage on tort reform is found in the chapters on products liability and workers' compensation.
- New material on the use of computers in a torts practice has been added such as software for the calculation of damages discussed in Chapter 14.
- New material on torts committed through e-mail and the Internet has been added to Chapters 20 and 21.
- The main negligence chapters now come after most of the chapters on the intentional torts in order to take advantage of the analytical foundation that intentional torts provide for negligence.
- New material on the purposes of tort law and the creation of tort law by statute has been added to Chapter 1.
- A new chapter on strict liability has been added (Chapter 9) covering areas other than products liability, which is covered in Chapter 16.
- The negligence chapters now include the special statutory protection for the Good Samaritan against tort liability.
- In the negligence and products liability chapters, greater attention is given to risk-benefit analysis in determining whether there has been a breach of duty.
- Chapter 15 on negligence defenses includes greater coverage on the impact of comparative negligence on assumption of risk and the other defenses to negligence.

TEACHING AIDS AND SUPPLEMENTS

- **Instructor's Manual with Test Bank** by William Statsky contains suggested answers to the assignments in the text, as well as teaching suggestions. The Test Bank contains true/false, multiple-choice, and discussion questions for each chapter. The questions are designed to test a student's knowledge of major chapter concepts.
- **Computerized Test Bank**—The Test Bank found in the Instructor's Manual is also available in a computerized format on CD-ROM. The platforms supported include Windows™ 3.1 and 95, Windows™ NT, and Macintosh. Features include:

  Multiple methods of question selection
  Multiple outputs—that is, print, ASCII, and RTF

Graphic support (black and white)
Random questioning output
Special character support

- **Survival Manual for Paralegal Students,** written by Bradene Moore and Kathleen Reed of the University of Toledo, provides tips for making the most of paralegal courses. ISBN 0-314-22111-5.
- **Strategies and Tips for Paralegal Educators,** written by Anita Tebbe of Johnson County Community College, provides teaching strategies specifically designed for paralegal educators. It concentrates on how to teach and is organized in three parts: the WHO of Paralegal education—students and teachers; the WHAT of paralegal education—goals and objectives; and the HOW of paralegal education—methods of instruction, methods of evaluation, and other aspects of teaching. A copy of this pamphlet is available to each adopter of a West text. ISBN 0-314-04971-1.
- **WESTLAW**® West's on-line computerized legal research system offers students hands-on experience with a system commonly used in law offices. Qualified adopters can receive 10 free hours of WESTLAW®. WESTLAW® can be accessed with Macintosh and IBM PC and compatibles. A modem is required.
- **Court TV Videos** West Legal Studies is pleased to offer the following videos from Court TV. Available for a minimal fee:
  - Fentress v. Eli Lilly & Co., et al—Prozac on Trial
    Joseph Wesbecker, a manic depressive on Prozac, returned to the printing plant from which he was on disability leave, shot and killed eight coworkers, wounded 12 others and then killed himself. Five years later, victims and relatives sue Eli Lilly, the manufacturer of Prozac, for product liability. First Aired August 1995. ISBN 0-7668-1099-5.
  - Ohio v. Alfieri—Road Rage
    A woman is tried under Ohio's new fetal homicide statute after she causes a car accident that injured a woman and killed her six-month-old fetus. First Aired October 1997. ISBN 0-7668-1099-2.
- **West's Paralegal Video Library** includes:
  - ABA Mock Trial Video—Anatomy of a Trial: A Contracts Case ISBN #0-314-07343-44
  - ABA Mock Trial Video—Product Liability ISBN #0-314-07342-6

These videos are available free to qualified adopters.

- **Web page** Come visit our Web site at *www.westlegalstudies.com,* where you will find a page dedicated to this text with sample material, hotlinks, and content updates. You will also find valuable information about our other West Legal Studies texts.

ACKNOWLEDGMENTS

Valuable contributions have been made to this edition by the team at West Legal Studies, an imprint of Delmar, a division of Thomson Learning. My thanks to Joan Gill, Acquisitions Editor, Rhonda Dearborn, Developmental Editor, Lisa Flatley, Editorial Assistant, and Betty Dickson, Production Editor.

Katherine Arnold
Loyola University, IL

Laura Barnard
Lakeland community College, OH

Anna Drummond
Chaplain College, VT

Paul D. Marsella, Ph.D.
Salem State College, MA

H. Margaret Nickerson
William Woods University, MO

> Please note the Internet resources are of a time sensitive nature and URL addresses may often change or be deleted.

Contact us at westlegalstudies@delmar.com.

Introduction to Tort Law and Practice

Chapter Outline

- Scope
- Definitions and Purposes
- Elements of All the Torts
- Categories of Torts
- Introduction to Causation
- Tort Law Outline

SCOPE

Unintentional injuries take a staggering toll on society. In 1997, for example, the total economic cost of unintentional injuries amounted to $478 billion according to the National Safety Council. This included medical expenses, vehicle damage, wage and productivity losses, other employer costs, fire losses, and administrative expenses such as police and legal costs. (See Figure 1–1.) In addition, lost quality of life from these injuries is valued at $1,052 billion. This brings the total annual cost of unintentional injuries to $1.5 trillion.

Some of these injuries lead to tort litigation, which brings us to the subject of this book. For an overview of the types of tort cases filed in court, the kinds of harm alleged, and the amount of time taken to process the cases through the courts, see Figure 1–2. Our goal is to understand the law behind these statistics and the roles played by paralegals in a legal system designed to identify who should be compensated for losses that have been suffered.

DEFINITIONS AND PURPOSES

When someone harms or damages the person or property of another, the primitive instinct of the victim is to strike back. Our legal system functions as a check against this instinct so that the peace of the realm is not disturbed. We ask everyone to resolve conflicts by seeking a **remedy** in court. In the medical world, a remedy is something that cures or treats an ailment. In the law, a remedy is a means by which the enforcement of a right is sought or the violation of a right is compensated for or otherwise redressed.

FIGURE 1–1 Costs of unintentional injuries by class, 1997 ($ billions).

Cost	Total[a]	Motor-Vehicle	Work	Home	Other
Total	$478.3	$200.3	$127.7	$99.9	$66.1
Wage and productivity losses	238.4	70.2	63.4	63.7	44.5
Medical expenses	76.3	21.9	20.7	21.9	12.9
Administrative expenses[b]	82.4	56.2	26.5	4.5	3.9
Motor-vehicle damage	49.8	49.8	2.0		
Employer cost	21.3	2.2	11.9	4.3	3.4
Fire loss	10.1		3.2	5.5	1.4

Source: National Safety Council, *Accident Facts, 1998 edition.*
[a]Duplication between work and motor-vehicle, which amounted to $15.7 billion, was eliminated in the total.
[b]Includes the administrative cost of public and private insurance and police and legal costs.

FIGURE 1–2
Types of tort cases in state courts in the nation's 75 largest counties, 1992.

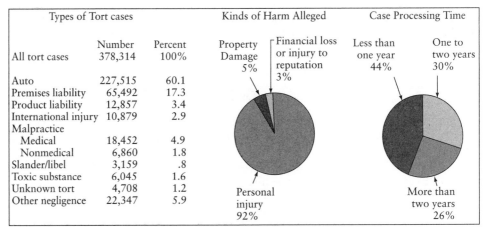

Types of Tort cases	Number	Percent
All tort cases	378,314	100%
Auto	227,515	60.1
Premises liability	65,492	17.3
Product liability	12,857	3.4
International injury	10,879	2.9
Malpractice		
Medical	18,452	4.9
Nonmedical	6,860	1.8
Slander/libel	3,159	.8
Toxic substance	6,045	1.6
Unknown tort	4,708	1.2
Other negligence	22,347	5.9

Kinds of Harm Alleged — Property Damage 5%, Financial loss or injury to reputation 3%, Personal injury 92%

Case Processing Time — Less than one year 44%, One to two years 30%, More than two years 26%

Source: "Tort Cases in Large Counties," by Steven K. Smith, Carol J. De Frances, and Patrick A. Langan, *Bureau of Justice Statistics Special Report,* 1995; *Bulletin,* 1997.

There are two kinds of disputes over which courts have **jurisdiction:** criminal disputes and civil disputes. (Jurisdiction is the authority or power of a court to resolve a dispute.) These disputes are based on the two major categories of law:

- **criminal law:** the law that governs crimes alleged by the government
- **civil law:** the law that governs rights and duties between private persons or between private persons and the government concerning matters other than the commission of a crime[1]

Criminal law covers those wrongs that are serious enough to be classified as crimes, e.g., murder, burglary. Civil law covers civil wrongs, which essentially consists of everything other than criminal wrongs. Tort law is one of the branches of civil law. Another familiar branch is contract law.

The word **tort** comes from the Latin word "tortus," meaning twisted, and from the French word "tort," meaning injury or wrong. The modern definition of tort is a civil wrong (other than a breach of contract) that causes injury or other damage for which our legal system deems it just to provide a remedy such as compensation. Although torts are different from crimes and breaches of contract, we will see later that there can be a close relationship among them. For example, a person's conduct may constitute both a crime and a tort.

> **EXAMPLE:** When Mary isn't looking, Jim takes jewelry out of Mary's purse. For this action, Jim may face prosecution for larceny (resolved in a criminal court proceeding) and liability for the tort of conversion (resolved in a civil court proceeding).

---

[1]Civil law also refers to the legal system and kind of law that exists in many Western European countries other than England.

When a crime is committed, public order is disrupted; therefore, the primary focus of criminal law is to vindicate a *public* wrong. The primary focus of tort law, however, is to vindicate a *private* wrong.

There are four major purposes of tort law:[2]

1. Peace: to provide a peaceful means for adjusting the rights of parties who might otherwise "take the law into their own hands." A courtroom is a neutral setting where the allegations can be aired in order to reach a rational resolution that the parties and the community can accept.

2. Deterrence: to deter wrongful conduct. Tort litigation takes place in public. The media is free to report what occurs in court. News that certain conduct forced someone into court and led to the payment of a large money judgment (called **damages**) can encourage the public to avoid that kind of conduct for fear of being subjected to a similar fate. This is sometimes called the "behavior modification" purpose of tort law. It has the effect of encouraging socially responsible behavior such as making safer automobiles and removing ice from your sidewalk.

3. Restoration: to restore injured parties to their original position, insofar as this is possible, by compensating them for their injury. This is sometimes referred to as being **made whole.** Of course, it is often impossible to restore someone to the condition that existed before the injury occurred. If you negligently break my leg, I may never be restored to full health. Yet by providing compensation (damages), I am being made as whole as is humanly possible.

4. Justice: to identify those who should be held accountable for the harm that resulted. A tort case can involve one or more victims and one or more defendants alleged to have a role in causing the victim's injury. The law of torts is designed to sort through the involvement of all of the participants in order to identify who is culpable or blameworthy and to determine who, in fairness, should be made to pay.

Someone has suffered a loss due to an injury. The overriding question of tort law—and the theme of this book—is whether that loss should be shifted to someone else in light of the peace, deterrence, restoration, and justice objectives of tort law.

ELEMENTS OF ALL THE TORTS

Every tort is a **cause of action,** which is simply a legally acceptable reason for bringing a suit. When you **state a tort cause of action,** you list the facts that give you a right to judicial relief against the **tortfeasor**—the wrongdoer who is alleged to have committed the tort. Causes of action are rules. Every rule can be broken down into the component parts that we call **elements.** (The complete definition of an element is as follows: a portion of a rule that is one of the preconditions of the applicability of the entire rule.) The elements of the torts and related causes of action that we will study in this book are listed in Figure 1–3. For each cause of action listed in Figure 1–3, you are told what elements must be supported by facts in order to "state" the cause of action.[3]

Most of the torts are part of the **common law,** which is judge-made law created in the absence of statutes or other controlling law. The legislature can create a tort cause of action by statute, but this is relatively rare. The overwhelming number of torts we will study in this book were created by the courts.

---

[2]Adapted from John W. Wade et al., *Torts* 1 (9th ed. 1994).
[3]When a party has offered sufficient evidence covering every element of a cause of action, that party has presented what is called a **prima facie case** that will entitle the party to prevail unless the other side offers convincing counterevidence.

Figure 1–3   Torts and related causes of action: The elements
(the page numbers in the first column tell you where the cause of action is discussed in this book).

The Cause of Action	Its Elements
1. Abuse of Process (p. 62)	i. Use of civil or criminal proceedings ii. Improper or ulterior purpose
2. Alienation of Affections (p. 235)	i. Intent to diminish the material relationship between spouses ii. Affirmative conduct iii. Affections between spouses are in fact alienated iv. Causation

3. Assault (Civil) (p. 33)	i. Act
	ii. Intent to cause either:
	  a. an imminent harmful or offensive contact, or
	  b. an apprehension of an imminent harmful or offensive contact
	iii. Apprehension of an imminent harmful or offensive contact to the plaintiff's person
	iv. Causation

4. Battery (Civil) (p. 25)	i. Act
	ii. Intent to cause either:
	  a. an imminent harmful or offensive contact, or
	  b. an apprehension of an imminent harmful or offensive contact
	iii. Harmful or offensive contact with the plaintiff's person
	iv. Causation

5. Civil Rights Violation (p. 321)	i. A person acting under color of state law ii. Deprives someone of a federal right
6. Conversion (p. 79)	i. Personal property (chattel) ii. Plaintiff is in possession of the chattel or is entitled to immediate possession iii. Intent to exercise dominion or control over the chattel iv. Serious interference with plaintiff's possession v. Causation
7. Criminal Conversation (p. 235)	Defendant has sexual relations with the plaintiff's spouse (adultery)

Defamation (two torts) (p. 259)
8. Libel
	i. Written defamatory statement by the defendant
	ii. Of and concerning the plaintiff
	iii. Publication of the statement
	iv. Damages:
	  a. In some states, special damages never have to be proven in a libel case
	  b. In other states, only libel on its face does not require special damages. In these states, libel per quod requires special damages
	v. Causation

9. Slander	i. Oral defamatory statement by the defendant
	ii. Of and concerning the plaintiff
	iii. Publication of the statement
	iv. Damages:
	  a. Special damages are not required if the slander is slander per se
	  b. Special damages must be proven if the slander is not slander per se
	v. Causation

10. Disparagement (p. 296)	i. False statement of fact ii. Disparaging the plaintiff's business or property iii. Publication iv. Intent v. Special damages vi. Causation

Figure 1–3 (Continued)

The Cause of Action	Its Elements

11. Enticement of a Child or Abduction of a Child (p. 236)	i. Intent to interfere with a parent's custody over his or her child
	ii. Affirmative conduct by the defendant:
	  a. to abduct or force the child from the parent's custody, or
	  b. to entice or encourage the child to leave the parent, or
	  c. to harbor the child and encourage him or her to stay away from the parent's custody
	iii. The child leaves the custody of the parent
	iv. Causation

12. Enticement of Spouse (p. 235)	i. Intent to diminish the marital relationship between the spouses
	ii. Affirmative conduct by the defendant:
	  a. to entice or encourage the spouse to leave the plaintiff's home, or
	  b. to harbor the spouse and encourage him or her to stay away from the plaintiff's home
	iii. The spouse leaves the plaintiff's home
	iv. Causation

13. False Imprisonment (p. 41)	i. An act that completely confines the plaintiff within fixed boundaries set by the defendant ii. Intent to confine plaintiff or a third person iii. Causation of the confinement iv. Plaintiff was either conscious of the confinement or suffered actual harm by it
14. Intentional Infliction of Emotional Distress (p. 66)	i. An act of extreme or outrageous conduct ii. Intent to cause severe emotional distress iii. Severe emotional distress is suffered iv. Causation
15. Interference with Contract Relations (p. 293)	i. An existing contract ii. Interference with the contract by defendant iii. Intent iv. Damages v. Causation
16. Interference with Prospective Advantage (p. 295)	i. Reasonable expectation of an economic advantage ii. Interference with this expectation iii. Intent iv. Damages v. Causation
Invasion of Privacy (four torts)	
17. Appropriation (p. 282)	i. The use of the plaintiff's name, likeness, or personality ii. For the benefit of the defendant
18. False Light (p. 283)	i. Publicity ii. Placing the plaintiff in a false light iii. Highly offensive to a reasonable person
19. Intrusion (p. 281)	i. An act of intrusion into a person's private affairs or concerns ii. Highly offensive to a reasonable person
20. Public Disclosure of Private Fact (p. 282)	i. Publicity ii. Concerning the private life of the plaintiff iii. Highly offensive to a reasonable person
21. Malicious Prosecution (p. 56)	i. Initiation or procurement of the initiation of criminal proceedings ii. Without probable cause iii. With malice iv. The criminal proceedings terminate in favor of the accused

Figure 1–3 (Continued)

The Cause of Action	Its Elements
22. Misrepresentation (p. 287)	i. Statement of fact ii. Statement is false iii. Scienter (intent to mislead) iv. Justifiable reliance v. Actual damages
23. Negligence (p. 97)	i. Duty ii. Breach of duty iii. Proximate cause iv. Damages
Nuisance (two torts) (p. 245)	
24. Private Nuisance	An unreasonable interference with the use and enjoyment of private land
25. Public Nuisance	An unreasonable interference with a right that is common to the general public
26. Prima Facie Tort (p. 299)	i. Infliction of harm ii. Intent to do harm (malice) iii. Special damages iv. Causation
27. Seduction (p. 236)	The defendant has sexual relations with the plaintiff's daughter, with or without consent
28. Strict Liability for Harm Caused by Animals (p. 88)	Domestic Animals: i. Owner has reason to know the animal has a specific propensity to cause harm ii. Harm caused by the animal was due to that specific propensity Wild Animals: i. Keeping a wild animal ii. Causes harm
29. Strict Liability for Abnormally Dangerous Conditions or Activities (p. 89)	i. Existence of an abnormally dangerous condition or activity ii. Knowledge of the condition or activity iii. Damages iv. Causation
30. Strict Liability in Tort (p. 209)	i. Seller ii. A defective product that is unreasonably dangerous to person or property iii. User or consumer iv. Physical harm (damages) v. Causation
31. Trespass to Chattels (p. 79)	i. Personal property (chattel) ii. Plaintiff is in possession of the chattel or is entitled to immediate possession iii. Intent to dispossess or to intermeddle with the chattel iv. Dispossession or intermeddling v. Causation
32. Trespass to Land (p. 242)	i. An act ii. Intrusion on land iii. In possession of another iv. Intent to intrude v. Causation of the intrusion

Figure 1–3 (Continued)

The Cause of Action	Its Elements
Warranty (three causes of action)	
33. Breach of Express Warranty (p. 202)	i. A statement of fact that is false ii. Made with the intent or expectation that the statement will reach the plaintiff iii. Reliance on the statement by the plaintiff iv. Damage v. Causation
34. Breach of Implied Warranty of Fitness for a Particular Purpose (p. 207)	i. Sale of goods ii. Seller has reason to know the buyer's particular purpose in buying the goods iii. Seller has reason to know that the buyer is relying on the seller's skill or judgment in buying the goods iv. The goods are not fit for the particular purpose v. Damage vi. Causation
35. Breach of Implied Warranty of Merchantability (p. 206)	i. Sale of goods ii. By a merchant of goods of that kind iii. The goods are not merchantable iv. Damage v. Causation

CATEGORIES OF TORTS

There are three main categories of torts:

- intentional torts
- negligence
- strict liability torts

These categories are not ironclad. There are some torts that overlap the categories, as we will see.

Intentional Torts

An **intentional tort** is a tort in which a person either desired to bring about the result or knew with substantial certainty that the result would follow from what the person did or failed to do. Some of the major intentional torts are battery, assault, trespass, and false imprisonment. Many of the cases asserting these torts are relatively straightforward. An easy battery case, for example, occurs when one person punches another in the nose. Other cases, however, are not so easy:

> **EXAMPLE:** Jim rides his bicycle through a large puddle of water directly in front of a bench where Mary is sitting. The water splashes on Mary who now sues Jim for battery. *Mary v. Jim* (battery)

When we study battery, we will see that this intentional tort can be committed by using an object such as a stick or water to make an offensive contact with someone. In the battery case of *Mary v. Jim,* a main issue will be whether Jim desired to hit Mary with the water or knew with substantial certainty that this would happen by riding through the water.

It is often difficult to get into someone's head to prove desire. Hence, plaintiffs use the alternative test of substantially certain knowledge. Compare the following two cases:

- I place a lighted match to the newspaper you are reading, which then catches fire. Assume that I was just joking around; I didn't want the newspaper to go up in flames.
- I light a cigarette in a room full of gasoline vapors, which then explode. Assume that I did not want this explosion to occur.

In the first case, a jury would probably conclude that I had substantially certain knowledge that your newspaper would catch fire when I placed a lighted match to it. To reach this result, the jury would rely on common sense and the everyday experience of all adults. The jury, however, might not conclude that I had substantially certain knowledge that the explosion would result in the second case. I may have been stupid to light a cigarette in that room, but stupidity or carelessness is not the same as substantially certain knowledge.

In the case of *Mary v. Jim*, suppose that the jury believes Jim when he asserts that he never wanted to splash Mary (perhaps because he never saw anyone on the bench) or that he did not know with substantial certainty that he would splash her (perhaps because he was riding the bike so slowly). In short, the jury believes Jim when he says that he splashed Mary by accident. If the jury accepts this version of the facts, there is no intentional tort because the element of intent has not been proven. There is, however, another tort that Jim may have committed: negligence.

Negligence

Negligence is harm caused by the failure to use reasonable care. An example might be colliding with someone while driving under the influence of medication that causes drowsiness. A critical distinction between a case of negligence and a case of an intentional tort is the distinction between an unreasonable risk of harm and the substantial certainty of harm:

- negligence: The heart of a plaintiff's negligence case is to show that the defendant created an *unreasonable risk of harm.*
- intentional tort: The heart of a plaintiff's intentional tort case is to show that the defendant wanted the harm to result or knew that there was a *substantial certainty of harm* based on what the defendant did or failed to do.

In our bicycle example of *Mary v. Jim*, assume that Mary does not sue for battery because of the difficulty of proving intent. Instead, she sues Jim under a negligence cause of action. Now the question will be whether Jim was so careless in riding the bike near the bench that he created an unreasonable risk of splashing people with water. The answer may depend on a variety of facts (which a paralegal might be asked to help uncover through interviewing and investigation) such as:

- how fast Jim was riding,
- how deep was the puddle,
- whether Jim knew his riding through other puddles in the area was causing splashes,
- how visible to Jim was Mary on the bench, etc.

A jury might believe Jim that he never wanted (desired) to splash Mary and that he did not have substantially certain knowledge that he would splash her, but still come to the conclusion that he created an unreasonable risk of splashing her. Hence, he committed negligence. In later chapters, we will examine other examples of this important distinction between negligence and intentional torts.

Strict Liability

The general meaning of **strict liability** (also called **absolute liability** or **liability without fault**) is responsibility regardless of blameworthiness or fault. If the defendant engages in a certain kind of conduct that causes harm, liability will result irrespective of intent, negligence, or innocence. An example would be performing an abnormally dangerous activity such as blasting. If the plaintiff is injured because of the explosion of the defendant's dynamite, the latter will be responsible (i.e., **liable**), regardless of whether the defendant desired to injure the plaintiff or knew with substantial certainty that the plaintiff or anyone else would be injured (intent), and regardless of whether the defendant acted unreasonably in setting off the explosive (negligence).

As we will see, however, it is sometimes difficult to distinguish strict liability from negligence, especially in the area of products liability.

One final caution about definitions of legal terminology: use the definitions as points of departure only. The most dangerous definitions are the ones that give the appearance of universality. The meaning of a word or phrase may change when the context changes. In the practice of law, great care is needed to *localize* all definitions by determining what a particular court in your state meant by a word or phrase. Also, keep in mind that as courts struggle to do justice, they sometimes stretch the definitions to accommodate the result they want to reach on the facts before them. Again, consider all definitions as no more than starting points from which you need to make further inquiry.

INTRODUCTION TO CAUSATION

In Chapter 13 we will study causation extensively. Since causation will be referred to throughout the book, a brief introduction is in order here. There are two main tests that are used to determine whether something has in fact caused something else:

- **but-for test:** Without (i.e., "but for") the act or omission, the event would not have occurred.
- **substantial factor test:** The act or omission had a significant role in bringing about the event.

Either test is sufficient to establish causation, or to establish what we call **cause in fact**. The but-for test is used when there is only one alleged cause of an event in question. The substantial factor test is used primarily when more than one causal entity is alleged.

> **EXAMPLES:**   George fires his gun at Bill. Bill's left arm is paralyzed in the area hit by the bullet. But for the gunshot wound, Bill's arm would not have been paralyzed. Therefore, George's act of firing the gun caused the paralysis—it was a cause in fact of the paralysis.
>
> Two companies, Ajax Manufacturing Co. and Winthrop, Inc., pour chemicals into a county stream. After this dumping of chemicals by both companies, the stream is no longer suitable for fishing.

- The dumping of chemicals by Ajax into the stream had a significant role in making it unsuitable for fishing. Therefore, Ajax was a substantial factor in making it unsuitable. Ajax was a cause in fact of the pollution that made the stream unsuitable for fishing.
- The dumping of chemicals by Winthrop into the stream had a significant role in making it unsuitable for fishing. Therefore, Winthrop was a substantial factor in making it unsuitable. Winthrop was a cause in fact of the pollution that made the stream unsuitable for fishing.

Again, we will have a lot more to say about these two tests for causation in Chapter 13.

TORT LAW ONLINE

It is now possible to obtain a great deal of **online** information that is relevant to a torts practice. In addition to research into cases, statutes, and other primary authority, a law firm often needs to do factual research. Examples include obtaining information about the manufacturer of a product, the weather conditions on the day of an accident, the assets of a defendant, or the location of a potential witness. "Nearly anything you can imagine is out there," commented one researcher.[4]

---

[4]Samuels, David (1998, August 2). The White House Shamus, *New York Times Magazine*, p. 40.

FIGURE 1–4
Internet sites relevant to tort law.

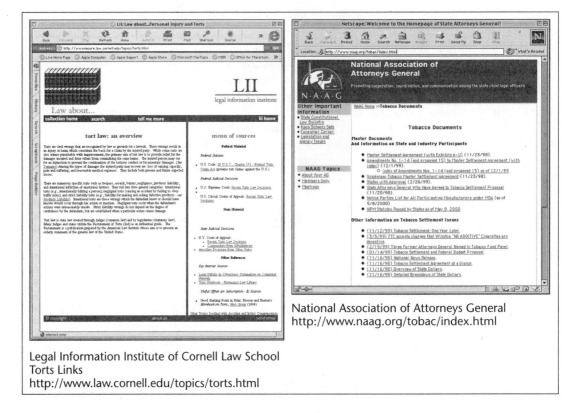

Legal Information Institute of Cornell Law School
Torts Links
http://www.law.cornell.edu/topics/torts.html

National Association of Attorneys General
http://www.naag.org/tobac/index.html

The two major commercial online services, for which you pay a subscription fee, are WESTLAW and LEXIS-NEXIS. An important jury verdict database in both of these services allows you to search court records to find out what jury verdicts have been returned for certain bodily injuries caused by specific products. Such information can be invaluable in deciding whether to settle a case and in making a presentation to a liability insurance company.

In addition to these fee-based, online services, you can obtain a great deal of information on the **Internet** through the **World Wide Web.** Most of it is free once you have the basic connection to the Internet. Greater care is needed, however, when using information found on the Internet. Unlike services such as WESTLAW and LEXIS-NEXIS, the Internet is not centrally regulated or monitored. Consequently, you cannot have the same assurance in the accuracy and quality of material obtained from the Internet sites that you can for material obtained from the fee-based services or, indeed, from traditional bound volumes. Nevertheless, the vast resources of the Internet are useful as starting points. See Figure 1–4 for two Internet sites relevant to tort law.

Here are some additional Internet sites that would be of interest to someone in a law office doing work on personal injury or property damage cases.

Torts, Accidents, and Injuries
- American Tort Reform Association
  http://www.atra.org

- Emory Law Library, Electronic Reference Desk, Tort Law Links
  http://www.law.emory.edu/LAW/refdesk/subject/tort.html

- FindLaw [find law firms practicing tort law]
  http://firms.findlaw.com/firms/pract46.html

- Hieros Gamos, Guide to Tort Law
  http://www.hg.org/torts.html

- LawJournal Extra
  http://www.ljx.com/practice/negligence/index.html

- Occupational Safety and Health Administration
  http://www.osha.gov

- Products Liability Sites
  http://ublib.buffalo.edu/libraries/units/law/remotesites/liability.html
  http://www.productslaw.com
  http://www.ljx.com/practice/productliability/index.html
  http://www.cpsc.gov

- Tobacco Litigation
  http://www.tobacco-litigation.net
  http://www.house.gov/commerce/TobaccoDocs/documents.html
  http://stic.neu.edu/settlement/6-20-settle.htm
  http://www.naag.org/tobac/index.html

- Toxic Torts
  http://www.toxlaw.com

- United States Consumer Product Safety Commission
  http://www.cpsc.gov

- World Wide Web Virtual Library: Law: Torts
  http://www.law.indiana.edu/law/v-lib/tort.html

- Workers' Compensation
  http://www.law.cornell.edu/topics/workers_compensation.html
  http://www.dol.gov/dol.esa/public/regs/statutes/owcp/stwclaw/stwclaw.htm
  http://www.prairielaw.com/wc

Medical Sites (for information on injuries and diseases)

- American Medical Association
  http://www.ama-assn.org

- Anatomy Sites
  http://www.ama-assn.org/insight/gen_hlth/atlas/atlas.htm
  http://www.vh.org/Providers/Textbooks/BrainAnatomy/BrainAnatomy.html

- Forensic Information Services [Zeno's Forensic Page]
  http://www.bart.nl:80/~geradts/forensic.html

- Internet Drug Index
  http://www.rxlist.com

- Internet Grateful Med [access to numerous resources such as MEDLINE]
  http://igm.nlm.nih.gov

- Mediconsult [general medical search engine]
  http://www.mediconsult.com

- MEDLINE
  http://www.nlm.nih.gov/databases/freemedl.html

- Medscape [medical search engine]
  www.medscape.com

- National Library of Medicine
  http://www.nlm.nih.gov

- National Patient Safety Foundation
  http://www.npsf.org

- PubMed [National Library of Medicine's search service to MEDLINE]
  http://www.ncbi.nlm.nih.gov/PubMed

ASSIGNMENT

1.1

When answering the following questions, give the full name and Internet address of the sites you use, the dates you visited the sites, and, if provided, the dates the sites were last updated. You can use any of the sites listed in this chapter as well as links within them.

a. Find a reference to a court opinion written by a state court in your state on any tort topic. What is the name of the opinion? What tort did it cover? What court wrote it?

b. Find a discussion of any disease that you select. Include a definition of the disease.

c. Find a federal regulation on air bags. Quote a line from the regulation.

SUMMARY

A remedy is a means by which the enforcement of a right is sought or the violation of a right is compensated for or otherwise redressed. Criminal law governs a suit brought by the government for the commission of a crime. Civil law governs a suit between private persons or between private persons and the government over a matter other than the commission of a crime. Tort law is one of the branches of the civil law. A tort is a civil wrong (other than a breach of contract) that causes injury or other damage for which our legal system deems it just to provide a remedy such as compensation. There are four major purposes of tort law: to provide a peaceful means for adjusting the rights of parties, to deter wrongful conduct, to try to restore injured parties to their original position, and to identify who in fairness should be responsible for the harm that resulted.

A cause of action is a legally acceptable reason for bringing a suit. Tort causes of action have elements. To state a tort cause of action is to list the facts that support each element of the tort. There are three main categories of torts: intentional torts (the actor desires the result or knows with substantial certainty that it will occur), negligence (the actor creates an unreasonable risk of harm), and strict liability torts (the actor engages in certain conduct for which the law imposes liability regardless of intent or reasonableness). The two tests for causation (cause in fact) are the but-for test and the substantial factor test.

There is a great deal of legal and factual information relevant to a torts litigation practice that is available online from commercial, fee-based services and from the Internet through the World Wide Web.

KEY TERMS

remedy   1
jurisdiction   2
criminal law   2
civil law   2
tort   2
damages   3
made whole   3
cause of action   3
state a tort cause of action   3

tortfeasor   3
elements   3
prima facie case   3
common law   3
intentional tort   7
negligence   8
strict liability   8
absolute liability   8
liability without fault   8

liable   8
but-for test   9
substantial factor test   9
cause in fact   9
online   9
Internet   10
World Wide Web   10

Foreseeability in Tort Law

Chapter Outline

- Introduction
- Defining Foreseeability
- Foreseeability Spectrum
- Objective Standard
- Phrasing the Foreseeability Question
- Foreseeability Determination "Formula"
- Review of Steps to Determine Foreseeability

INTRODUCTION

Foreseeability is a critical concept in tort law. In three of the elements of negligence, for example, foreseeability often plays a major role:

- duty
- breach of duty
- proximate cause

In later chapters we will discover that foreseeability is relevant to some of the intentional and strict-liability torts as well as to negligence. Before studying any of these torts, we need to spend some time analyzing the concept of foreseeability. Given its critical importance, we will be referring back to this discussion throughout the remainder of the book.

The central question of this chapter is: How do we determine foreseeability? This question is explored through the following topics:

- the meaning of foreseeability
- the spectrum of foreseeability
- foreseeability as an objective standard
- phrasing the foreseeability question
- the foreseeability determination "formula"

The legal consequences of foreseeability will be considered in later chapters. For now, our concern is the nature of foreseeability itself.

DEFINING FORESEEABILITY

In everyday language, foresee means "to see or know beforehand." **Foreseeable**, the adjective, simply describes that which one can see or know beforehand. From a legal perspective, however, the emphasis is on the *extent* to which something can be known beforehand. It is important to understand that the question, "Is it foreseeable?", is less significant than the question, "How foreseeable is it?" Or, to combine the two questions: "How foreseeable is it, if at all?" Foreseeability is primarily a question of the *extent* to which something is predictable or "occurable."

It is also important to understand that foreseeability is determined *before the fact*. If you want to know, for example, whether a fire was foreseeable, you mentally turn the clock back to the period of time *before* the fire occurred and ask: how likely was it, if at all, that a fire would occur? This determination is not made on the basis of what happens after the fact. An event or result is not foreseeable simply because it happened.

FORESEEABILITY SPECTRUM

To assess the foreseeability of an event or result, you must pinpoint it on a scale or **spectrum of foreseeability**. Figure 2–1 presents this spectrum. The threshold question is whether the event or result was foreseeable in any shape, fashion, or form. If the answer is no, the inquiry is ended. If, however, the answer is yes, then the next and most important inquiry is *how* foreseeable was the event or result. Where on the spectrum did it fall before it happened?

The categories on the spectrum are not mutually exclusive. There is no scientific or measurable distinction among all the items on the spectrum. The categories are rough approximations on the higher-to-lower ranges of "occurability."

Note the last item on the spectrum: foreseeability to a certainty. When something is that foreseeable, the law says that you *intended* the event or result to occur. **Intent** has two meanings in the law: the desire to have something happen or the **knowledge with substantial certainty** that it will happen from what you do or fail to do. If you pull the trigger of a gun aimed at a crowd a few feet in front of where you are standing, you cannot claim that you did not intend to shoot the person who was hit. You may have hoped and prayed that no one would be hit, but a court will probably find that you had substantially certain knowledge that someone would be hit. In the eyes of the law, you intended this result. You have committed a battery.

FIGURE 2–1
Foreseeability spectrum: How foreseeable, if at all?

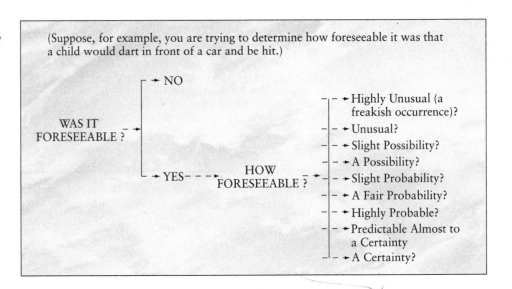

(Suppose, for example, you are trying to determine how foreseeable it was that a child would dart in front of a car and be hit.)

WAS IT FORESEEABLE?
→ NO
→ YES → HOW FORESEEABLE?
- Highly Unusual (a freakish occurrence)?
- Unusual?
- Slight Possibility?
- A Possibility?
- Slight Probability?
- A Fair Probability?
- Highly Probable?
- Predictable Almost to a Certainty
- A Certainty?

OBJECTIVE STANDARD

When foreseeability is an issue in the law, we often ask two questions:

- Was the event or result foreseeable to the defendant? (You answer this question by applying a **subjective standard.**)
- Would the event or result have been foreseeable to a reasonable person? (You answer this question by applying an **objective standard.**)

In most cases, the second question is asked only when the answer to the first question is no.

A subjective standard simply means that everything is measured solely by what the defendant actually knew or understood. Suppose, for example, we want to know whether it was foreseeable that Ted Vinson's dog would bite the mail carrier last Monday morning. Assume that the dog has bitten mail carriers (and others) in the past and that the dog runs loose in the front yard where the mailbox is located. Assume further that Ted is totally oblivious of the dog's biting habits and believes he owns the most gentle and friendly dog in the world. He has forgotten that the dog has bitten people before. By a subjective standard, the Monday bite was not foreseeable to Ted. He may have been silly in thinking the dog is harmless, but if he honestly believed the dog would not bite anyone, then the Monday bite was not foreseeable to him.

Suppose, however, we apply an objective standard to the dog bite case. An objective standard measures something by reference to what a **reasonable person** under the same or similar circumstances would have known or understood. What do we mean by a reasonable person? We will spend a great deal of time on this topic in later chapters. For now, suffice it to say that a reasonable person is an ordinary, prudent person.

Would a reasonable person have foreseen that the dog would bite the mail carrier last Monday? An ordinary, prudent person would *not* have been oblivious of this dog's prior biting habit and would have understood that an untied dog with such a habit will probably bite again. Hence, by an objective standard, the bite was foreseeable, particularly since the dog was kept near the mailbox.

If a defendant did not foresee something that a reasonable person would have foreseen, we are able to say that the defendant *should have foreseen* it. We cannot reach this conclusion, however, until we make an assessment of what a reasonable person would have foreseen—using an objective standard. This is the process that we will go through in most of the cases in this book when foreseeability is an issue.

PHRASING THE FORESEEABILITY QUESTION

There are two ways to phrase the foreseeability question: general and particular. Assume that Mary Jefferson crashes her car into a lamp post by a local beach two weeks after Christmas. She claims that Mrs. X is responsible for the crash because of how she disposed of her Christmas tree. Compare the following two foreseeability questions concerning this case:

A. Was harm foreseeable to Mrs. X when she allowed Tommy to take the Christmas tree she had just thrown into the garbage two weeks after Christmas, which led to Mary Jefferson's injury?

B. When Mrs. X allowed ten-year-old Tommy to take the Christmas tree that she had just thrown into the garbage two weeks after Christmas, how foreseeable was it to Mrs X:
   1. that an older child, Ted, would steal the tree from Tommy,
   2. that Ted would organize a tree-collection project so that the trees could be burned together at a big bonfire at a local beach,
   3. that about thirty children would drag the trees across busy streets to get to the beach,

4. that traffic would be interrupted, and
5. that Mary Jefferson would be injured when she crashed her car into a lamp post in an effort to avoid hitting Ted crossing the street with Mrs. X's tree?

The first statement is a very general phrasing of the foreseeability question: Was harm foreseeable? The second statement, however, is highly particularized. Everything is segmented into events that raise a series of isolated foreseeability subquestions.

When do you use a general foreseeability question and when do you use a particularized one? The answer, in part, is governed by the following advocacy principles:

Advocacy Principles: Arguments on Foreseeability

- The party who wants to reach the conclusion that something was *foreseeable* will seek to phrase the foreseeability question in the most broad, *generalized* form possible. (In our Christmas tree case, Mary Jefferson wants to argue that the injury she suffered was foreseeable to Mrs. X; therefore, she will phrase the foreseeability question broadly. See question A.)
- The party who wants to reach the conclusion that something was *unforeseeable* will seek to phrase the foreseeability question in the most narrow, *particularized* form possible. (Mrs. X wants to argue that the injury Mary Jefferson suffered was unforeseeable; therefore, she will phrase the foreseeability question narrowly. See question B.)

A particularized statement of the foreseeability question itemizes the major chain of events that led up to the accident or injury. The more events listed, the more self-evident the answer becomes: a particularized question is stacked in favor of *un*foreseeability. After reading all the events in the question, we are often inclined to say that all of it could not possibly have been foreseen. Care must be used, however, not to overparticularize the question to the point of absurdity.

Later, we will learn what the courts have said on how foreseeable something must be in given areas of tort law such as proximate cause in negligence. Knowing the law, however, will not eliminate the need for advocacy in the statement of the foreseeability question. The more an advocate wants to conclude that something was very foreseeable on the foreseeability spectrum, the more generalized the advocate will try to make the foreseeability question. The more an advocate wants to conclude that there was low foreseeability, the more particularized the advocate will try to make the foreseeability question.

ASSIGNMENT

2.1

You are a paralegal who works in the office of Smith & Smith. The firm represents Dan in a suit by Pete who claims that Dan caused Pete to suffer a seizure. Pete is represented by Karen Wilson, Esq. Read the following fact situation carefully. Focus on the foreseeability of Pete's seizure. First, phrase the foreseeability question that Karen Wilson would try to use on behalf of Pete. Her phrasing will be broad and generalized. Next, phrase the foreseeability question that Smith & Smith would try to use on behalf of Dan. Its phrasing will be narrow and particularized. Assume that Dan wants to reach the conclusion that the seizure was very unforeseeable and that Pete wants to reach the conclusion that an injury was foreseeable.

Dan has a weekend job operating a ferris wheel at the state fair. Pete buys a ticket and gets on. Soon after the ride begins, Dan notices that Pete is throwing objects onto the people below. Dan decides to stop the wheel in order to remove Pete. When Dan grabs the brake lever, he immediately notices that it is stuck. He has an emergency brake, but is very reluctant to use it because it might cause the entire wheel to come to a jolting halt. He fears that some of the riders could be thrown out. The more he thinks about it, the more frantic he becomes. This is only his first week on the job. While he stands there thinking about what to do, some of the people on the ground, who have been hit by the objects Pete threw on them, begin shouting at Dan to do something. Dan becomes more and more dizzy as he tries to think of what to do. Someone in the crowd yells out at Dan to turn the electricity off as a way to stop the wheel. Dan thinks it is a good idea, but by this time, he is so confused that he does not know what to do. Suddenly, he dashes away from the crowd so that he can try to collect his thoughts. Luckily, he spots his boss at the other end of the fair. He runs toward her for help. When he reaches her, he is so up-set and frantic that it takes his boss close to a minute to figure out what he is talk-ing about. When the boss finally does understand, she goes to the still-turning fer-ris wheel and stops it safely by skillfully using the emergency brake. When Pete gets off this twenty-eight-minute ride, he suffers a seizure. Later, he sues Dan.

FORESEEABILITY DETERMINATION "FORMULA"

It is probably accurate to say that you will rarely have enough facts to determine how foreseeable something was or was not. Hence, determining foreseeability requires a probing for further facts. Questions need to be asked about the facts that you do not have, and often, about the facts that you do have. For this reason, effective inter-viewing and investigation are critical to reaching intelligent conclusions about fore-seeability.

The foreseeability "formula" in Figure 2–2 is designed to provide a framework for asking the right questions about foreseeability. The starting point in the use of the formula is to identify the subject matter of the foreseeability question. What is the event or result whose foreseeability or unforeseeability you want to assess? As pointed out earlier, the subject matter of the foreseeability inquiry can be stated in *generalized* terms (e.g., was any harm or injury of any kind foreseeable), or in very *particularized* terms (e.g., was it foreseeable that customers in a department store would run toward an exit because of a light failure during the day, push each other in an effort to get out, and then fail to. . .). After you have identified the question, you then apply the "formula."

There are eight factors to consider:

area	human nature
activity	history
people	sensory data
preparation	common sense

The factors may appear complicated. In fact, however, the list is simply a detailed overview of the process we naturally go through whenever we want to determine whether something is foreseeable. Examine each of the eight factors separately, even though there will be considerable overlap among them. As you focus on each factor, ask yourself factual questions that relate to foreseeability. Do not, however, expect definitive answers at this point. The "formula" is not a mathematical equation. It is no more than an aid to give you some direction as you try to place an event or result on the foreseeability spectrum. Later, you will want to pursue answers to the ques-tions during client interviews and field investigation.

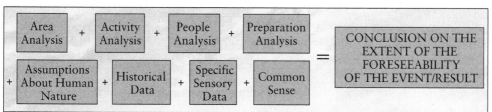

FIGURE 2–2
Foreseeability determination "formula."

Area Analysis

The nature of the area can sometimes be very important. If, for example, a child is hit by a car, it is important to know whether the accident occurred in a residential area, near a school, at a playground, etc. From the nature of the area, how foreseeable is it that children will be around? If an accident occurs in a supermarket, it is equally important to assess the area. It is usually a crowded, closed area with many products stacked on shelves or on the floor. What is foreseeable given these conditions? A rotted tree branch falls and hits the plaintiff. Where did this occur? In the country? In a city? A suburb? A zoo? A park? How, if at all, would the area affect the foreseeability of what happened? An explosion occurs in a university lab. A lab is a place for experiments and the storage of chemicals. Danger is usually more foreseeable in a lab than in other areas.

Activity Analysis

Area and activity are intimately related. What specific activities were going on at the time of the accident or event whose foreseeability we are assessing? Swimming? Driving? Walking? Running? Eating? Selling? Dynamiting? What occurs during this activity? What is frequently foreseeable? Occasionally foreseeable? Rarely foreseeable? Examine the nature of the activity or activities themselves. What does human experience tell you (or what should it tell you) about what might be anticipated from this activity?

People Analysis

What kind of people were involved in the activities that led to the event or result whose foreseeability is being examined? How would you characterize them, and does this characterization tell you something about what should have been foreseeable by them or by others interacting with them? Were they children? Adults? Trespassers? Doctors? Mechanics or others with special knowledge and skills? What is normally expected from such people? What precautions do they usually take or fail to take? We have certain expectations from certain classes or kinds of people. What are the expectations in this case? Do these expectations help us determine what should have been foreseeable?

Preparation Analysis

What do people usually do before they engage in the activity you listed? Is any long-term preparation needed, e.g., training, testing? Short-term preparation, e.g., checking equipment, looking out for obstacles? No preparation? The data received from any preparation will usually be very relevant to foreseeability.

Assumptions About Human Nature

This factor is very similar to the people analysis except that it is more general. What kind of behavior is usually expected of anyone engaged in the kind of activity in question? In driving a car, for example, can you assume that other drivers will *not* always obey all traffic laws? When people are in danger, can you assume that they will act in self-defense? Can you assume that people will gravitate toward pleasurable, attractive things or events? Can you assume that many people will not read five pages of fine-print instructions? Such assumptions, when they can be made, are often relevant to what might be anticipated from people.

This is not to say that any of these assumptions are to be condoned or that they justify conduct in any way. The law that applies to conduct is a separate matter that will be considered in later chapters. Here we are limiting ourselves to a consideration of the extent of foreseeability, independent of any legal consequences.

Historical Data

The more something has occurred in the past, the more foreseeable is its reoccurrence. Have incidents of a similar nature occurred in the past? If so, under what circumstances? How often? How well known were they? A customer sues a grocery store owner for injuries received when opening a can of tuna. We want to know if this injury was foreseeable to the owner of the store. Has the owner had similar complaints about this tuna brand in the past? Has the owner heard of problems other stores have had? Is this the first time the owner became aware of such a problem? Historical data can be quite relevant to foreseeability.

Specific Sensory Data

What did the eyes, ears, nose, fingers, feet, etc. tell the parties just before the incident? Did any of this sensory data provide signs of what might happen? Are certain things foreseeable in certain kinds of weather? (Was this kind of weather foreseeable?) Visibility is often relevant to foreseeability. What factors affected visibility, e.g., weather, time of day, and presence of obstructions? Were there distractions that prevented people from being aware of a danger? If so, were these distractions foreseeable?

Common Sense

Common sense is a catchall factor. All of the other factors should have led you to questions and observations grounded in common sense. Here we simply reinforce the central role of this factor and ask ourselves to what extent something was or was not foreseeable based on common sense.

> **EXAMPLE:**   Jones builds a swimming pool in his backyard. The use of the pool is restricted to Jones family members and guests who are present when an adult is there to supervise. One hot, summer night, a neighbor's child opens an unlocked door of a fence that surrounds the Jones yard and goes into the pool. (There is no separate fence around the pool.) The child knows he is not supposed to be there without an adult. No one else is at the pool. The child drowns.
>
> **Foreseeability question (general):** Was it foreseeable that someone would be injured in the pool?
>
> **Foreseeability question (particular):** Was it foreseeable that a neighbor's child would violate a rule of the owner of the pool not to use it unless an adult was present, open a closed fence door to get to the pool, and drown in it?

From the facts, it appears that Jones built his pool in a residential area. If so, it certainly was foreseeable that children would be in the area. Jones should have anticipated that children would be drawn to the pool. The neighbor's child used the pool while no one was around. (We need to know how old the child was.) It would help to know whether people use each other's pools in this way in the neighborhood. If it is common, then it is more foreseeable to Jones that a child would use his pool without permission or supervision in spite of his rule to the contrary. Why did he impose this rule? Because of prior pool trespassing in the neighborhood? Swimming is generally considered a dangerous activity, particularly for children. It is foreseeable, however, that children will not be able to fully protect themselves in water, hence the need to take additional precautions when children could be swimming.

There was no separate fence around Jones's pool; there was simply an unlocked door to a fence around the yard. Was it foreseeable to Jones that this might be an inadequate precaution? Again, this may depend on the frequency with which children have made unauthorized use of pools in the area and the extent to which Jones knew about this or should have known about it. Are other pools in the area left unlocked and unguarded at night? Should Jones have checked on this? It is true that Jones had a rule that adults must be present. But is this rule enough? Shouldn't Jones have assumed that a child would *not* obey such a rule? Has any child ever violated this rule in the past? Have there ever been children using the Jones pool without adults present? If so, then Jones was on notice that it could happen again and that additional precautions would be needed. What steps did Jones take, if any, to make sure that neighborhood children and their parents knew about his rule?

We also need to know whether there have been any recent swimming pool accidents in the area. The drowning took place at night. (We do not know whether any of the Jones family members were at home at the time.) Common sense tells us that a child will be tempted to use an easily accessible swimming pool in the summer and that drowning is a fair probability when there is no supervision.

ASSIGNMENT

2.2

You have just read a series of facts and factual questions relevant to whether the swimming pool tragedy was foreseeable. Categorize each of these facts and questions under the eight categories of the foreseeability determination formula. Specify what falls under area analysis, activity analysis, people analysis, preparation analysis, assumptions about human nature, historical data, specific sensory data, and common sense. Place a fact or a question under more than one category if there is overlap.

REVIEW OF STEPS TO DETERMINE FORESEEABILITY

1. Turn the clock back to the time before the event/result in question occurred—foreseeability is determined *before* the fact.
2. Decide how broadly (generalized) or narrowly (particularized) you want to phrase the foreseeability question.
3. Apply the factors in the foreseeability determination formula that are applicable to the situation.
4. From the range of "highly unusual" to "a certainty," draw your conclusion of where the event/result falls on the foreseeability spectrum.
5. Give a counteranalysis. If both sides are not going to agree on the extent to which the event/result was foreseeable, state the other side.

ASSIGNMENT

2.3

Assess the foreseeability of the events listed in the following situations. Go through the five steps just listed. Include a large number of factual questions you would raise, and state how these factual questions might be relevant to the foreseeability of the result or event in question.

a. The ABC Company manufactures kitchen stoves. Smith buys one of the stoves. There is no heat in Smith's kitchen. Hence, Smith often turns the stove on, opens the oven door, and rests his feet on the door while sitting on a chair in front of the stove. One day, the stove collapses forward onto Smith while he is warming his feet in this way. Smith is severely injured. Was this injury foreseeable to the ABC Company?

b. A hobo hitching a ride on a railroad train falls off and injures himself. Was this injury foreseeable to the railroad?

c. Examine the facts of Assignment 2.1. Was the injury foreseeable to Dan's boss?

Accidents happen to all of us throughout our lives. Think of an event in your life involving an accident that was somewhat of a surprise to you when it occurred. It can be a major or a minor accident. In class the teacher will select one student to be interviewed by the rest of the class (i.e., to be the interviewee) in order to determine how foreseeable the accident was to you (subjective standard) and how foreseeable it would have been to a reasonable person (objective standard).

Instructions to interviewee: If you are selected, start by telling the class what the accident was. The class will then ask you questions relevant to foreseeability. (Feel free to change any facts to preserve privacy.)

Instructions to class: Assume that each of you is conducting the interview. Start asking questions of the interviewee in class. Your questions should cover the eight categories of area, activity, people, preparation, assumptions about human nature, historical data, specific sensory data, and common sense. When the teacher indicates that the interview is over, write down your answers to the two following questions. The teacher will then lead a class discussion on the differences and similarities in the answers among the students in the class.

a. Was the accident foreseeable to the interviewee? Where on the foreseeability spectrum would you place it?

b. Would the accident have been foreseeable to a reasonable person? Where on the foreseeability spectrum would you place it?

SUMMARY

Foreseeability means the extent to which we can see or know something beforehand. It is determined before the fact; something is not foreseeable simply because it happened. The spectrum of foreseeability ranges from highly unusual to a virtual certainty. (If something falls into the latter category, it was intended.) When foreseeability is an issue, we ask if the event or result was foreseeable to the defendant (answered by using a subjective standard). If not, we often ask if the event or result would have been foreseeable to a reasonable person (answered by applying an objective standard). Advocates tend to generalize the foreseeability question when they want to argue that something was foreseeable; they particularize the question when they are hoping for a finding of unforeseeability. Assessing foreseeability requires an analysis of the area involved, the activity undertaken, the people involved, the preparation involved, assumptions about human nature, historical data, specific sensory data, and common sense.

KEY TERMS

foreseeable   14

spectrum of foreseeability   14

intent   14

knowledge with substantial
   certainty   14

subjective standard   15

objective standard   15

reasonable person   15

Battery

Chapter Outline

- Introduction
- Act
- Person
- Intent
- Harmful or Offensive Contact
- Consent and Privilege

INTRODUCTION

Battery—civil battery—is a harmful or offensive contact with a person that results from the defendant's intent to cause the contact or to cause an apprehension of imminent contact. The easiest case is when the defendant punches the plaintiff in the nose. Many make the mistake of saying that the punch was an "assault." Although the words *battery* and *assault* are sometimes confused, we need to keep the concepts separate. As we will see in the next chapter, assault is a separate tort that does not require actual contact with the plaintiff. By the time you finish studying this chapter and the next one, you should know why Sleeping Beauty, if she woke up angry, could have sued the kissing prince for battery, but not for assault.

Battery is frequently committed, but rarely litigated. A major reason for this is that most batterers are not **deep pockets,** meaning individuals who have enough resources from which a plaintiff can collect a judgment. The vast majority of people who commit intentional torts such as battery are **shallow pockets**—individuals without assets. Furthermore, liability insurance policies generally do not cover intentional torts, whereas they do cover the most common cause of injury, automobile negligence. For most victims of battery, therefore, the cost and hassle of suing under a battery cause of action is simply not worth it. If, however, the person committing battery has assets, i.e., is a deep pocket, a battery suit is likely. Sports figures or other celebrities, for example, are relatively common defendants in battery actions.

Of course, criminal law may be an option. The same conduct can constitute both a criminal battery and a civil battery. (Criminal battery is sometimes called "assault" or "assault and battery.") Our focus in this chapter is civil battery, which is a tort. Criminal battery is a crime prosecuted by the state.

Before beginning our study of the substantive law of civil battery, you will find a comprehensive checklist of definitions, defenses, relationships, paralegal roles, and research references for this tort. It is designed to make connections between the battery chapter and related material discussed in other chapters and in other courses in the curriculum. It can also serve as an on-the-job checklist after graduation. We will provide a comparable checklist at the beginning of our discussion of every major tort in this book.

Battery Checklist

Definitions, Relationships, Paralegal Roles, and Research References

Category
Battery is an intentional tort.

Interest Protected by This Tort
The right to be free from a harmful or offensive bodily contact.

Elements
   i. Act
   ii. Intent to cause either:
      a. an imminent harmful or offensive contact, or
      b. an apprehension of an imminent harmful or offensive contact
   iii. Harmful or offensive contact with the plaintiff's person
   iv. Causation of the harmful or offensive contact

Definitions of Major Words/Phrases in the Elements
Act: A voluntary movement of the defendant's body.
Intent: Either
a. the desire to bring about the consequences of the act (i.e., the desire to cause the contact or the apprehension of an imminent contact), or
b. the substantially certain knowledge that the consequences (i.e., the contact or the apprehension) will follow from the act.
Harmful: Involving physical damage, impairment, pain, or illness to the body.
Offensive: Offending the personal dignity of an ordinary person who is not unduly sensitive.
Person: One's body, something attached to the body, or something so closely associated with the body as to be identified with it.
Causation: Either
a. but for the defendant's act, the consequences would not have occurred (i.e., the contact would not have occurred), or
b. the defendant's act was a substantial factor in bringing about the consequences (i.e., the contact).

Major Defense and Counterargument Possibilities That Need to Be Explored
1. There was no voluntary movement of the defendant's body (no act).
2. The defendant had no desire to make contact with the plaintiff, nor any substantially certain knowledge that such contact would result from what the defendant did (no intent).
3. The contact was neither harmful nor offensive.
4. But for what the defendant did, the contact would have resulted anyway. The defendant was not a substantial factor in producing the contact. (No causation.)
5. The plaintiff consented to the defendant's contact (on the defense of consent, see Chapter 23).
6. The contact resulted while the defendant was defending him- or herself from the plaintiff (on self-defense and other self-help privileges, see Chapter 23).
7. The contact occurred while the defendant was defending someone else from the plaintiff (on the defense of others and other self-help privileges, see Chapter 23).
8. The contact occurred while the defendant was defending property or recapturing chattels from the plaintiff (on the privileges of necessity, defense of property, recapture of property, and other self-help privileges, see Chapter 23).

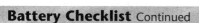

Battery Checklist Continued

9. The contact occurred while the defendant was disciplining the plaintiff (on discipline and other self-help privileges, see Chapter 23).
10. The contact occurred while the defendant was arresting the plaintiff (on the privilege of arrest, see Chapter 5).
11. The plaintiff's suit against the government for a battery committed by a government employee may be barred by sovereign immunity (on sovereign immunity, see Chapter 23).
12. The plaintiff's suit against the government employee for battery may be barred by public official immunity (on official immunity, see Chapter 23).
13. The plaintiff's suit against the charitable organization for a battery committed by someone working for the organization may be barred by charitable immunity (on charitable immunity, see Chapter 23).
14. The plaintiff's suit against a family member for battery may be barred by intrafamily immunity (on intrafamily immunity, see Chapter 18).
15. The plaintiff failed to take reasonable steps to mitigate the harm caused when the defendant committed battery; therefore, damages should not cover the aggravation of the harm caused by the plaintiff (on the doctrine of avoidable consequences, see Chapter 14).

Damages

The plaintiff can recover compensatory damages for the contact, including pain and suffering, medical bills, and loss of wages. Since the defendant often acts out of hatred and malice in committing the battery, punitive damages are commonly awarded as well. (On the categories of damages, see Chapter 14.)

Relationship to Criminal Law

The same act of the defendant can constitute a *civil* battery (for which the plaintiff recovers damages) and a *criminal* battery (for which the state collects a fine or imposes jail or imprisonment). The crime may be called assault and battery, aggravated assault, assault with intent to kill, etc.

Other Torts and Related Actions

Assault: If there was no contact, but the plaintiff was placed in apprehension of a contact, the tort of assault may have been committed.

False Imprisonment: While committing the tort of false imprisonment, battery may also have been committed if contact was made with the plaintiff's person during or just before the confinement.

Negligence: (a) There may have been a harmful or offensive contact that was not intentional, hence no battery. Yet if the contact was due to unreasonable conduct by the defendant, negligence should be explored. (b) A doctor must have informed consent before making contact with a part of the patient's body. The failure to obtain such consent is a battery in some states. In most states, however, as we will see in Chapter 12, the patient must sue under a negligence cause of action in such cases.

Wrongful Death: A wrongful death action can be brought by the survivors of the deceased if death resulted from the battery.

Federal Law

a. Under the Federal Tort Claims Act, the United States Government will *not* be liable for a battery committed by one of its federal employees within the scope of employment (respondeat superior) *unless* the federal employee is an investigative or law enforcement officer. (See Figure 23–7 in Chapter 23.)
b. There may be liability under the Civil Rights Act if the battery was committed while the defendant was depriving the plaintiff of federal rights under color of law. (See Figure 23–8 in Chapter 23.)

Employer-Employee (Agency) Law

An employee who commits a battery is personally liable for this tort. His or her employer will *also* be liable for battery if the conduct of the employee was within the scope of employment (respondeat superior). The employee must be furthering a business objective of the employer at the time. Intentional torts such as battery, however, are often outside the scope of employment. If so, only the employee is liable for the battery. (On the factors that determine the scope of employment, see Figure 12–7 in Chapter 12.)

Battery Checklist Continued

Paralegal Roles in Battery Litigation

Fact finding (help the office collect facts relevant to prove the elements of battery, the elements of available defenses, and extent of injuries or other damages):
- client interviewing
- field investigation
- online research (e.g., find newspaper accounts of a public brawl)

File management (help the office control the volume of paperwork in a battery litigation):
- open client file
- enter case data in computer database
- maintain file documents

Litigation assistance (help the trial attorney prepare for a battery trial and appeal, if needed):
- draft discovery requests
- draft answers to discovery requests
- draft pleadings
- digest and index discovery documents
- help prepare, order, and manage trial exhibits (visuals or demonstratives)
- prepare trial notebook
- draft notice of appeal
- order trial transcript
- cite check briefs
- perform legal research

Collection/enforcement (help the trial attorney for the judgment creditor to collect the damages award or to enforce other court orders at the conclusion of the battery case):
- draft postjudgment discovery requests
- field investigation to monitor compliance with judgment
- online research (e.g., location of defendant's business assets)

Research References for Battery

Digests

In the digests of West, look for case summaries on battery under key topics such as:

Assault and Battery	Damages
Torts	Death

Corpus Juris Secundum

In this legal encyclopedia, see the discussion under topic headings such as:

Assault and Battery	Damages
Torts	Death

American Jurisprudence 2d

In this legal encyclopedia, see the discussion under topic headings such as:

Assault and Battery	Damages
Torts	Death

Legal Periodical Literature

There are two index systems to use to try to locate legal periodical literature on battery:

INDEX TO LEGAL PERIODICALS AND BOOKS (ILP)	CURRENT LAW INDEX (CLI)
See literature in *ILP* under subject headings such as:	See literature in *CLI* under subject headings such as:
Assault and Battery	Assault and Battery
Damages	Torts
Federal Tort Claims Act	Damages
Personal Injuries	Personal Injuries
Torts	
Wrongful Death	

Battery Checklist Continued

Example of a legal periodical article you will find by using *ILP* or *CLI:*

Smoker Battery: An Antidote to Second-Hand Smoke by Donald B. Ezra, 63 Southern California Law Review 1061 (1991).

A.L.R., A.L.R.2d, A.L.R.3d, A.L.R.4th, A.L.R.5th, A.L.R. Fed.

Use the *ALR Index* to locate annotations on battery. In this index, check subject headings such as:

Assault and Battery
Damages
Torts

Example of an annotation on battery you can locate through this index:

Civil Liability of Insane or Other Disordered Person for Assault or Battery, by C. R. McCorkle, 77 A.L.R.2d 625 (1961).

Words and Phrases

In this multivolume legal dictionary, look up *battery, harmful, offensive, apprehension,* and every other word or phrase connected with the tort discussed in this chapter. The dictionary will give you definitions of these words or phrases from court opinions.

CALR: Computer-Assisted Legal Research

Example of a query you could ask on WESTLAW or on LEXIS to try to find cases, statutes, or other legal materials on battery: **battery /p damages**

Example of search terms you could use on an Internet legal search engine such as LawCrawler (http://lawcrawler.findlaw.com) to find cases, statutes, or other legal materials on battery: **civil AND battery AND tort**

Example of search terms you could use on an Internet general search engine such as Alta Vista (http://www.altavista.com) to find cases, statutes, or other legal materials on battery: +**civil** +**battery** +**tort**

More Internet sites to check for materials on battery and other torts:
Jurist: (http://jurist.law.pitt.edu/sg_torts.htm)
LawGuru: (http://www.lawguru.com/search/lawsearch.html)
See also Tort Law Online at the end of Chapter 1.

ACT

There must be an **act** by the defendant that leads to contact with the plaintiff's person. An act is a voluntary movement of the body. Not all harmful or offensive contacts are the result of acts. For example, if Dan's arm hits Linda during a sleep walk, no battery exists because there is no act—no voluntary movement of Dan's body that caused the contact.

PERSON

The definition of **person** is broad. It means one's body, anything attached to one's body, or anything so closely associated with one's body as to be identified with it. A kick in the shin is clearly a contact with the body. So is a yank on a tie or other item of clothing worn by the plaintiff. The following cases also illustrate the broader definition of person:

- the defendant knocks off the plaintiff's hat
- the defendant pulls a plate out of the plaintiff's hand
- the defendant stabs or shoots a horse while the plaintiff is riding it

The hat, plate, and horse are so closely associated with the body in these cases as to be practically identified with it at the time of the contact. There does not have to be contact with the physical body.

Consciousness

The tort of battery is designed to protect the personal integrity of one's body against intentional invasions, which can occur even if one does not know it at the time. The plaintiff does not have to be conscious of the invasion.

> ▪ **EXAMPLE:** Jim kisses Lena while she is asleep or under anesthesia.

Lena has been battered by Jim.

INTENT

For purposes of battery, **intent** is the desire to bring about **imminent** harmful or offensive contact or to bring about an imminent apprehension of that contact. Imminent means immediate in the sense of no significant delay. In most cases, intent is not difficult to prove, because it is clear that the defendant wants to make contact with the plaintiff, e.g., the defendant picks up a bucket of water and pours it on the plaintiff's head. It is more difficult to prove intent when the defendant does not want contact to occur, but merely wants the plaintiff to think it will occur.

> **EXAMPLE:** Mary throws a hammer at George. She aims it several feet above George's head, hoping to scare him. Unfortunately, it hits him in the eye.

Mary can accurately say that she did not intend to hit George, but this is not a defense. She wanted him to think he was about to be hit. She intended to cause an **apprehension** (i.e., an understanding or awareness) of an imminent contact. This is sufficient to establish the element of intent.

Suppose that there is no desire to cause a contact or even an apprehension of one.

> **EXAMPLE:** Fred throws a stone through an open window of a crowded moving bus. His purpose is to have it pass through another open window at the other side of the bus without anyone noticing. One of the passengers, however, is hit by the stone.

Did Fred intend to hit the passenger? In general, intent is the desire to bring about the consequences of an act or the **knowledge with substantial certainty** that the consequences will follow from the act. If Fred had substantially certain knowledge that a passenger would be hit (or would have an apprehension of being hit), then he intended that result. Note, however, that merely being careless or even reckless is not enough to establish intent. There must be substantially certain knowledge. If all you can show is carelessness or recklessness, the tort to bring is *negligence* in creating an unreasonable risk of injuring someone, not the intentional tort of battery.

Transferred Intent

It is no defense to argue that the person hit is not the one the defendant intended to hit.

> **EXAMPLE:** Helen fires a gun at Paul. She misses him, but strikes Rich, whom she did not see.

Helen has battered Rich. Under the rule of **transferred intent,** her intent to hit Paul is transferred to Rich. (For more on transferred intent, see Figure 4–1 in Chapter 4.)

Motive

Motive is irrelevant. If the defendant intends a harmful or offensive contact, a battery has been committed, even if the defendant was trying to help the plaintiff through the contact.

> **EXAMPLE:**   On a rainy night, John falls off the curb. When a passerby tries to help, John says, "Don't touch me." Nevertheless, the passerby lifts John to carry him out of the rain.

The passerby has battered John. The fact that the motive may have been to be of help is no defense. As long as the contact is harmful or offensive (see next section), the tort has been committed. When we study medical malpractice in Chapter 12, we will see that treatment by a doctor without the informed consent of the patient is a battery in some states. Here again, the fact that the doctor had a benevolent motive would not be a defense. Most states, however, prefer that patients use negligence as the cause of action when they are treated without their informed consent.

HARMFUL OR OFFENSIVE CONTACT

Contact is **harmful** if it brings about physical damage, impairment, pain, or illness. It is **offensive** if it offends the personal dignity of an ordinary person who is not unduly sensitive.

Any physical damage, impairment, pain, or illness—no matter how trivial or slight—is considered harmful. The jury award that the plaintiff can recover for modest harm may be nominal, but even technical violations will give rise to a cause of action for battery.

If there is no harmful contact, the plaintiff may still be able to recover if the contact is offensive. An **objective standard** is used to determine when contact is offensive. The test is whether a reasonable person—someone not unduly sensitive—would be offended by the contact. If not, there is no battery, even though the plaintiff considered the contact offensive.

> **EXAMPLE:**   In a noisy, crowded subway, Jim approaches Cecile, a stranger. He gently taps her on the shoulder and says, "Would you please tell me the time?" Cecile is absolutely outraged by this contact, and screams.

A reasonable person would not consider this contact offensive, even though Cecile clearly does. In city life, a reasonable person expects a certain amount of contact as part of everyday living.

There is an exception to this rule when the defendant knows that the plaintiff has peculiar—even unreasonable—sensibilities about being touched. In such a case, the court will find the contact to be offensive even though someone of ordinary sensibilities would not be offended by it. The test of offensiveness is no longer objective when the defendant has such knowledge.

> **EXAMPLE:** Same situation involving Jim and Cecile, except that she is not a stranger, and Jim knows that she would be angered by the tap.

Here the contact is offensive. Jim's knowledge of her idiosyncrasy makes it so. (Depending on the severity of the circumstances, she may even have an action for the separate tort of intentional infliction of emotional distress. See Chapter 7.)

CONSENT AND PRIVILEGE

Consent is a complete defense. There is no liability for battery if the plaintiff permitted the contact.

> **EXAMPLE:** The plaintiff offers her arm to a doctor who is inoculating everyone in line.

The plaintiff cannot later say that the doctor battered her. She consents to the contact if certain conditions are met, e.g., she has the capacity to consent, she voluntarily does so, and she knows what she is consenting to. For an extensive discussion of consent, see Chapter 23.

Similarly, if the plaintiff has a **privilege** to cause a contact with the plaintiff, the latter cannot win a suit for battery. The privileges include self-defense, the defense of others, the defense of property, discipline, and arrest. The elements of these privileges are discussed in Chapters 5 and 23.

ASSIGNMENT

3.1

a. Bill is behind the steering wheel of his parked car. He sees Helen take a baseball bat and swing it at the windshield directly in front of him. The windshield cracks but does not shatter. Has a battery been committed? Why or why not? What other torts, if any, might have been committed?

b. Ed throws a snowball at Dan's house, knowing that Dan is inside. The moment Dan hears the snowball, he is afraid that he will be hit. Battery?

c. Sam makes a batch of cookies with poison in them. He leaves them in a hall next to a telephone booth. A stranger eats one after making a call. Has Sam battered the stranger? If not, has another tort been committed?

d. Diane and Bob are walking across the street. Bob is daydreaming and doesn't see a car about to hit him. Diane pushes him away from the path of the car into safety. But he falls and breaks his ankle from the push. Bob sues Diane for battery. What result?

e. In the case discussed in the text in which Fred threw a stone through the window of a moving bus, do you think that intent can be proven? What further facts would you like to have?

SUMMARY

Battery is a harmful or offensive contact with a person that results from the defendant's intent to cause either imminent contact or apprehension of imminent contact. There must be a voluntary movement of the defendant's body—an act. There must be actual contact with the person of the plaintiff. The plaintiff's person can include the plaintiff's body, anything attached to it, or anything so closely associated with the body as to be identified with it. The plaintiff does not have to be aware of the contact. The intent must be either the desire to bring about the contact or an imminent apprehension of the contact.

The law presumes the defendant had the requisite intent if he or she knew with substantial certainty that the contact or apprehension would result from his or her act. If the defendant intended to make contact with one person but in fact hit another, the law will transfer the intent to cover the latter. The defendant's motive is not relevant, even if it was to help (and even if the defendant does in fact help) the plaintiff through the contact.

The contact is harmful if it brings about physical damage, impairment, pain, or illness. It is offensive if it offends the personal dignity of an ordinary person who is not unduly sensitive. This objective test of offensiveness is used unless the defendant has reason to know that the plaintiff has an overly sensitive reaction to contact.

Consent and privilege are defenses to the cause of action of battery.

KEY TERMS

battery   23

deep pockets   23

shallow pockets   23

act   27

person   27

intent   28

imminent   28

apprehension   28

knowledge with substantial certainty   28

transferred intent   28

motive   28

harmful   29

offensive   29

objective standard   29

consent   30

privilege   30

Assault

Chapter Outline

- Introduction
- Act
- Apprehension
- Harmful or Offensive
- Transferred Intent
- Assault and Civil Rights

INTRODUCTION

Assault is an act that intentionally causes an apprehension of a harmful or offensive contact. Phrased another way, it means intentionally causing an awareness of a battery. The average citizen thinks of assault as an unwanted, and usually violent, contact with someone. But the tort of assault does not require actual contact. If someone hits you with a stick, a battery has been committed against you. If you were aware of the stick coming at you, an assault has also been committed against you. The contact and the apprehension (awareness) of the contact constitute separate torts. In criminal law, assault often means a violent contact; in the law of torts, however, it is the apprehension of a harmful or offensive contact.

 Assault Checklist

Definitions, Relationships, Paralegal Roles, and Research References

Category
Assault is an intentional tort.

Interest Protected by This Tort
The right to be free from the apprehension of a harmful or offensive contact.

Elements of This Tort
    i. Act ✓
    ii. Intent to cause either:
        a. an imminent harmful or offensive contact, or
        b. an apprehension of an imminent harmful or offensive contact

Assault Checklist Continued

   iii. Apprehension of an imminent harmful or offensive contact to the plaintiff's person
   iv. Causation

Definitions of Major Words/Phrases in the Elements

Act: A voluntary movement of the defendant's body.
Intent: Either:
  a. the desire to bring about the consequence of the act (i.e., the desire to cause the apprehension), or
  b. the substantially certain knowledge that the consequence (i.e., the apprehension) will follow from the act.
Apprehension: Anticipation, knowledge, or belief (fear is *not* required).
Imminent: Immediate in the sense of no significant delay (something can be imminent without being instantaneous).
Harmful: Involving physical impairment, pain, or illness.
Offensive: Offending the personal dignity of an ordinary person who is not unduly sensitive.
Causation: Either:
  a. but for the defendant's act, the consequence would not have occurred (i.e., the apprehension would not have occurred), or
  b. the defendant's act was a substantial factor in bringing about the consequence (i.e., the apprehension).

Major Defense and Counterargument Possibilities That Need to Be Explored

1. Defendant's conduct was involuntary (no act).
2. Defendant did not desire a contact or apprehension, or know with substantial certainty that the apprehension would result from what he or she did (no intent).
3. There was no apprehension.
4. The apprehension pertained to a future contact (no imminence).
5. The apprehension would have occurred even if the defendant did not do what he or she did. The defendant was not a substantial factor in producing the apprehension. (No causation.)
6. The plaintiff consented to the conduct of the defendant that led to the apprehension (on the defense of consent, see Chapter 23).
7. The apprehension resulted while the defendant was defending him- or herself from the plaintiff (on self-defense and other self-help privileges, see Chapter 23).
8. The apprehension occurred while the defendant was defending someone else from the plaintiff (on the defense of others and other self-help privileges, see Chapter 23).
9. The apprehension occurred while the defendant was defending property or recapturing chattels from the plaintiff (on the privileges of necessity, defense of property, recapture of property, and other self-help privileges, see Chapter 23).
10. The apprehension occurred while the defendant was disciplining plaintiff (on discipline and other self-help privileges, see Chapter 23).
11. The apprehension occurred while the defendant was arresting the plaintiff (on the privilege of arrest, see Chapter 5).
12. The plaintiff's suit against the government for an assault committed by a government employee may be barred by sovereign immunity (on sovereign immunity, see Chapter 23).
13. The plaintiff's suit against the government employee for assault may be barred by public official immunity (on official immunity, see Chapter 23).
14. The plaintiff's suit against the charitable organization for assault committed by someone working for the organization may be barred by charitable immunity (on charitable immunity, see Chapter 23).
15. The plaintiff's suit against a family member for assault may be barred by intrafamily immunity (on intrafamily immunity, see Chapter 23).

Damages

The plaintiff can recover compensatory damages for the apprehension, including pain and suffering, medical bills, and loss of wages. If the defendant acts out of hatred and malice in committing the assault, punitive damages are often awarded as well. (On the categories of damages, see Chapter 14.)

Assault Checklist Continued

Relationship to Criminal Law
The same act of the defendant can constitute a *civil* assault (for which the plaintiff recovers damages) and a *criminal* assault (for which the state collects a fine or imposes jail or imprisonment). The word "assault" in criminal law is often used interchangeably with the word "battery."

Other Torts and Related Actions
Battery: The defendant may intend to batter the plaintiff, but fail to do so. If, in the process, the plaintiff is aware of the attempted battery, the tort of assault is probably committed.

False Imprisonment: If the plaintiff is aware of the defendant's attempt to confine the plaintiff, there may be an apprehension of contact, and hence an assault as well as false imprisonment.

Intentional Infliction of Emotional Distress: Assaults frequently accompany this tort.

Negligence: If the defendant does not intentionally cause apprehension in the plaintiff, the defendant may be negligent in causing it. For the negligence action to succeed, there must be actual harm in addition to the apprehension.

Wrongful Death: A wrongful-death action can be brought by the survivors of the plaintiff if death results from the assault.

Federal Law
a. Under the Federal Tort Claims Act, the United States Government will *not* be liable for an assault committed by one of its federal employees within the scope of employment (respondeat superior) *unless* the federal employee is an investigative or law enforcement officer. (See Figure 23–7 in Chapter 23.)
b. There may be liability under the Civil Rights Act if the assault was committed while the defendant was depriving the plaintiff of federal rights under color of law. (See Figure 23–8 in Chapter 23.)
c. There may be liability under the federal Free Access to Clinic Entrances Act (FACE) for assaults committed against people seeking or providing "reproductive health services."

Employer-Employee (Agency) Law
An employee who commits an assault is personally liable for this tort. His or her employer will *also* be liable for assault if the conduct of the employee was within the scope of employment (respondeat superior). The employee must be furthering a business objective of the employer at the time. Intentional torts such as assault, however, are often outside the scope of employment. If so, only the employee is liable for the assault. (On the factors that determine the scope of employment, see Figure 12–7 in Chapter 12.)

Paralegal Roles in Assault Litigation
Fact finding (help the office collect facts relevant to prove the elements of assault, the elements of available defenses, and extent of injuries or other damages):
- client interviewing
- field investigation
- online research

File management (help the office control the volume of paperwork in an assault litigation):
- open client file
- enter case data in computer database
- maintain file documents

Litigation assistance (help the trial attorney prepare for an assault trial and appeal, if needed):
- draft discovery requests
- draft answers to discovery requests
- draft pleadings
- digest and index discovery documents
- help prepare, order, and manage trial exhibits (visuals or demonstratives)
- prepare trial notebook
- draft notice of appeal
- order trial transcript
- cite check briefs
- perform legal research

Assault Checklist Continued

Collection/enforcement (help the trial attorney for the judgment creditor to collect the damages award or to enforce other court orders at the conclusion of the assault case):
- draft postjudgment discovery requests
- field investigation to monitor compliance with judgment
- online research (e.g., location of defendant's business assets)

Research References for Assault

Digests

In the digests of West, look for case summaries on assault under key topics such as:

Assault and Battery	Damages
Torts	

Corpus Juris Secundum

In this legal encyclopedia, see the discussions under topic headings such as:

Assault and Battery	Damages
Torts	

American Jurisprudence 2d

In this legal encyclopedia, see the discussions under topic headings such as:

Assault and Battery	Damages
Torts	

Legal Periodical Literature

There are two index systems to use to try to locate legal periodical literature on assault:

INDEX TO LEGAL PERIODICALS AND BOOKS (ILP)	CURRENT LAW INDEX (CLI)
See literature in *ILP* under subject headings such as:	See literature in *CLI* under subject headings such as:
Assault and Battery	Assault and Battery
Damages	Torts
Federal Tort Claims Act	Damages
Personal Injuries	Personal Injuries
Torts	
Wrongful Death	

Example of a legal periodical article you will find by using *ILP* or *CLI:*

> *Respondeat Superior and the Intentional Tort: A Short Discourse on How to Make Assault and Battery a Part of the Job* by J. Terry Griffith, 45 University of Cincinnati Law Review 235 (1976).

A.L.R., A.L.R.2d, A.L.R.3d, A.L.R.4th, A.L.R.5th, A.L.R. Fed.

Use the *ALR Index* to locate annotations on assault. In this index, check subject headings such as:

Assault and Battery	Damages
Torts	

Example of an annotation on assault you can locate through this index:

> *Federal Tort Claims Act Provision Exempting from Coverage Claim Arising out of Assault, Battery, False Imprisonment, False Arrest, Malicious Prosecution, etc.* by W. J. Dunn, 23 A.L.R.2d 574 (1952).

Words and Phrases

In this multivolume legal dictionary, look up *assault, apprehension, imminent, harmful, offensive, transferred intent,* and every other word or phrase connected with assault discussed in this chapter. The dictionary will give you definitions of these words or phrases from court opinions.

CALR: Computer-Assisted Legal Research

Example of a query you could ask on WESTLAW or on LEXIS to try to find cases, statutes, or other legal materials on assault: **assault/p damages**

Assault Checklist Continued

Example of search terms you could use on an Internet legal search engine such as Law-Crawler (http://lawcrawler.findlaw.com) to find cases, statutes, or other legal materials on assault: **civil AND assault AND tort**

Example of search terms you could use on an Internet general search engine such as Alta Vista (http://www.altavista.com) to find cases, statutes, or other legal materials on assault: **+civil +assault +tort**

More Internet sites to check for materials on assault and other torts:
Jurist: (http://jurist.law.pitt.edu/sg_torts.htm)
LawGuru: (http://www.lawguru.com/search/lawsearch.html)
See also Tort Law Online at the end of Chapter 1.

ACT

The apprehension of a harmful or offensive contact must be caused by an **act,** which is a voluntary movement of the body.

> **EXAMPLE:**   A stranger pushes Jim, who then falls toward Ed. When Ed sees Jim coming, he quickly gets out of the way.

Ed, concerned about being hit by Jim, clearly had an apprehension of a harmful or offensive contact. But Jim did not commit an act that caused this apprehension. Because of the stranger's push, Jim involuntarily moved toward Ed. The stranger committed an act; Jim did not.

APPREHENSION

Apprehension is an understanding, awareness, anticipation, belief, or knowledge of something. It is not the equivalent of fear, although fear certainly qualifies as apprehension.

> **EXAMPLES:**
>
> * Greg (a 300-pound wrestler) swings his fist at Martha (a seventy-year-old, petite widow) because she called him a "bum" at a match. Terrified, Martha ducks just in time to avoid his punch.
> * Later, Martha raises her newspaper to strike Greg in the stomach. Laughing, Greg steps back to avoid Martha's swing.

Greg and Martha have assaulted each other. Both had an awareness—an apprehension—of a harmful or offensive contact. Martha was afraid; Greg was not. But fear or intimidation is not required.

Greg laughed. Doesn't this mean he didn't think Martha was going to do something harmful or offensive? It depends on the meaning of harmful and offensive. This brings us to the third element of assault.

HARMFUL OR OFFENSIVE

As we saw in Chapter 3 on battery, **harmful** means bringing about physical damage, impairment, pain, or illness; and **offensive** means offending the dignity of an ordinary person who is not unduly sensitive. A smack on the stomach with a newspaper could cause pain, no matter how slight. Also, it is hardly a friendly gesture. Furthermore, most people would take offense at being hit under these circumstances. Greg may have thought it was all a big joke. Yet note that he stepped back to avoid the newspaper. To him, the idea of a fight with an old lady may have been ludicrous, but he clearly didn't appreciate being hit. Most people wouldn't. He was not *afraid* of a harmful or offensive contact, but he surely had an *apprehension* of one, however minor it might have been.

Reasonable

The plaintiff must be **reasonable** in claiming that he or she experienced an apprehension of the contact. The plaintiff may actually feel that a harmful or offensive contact is coming, but if this concern is peculiar or excessive, there is no tort of assault. There may, however, be an exception if the defendant knows that the plaintiff is unreasonably sensitive but proceeds to cause the apprehension anyway.

Imminent

The apprehension must be of an **imminent** harmful or offensive contact. A future or **conditional threat** is not enough.

> **EXAMPLE:**   On Monday, Ted calls Don on the phone and says, "If you don't pay your debt to me by this Friday, I'll be by Saturday to kill you." When Don hangs up the phone, he breaks out in a sweat because he knows Ted can be very violent.

There is no doubt that Don apprehends a very dangerous harmful and offensive contact. Yet it is not an imminent contact. It is scheduled to happen in the future (Saturday), and is conditional (on not paying the debt by Friday). Imminent means immediate, without significant delay. Verbal threats alone are often not sufficient when they explicitly relate to future conduct. Furthermore, the defendant must have the **apparent present ability** to carry out the threat. If the defendant points a toy gun at the plaintiff and threatens to shoot, there is no imminent apprehension if the plaintiff knows that the gun is a toy that is incapable of firing anything.

ASSIGNMENT

4.1

a. Recall the example given in the text of the stranger pushing Jim, who then falls toward Ed. When Ed sees Jim coming toward him, he quickly gets out of the way. As we said in the text, Jim did not commit an assault on Ed. What torts, if any, did the stranger commit?

b. Several Ku Klux Klan members in white robes march on the sidewalk five feet in front of a black person's house for about thirty minutes. The black person is terrified. Have the KKK members assaulted this person?

c. Sam puts an unloaded gun on the table in front of Mary and says, "This is for you if you don't cooperate." Mary knows the gun is unloaded but is terrified because Sam has thrown things at her in the past. Did Sam assault Mary with the gun?

TRANSFERRED INTENT

Assume that the defendant intends to assault one person, but in fact assaults the plaintiff, whom the defendant never knew existed. In spite of this mistake, the plaintiff has been assaulted by the defendant. This result is due to the doctrine of **transferred intent**. The defendant's intent to assault one person has been transferred to another person—the unintended plaintiff. Assault is not the only intentional tort that protects unintended plaintiffs through transferred intent. There are four others: battery, false imprisonment, trespass to land, and trespass to chattels.

In addition to unintended plaintiffs, there also can be unintended torts that are subject to a similar transfer under the doctrine of transferred intent. For an overview of unintended plaintiffs and unintended torts involving these five torts, see Figure 4–1.

FIGURE 4–1   Doctrine of transferred intent: What to do about an unintended plaintiff and/or an unintended tort?

Unintended Plaintiff

a. Defendant (D) intends to commit one of the following five torts against P_1:

Assault
Battery
False Imprisonment
Trespass to Land
Trespass to Chattel

b. In fact, this tort is committed against P_2.
c. D did not intend to commit this tort against P_2.

Result: The law will transfer D's intent from P_1 to P_2 in order to make D liable for this tort to P_2.

Examples:

• D wants to lock Mary in a room. D mistakes Fran for Mary and falsely imprisons Fran. Fran can sue D for false imprisonment.
• D throws a rock, intending to hit Paul's car. The rock misses Paul's car and hits Bill's van. Bill can sue D for trespass to chattels.

In the above two examples, it is irrelevant that D did not intend to commit any tort against Fran or Bill. They are unintended plaintiffs to whom D is liable under the doctrine of transferred intent.

Unintended Tort

a. Defendant (D) intends to commit acts that would constitute one of the following five torts:

Assault
Battery
False Imprisonment
Trespass to Land
Trespass to Chattel

b. In fact, D commits one of the other four torts.
c. D did not intend to commit the tort that occurred.

Result: The law will transfer D's intent from the tort D intended to commit to the tort that in fact resulted in order to make D liable for the latter tort.

Example:

• D wants to lock Joe in a room. D does not succeed because the door to the room has no lock. By mistake, however, D causes Joe to be in apprehension of being hit. Joe can sue D for assault.

In the above example, it is irrelevant that D did not intend to commit assault against Joe. An unintended tort has been committed for which D is liable under the doctrine of transferred intent.

ASSAULT AND CIVIL RIGHTS

In Chapter 23 we will examine the Civil Rights Act, which is a federal statute that gives someone a right to damages for being deprived of federal rights under color of law. (See Figure 23–8 in Chapter 23.) There are other statutes that also provide similar remedies for civil rights violations. An example is the federal Free Access to Clinic Entrances Act (**FACE**). Between 1977 and 1993, over 1,000 acts of violence were committed against abortion providers. Thousands of clinic blockades also occurred. In response, Congress passed FACE, which provides a remedy for anyone who is a victim of assault or other attack while seeking or providing "reproductive health services." 18 U.S.C.A. § 248. The statute provides that "civil remedies" will be available against anyone who:

> "by force or threat of force or by physical obstruction, intentionally injures, intimidates or interferes with or attempts to injure, intimidate or interfere with any person because that person is or has been, or in order to intimidate such person or any other person or any class of persons from obtaining or providing reproductive health services. . . ." § 248(a)(1).

SUMMARY

An assault is an act (usually an attempted battery) that causes apprehension of an imminent harmful or offensive contact. There is no requirement that the plaintiff fear—he or she need only be aware of—a coming harmful or offensive contact. "Harmful" means bringing about physical damage, impairment, pain, or illness; "offensive" means offending the dignity of an ordinary person who is not unduly sensitive.

The plaintiff must be reasonable in claiming that he or she experienced the apprehension. Furthermore, the apprehension must pertain to an imminent (not a future or conditional) harmful or offensive contact.

If the defendant intends to assault one person, but mistakenly assaults another, the defendant is liable for assault to the unintended plaintiff. This doctrine of transferred intent also covers the intentional torts of battery, false imprisonment, trespass to land, and trespass to chattels. In addition, under this doctrine, the defendant's intent to commit one of these five torts will also make the defendant liable for one of the other four unintended torts that results from what the defendant did.

The federal Free Access to Clinic Entrances Act (FACE) provides a civil cause of action for a person who has been threatened or otherwise attacked while seeking or providing reproductive health services.

KEY TERMS

assault 33

act 33

apprehension 33

harmful 33

offensive 33

reasonable 38

imminent 38

conditional threat 38

apparent present ability 38

transferred intent 38

FACE 39

False Imprisonment

Chapter Outline

- Introduction
- False Imprisonment
- False Arrest

INTRODUCTION

The tort of **false imprisonment** covers much more than prisons and jails. It protects the right of everyone to move about freely. The most obvious example of this tort is being locked in a room. But imprisonment is not limited to forcing a person to remain within an enclosed structure. It is possible to falsely imprison someone in an area where there are no walls. Recently, a celebrity brought a false imprisonment suit against *paparazzi*—photographers who stalk celebrities for photographs outside restaurants, in parking lots, on the sidewalk, on the freeway, etc. To understand how such conduct might constitute false imprisonment, we need to explore the broader dimension of this intentional tort.

FALSE IMPRISONMENT

 False Imprisonment Checklist

Definitions, Relationships, Paralegal Roles, and Research References

Category
False imprisonment is an intentional tort.

Interest Protected by This Tort
The right to be free from intentional restraints on one's freedom of movement.

False Imprisonment Checklist Continued

Elements of This Tort
  i. An act that completely confines the plaintiff within fixed boundaries set by the defendant
  ii. Intent to confine the plaintiff or a third party
  iii. Causation of the confinement
  iv. The plaintiff was either conscious of the confinement or suffered actual harm by it

Definitions of Major Words/Phrases in These Elements
Act: A volitional movement of the defendant's body by words or other conduct.
Confine: To restrain the plaintiff's freedom of movement:
  a. by physical barriers, or
  b. by physical force, or
  c. by the threat of present physical force, or
  d. by asserting legal authority to confine, or
  e. by refusing to release the plaintiff.
Complete: A total confinement where the plaintiff knows of no safe or inoffensive means of escape.
Intent to Confine: The desire to confine the plaintiff or the knowledge with substantial certainty that the defendant's act will result in the confinement.
Causation: But for the defendant's act, the plaintiff would not have been confined, or the defendant was a substantial factor in producing the confinement.
Harmed: Actual damage or injury in addition to the confinement itself.

Major Defense and Counterargument Possibilities That Need to Be Explored
  1. There was no confinement.
  2. The confinement was not total; there was a safe and inoffensive means of escape that the plaintiff did not take.
  3. The threat of force related to the future.
  4. The confinement was accidental. It may have been negligently or recklessly caused, but it was not intentional.
  5. The defendant was not a substantial factor in producing the confinement.
  6. The plaintiff either did not know about the confinement or was not physically harmed by it.
  7. The plaintiff consented to the confinement by the defendant (on the defense of consent, see Chapter 23).
  8. The confinement resulted while the defendant was defending him- or herself from the plaintiff (on self-defense and other self-help privileges, see Chapter 23).
  9. The confinement occurred while the defendant was defending someone else from the plaintiff (on the defense of others and other self-help privileges, see Chapter 23).
  10. The confinement occurred while the defendant was legitimately defending property or recapturing chattels from the plaintiff (on the privileges of necessity, defense of property, recapture of property, and other self-help privileges, see Chapter 23).
  11. The confinement occurred while the defendant was detaining plaintiff for investigation to determine whether the plaintiff had stolen property or services (shopkeeper's privilege, covered in this chapter).
  12. The confinement occurred while the defendant was disciplining the plaintiff (on discipline and other self-help privileges, see Chapter 23).
  13. The confinement occurred while the defendant was arresting the plaintiff (privilege of arrest, covered in this chapter).
  14. The plaintiff's suit against the government for false imprisonment committed by a government employee may be barred by sovereign immunity (on sovereign immunity, see Chapter 23).
  15. The plaintiff's suit against the government employee for false imprisonment may be barred by public official immunity (on official immunity, see Chapter 23).
  16. The plaintiff's suit against the charitable organization for a false imprisonment committed by someone working for the organization may be barred by charitable immunity (on charitable immunity, see Chapter 23).
  17. The plaintiff's suit against a family member for false imprisonment may be barred by intrafamily immunity (on intrafamily immunity, see Chapter 18).

False Imprisonment Checklist Continued

18. The plaintiff failed to take reasonable steps to mitigate the harm caused when the defendant committed false imprisonment; therefore, damages should not cover the aggravation of the harm caused by the plaintiff (on the doctrine of avoidable consequences, see Chapter 14).

Damages

The plaintiff does not have to prove actual harm to establish a prima facie case of false imprisonment (unless the plaintiff was unaware of the confinement). In most cases, the confinement is harm enough. Once the elements of false imprisonment have been proven, the jury will be allowed to consider compensatory damages for humiliation, injury to plaintiff's reputation, illness or other physical discomfort, loss of earnings or other damage to personal property due to the confinement, etc. If the defendant acted out of hatred or malice, punitive damages are also possible.

Relationship to Criminal Law

In many states, false imprisonment is also a crime if the confinement is serious enough. The crime may be called false imprisonment, abduction, kidnapping, etc.

Relationship to Other Torts

Assault: An assault may also be committed if the defendant puts the plaintiff in apprehension of a harmful or offensive contact while falsely imprisoning him or her.

Battery: It is common for the defendant to touch the plaintiff while falsely imprisoning him or her. If this touching was without consent, the defendant may also be liable for a battery.

Defamation: Defamation may occur during the false imprisonment. For example, the defendant may use derogatory language while confining the plaintiff. Also, the very act of being confined may be a derogatory "communication," especially if the defendant is a police officer and the confinement is seen by others.

Intentional Infliction of Emotional Distress: This tort may also be committed if the intent of the defendant who falsely imprisoned the plaintiff was to subject the plaintiff to severe emotional trauma by the confinement.

Malicious Prosecution: If the defendant has instigated an unlawful arrest of the plaintiff, the defendant may be liable for false imprisonment and for malicious prosecution if the defendant acted with malice, without probable cause, and if the criminal case terminated favorably to the plaintiff.

Negligence: The defendant may have caused the confinement of the plaintiff by carelessness or recklessness rather than with the intent to confine him or her, e.g., the defendant accidentally, but carelessly or recklessly, locks the plaintiff in a room. If so, there is no false imprisonment, but there may be negligence if the plaintiff has suffered actual harm in addition to the confinement itself.

Federal Law

a. Under the Federal Tort Claims Act, the United States Government will *not* be liable for a false imprisonment committed by one of its federal employees within the scope of employment (respondeat superior) *unless* the federal employee is an investigative or law enforcement officer. (See Figure 23–7 in Chapter 23.)

b. There may be liability under the Civil Rights Act if the false imprisonment was committed while the defendant was depriving the plaintiff of federal rights under color of law. (See Figure 23–8 in Chapter 23.)

Employer-Employee (Agency) Law

An employee who commits false imprisonment is personally liable for this tort. His or her employer will *also* be liable for false imprisonment if the conduct of the employee was within the scope of employment (respondeat superior). The employee must be furthering a business objective of the employer at the time. Intentional torts such as false imprisonment, however, are often outside the scope of employment. If so, only the employee is liable for the false imprisonment. (On the factors that determine the scope of employment, see Figure 12–7 in Chapter 12.)

False Imprisonment Checklist Continued

Paralegal Roles in False Imprisonment Litigation

Fact finding (help the office collect facts relevant to prove the elements of false imprisonment, the elements of available defenses, and extent of injuries or other damages):
- client interviewing
- field investigation
- online research

File management (help the office control the volume of paperwork in a false imprisonment litigation):
- open client file
- enter case data in computer database
- maintain file documents

Litigation assistance (help the trial attorney prepare for a false imprisonment trial and appeal, if needed):
- draft discovery requests
- draft answers to discovery requests
- draft pleadings
- digest and index discovery documents
- help prepare, order, and manage trial exhibits (visuals or demonstratives)
- prepare trial notebook
- draft notice of appeal
- order trial transcript
- cite check briefs
- perform legal research

Collection/enforcement (help the trial attorney for the judgment creditor to collect the damages award or to enforce other court orders at the conclusion of the false imprisonment case):
- draft postjudgment discovery requests
- field investigation to monitor compliance with judgment
- online research (e.g., location of defendant's business assets)

Research References for False Imprisonment

Digests
In the digests of West, look for case summaries on false imprisonment under key topics such as:

False Imprisonment	Torts
Arrest	Damages

Corpus Juris Secundum
In this legal encyclopedia, look for discussions under topic headings such as:

False Imprisonment	Torts
Arrest	Damages

American Jurisprudence 2d
In this legal encyclopedia, look for discussions under topic headings such as:

False Imprisonment	Torts
Arrest	Damages

Legal Periodical Literature
There are two index systems to use to try to locate legal periodical literature on false imprisonment:

INDEX TO LEGAL PERIODICALS AND BOOKS (ILP)	CURRENT LAW INDEX (CLI)
See literature in *ILP* under subject headings such as:	See literature in *CLI* under subject headings such as:
False Imprisonment	False Imprisonment
Arrest	Arrest

False Imprisonment Checklist Continued

INDEX TO LEGAL
PERIODICALS AND BOOKS (ILP)
- Damages
- Torts
- Personal Injuries

CURRENT LAW INDEX
(CLI)
- Tort
- Damages
- Duress
- Personal Injuries
- Privileges and Immunities

Example of a legal periodical article on this tort you will find by using *ILP* or *CLI*:

"Nowhere to Go and Chose to Stay"; Using the Tort of False Imprisonment to Redress Involuntary Confinement of the Elderly in Nursing Homes and Hospitals by Cathrael Kazin, 137 University of Pennsylvania Law Review 903 (1989).

A.L.R., A.L.R.2d, A.L.R.3d, A.L.R.4th, A.L.R.5th, A.L.R. Fed.
Use the *ALR Index* to locate annotations on false imprisonment. In this index, check subject headings such as:

False Imprisonment	Shoplifting
Arrest	Torts
Privileges and Immunities	Damages

Example of an annotation on false imprisonment you can locate through this index:

Liability of Attorney Acting for Client for False Imprisonment or Malicious Prosecution of Third Party, 27 A.L.R.3d 1113 by J. Kraut (1969).

Words and Phrases
In this multivolume legal dictionary, look up *false imprisonment, confinement, false arrest,* and every other word or phrase connected with the torts discussed in this chapter. The dictionary will give you definitions of these words or phrases from court opinions.

CALR: Computer-Assisted Legal Research
Example of a query you could ask on WESTLAW to try to find cases, statutes, or other legal materials on false imprisonment: **"false imprisonment" /p damages**

Example of a query you could ask on LEXIS to try to find cases, statutes, or other legal materials on false imprisonment: **false imprisonment /p damages**

Example of search terms you could use on an Internet legal search engine such as Law-Crawler (http://lawcrawler.findlaw.com) to find cases, statutes, or other legal materials on false imprisonment: **"false imprisonment"**

Example of search terms you could use on an Internet general search engine such as Alta Vista (http://www.altavista.com) to find cases, statutes, or other legal materials on false imprisonment: **"false imprisonment" -crime**

More Internet sites to check for materials on false imprisonment and other torts:
Jurist: (http://jurist.law.pitt.edu/sg_torts.htm)
LawGuru: (http://www.lawguru.com/search/lawsearch.html)
See also Tort Law Online at the end of Chapter 1.

Confinement

The first element of false imprisonment is an act that completely confines the plaintiff within fixed boundaries set by the defendant. The word "imprisonment" is very misleading. To commit this tort, you do not have to place someone behind bars without authority. Such an act will constitute false imprisonment, as will an illegal delay in releasing someone from jail or prison. But false imprisonment is not limited to such extreme situations. It can also occur when there is a **confinement** of one's freedom of movement. This confinement or restraint can happen in five ways:

Confinement by Physical Barrier
Tangible, physical restraints or barriers are imposed on the plaintiff.

> **EXAMPLES:**
>
> - The defendant locks the plaintiff in a room.
> - The defendant takes away the plaintiff's wheelchair.
> - The defendant takes away the plaintiff's ladder that is necessary to climb out of a deep ditch.

Confinement by Physical Force Against the Plaintiff, the Plaintiff's Immediate Family, or the Plaintiff's Property

> **EXAMPLES:**
>
> - If the defendant grabs or holds the plaintiff, confinement results from physical force on the plaintiff's body.
> - The plaintiff can also be confined if the defendant uses physical force on the plaintiff's child or other members of his or her immediate family. Suppose that the defendant ties up the plaintiff's son. The plaintiff may be able to escape, but it is highly unlikely that he or she will do so while the child is in danger. Hence, the defendant has confined *both* the child and the plaintiff. The physical force used against the child has also resulted in the confinement of the parent.
> - Finally, suppose that the defendant uses physical force against the plaintiff's valuable property, such as by seizing the plaintiff's watch. The plaintiff stays in order to try to get the watch back. (As we will see in Chapter 23, the plaintiff has a **privilege to recapture** such property.)

In the last two examples, the parent who remains because his or her child is tied up and the plaintiff who remains to see about a watch that has been taken, have "agreed" to stay, but they have done so under such severe **duress** that the confinement is not voluntary. The confinement is imposed on the plaintiffs as effectively in these situations as when actual physical force is used on a plaintiff's body.

Confinement by Threat of Present Physical Force Against the Plaintiff, Against the Plaintiff's Immediate Family, or Against the Plaintiff's Property
A plaintiff's freedom of movement is certainly restricted if the defendant threatens present force or violence against the plaintiff, against a member of the plaintiff's immediate family, or against the plaintiff's valuable property if the plaintiff tries to escape or move out of an area designated by the defendant. If the plaintiff submits to the threat and remains, a confinement has occurred for purposes of establishing the first element of the tort of false imprisonment. The plaintiff does not have to be reasonable in submitting as long as the defendant has the intent to confine the plaintiff through the threat of immediate physical force.[1]

Confinement by Asserted Legal Authority
Here the defendant claims the legal authority or right to confine or arrest the plaintiff. Confinement occurs when the plaintiff is taken into custody. If the defendant does not have the privilege of arresting the plaintiff, as defined later in the chapter, the first element of false imprisonment has been met. No physical force or touching need be used as long as the plaintiff has reason to believe that such force will be used if the plaintiff either moves outside an area designated by the defendant or fails to follow the defendant.

Confinement by Refusal to Release
Assume that the plaintiff has been validly confined, e.g., imprisoned. At the time when the plaintiff has a right to be released, he or she has been improperly confined if the defendant interferes with the release.

Confinement in any of the five ways must be complete or total, meaning that the plaintiff must know of no safe or inoffensive means of escape out of the fixed bound-

---

[1] *Restatement (Second) of Torts* § 40 comment d (1965).

aries set by the defendant. There is no confinement, for example, if the defendant blocks the plaintiff's path when there is a clear and accessible way around the defendant. Nor is there confinement when the defendant locks all the doors of a house if the plaintiff is able to escape by climbing out of a window that is very close to the ground and if the inconvenience in climbing out is slight. A different result would follow, however, if the plaintiff had little or no clothing on, or would have substantial difficulty climbing out because of age or illness.

Finally, there is no set length of time that the confinement must last. A person can be confined for a brief or a prolonged period.

A great many false imprisonment cases result from detention in shops and department stores when a customer is suspected of stealing merchandise or services. A **shopkeeper's privilege** gives a shopkeeper the right to detain someone temporarily for the sole purpose of investigating whether theft has occurred. Reasonable force can be used to carry out this temporary investigation. The shopkeeper must be reasonable in suspecting that the person has committed the crime. If it turns out that the person is innocent and that the shopkeeper has made a mistake, the latter is still protected if the mistake was reasonable.

Every state has a shopkeeper's privilege in one form or another. The privilege may have been created by the courts as part of the **common law** or by the legislature as part of its statutory code.

The following example demonstrates the operation of the privilege.

> **EXAMPLE:**   George is a store clerk at Macy's. He sees Fred, a teenager, take a watch from the counter, put it in his pocket, and walk out the door without paying. In the parking lot, George orders Fred to the back room of the store. After about ten minutes of questioning, George concludes that Fred stole the watch. As Fred breaks down and cries, George spends about an hour lecturing Fred about the morality of stealing. He then calls the police. Later, Fred sues Macy's for false imprisonment.

The store can raise the defense of shopkeeper's privilege to cover the time when Fred was escorted to the back room and questioned about payment for the watch. The privilege, however, would *not* cover the period after George completed his investigation of Fred. There is no shopkeeper's privilege to lecture thieves about the morality of what they are doing. During the time of the lecture, Fred was falsely imprisoned.

ASSIGNMENT
5.1

Jim is soliciting religious contributions in Leo's department store. Leo tells Jim that this is not allowed in the store. Jim nevertheless continues. Leo and four of his security guards surround Jim and tell him to come to the manager's office. Jim does so. In the manager's office, Leo shouts at Jim and tells him, "you've got thirty seconds to get out the back door." Jim leaves and sues Leo for false imprisonment. Discuss Jim's chances of winning.

Intent

False imprisonment is an intentional tort. To establish **intent,** the defendant must desire to confine or know with substantial certainty that confinement will result from what he or she does. If the defendant is merely negligent or reckless in causing the confinement, the intentional tort of false imprisonment has not been committed. The tort of **negligence** might be possible. A negligence suit, however, requires proof of actual damages, whereas for false imprisonment, no more damages than the confinement itself need be shown. (See, however, an exception in the next section on causation covering cases in which the plaintiff was unaware of the confinement.)

> **EXAMPLE:** The defendant locks up an old building and carelessly or even recklessly fails to check whether anyone is still inside. This is not enough to establish intent to confine, because the defendant neither desired nor knew with substantial certainty that someone would be confined.

The doctrine of **transferred intent** applies. If the defendant intends to confine one person, but mistakenly confines a plaintiff whom the defendant never even knew existed, the requisite intent has been established. The defendant's intent to confine one person is transferred to another person who is in fact confined by the defendant's intentional conduct. (On transferred intent, see Figure 4–1 in Chapter 4.)

Causation

To establish the element of **causation,** the plaintiff must be able to show that either:

- but for the act of the defendant the plaintiff would not have been confined, or
- the defendant was a substantial factor in producing the plaintiff's confinement.

The defendant need not be the sole cause of the confinement.

> **EXAMPLE:** A citizen makes a complaint about a person to a police officer. The latter makes an arrest of the person—a false arrest, because the privilege to arrest, to be discussed later, does not apply.

The question arises whether the citizen who made the complaint to the police officer is liable for the false imprisonment that resulted from the false arrest. Was the citizen a substantial factor in the false arrest? The answer depends on whether the citizen instigated the arrest, as opposed to simply reporting the facts to the police officer who made up his or her own mind on whether to arrest. **Instigation** consists of insisting, directing, encouraging, or participating in the arrest. There must be persuasion or influencing of some kind in order for the citizen to have been a substantial factor in producing the arrest by the police officer. Without this instigation, the citizen has not caused the confinement.

Consciousness or Harm

The courts are split on whether the plaintiff must *know* that he or she is being confined. Some courts do not require consciousness of the confinement. The tort of false imprisonment can exist even if the plaintiff was ignorant of the confinement.

> **EXAMPLE:** Sam walks into a room to sleep. After he falls asleep, someone locks the door to the room for one hour. By the time Sam wakes up, however, the door has been unlocked.

Sam was unaware that he had been confined for one hour. In some states, this is not relevant. False imprisonment has still been committed. Other states require consciousness of confinement. These states, however, make an exception if the victim suffered actual harm (e.g., an illness) during the confinement. If such harm can be shown, recovery will be allowed even though the victim was unaware of the confinement. In general, actual harm is not an element of false imprisonment. The confinement itself is sufficient. In cases where the plaintiff was unaware of the confinement, however, some states require a showing of actual harm.

ASSIGNMENT

5.2

In each of the following four situations, determine whether false imprisonment has been committed.

a. Luis is driving a car down the highway. His two-year-old son, Fred, is in the back seat playing. It is a three-lane highway going one way; Luis is in the middle lane. Dan's car is in the far right lane. Luis gives a right-turn signal. He wants to go to the far right lane in order to make a right turn. Dan is driving to the immediate right of Luis. Dan refuses to yield, forcing Luis to miss his turn. Luis loses fifteen minutes in taking an alternate route to where he was headed. Luis and Fred sue Dan for false imprisonment.

b. Mary calls John on the phone and threatens to kill him by 2 P.M. tomorrow unless John goes downtown to pay a debt that John owes Mary's company. John does so. He later sues Mary for false imprisonment.

c. Jane is one of the guests on the talk show called, "How Nasty Can You Get?" She says she was invited on the show to receive a surprise on the air. She thought the surprise might be that she was going to receive a free trip to Germany to visit her husband who was stationed at a military base there. Instead she was told by her sister, Ann, that Jane's husband was the father of Ann's recently born baby. Jane was stunned and disgusted. She immediately stood up and tried to take her microphone off so that she could leave. Because the wire was attached through Jane's clothes, she was unable to disconnect the wire. After about five minutes, a stagehand helped her remove the microphone so that she could leave. She now brings a false imprisonment suit against the TV station for inviting her on the program under false pretenses and for the five minutes of humiliation when she could not unhook the microphone.

d. Paul Richardson is a photographer for the SinSational Daily News. He is in the parking lot of the Fillmore Maternity Clinic waiting for Sally Starr to emerge with her first-born child. Sally is an international recording artist. Suddenly he spots her coming out through a side door. He sees Sally's husband help her into a car. Paul quickly gets into his own car and races toward the exit where Sally's car is headed. Paul blocks this exit, jumps out of his car, goes over to Sally's car, and takes her picture through the car window. He then gets back into his own car and drives it out of the way of the exit. Sally's husband drives through. Paul follows behind through city streets for over three hours. Sally's husband wants to stop and confront Paul. But Sally says, "No, don't stop. I'm too sick to stop. He's got us trapped on this road." Finally Paul gives up and returns without obtaining any more pictures. Sally and her husband now sue Paul for false imprisonment.

FALSE ARREST

One way to commit false imprisonment is to make a **false arrest.** An arrest is false when it is not privileged. Private citizens as well as peace officers have a privilege to arrest. A summary of the privilege each enjoys is presented in Figure 5–1.

Throughout this discussion, our concern is the **personal liability** of the individual making the arrest. When someone is personally liable for a wrong, the consequence is that an adverse judgment is paid out of the pocket of the wrongdoer. When the defendant is a peace officer, a separate question arises as to whether the government that employs the officer is *also* liable for the tort on a theory of **respondeat superior.** The answer depends upon whether the government has waived its sovereign immunity for this kind of claim. Sovereign immunity is considered in Chapter 23.

Peace Officer's Privilege to Arrest

When a **peace officer** has a **warrant** to arrest someone, the arrest is privileged as long as the warrant is **fair on its face.** Courts differ on the meaning of this phrase. Most courts will give it a broad interpretation in order to protect the peace officer. A warrant is not fair on its face if it is obviously defective, e.g., the warrant does not name the party to be arrested or does not state the crime charged. An officer is not required to be an attorney who knows how to analyze the warrant in all its

FIGURE 5–1 Comparison of Peace Officer's and Private Citizen's Privilege to Arrest without a Warrant.

<table>
<tr><td colspan="2" align="center">**Elements of Privilege**</td></tr>
<tr><td align="center">**Peace Officer's Privilege**</td><td align="center">**Private Citizen's Privilege**</td></tr>
<tr><td valign="top">

1. Criminal Arrest: Felony
a. The peace officer has reasonable grounds to believe a felony has been committed.
b. The peace officer has reasonable grounds to suspect that the person arrested by the peace officer probably committed the felony.
c. The peace officer uses reasonable force in making the arrest or in preventing the person from fleeing.

Notes:
• States differ on whether deadly force can be used to make the arrest or to prevent fleeing.
• Deadly force can be used if the peace officer's life becomes endangered while making the arrest or preventing fleeing (self-defense).
• A reasonable mistake on any of the three elements will still protect the officer.

2. Criminal Arrest: Misdemeanor
a. The misdemeanor must be a breach of the peace.
b. The misdemeanor must be committed in the presence of the officer.
c. The arrest must be made immediately or in fresh pursuit.
d. Reasonable force is used to make the arrest or to prevent fleeing.

Notes:
• The peace officer's privilege to arrest for a misdemeanor is the same as that of a private citizen.
• In most states, a mistake on the first three elements will not protect the peace officer, even if the mistake is reasonable.
• The officer can use deadly force only if the officer's life is in danger in making the arrest or in preventing fleeing (self-defense).
• Statutes may exist in a state to extend the privilege to arrest for misdemeanors not committed in the officer's presence and for misdemeanors that are not breaches of the peace.

3. Civil Arrest
a. The officer must reasonably believe that an insane or mentally ill person poses a serious threat of danger to him- or herself or to others.
b. Reasonable force is used to bring the person to the authorities for medical attention.

</td><td valign="top">

1. Criminal Arrest: Felony
a. A felony has in fact been committed.
b. The felony committed is the one for which the citizen has made the arrest.
c. The citizen has reasonable grounds to suspect that the person arrested by the citizen probably committed the felony.
d. The citizen uses reasonable force in making the arrest or in preventing the person from fleeing.

Notes:
• States differ on whether deadly force can be used to make the arrest or to prevent fleeing.
• Deadly force can be used if the citizen's life becomes endangered while making the arrest or preventing fleeing (self-defense).
• A reasonable mistake on any of the four elements will not protect the citizen. Some states, however, have passed statutes that say the privilege is not lost if the citizen has reasonable grounds to believe that a felony has been committed by the person arrested—a reasonable mistake will protect the citizen in these states.

2. Criminal Arrest: Misdemeanor
a. The misdemeanor must be a breach of the peace.
b. The misdemeanor must be committed in the presence of the citizen.
c. The arrest must be made immediately or in fresh pursuit.
d. Reasonable force is used to make the arrest or to prevent fleeing.

Notes:
• The citizen's privilege to arrest for a misdemeanor is the same as that of a peace officer.
• In most states, a mistake on the first three elements will not protect the citizen, even if the mistake was reasonable.
• The citizen can use deadly force only if the citizen's own life was in danger in making the arrest or in preventing fleeing (self-defense).
• Statutes may exist in a state to extend the privilege to arrest for misdemeanors not committed in the citizen's presence and for misdemeanors that are not breaches of the peace.

3. Civil Arrest
a. The citizen must reasonably believe that an insane or mentally ill person poses a serious threat of danger to him- or herself or to others.
b. Reasonable force is used to bring the person to the authorities for medical attention.

</td></tr>
</table>

Major Definitions
• **Warrant:** a written order issued by an authorized government body directing the arrest of a person.
• **Peace Officer:** a person appointed by the government to keep the peace.
• **Arrest:** taking another into custody to bring before the proper authorities.
• **Felony:** a serious crime that is defined as a felony by the government. The common definition is a crime punishable by incarceration for a term exceeding a year.
• **Misdemeanor:** a less serious crime that is defined as a misdemeanor by the government. The common definition is a crime punishable by incarceration of a year or less, or a crime that is less serious than a felony.

FIGURE 5–1 Continued

- **Breach of the Peace:** an offense committed by violence or by acts likely to cause immediate disturbance of the public order.
- **Fresh pursuit:** promptly, without undue delay.
- **Civil Arrest:** arrest for the purpose of treatment or protection, and not because of the alleged commission of a crime.

Paralegal Investigation Tasks
Relevant to the Privilege to Arrest

- What crime was reported? To whom?
- What evidence existed that a crime had been committed? Who was aware of this evidence?
- What evidence led X (the person who arrested Y) to conclude that Y committed this crime? Did anyone else reach this conclusion? If so, on what basis?
- Were there any other suspects?
- What did other people say to X about Y?
- Was X present when Y committed the crime? Did X see Y commit the crime? Did anyone witness the crime?
- Did X know Y before the incident leading to the arrest? If so, how?
- Did Y have a reputation for criminal behavior in the area?
- What did Y say to X before and during the arrest? What did X say to Y? Did Y admit to X that Y committed a crime?
- How soon after X concluded that Y committed a crime did X arrest Y?
- What caused the delay, if any?
- Did Y resist the arrest? If so, how? What force, if any, did X use to make the arrest? Why did X think this force was needed? Was less force possible? Why or why not?
- What are the physical differences between X and Y, e.g., age, weight, bodily strength?
- Where did X take Y after the arrest and how long did it take to get there?
- If X made a civil arrest, what indications were there that Y's mental condition was a threat to the safety of Y or to anyone else?

---

technicalities. The officer is required, however, to be able to recognize blatant irregularities such as these.

If the officer arrests the wrong person under the warrant, the privilege is lost in most states. In some states, however, the privilege is not lost if the officer's mistake was reasonable under the circumstances.

An officer may also make an arrest without a warrant. As Figure 5–1 shows, the principles of the privilege to arrest without a warrant differ depending on why the arrest is being made:

- criminal arrest for a felony
- criminal arrest for a misdemeanor
- civil arrest for treatment or protection rather than for the commission of an alleged crime

ASSIGNMENT
5.3

At a rock concert, a police officer smells marijuana coming from a section where Mary and her seven friends are sitting. The officer arrests all of them. The officer thinks that one or two are doing the smoking, but he wants to take them all in for questioning so that he can find out which ones are guilty. Mary tries to run away. The officer shoots her. An investigation reveals that none of the arrested individuals possessed or used any drugs. The police officer is sued for false arrest, false imprisonment, and battery. What result based on the principles in Figure 5–1?

Private Citizen's Privilege to Arrest

The privilege of a **private citizen** to make an arrest without a warrant must be considered under the same three categories covered in Figure 5–1 for peace officers:

- criminal arrest for a felony
- criminal arrest for a misdemeanor
- criminal arrest for treatment or protection rather than for the commission of an alleged crime

ASSIGNMENT 5.4

a. For this assignment, the facts are the same as in Assignment 5.3, except that the person who made the arrests, did the shooting, and is sued is a private citizen, rather than a peace officer. What result based on the principles in Figure 5–1?

b. Sam is a private citizen. Someone has just stolen his $200 watch, but he is not sure who did it. Len, a stranger, comes up to Sam and tells him that he just saw a woman named Cindy steal the watch. Len points Cindy out to Sam as she is about to board a train. Sam follows the train in his car until Cindy gets off. He arrests her immediately. When she resists, he pushes her into his car. At the trial, Cindy is found innocent of the crime. Cindy now sues Sam for false arrest, false imprisonment, and battery. Does Sam have any defense?

SUMMARY

False imprisonment is an intentional confinement within fixed boundaries set by the defendant. The confinement can be by physical barriers; by physical force or threat of physical force against the plaintiff, against his or her immediate family, or against his or her property; by asserted legal authority; or by a refusal to release someone who was initially confined properly. The confinement must be complete or total. Shopkeepers have a limited privilege to detain someone temporarily to investigate whether merchandise has been stolen.

The defendant must desire to confine the plaintiff or know with substantial certainty that the confinement will result from what the defendant does. The plaintiff must either be aware of the confinement or suffer physical harm as a result of it.

An arrest is false when it is unprivileged. A peace officer has a privilege to arrest someone if the officer is acting on a warrant that is fair on its face. If no warrant exists, the peace officer has a privilege to make a felony arrest if there are reasonable grounds to believe the plaintiff committed the felony and if the officer uses reasonable force; to make a misdemeanor arrest if the misdemeanor is a breach of the peace, if it is committed in the officer's presence, if the arrest is made immediately or in fresh pursuit, and if the officer uses reasonable force; or to make a civil arrest if the officer reasonably believes the insane or mentally ill plaintiff poses a serious danger to him- or herself or to others, and if the officer uses reasonable force.

A private citizen has a privilege to make a felony arrest if a felony has in fact been committed, if it is the felony the citizen arrested the plaintiff for, if the citizen has reasonable grounds to believe the plaintiff committed the felony, and if the citizen uses reasonable force; to make a misdemeanor arrest if the misdemeanor is a breach of the peace, if it is committed in the citizen's presence, if the arrest is made immediately or in fresh pursuit, and if the citizen uses reasonable force; or to make a civil arrest if the citizen reasonably believes the insane or mentally ill plaintiff poses a serious danger to him- or herself or to others, and if the citizen uses reasonable force.

KEY TERMS

false imprisonment   41

confinement   45

privilege to recapture   46

duress   46

shopkeeper's privilege   47

common law   47

intent   47

negligence   47

transferred intent   48

causation   48

instigation   48

false arrest   49

personal liability   49

respondeat superior   49

peace officer   49, 50

warrant   49, 50

fair on its face   49

arrest   50

felony   50

misdemeanor   50

breach of the peace   51

fresh pursuit   51

civil arrest   51

private citizen   52

Misuse of Legal Proceedings

Chapter Outline

- Introduction
- Malicious Prosecution
- Wrongful or Unjustified Civil Proceedings
- Abuse of Process

INTRODUCTION

Think of the devastating feeling you would have if:

- a police officer comes to your home or your place of employment to tell you that you are under arrest for a crime (e.g., passing a forged check) that you know you did not commit; or
- a process server comes to your home or place of employment to hand you a summons and complaint notifying you that you are the defendant in a civil action (e.g., negligence) that you know is frivolous.

You would not be able to close the door and refuse to cooperate with the police or refuse to accept the summons and complaint. Once the system is set in motion, the process must go forward to the next step. The costs to you can be substantial: damage to reputation, disruption in schedule, expense of defending yourself, emotional stress, etc. Surprisingly, it is relatively easy for a criminal or civil proceeding to be launched. Essentially, all that is needed is an allegation by someone against you.

Since you cannot walk away from legal proceedings that have been commenced, what remedy do you have once you are able to convince the system that the criminal or civil case against you was groundless? You can bring a tort action. Three torts are possible: malicious prosecution, wrongful civil proceedings, and abuse of process. These torts are our concern in this chapter.

We begin with **malicious prosecution**. It primarily covers wrongful *criminal* proceedings launched against you. Wrongful *civil* proceedings may also be covered under the tort of malicious prosecution or a state may have a separate tort called "malicious civil prosecution" or "wrongful civil proceedings" to cover civil matters. At the end of the chapter, we will examine abuse of process, a distinct tort that covers legal proceedings that are properly initiated, but for an improper purpose.

This is a delicate area of the law. We want to provide some protection against defendants who have been subjected to wrongful legal proceedings. At the same time, we do not want to discourage the public at large from filing grievances. Arguably, people will be less inclined to complain to the police or to the courts if they know that they might end up being sued themselves for the torts of malicious prosecution, wrongful civil proceedings, or abuse of process if they turn out to be wrong. One way in which the system tries to balance these concerns is to make these torts available, but relatively difficult to win.

MALICIOUS PROSECUTION

 Malicious Prosecution Checklist

Definitions, Relationships, Paralegal Roles, and Research References

Category
Malicious prosecution is an intentional tort.

Interest Prosecuted by This Tort
The right to be free from unreasonable or unjustifiable criminal litigation brought against you. Secondarily, the tort protects your interest in not having your reputation harmed by such litigation. (The tort may also cover unjustified civil proceedings, although many states have a separate tort to cover the latter.)

Elements of This Tort
  i. Initiation or procurement of the initiation of criminal proceedings
 ii. Without probable cause
iii. With malice
 iv. The criminal proceedings terminate in favor of the accused

Definitions of Major Words/Phrases in These Elements
Initiation: Instigation, urging, inciting, exertion of pressure to begin something.
Criminal Proceedings: Formal action commenced by criminal justice officials.
Probable Cause: A suspicion based on the appearance of circumstances that are strong enough to allow a reasonable person to believe that a criminal charge against an individual is true.
Malice: An improper motive. If the primary motive for initiating criminal proceedings is not the desire to bring the accused to justice, then the motive is improper.
Terminate in Favor of the Accused: The ending of the criminal proceedings expressly or by fair implication shows that the accused is innocent of the charge.

Major Defense and Counterargument Possibilities That Need to Be Explored
  1. Criminal proceedings never actually began.
  2. The accuser did not instigate the prosecution, but simply gave the facts to the authorities who decided to prosecute without urging from the accuser.
  3. There was probable cause.
  4. The primary purpose of the accuser was to bring the accused to justice (i.e., to use the court for its *proper* purpose).
  5. The criminal proceedings have not yet terminated.
  6. The criminal proceedings did not terminate in favor of the accused.
  7. The plaintiff's suit against the government for malicious prosecution may be barred by sovereign immunity (on sovereign immunity, see Chapter 23).
  8. The plaintiff's suit against the government employee for malicious prosecution may be barred by public official immunity, e.g., prosecutors have an absolute immunity (on official immunity, see Chapter 23).
  9. The criminal case against the plaintiff began when the defendant arrested the plaintiff (on the privilege of arrest, see Chapter 5).
 10. The plaintiff's suit against the charitable organization for malicious prosecution committed by someone working for the organization may be barred by charitable immunity (on charitable immunity, see Chapter 23).
 11. The plaintiff's suit against a family member for malicious prosecution may be barred by intrafamily immunity (on intrafamily immunity, see Chapter 18).

Malicious Prosecution Checklist Continued

Damages

Malicious prosecution (unlike negligence) does not require proof of actual damages. There can be recovery for the humiliation and mental suffering. Other compensatory damages include the costs of defending the underlying criminal case, medical bills, and loss of business or employment. Punitive damages are often possible when the defendant (the accuser in the criminal case) acted out of hatred for the accused. (On the categories of damages, see Chapter 14.)

Relationship to Criminal Law

One of the main purposes of the malicious prosecution tort is to provide a remedy against a person who has unjustifiably caused the criminal justice system "to go after you" because of an accusation that you have committed a crime.

Relationship to Other Torts

Abuse of Process: Abuse of process is the improper use of legal proceedings that may have been properly initiated. If proceedings have been properly initiated, there is no malicious prosecution, but there may be abuse of process if the proceedings are used for an improper goal, e.g., to coerce the accused to pay a debt.

Battery: If the accused was touched, e.g., as part of an arrest, as criminal proceedings were initiated, the tort of battery as well as malicious prosecution may have been committed.

Defamation: Defamation (libel or slander) as well as malicious prosecution may be committed when the accuser initiates criminal proceedings against the accused. Things are probably said or written that are derogatory of the accused's character.

Disparagement: In the process of initiating criminal proceedings against the accused, the accuser may utter false statements injurious to the accused's business or property. The tort of disparagement as well as malicious prosecution may have been committed.

False Imprisonment: The accused may have been improperly restrained in his or her liberty while being maliciously prosecuted.

Intentional Infliction of Emotional Distress: It may be that the objective of the accuser was to subject the accused to severe emotional trauma by initiating criminal proceedings against the accused. A court might consider such conduct sufficiently outrageous so that the tort of intentional infliction of emotional distress is committed along with malicious prosecution.

Wrongful Civil Proceedings: Malicious prosecution covers wrongful criminal proceedings. It may also cover wrongful civil proceedings. In some states, however, wrongful civil proceedings is covered by a separate tort, sometimes called wrongful civil proceedings.

Federal Law

a. Under the Federal Tort Claims Act, the United States Government will *not* be liable for malicious prosecution committed by one of its federal employees within the scope of employment (respondeat superior) *unless* the federal employee is an investigative or law enforcement officer. (See Figure 23–7 in Chapter 23.)

b. There may be liability under the Civil Rights Act if the malicious prosecution was committed while the defendant was depriving the plaintiff of federal rights under color of law. (See Figure 23–8 in Chapter 23.)

Employer-Employee (Agency) Law

An employee who commits malicious prosecution is personally liable for this tort. His or her employer will *also* be liable for malicious prosecution if the conduct of the employee was within the scope of employment (respondeat superior). The employee must be furthering a business objective of the employer at the time. Intentional torts such as malicious prosecution, however, are often outside the scope of employment. If so, only the employee is liable for the malicious prosecution. (On the factors that determine scope of employment, see Figure 12–7 in Chapter 12.)

Paralegal Roles in Malicious Prosecution Litigation

Fact finding (help the office collect facts relevant to prove the elements of malicious prosecution, the elements of available defenses, and extent of injuries or other damages):

• client interviewing
• field investigation
• online research (e.g., court records)

Malicious Prosecution Checklist Continued

File management (help the office control the volume of paperwork in a malicious prosecution litigation):
- open client file
- enter case data in computer database
- maintain file documents

Litigation assistance (help the trial attorney prepare for a malicious prosecution trial and appeal, if needed):
- draft discovery requests
- draft answers to discovery requests
- draft pleadings
- digest and index discovery documents
- help prepare, order, and manage trial exhibits (visuals or demonstratives)
- prepare trial notebook
- draft notice of appeal
- order trial transcript
- cite check briefs
- perform legal research

Collection/enforcement (help the trial attorney for the judgment creditor to collect the damages award or to enforce other court orders at the conclusion of the malicious prosecution case):
- draft postjudgment discovery requests
- field investigation to monitor compliance with judgment
- online research (e.g., location of defendant's business assets)

Research References for Malicious Prosecution

Digests of West such as the American Digest System
In these digests, check key topics such as:

Malicious Prosecution	Arrest (especially key number 63.4 on probable cause)
False Imprisonment	
Torts	Damages
Extortion	Compromise and Settlement
Indictment and Information	Attorney and Client (especially key number 159)

Corpus Juris Secundum
In this legal encyclopedia, see the discussions under topic headings such as:

Malicious Prosecution	Indictment and Information
Malice	Arrest
False Imprisonment	Damages
Agency	Accord and Satisfaction
Torts	Compromise and Settlement
Extortion	

American Jurisprudence 2d
In this legal encyclopedia, see the discussions under topic headings such as:

Malicious Prosecution	Master and Servant
Abuse of Process	Damages
Attachment and Garnishment (see sections 596ff)	Arrest
	Criminal Law
Executions (sections 750ff)	Extortion, Blackmail and Threats
Malice	Indictment and Information
False Imprisonment	Compromise and Settlement
Torts	Prosecuting Attorneys

Legal Periodical Literature
There are two index systems to use to locate articles on this tort:

Malicious Prosecution Checklist Continued

*INDEX TO LEGAL PERIODICALS
AND BOOKS (ILP)*

See literature in *ILP* under subject
headings such as:

    Malicious Prosecution
    Damages
    False Imprisonment
    Master and Servant
    Personal Injuries
    Settlements
    Torts

CURRENT LAW INDEX (CLI)

See literature in *CLI* under subject
headings such as:

    Malicious Prosecution
    False Imprisonment
    Torts
    Damages
    Personal Injuries
    Employers' Liability

Example of a legal periodical article on malicious prosecution you can locate by using these
index systems:

    Damages for Injury to Feelings in Malicious Prosecution and Abuse of Process by A.M.
    Witte, 15 Cleveland Marshall Law Review 15 (1969).

A.L.R., A.L.R.2d, A.L.R.3d, A.L.R.4th, A.L.R.5th, A.L.R. Fed.

Use the *ALR Index* to find annotations relevant to malicious prosecution. In this index, check
headings such as:

    Malicious Prosecution
    Malice
    Malicious Use of Process
    Torts
    Damages

    Libel and Slander
    Master and Servant
    Federal Tort Claims Act
    Criminal Law

Example of an annotation on malicious prosecution you can locate by using this index:

    Malicious Prosecution: Effect of Grand Jury Indictment on Issue of Probable Cause by J.D.
    Perovich, 28 A.L.R.3d 748 (1969).

Words and Phrases

In this multivolume legal dictionary, look up *malicious prosecution, probable cause, malice,
nolle prosequi, abuse of process,* and every other word or phrase discussed in this chapter. The
dictionary will give you definitions of these words or phrases from court opinions.

CALR: Computer-Assisted Legal Research

Example of a query you could ask on WESTLAW to try to find cases, statutes, or other legal
materials on malicious prosecution: **"malicious prosecution"/p damages**

Example of search terms you could use on an Internet legal search engine such as
LawCrawler (http://lawcrawler.findlaw.com) to find cases, statutes, or other legal
materials on malicious prosecution: **"malicious prosecution"**

Example of search terms you could use on an Internet general search engine such as
Alta Vista (http://www.altavista.com) to find cases, statutes, or other legal materials on
malicious prosecution: **+"malicious prosecution" +tort -crime**

More Internet sites to check for materials on malicious prosecution and other torts:
Jurist: (http://jurist.law.pitt.edu/sg_torts.htm)
LawGuru: (http://www.lawguru.com/search/lawsearch.html)
See also Tort Law Online at the end of Chapter 1.

Initiation or Procurement
of the Initiation of Criminal Proceedings

The first element of malicious prosecution is that the wrongdoer initiates or procures
the initiation of criminal proceedings.

> **EXAMPLE:**   Dan calls the police to complain that Linda stole his car.
> The police then arrest Linda. After an investigation, she is indicted for
> grand larceny.

In many states, Dan would be called the complaining witness. By his specific accusation, he has set official action in motion against Linda who will become the defendant in a criminal case. To **initiate** means to instigate, urge on, or incite. The instigator in the criminal case later becomes the defendant in the civil case of malicious prosecution brought by whoever was accused in the criminal case. The two separate proceedings are as follows:

State v. Linda (criminal case of grand larceny)

Linda v. Dan (civil case of malicious prosecution)

Without Probable Cause

The legal proceedings must be initiated without **probable cause.** Probable cause is a suspicion based on the appearance of circumstances that are strong enough to allow a reasonable person to believe that a criminal charge against a person is true. If there *is* probable cause, then the tort of malicious prosecution cannot succeed no matter how much ill will or malice the initiator may have against the accused.

Some of the factors that a court will use to determine whether probable cause exists are outlined in Figure 6–1.

With Malice

Malice, for purposes of this tort, means doing something for an improper motive. It does not necessarily require a showing of hatred or ill will. The proper motive for initiating criminal proceedings is to bring an alleged criminal to justice. If this is not the initiator's primary purpose, then he or she is acting with malice. Examples of improper (and hence malicious) purposes are to exert pressure on the accused to pay a debt, to return property, or to vote a certain way in an election. Often the initiator has more than one motive. If the primary motive is proper, the contemporaneous presence of improper incidental motives will not lead to the conclusion that the proceeding was initiated with malice.

FIGURE 6–1 Probable cause in malicious prosecution suits.

> **Factors Considered by the Court in Determining Whether the Accuser Had Probable Cause to Initiate the Criminal Process against the Accused.**
>
> 1. Did the accuser honestly believe that the accused committed the crime charged?
> 2. Did the accuser have first-hand knowledge/observation of what the accused allegedly did?
> 3. If the accuser used second-hand knowledge/observation, how reliable was the source used? If, for example, an informer gave information to the accuser (which the latter used in initiating the criminal case against the accused), what was the informer's reputation for reliability? Did the accuser check into this before initiating the criminal case?
> 4. What was the accused's reputation in the community? Notorious? The type of person who would commit this kind of crime? Or an honest, upright citizen?
> 5. Did the accuser know of the accused's reputation? If not, was there time to find out?
> 6. Did the accuser first confront the accused before going to the authorities? If not, why not? Impractical? No time? Danger to the accuser? Fear the accused would flee?
> 7. Was there any time for the accuser to do any further informal or formal investigation before contacting the authorities? If there was time, was it practical to use it?
> 8. Did the accuser seek the advice of his or her own attorney on whether there was a basis for the accuser to initiate criminal proceedings against the accused? If so, and if the advice was that the accuser should go to the authorities, did the accuser give the attorney all the relevant facts known to the accuser so that the attorney could provide informed advice?
> 9. Was there any other information that was reasonably available to the accuser that should have been obtained by the accuser before he or she initiated the criminal case against the accused?

Criminal Proceedings Terminate in Favor of the Accused

The criminal proceedings must be over, and the accused must have won the case. Most states require the victory to be on the merits, rather than be a mere technical or procedural victory. If the accused did not win the case, the strong likelihood is that the initial prosecution against the accused was made with probable cause rather than with malice. Examples of criminal proceedings that terminate in favor of the accused would include a verdict of not guilty, a discharge of the case because the grand jury fails to indict, and a **nolle prosequi** (i.e., a statement by the district attorney that he or she is unwilling to prosecute).

The malicious prosecution case is not necessarily won, however, just because the criminal proceedings end in favor of the accused. As we have seen, the accused must also show that there was no probable cause. Winning the criminal case does not necessarily mean that there was no probable cause.

> **EXAMPLE:**   While walking in the corridor, Mary overhears Fred say on a cell phone that he is going to "bomb a federal building." They were in a federal building at the time. He was carrying a suspicious suitcase and acting erratically when Mary heard him talking. In a panic, she immediately calls the police and demands that Fred be arrested. Fred is tried but found not guilty because he convinced the jury that the statement he actually made was that "anyone who would bomb a federal building should be executed." Mary had misunderstood what he was saying. Fred now sues Mary for malicious prosecution.

The criminal proceedings certainly terminated in favor of the accused—Fred was acquitted. In the malicious prosecution case, however, he must show that Mary had no probable cause to instigate his arrest and prosecution. But Mary did have probable cause based on what she thought she heard, the suspicious suitcase, and the erratic behavior. She simply made a reasonable mistake in failing to hear Fred correctly. Hence, Fred loses the malicious prosecution case for failure to establish that Mary acted without probable cause. This is a case in which there was probable cause to believe that an innocent person committed a crime.

ASSIGNMENT

6.1

Elaine arrives home one night to find that her home has been burglarized. She calls the police. When questioned by the police, she says she does not know who did it, but that her uncle Bob recently threatened to harm her. The police conduct an investigation of Bob. He is indicted for burglary. At his trial, Elaine testifies that he once threatened her. The jury is deadlocked, and a mistrial is declared. The District Attorney (D.A.) is unsure whether to reprosecute him. By this time, Elaine is convinced Bob is guilty of the burglary. She urges the D.A. to retry Bob for the burglary. She constantly calls the D.A. Once she carries a sign outside the D.A.'s office urging prosecution. The D.A.'s decision, however, is to drop the charges. After the case is dismissed, Bob sues Elaine for malicious prosecution. What result?

WRONGFUL OR UNJUSTIFIED CIVIL PROCEEDINGS

The tort of malicious prosecution covers wrongful criminal litigation. Suppose that **wrongful civil proceedings** are initiated.

> **EXAMPLE:**   Charles files a complaint against Ted for negligence. Ted is served with process, which orders Ted to file an answer within thirty days. After a trial, Ted is found not liable for negligence.

Charles has initiated civil proceedings that have terminated in favor of Ted. Many states will now allow Ted to assert a tort action against Charles for bringing wrongful civil proceedings. The action may still be called malicious prosecution, although this term is more appropriate when the underlying proceedings are criminal.

Generally, the same elements apply for the causes of action of wrongful civil proceedings and wrongful criminal proceedings. The defendant must maliciously initiate civil proceedings without probable cause, and the proceedings must terminate in favor of the person charged in the civil proceedings. (The latter was the defendant in the civil proceedings case and is now the plaintiff in the wrongful civil proceedings case.) Probable cause here means a reasonable belief that good grounds exist for initiating the civil proceeding. Some courts impose an additional requirement for parties bringing wrongful civil proceedings suits: they must show some special interference with person or property as a result of the wrongful civil proceedings. Evidence of such a special injury or grievance is not required of parties suing because of wrongful criminal proceedings.

ABUSE OF PROCESS

The elements of the tort of **abuse of process** are:

 i. Use of civil or criminal proceedings, and
 ii. Improper or ulterior motive.

Some states also require a showing of injury to person or property beyond mere injury to name or reputation.

Unlike malicious prosecution, abuse of process involves a civil or criminal case that was *properly* initiated. Probable cause may exist, and the proceeding does not have to terminate in favor of the person now bringing the abuse-of-process action. Yet, the civil or criminal proceeding was used for an improper or ulterior motive.

> **EXAMPLE:** Bob and Mary are married, but have been separated for over five years. They have two children. Mary believes that she is the better parent and tells Bob that if he does not agree to give her full custody, she will tell the Internal Revenue Service that he has been cheating on his business taxes for years. Bob refuses. Mary tells the IRS, which begins a criminal fraud case against Bob. He is convicted. He then sues Mary for abuse of process.

Bob would win. Mary had an ulterior motive in initiating the criminal case against Bob. She was using the courts for a purpose for which they are not designed. She may have had probable cause to accuse Bob of tax fraud, but it is improper to initiate a criminal tax proceeding against someone in order to gain agreement on a child custody matter.

SUMMARY

Malicious prosecution requires initiating, or procuring the initiation of, criminal proceedings against an accused. There must be no probable cause to initiate the proceedings. This means that a reasonable person would not have suspected that the accused was guilty. Malice is also required, meaning that the primary purpose in initiating the proceedings was improper because the purpose was something other than to bring someone to justice. Finally, the legal proceedings must terminate in favor of the accused, usually on the merits.

Initiating wrongful civil proceedings is a tort in many states. The defendant must maliciously initiate civil proceedings without probable cause, and the proceedings must terminate in favor of the person charged in the civil proceedings.

Some courts also require the defendant to show that he or she suffered a special injury or grievance as a result of the wrongdoing civil proceedings.

Abuse of process covers criminal or civil litigation that is properly initiated because probable cause exists, but it is used for an improper motive or purpose. The civil or criminal litigation does not have to terminate in favor of the defendant in the litigation.

KEY TERMS

malicious prosecution   55

initiate   60

probable cause   60

malice   60

nolle prosequi   61

wrongful civil proceedings   61

abuse of process   62

Infliction of Emotional Distress

Chapter Outline

- Introduction
- Intentional Infliction of Emotional Distress
- Tort Law and the Impeachment of the President
- Media Defendants and the Constitution
- Negligent Infliction of Emotional Distress

INTRODUCTION

Emotional distress can be damaging to a person. Our concern in this chapter is whether the sufferer can bring a tort action against the person who caused this suffering. When someone commits a traditional tort such as battery, false imprisonment, or negligence, there is usually little difficulty recovering for the emotional distress (called **pain and suffering**) that results from this tort. In fact, damages for pain and suffering often constitute the largest portion of a successful plaintiff's judgment. Suppose, however, that the defendant causes mental distress without committing one of these traditional torts. For example, George is emotionally upset when Mary refuses to date him and tells him that she never wants to see him again as long as she lives. Although this statement could cause George enormous pain and suffering (in fact, an emotional breakdown), Mary has not committed a tort. The facts do not fit any of the traditional torts.

A floodgate of litigation would result if every victim of every emotional distress is allowed to sue. Courts are also concerned about the filing of fraudulent lawsuits because it is fairly easy to fabricate a claim of emotional distress.

One of the ways the law has dealt with these concerns is to create a new tort called **intentional infliction of emotional distress** (also called the tort of **outrage**). To prevent this tort from opening a floodgate of litigation, the tort is relatively difficult to win, as President Bill Clinton discovered to his relief in the famous case of *Jones v. Clinton* that we will discuss. After we examine the boundaries of this narrow intentional tort, we need to determine when *negligently* inflicted emotional distress can also be a basis of recovery.

INTENTIONAL INFLICTION OF EMOTIONAL DISTRESS

 Intentional Infliction of Emotional Distress Checklist

Definitions, Relationships, Paralegal Roles, and Research References

Category

Intentional infliction of emotional distress is an intentional tort. Some courts have expanded it to include recovery for reckless infliction of emotional distress.

Interest Protected by This Tort

The right to be free from emotional distress that is intentionally (or recklessly) caused by someone else.

Elements of This Tort

   i. An act of extreme or outrageous conduct
   ii. Intent to cause severe emotional distress
   iii. Severe emotional distress is suffered
   iv. Defendant is the cause of this distress

Definitions of Major Words/Phrases in These Elements

Act: Voluntary movement of the defendant's body.
Extreme or outrageous conduct: Atrocious and totally intolerable behavior—shocking conduct.
Intent: The desire to inflict severe emotional distress on the plaintiff or the knowledge with substantial certainty that such distress will result from what the defendant does. (In some states, recklessness, or wanton and willful conduct, will be sufficient.)
Severe emotional distress: Substantial mental anguish.
Cause: "But for" what the defendant did, the plaintiff would not have suffered severe emotional distress, or the defendant was a substantial factor in producing such distress.

Major Defense and Counterargument Possibilities That Need to Be Explored

1. The defendant did not act voluntarily.
2. The defendant's conduct may have been unpleasant and wrongful, but it was not extreme or outrageous.
3. The defendant did not desire the plaintiff to suffer severe emotional distress nor know with substantial certainty that such distress would result from what the defendant did (no intent). In a state where recklessness can be a substitute for intent, the defendant did not recklessly cause such distress.
4. The plaintiff may have been embarrassed or upset, but did not suffer severe emotional distress.
5. The plaintiff may have suffered severe emotional distress, but a reasonable person would not have reacted in this way.
6. The plaintiff suffered severe emotional distress because he or she is unusually sensitive and the defendant had no reason to know of this sensitivity.
7. "But for" what the defendant did, the plaintiff would still have suffered severe emotional distress; the defendant was not a substantial factor in producing plaintiff's emotional distress (no causation).
8. The plaintiff consented to the defendant's conduct that led to the severe emotional distress (on the defense of consent, see Chapter 23).
9. The plaintiff's severe emotional distress resulted while the defendant was defending himself or herself from the plaintiff (on self-defense and other self-help privileges, see Chapter 23).
10. The plaintiff's severe emotional distress occurred while the defendant was defending someone else from the plaintiff (on the defense of others and other self-help privileges, see Chapter 23).
11. The plaintiff's severe emotional distress occurred while the defendant was defending property or recapturing chattels from the plaintiff (on necessity, defense of property, recapture of property, and other self-help privileges, see Chapter 23).

Intentional Infliction of Emotional Distress Checklist Continued

12. The plaintiff's severe emotional distress occurred while the defendant was disciplining the plaintiff (on discipline and other self-help privileges, see Chapter 23).
13. The plaintiff's severe emotional distress occurred while the defendant was arresting the plaintiff (on the privilege of arrest, see Chapter 5).
14. The plaintiff's suit against the government for intentional infliction of emotional distress committed by a government employee may be barred by sovereign immunity (on sovereign immunity, see Chapter 23).
15. The plaintiff's suit against the government employee for intentional infliction of emotional distress may be barred by public official immunity (on official immunity, see Chapter 23).
16. The plaintiff's suit against the charitable organization for intentional infliction of emotional distress committed by someone working for the organization may be barred by charitable immunity (on charitable immunity, see Chapter 23).
17. The plaintiff's suit against a family member for intentional infliction of emotional distress may be barred by intrafamily immunity (on intrafamily immunity, see Chapter 18).
18. The plaintiff failed to take reasonable steps to mitigate the harm caused when the defendant committed intentional infliction of emotional distress; therefore, damages should not cover the aggravation of the harm caused by the plaintiff (on the doctrine of avoidable consequences, see Chapter 14).

Damages

The plaintiff can recover compensatory damages for the mental distress suffered as well as for any physical harm or illness that may have resulted from the defendant's conduct. Punitive damages are also likely if the defendant acted out of hatred or malice. (On the categories of damages, see Chapter 14.)

Relationship to Criminal Law

The defendant's conduct may also constitute the crime of extortion, criminal assault, breach of the peace, criminal battery, etc.

Other Torts and Related Actions

Abuse of process: While using the criminal process for an improper purpose, the defendant may have intended to cause the plaintiff severe emotional distress.

Assault: While intending to cause severe emotional distress in the plaintiff, the defendant may have intentionally placed the plaintiff in apprehension of an imminent harmful or offensive contact.

Battery: While intending to cause severe emotional distress in the plaintiff, the defendant may have intentionally made harmful or offensive contact with the plaintiff.

Conversion: Defendant may have intended to have the plaintiff suffer severe emotional distress by destroying plaintiff's personal property.

Defamation: While intentionally causing the plaintiff to suffer severe emotional distress, the defendant may have published derogatory statements that injured the reputation of the plaintiff.

False imprisonment: By intentionally locking the plaintiff up or otherwise restricting his or her movement, the defendant may have had the intent to cause the plaintiff severe emotional distress.

False light (invasion of privacy): By giving unreasonable publicity to false private facts, the defendant may have had the intent to cause the plaintiff severe emotional distress.

Intrusion (invasion of privacy): By unreasonably intruding on the plaintiff's privacy, the defendant may have had the intent to cause the plaintiff severe emotional distress.

Malicious prosecution: The defendant may have initiated legal proceedings against the plaintiff with the intent to cause the plaintiff severe emotional distress.

Negligence: If the defendant negligently caused physical harm to the plaintiff, the latter can also recover for resulting emotional distress that was not intended. Some states also allow recovery for negligent infliction of emotional distress.

Trespass to land: While trespassing on the plaintiff's land, the defendant may have had the intent to subject the plaintiff to severe emotional distress.

Wrongful death: If the plaintiff died as a result of intentional infliction of emotional distress, designated survivors may be able to bring a wrongful death action.

Intentional Infliction of Emotional Distress Checklist Continued

Federal Law

   a. Under the Federal Tort Claims Act, there is no explicit exclusion that says the United States Government will not be liable for intentional infliction of emotional distress committed by one of its federal employees within the scope of employment (respondeat superior). (See Figure 23–7 in Chapter 23.)

   b. There may be liability under the Civil Rights Act if the intentional infliction of emotional distress was committed while the defendant was depriving the plaintiff of federal rights under color of law. (See Figure 23–8 in Chapter 23.)

Employer-Employee (Agency) Law

An employee who commits intentional infliction of emotional distress is personally liable for this tort. His or her employer will *also* be liable for the tort if the conduct of the employee was within the scope of employment (respondeat superior). The employee must be furthering a business objective of the employer at the time. Intentional torts such as intentional infliction of emotional distress, however, are often outside the scope of employment. If so, only the employee is liable for the tort. (On the factors that determine the scope of employment, see Figure 12–7 in Chapter 12.)

Paralegal Roles in Intentional Infliction of Emotional Distress Litigation

Fact finding (help the office collect facts relevant to prove the elements of intentional infliction of emotional distress, the elements of available defenses, and extent of injuries or other damages):
- client interviewing
- field investigation
- online research

File management (help the office control the volume of paperwork in an intentional infliction of emotional distress litigation):

- open client file
- enter case data in computer database
- maintain file documents

Litigation assistance (help the trial attorney prepare for an intentional infliction of emotional distress trial and appeal, if needed):
- draft discovery requests
- draft answers to discovery requests
- draft pleadings
- digest and index discovery documents
- help prepare, order, and manage trial exhibits (visuals or demonstratives)
- prepare trial notebook
- draft notice of appeal
- order trial transcript
- cite check briefs
- perform legal research

Collection/enforcement (help the trial attorney for the judgment creditor to collect the damages award or to enforce other court orders at the conclusion of the intentional infliction of emotional distress case):
- draft postjudgment discovery requests
- field investigation to monitor compliance with judgment
- online research (e.g., location of defendant's business assets)

Research References for Intentional Infliction of Emotional Distress

Digests
In the digests of West, look for case summaries on this tort under key topics such as:

Torts	Death
Threats	Damages

Intentional Infliction of Emotional Distress Checklist Continued

Corpus Juris Secundum
In this legal encyclopedia, look for discussions on this tort under topic headings such as:

Torts	Telegraph, telephone, radio
Threats and unlawful	and television
communications	Death
Damages	

American Jurisprudence 2d
In this legal encyclopedia, look for discussions on this tort under topic headings such as:

Torts	Damages
Fright, shock and	Death
mental disturbance	

Legal Periodical Literature
There are two index systems to use to try to locate articles on this tort:

INDEX TO LEGAL PERIODICALS AND BOOKS (ILP)	CURRENT LAW INDEX (CLI)
See literature in *ILP* under subject headings such as:	See literature in *CLI* under subject headings such as:
Torts	Privacy, Right of
Collection	Mental Distress
Agencies	Negligence
Damages	Damages
Negligence	Torts
Personal Injuries	Personal Injuries
Privacy	Death by
Wrongful Death	Wrongful Act
	Collection Agencies

Example of legal periodical literature you can locate through the *ILP* or *CLI* on this tort:

> *Intentional Infliction of Mental Distress—Seventeen Years Later* by Arthur J. Sabin, 66 Illinois Bar Journal 248 (1978).

A.L.R., A.L.R.2d, A.L.R.3d, A.L.R.4th, A.L.R.5th, A.L.R. Fed.
Use the *ALR Index* to locate annotations on this tort. In this index, check subject headings such as:

Mental Anguish	Torts
Shock	Death
Emotional Disturbance	Intentional Tort
Debtors and Creditors	

Example of an annotation you can locate through this index on this tort:

> *Recovery by Debtor, under Tort of Intentional or Reckless Infliction of Emotional Distress, for Damages Resulting from Collection Methods* by Joel E. Smith, 87 A.L.R.3d 201 (1978).

Words and Phrases
In this multivolume legal dictionary, look up *intentional infliction of emotional distress, emotional distress, outrageous, reckless, negligent infliction of emotional distress,* and every other word or phrase connected with the tort(s) discussed in this chapter. The dictionary will give you definitions of these words or phrases from court opinions.

CALR: Computer-Assisted Legal Research
Example of a query you could ask on WESTLAW to try to find cases, statutes, or other legal materials on this tort: **"intentional infliction of emotional distress"/p damages**

Example of a query you could ask on LEXIS to try to find cases, statutes, or other legal materials on this tort: **intentional infliction of emotional distress/p damages**

Intentional Infliction of Emotional Distress Checklist Continued

Example of search terms you could use on an Internet legal search engine such as LawCrawler (http://lawcrawler.findlaw.com) to find cases, statutes, or other legal materials on this tort: **"intentional infliction of emotional distress"**

Example of search terms you could use on an Internet general search engine such as Alta Vista (http://www.altavista.com) to find cases, statutes, or other legal materials on this tort: **"intentional infliction of emotional distress"**

More Internet sites to check for materials on intentional infliction of emotional distress and other torts:
Jurist: (http://jurist.law.pitt.edu/sg_torts.htm)
LawGuru: (http://www.lawguru.com/search/lawsearch.html)
See also Tort Law Online at the end of Chapter 1.

Extreme or Outrageous Conduct

The conduct of the defendant must be so **extreme or outrageous** that it would be regarded as atrocious and totally intolerable. Avoid the mistake of concluding that it is atrocious and intolerable to commit any intentional tort, and that therefore, any battery, assault, false imprisonment, or malicious prosecution is *also* the tort of intentional infliction of emotional distress. This is not always so. As indicated in the chart, it is possible for the tort of intentional infliction of emotional distress to be committed simultaneously with other torts. This, however, is not necessarily the case. The act required for intentional infliction of emotional distress must shock the conscience of society.

> **EXAMPLES:**
>
> * playing a practical joke on a mother by telling her that her son has just committed suicide
> * putting a knife to the throat of a ten-year-old child as a threat
> * surrounding a debtor and threatening to kill him and to destroy all of his business machinery if he does not pay a debt
> * pushing a pregnant woman down a flight of stairs or threatening to do so

If the defendant knows that the plaintiff is vulnerable because of age, mental illness, or physical illness, it is usually easier to establish that the conduct was extreme or outrageous. Yet, vulnerability in this sense is not required. It would be extreme or outrageous, for example, for a defendant to drive a car at a high rate of speed on the sidewalk in order to scare a pedestrian directly in front of the car, whether the pedestrian is on crutches or is a healthy boxer.

As we will see elsewhere in this book, common carriers, innkeepers, and public utilities are more likely to be found liable for a tort than other categories of defendants. This is particularly true with the tort of intentional infliction of emotional distress. For most defendants, the first element of this tort is not established by mere insults, threats, or obscenities directed at the plaintiff—they are not atrocious enough. Yet, such conduct might be sufficient if the defendant is a hotel or a public transit facility.

ASSIGNMENT
7.1

Has extreme or outrageous conduct taken place in the following cases?
a. A creditor threatens to force the debtor into involuntary bankruptcy if a debt is not paid immediately.
b. The principal of the school suspects that a student has been smoking marijuana in the restroom. The principal threatens to use the student as an example of delinquency before the entire school assembly if the student does not confess to smoking the marijuana.

c. Defendant pretends to be a police detective and threatens to arrest the plaintiff for espionage if the plaintiff does not turn over letters received by the plaintiff from a friend in Asia.

d. A bus driver tells a seventy-five-year-old passenger that her hat is so ridiculous that she would look better bald.

Intent

In most states, the defendant must have the **intent** to cause the severe emotional distress. This means that the defendant must either desire such a consequence or know with substantial certainty that it will result from what he or she does.

In a few states, **recklessness** (or willful and wanton conduct) is enough. In such states, the second element is met if the defendant knows that his or her conduct creates a very great risk that the plaintiff will suffer severe emotional distress. The following is a classic example of the kind of case that meets this standard:

> **EXAMPLE:** Bob is a good friend of Mary's. He attempts to commit suicide with a knife in Mary's kitchen. She suffers severe emotional distress upon seeing the blood and gore.

Mary sues Bob for intentional infliction of emotional distress. In a state that requires intent, Mary loses because there is no indication that Bob desired Mary to suffer this distress or that Bob knew with certainty that it would result. Mary has a better chance in a state where recklessness will suffice, because a strong argument can be made that Bob knew he created a very great risk that Mary would suffer this distress.

The line between desiring something or knowing something with substantial certainty (intent), and knowing that you create a very great risk of something (recklessness) is often very difficult to draw. Yet the line may have to be drawn in a state where recklessness is not enough to establish the second element of this tort.

If the defendant is merely *negligent* in causing the severe emotional distress, there is no intentional infliction of emotional distress. In the next section, we will consider the question of whether the plaintiff might be able to recover under a theory of negligence.

What happens if the defendant intends to cause severe emotional distress in one person, but in fact causes such distress in another person whom the defendant had no intent to bother? What happens if two individuals suffer severe emotional distress, even though defendant's intent was directed at only one of them? Rodney, for example, intentionally terrifies Mary and then maims her. Mary's mother suffers severe emotional distress because of this injury and the way it was brought about. Can both Mary and her mother sue Rodney for intentional infliction of emotional distress? Mary certainly can. In most states, however, her mother cannot sue unless the defendant either desired to cause her severe emotional distress or knew with substantial certainty that it would result from what he did. The doctrine of **transferred intent** (see Figure 7–1 in Chapter 4) does not apply to this tort. If, however, Rodney knew that the mother was present when he terrified and maimed Mary, a good argument can be made that he was at least reckless in creating a very grave risk that the mother would suffer severe emotional distress along with the daughter. In those states where recklessness is sufficient, the mother would be able to sue for intentional infliction of emotional distress if she could convince a jury that Rodney knew that he was creating this very grave risk.

Even states that accept recklessness, however, are reluctant to permit third persons to sue under this tort, and sometimes impose the requirements that the third person be a close relative of the person whom the defendant intends to injure, that this third person be present at the time of the act, and that the defendant know this third person is present.

Whether the mother can sue under a theory of negligence will be considered in the next section of this chapter.

Severe Emotional Distress

It is not enough that the defendant commit an outrageous act intended to cause **severe emotional distress** in the plaintiff. The plaintiff must in fact experience such distress. Minor inconvenience or annoyance is not enough. There must be severe fright, horror, grief, humiliation, embarrassment, anger, worry, or nausea. The severity of these feelings is, of course, measured by their intensity and duration as well as other factors, such as the relative size and weight of the plaintiff and defendant, and how the defendant approached the plaintiff. It is not necessary in the vast majority of states that the plaintiff suffer any **physical injury** or harm as a result of what the defendant did. Such physical illness or harm, if it exists, will increase the damages and help to prove that the plaintiff is telling the truth about the severity of the emotional distress that is alleged, but the plaintiff need not prove physical illness or harm in order to establish the tort.

Suppose the plaintiff is unusually sensitive and experiences severe emotional distress even though anyone else would not, e.g., the plaintiff goes into shock when the defendant plays a practical joke by telling the plaintiff that one of his flowers has just died. If the defendant knew of this vulnerability and still proceeded with the intent to cause severe emotional distress, the third element of the tort is established. Otherwise, the test is objective: the plaintiff will not be able to recover unless an ordinary person, not unduly sensitive, would have suffered severe emotional distress from what the defendant did.

ASSIGNMENT

7.2

For months Tom has been having difficulty finding work. Finally he gets a job at the XYZ gym as a judo instructor. It is the first time he has had a job in over a year and a half. A collection agency has been after Tom to pay a $500 debt. An employee of the agency calls Tom and says, "I understand that you now have a job and that you have had to go through a lot to get it. Don't do anything silly, which might cost you that job. Don't make me call your new boss to let him know that you're the kind of guy who doesn't pay his debts. You've got one week to pay up or else." Tom is terrified at the thought of losing his job. He has many sleepless nights worrying about the possibility that the collection agency might call his boss. Tom sues the agency for intentional infliction of emotional distress. What result?

Causation

Plaintiff can use either of the following tests to establish **causation:**

- But for what the defendant did, the plaintiff would not have suffered severe emotional distress.
- The defendant was a substantial factor in producing the plaintiff's severe emotional distress.

The second test is used when there is more than one potential cause of the severe emotional distress. The plaintiff is not required to prove causation by the but-for test. The broader substantial factor test is sufficient.

TORT LAW AND THE IMPEACHMENT OF THE PRESIDENT

In 1991, Paula Corbin Jones was a low-level employee of the state of Arkansas. While attending a conference in a Little Rock hotel, Governor Bill Clinton invited her to his hotel suite after he thought she displayed "that come-hither look" because of the suggestive way she dressed. Their encounter in the suite led to an allegation that he committed intentional infliction of emotional distress, called the tort of outrage in Arkansas. After he became President Clinton, she brought a tort action against him in which she alleged this tort as well as other wrongs.

According to plaintiff Jones:

[U]pon arriving at the suite and announcing herself, the Governor shook her hand, invited her in, and closed the door. She states that a few minutes of small talk ensued, which included the Governor asking her about her job and him mentioning the Dave Harrington, plaintiff's ultimate superior . . . and a Clinton appointee, was his "good friend." Plaintiff states that the Governor then "unexpectedly reached over to [her], took her hand, and pulled her toward him, so that their bodies were close to each other." She states she removed her hand from his and retreated several feet, but that the Governor approached her again and, while saying, "I love the way your hair flows down your back" and "I love your curves," put his hand on her leg, started sliding it toward her pelvic area, and bent down to attempt to kiss her on the neck, all without her consent. Plaintiff states that she exclaimed, "What are you doing?," told the Governor that she was "not that kind of girl," and "escaped" from the Governor's reach "by walking away from him." She states she was extremely upset and confused and, not knowing what to do, attempted to distract the Governor by chatting about his wife. Plaintiff states that she sat down at the end of the sofa nearest the door, but that the Governor approached the sofa where she had taken a seat and, as he sat down, "lowered his trousers and underwear, exposed his penis (which was erect) and told [her] to 'kiss it.' " She states that she was "horrified" by this and that she "jumped up from the couch" and told the Governor that she had to go, saying something to the effect that she had to get back to the registration desk. Plaintiff states that the Governor, "while fondling his penis," said, "Well, I don't want to make you do anything you don't want to do," and then pulled up his pants and said, "If you get in trouble for leaving work, have Dave call me immediately and I'll take care of it." She states that as she left the room (the door of which was not locked), the Governor "detained" her momentarily, "looked sternly" at her, and said, "You are smart. Let's keep this between ourselves."

. . .

[In her tort action, she alleged that she was "stunned" and in a state of "shock".] She states that "Mr. Clinton's outrageous conduct includes offensive language, an offensive proposition, offensive touching (constituting sexual assault under both federal and state definitions), and *actual exposure of an intimate private body part*," and that "[t]here are few more outrageous acts than a criminal sexual assault followed by unwanted exposure, coupled with a demand for oral sex by the most powerful man in the state against a very young, low-level employee." *Jones v. Clinton*, 990 F. Supp. 657, 663–64, 677 (E.D. Ark 1998).

The trial judge, Susan Webber Wright, disagreed. She dismissed the tort claim by granting the president's motion for a summary judgment.

While the Court will certainly agree that plaintiff's allegations describe offensive conduct, the . . . conduct as alleged by plaintiff describes a mere sexual proposition or encounter, albeit an odious one, that was relatively brief in duration, did not involve any coercion or threats of reprisal, and was abandoned as soon as plaintiff made clear that the advance was not welcome. The Court is not aware of any authority holding that such a sexual encounter or proposition of the type alleged in this case, without more, gives rise to a claim of outrage . . . . Moreover, notwithstanding the offensive nature of the Governor's alleged conduct, plaintiff admits that she never missed a day of work following the alleged incident, . . . , she continued to go on a daily basis to the Governor's Office to deliver items and never asked to be relieved of that duty, she never filed a formal complaint or told her supervisors of the incident . . ., she never consulted a psychiatrist, psychologist, or incurred medical bills and a result of the alleged incident, and she acknowledges that her two subsequent contacts with the Governor involved comments made "in a light vein" and nonsexual contact that was done in a "friendly fashion.". . . Plaintiff's actions and statements in this case do not portray someone who experienced emotional distress so severe in nature that no reasonable person could be expected to endure it. *Jones v. Clinton,* 990 F. Supp. at 677–78.

While this tort victory was welcomed by President Clinton, his troubles were far from over. Before Judge Wright rendered her decision, the president gave a deposition that gained worldwide notoriety and eventually was a major factor in his impeachment, only the second time in history that a president of the United States has been impeached. During the deposition the president answered "none" when asked whether there were any female employees of the federal government with whom he had had sexual relations. In particular, he denied having such relations with Monica Lewinsky, a White House intern. A special prosecutor and almost all Republicans in Congress charged that his answers were intentionally false. They believed that lying in a deposition was one of the "high crimes and misdemeanors" that should lead to his removal from office. Ultimately, the Senate as a whole disagreed when it failed to convict the president by the required two-thirds vote. By acquitting the president, the Senate was saying either that it did not believe the president lied or that even if he did, the lie and the other charges were not serious enough to remove him from office.

While the president won the tort case, Judge Susan Webber Wright ruled that he *did* lie during his deposition and held him in civil contempt. One of the consequences of the lie was that the legal team of Jones had to spend extra time preparing its case. Hence the judge ordered the president to pay a fine of $90,000 for reasonable legal fees covering this time. The fee request included $60 an hour for the work of two paralegals on the Jones legal team.

In the meantime, Jones was set to appeal Judge Wright's ruling that granted the president's motion for a summary judgement and dismissed her tort claim. The president, however, did not relish the prospect of fighting the appeal, particularly since the appeal would have taken place before the impeachment proceeding in Congress was concluded. Hence the president decided that the safest legal and political strategy was to settle the case to prevent the appeal from going forward. He agreed to pay Jones $850,000 in exchange for her decision to drop the appeal.

MEDIA DEFENDANTS AND THE CONSTITUTION

The First Amendment of the United States Constitution gives special protection to newspapers, magazines, TV, theater, and other media entities when they are sued because of something they publish. This includes a suit for intentional infliction of emotional distress. In a famous case that reached the United States Supreme Court, Reverend Jerry Falwell asserted this tort against *Hustler Magazine* and its publisher, Larry Flynt, after the magazine printed a crude parody about him. Falwell was the host of a nationally syndicated television show and the founder and president of a political organization formerly known as the Moral Majority. Here is the Court's description of Falwell's grievance:

Petitioner Hustler Magazine, Inc., is a magazine of nationwide circulation. Respondent Jerry Falwell, a nationally known minister who has been active as a commentator on politics and public affairs, sued petitioner and its publisher, petitioner Larry Flynt, to recover damages for . . . intentional infliction of emotional distress. . . . The inside front cover of the November 1983 issue of Hustler Magazine featured a "parody" of an advertisement for Campari Liqueur that contained the name and picture of respondent and was entitled

"Jerry Falwell talks about his first time." This parody was modeled after actual Campari ads that included interviews with various celebrities about their "first times." Although it was apparent by the end of each interview that this meant the first time they sampled Campari, the ads clearly played on the sexual double entendre of the general subject of "first times." Copying the form and layout of these Campari ads, Hustler's editors chose respondent as the featured celebrity and drafted an alleged "interview" with him in which he states that his "first time" was during a drunken incestuous rendezvous with his mother in an outhouse. The Hustler parody portrays respondent and his mother as drunk and immoral, and suggests that respondent is a hypocrite who preaches only when he is drunk. In small print at the bottom of the page, the ad contains the disclaimer, "ad parody—not to be taken seriously." The magazine's table of contents also lists the ad as "Fiction; Ad and Personality Parody." *Hustler Magazine and Larry C. Flynt v. Jerry Falwell,* 485 U.S. 46, 47–8, 108 S. Ct. 876, 887–8, 99 L. Ed. 2d 41, 47 (1988).

The question before the Court was whether Falwell had to prove an additional element of the tort because he was suing a media defendant. The Court concluded that he did. It is not enough to show that the defendant acted outrageously. When a public official or a public figure such as Falwell sues the media for intentional infliction of emotional distress, there must be proof that the media published a false statement of fact with **actual malice** (also called constitutional malice). This means that the media knew the statement was false or that it published the statement in reckless disregard of whether it was true or false. This is a standard that is very difficult for most plaintiffs to meet. It would, therefore, tend to discourage an onslaught of tort claims against the media and thereby help ensure the robust exchange of ideas that the First Amendment is designed to encourage.

In the *Hustler* case, the Court ruled against Falwell because the ad parody could not reasonably be understood as describing actual facts about Falwell. Given the context of the publication, the caricature was simply not reasonably believable. Therefore, the magazine did not publish a false statement of fact about Falwell, and, by definition could not have acted with actual malice. Consequently, the plaintiff cannot assert the tort of intentional infliction of emotional distress.

When the media is sued for something it publishes, the more common tort asserted against it is libel. This is the area of tort law that gave birth to the Supreme Court's imposition of the actual malice standard for media defendants. When we discuss defamation in Chapter 20, we will provide a fuller treatment of actual malice, particularly when the plaintiff is a public official or a public figure.

NEGLIGENT INFLICTION OF EMOTIONAL DISTRESS

Traditional Negligence

A traditional negligence action alleges that the defendant caused physical harm or injury for which damages can be recovered (see Chapter 10). The plaintiff can also recover damages for the emotional distress (*pain and suffering*) that accompany this physical harm or injury.

> **EXAMPLE:** Dan negligently drives his car into Rose, a pedestrian crossing the street. She suffers a broken back.

Rose can recover damages for the injury to her back (a direct physical injury) as well as for the pain and suffering she experienced during and since the accident.

Suppose, however, a person suffers emotional distress but no direct or immediate physical injury.

EXAMPLES: Case A. Bob negligently drives his car past Mary, a pedestrian crossing the street. She is not hit, but is extremely distressed by the way Bob was driving.

Case B. Bob negligently drives his car past Mary, a pedestrian crossing the street. She is not hit, but is extremely distressed by the way Bob was driving. Two days after this incident, Mary develops ulcers brought on by her memories of Bob's driving.

Case C. Bob negligently drives his car past Mary, a pedestrian crossing the street. His car runs into and kills another pedestrian. Mary is not hit, but is extremely distressed by witnessing the death.

If Bob intentionally caused Mary's distress in any of these cases, she may be able to sue him for intentional infliction of emotional distress. Suppose, however, that he negligently caused Mary's emotional distress in Cases A, B, or C. When emotional distress is negligently caused, we need to determine whether there can be a suit for **negligent infliction of emotional distress (NIED)**. Several variations are possible:

- The plaintiff does not suffer physical harm or injury along with the emotional distress (Case A).
- The plaintiff suffers emotional distress now and physical harm or injury at a later time (Case B).
- The plaintiff suffers emotional distress from witnessing someone else's injury and may or may not also suffer physical harm or injury (Case C).

No Physical Harm or Injury

We begin our discussion with Case A. Assume that the defendant's negligently driven car just misses the plaintiff. The latter suffers no *physical* harm or injury at any time, but does suffer substantial fright, anxiety, or other emotional distress. There can be no recovery according to the traditional rule. Courts take the position that the emotional distress is too trivial if it does not grow out of or cause a physical harm or injury, e.g., a heart attack. Courts are also concerned that it would be too easy to fabricate the emotional distress if it were not connected to physical harm or injury. A small number of courts provide an exception to this rule in certain kinds of cases, e.g., the defendant is a telegraph company that has negligently misdelivered a message (e.g., of death) to the wrong relative; the defendant is a funeral home that has negligently handled the body of the deceased. Relatives suffering emotional distress in such cases *can* recover even if they did not also suffer direct physical harm or injury. These are exceptions, however. In the vast majority of other cases, recovery is denied.

Later Physical Harm or Injury

Next we examine the case in which the negligence of the defendant causes emotional distress that *later* leads to physical harm or injury (Case B). The negligence does not directly produce this harm or injury. The classic case is the woman who suffers a miscarriage due to anxiety two weeks after the defendant *almost* hit her while negligently driving a truck close to the sidewalk. Assuming that the plaintiff can establish the causal link between the emotional distress and the physical harm or injury (not an easy task), can there be recovery? Courts answer this question differently; considerable confusion exists.

- Some courts will deny recovery unless the emotional distress and physical harm or injury are simultaneous.
- Most courts will allow recovery, but only if there is some **physical impact** on the plaintiff at the time of the defendant's negligence; the impact need not be substantial (a slight jar, or smoke in the face will be sufficient); the impact itself does not have to produce any physical harm or injury as long as harm or injury is caused by the emotional distress.

- Some courts allow recovery even if there is no impact as long as the evidence is strong enough to establish the causal connection between the emotional distress and the physical harm or injury that later develops.
- Some courts will allow recovery, but only if the plaintiff is in the **zone of danger** of physical impact due to the defendant's negligence even if there is no actual impact on the plaintiff.

When recovery is denied, it is sometimes based on the theory that the defendant owed no duty to the plaintiff to prevent the injury that resulted (see Chapter 11 on duty), or that the defendant was not the proximate cause of the injury (see Chapter 13 on proximate cause).

Witnessing Someone Else's Injury

The situation becomes even more complicated when the plaintiff is a witness to an injury negligently caused to someone else (Case C). What happens when the plaintiff suffers emotional distress in such a case (e.g., the plaintiff witnesses her son being hit by the defendant's negligently driven truck) and there is no impact on the plaintiff? Can the plaintiff recover damages if he or she has a physical injury caused by the emotional distress? Can the plaintiff recover damages if no physical injury results from the emotional distress? Again, the courts do not handle these questions in the same way.

- Some courts deny recovery in all such cases.
- Some courts will allow recovery but only if the plaintiff suffered a physical injury and was close enough to also be in the zone of danger when he or she witnessed the other person being injured.
- Some courts will allow recovery but only if the plaintiff suffered a physical injury, was close enough to also be in the zone of danger, and was very closely related to the person the plaintiff witnessed being injured.
- Some courts will allow recovery even if the plaintiff did not suffer a physical injury as long as the emotional distress from witnessing the injury was foreseeable and was serious or severe.

When recovery is denied, it is sometimes based on the theory that the defendant owed no duty to the plaintiff witnessing the accident (see Chapter 11), or that the defendant was not the proximate cause of what the plaintiff suffered by witnessing someone else's injury (see Chapter 13).

ASSIGNMENT
7.3

In the following situations, determine whether there can be recovery for negligent infliction of emotional distress (NIED).

a. Eight-year-old Johnny is on his first trip to Disneyland. While walking through the park, he is shocked to see Mickey Mouse remove his mask to get a drink of water at a fountain. Johnny is traumatized to learn that the character he idolized is not real. Johnny sues the person in the costume and Disneyland for NIED.

b. Mary is a passenger on a flight across the country. Suddenly the plane jerks. Mary looks out the window and sees that part of the wing has broken off. The pilot announces that everyone should be prepared for an emergency landing. Forty-five minutes of terror later, the plane lands safely in a farm field. Mary sues the airline for NIED.

c. While eating a sandwich, Bill senses something strange in the mustard. He immediately spits out what is in his mouth and discovers very small glass particles in the mustard. Bill suffers great anxiety at the thought of the glass in his mouth. He sues the manufacturer of the mustard for NIED.

d. Helen and Laura work for the railroad. Due to Laura's negligence, Helen's foot is trapped for a few seconds on a track with a train approaching directly at her. At the last moment, Helen is able to move out of the way. Helen is numb from fright. At home that night and for three nights thereafter, she suffers excruciating anguish at the thought of almost being hit by a train. Helen sues Laura for NIED.

e. Fred is on a hill overlooking his house. He watches a huge truck being carelessly driven by Jim heading right for his house. Fred knows that there is no one in the house, but is extremely concerned because he just had $50,000 in repairs made on the front of the house. Jim smashes into the front of the house. Fred is frantic. He starts running toward the house, trips, and has a heart attack. Fred sues Jim for NIED.

SUMMARY

The tort of intentional infliction of emotional distress requires an act of extreme or outrageous conduct. It must shock the conscience. For defendants such as common carriers and innkeepers, however, courts sometimes say that less severe conduct will suffice. In most states, there must be intent to cause the severe emotional distress; in some states, recklessness is enough. The defendant's intent to cause distress in one person will not be transferred to another person who suffered the distress if the defendant did not intend to harm the latter. The plaintiff must in fact suffer severe emotional distress. Physical illness or harm is not required. The test of whether the distress was severe is an objective test unless the defendant is aware of (and takes advantage of) the plaintiff's unusual susceptibility to such distress. The plaintiff must show either that but for what the defendant did the distress would not have resulted, or that the defendant was a substantial factor in producing it.

When a media defendant is sued for intentional infliction of emotional distress and the plaintiff is a public official or public figure, the plaintiff must prove that the media published a false statement of fact and either knew the statement was false or published it in reckless disregard of whether it was true or false (actual malice).

In a standard negligence action, the plaintiff can recover for emotional distress arising out of direct and immediate physical harm or injury. With few exceptions, if the plaintiff never suffers physical harm or injury, courts deny recovery for the negligently caused emotional distress. If this distress later results in physical harm or injury, courts sometimes grant recovery. It may depend on whether there was some physical impact on the plaintiff or whether the plaintiff was in the zone of danger of impact. If the plaintiff witnesses someone else's injury, recovery may depend on whether the plaintiff suffered a physical injury, was also in the zone of danger, was closely related to the person whose injury the plaintiff witnessed, suffered serious or severe emotional distress that was foreseeable, etc.

KEY TERMS

pain and suffering 65
intentional infliction of emotional distress 65
outrage 65
extreme or outrageous 70
intent 71

recklessness 71
transferred intent 71
severe emotional distress 72
physical injury 72
causation 72

actual malice 75
negligent infliction of emotional distress (NIED) 76
physical impact 76
zone of danger 77

Conversion and Trespass to Chattels

Chapter Outline

- Introduction
- Damages
- Kind of Interference
- Mistake Defense

INTRODUCTION

If someone accidently damages your personal property (also called a **chattel**) e.g., a motorist dents the right fender of your car in a collision, you may be able to sue for negligence. Suppose, however, that the interference is *intentional* rather than accidental, e.g., someone steals your fountain pen from your bag or decides to "borrow" your car for an hour without your permission. Your remedy in such cases is the tort of **conversion** or the tort of **trespass to chattels.** The major distinction between the two torts is the degree of interference that is involved. If the interference is relatively minor, the tort to use is trespass to chattels. A more serious interference justifies an action for conversion.

 Conversion and Trespass to Chattels Checklist

Definitions, Relationships, Paralegal Roles, and Research References

Category of These Torts
They are both intentional torts.

Interests Protected by These Torts
    Conversion: The right to be free from serious intentional interferences with personal property.
    Trespass to Chattels: The right to be free from intentional interferences with personal property resulting in dispossession or intermeddling.

Elements of These Torts
Conversion:

    i. Personal property (chattel)
    ii. The plaintiff is in possession of the chattel or is entitled to immediate possession
    iii. Intent to exercise dominion or control over the chattel
    iv. Serious interference with plaintiff's possession
    v. Causation (of element iv)

Conversion and Trespass to Chattels Checklist Continued

Trespass to Chattels:

   i. Personal property (chattel)
   ii. The plaintiff is in possession of the chattel or is entitled to immediate possession
   iii. Intent to dispossess or to intermeddle with the chattel
   iv. Dispossession or intermeddling
   v. Causation (of element iv)

Definitions of Major Words/Phrases in the Elements

Chattel: Tangible or intangible property other than land or things attached to land.
Intent: The desire to exercise control or dominion over the chattel, or the knowledge with substantial certainty that this control or dominion will result from what the defendant does (for conversion). The desire to dispossess or to intermeddle, or the knowledge with substantial certainty that dispossession or intermeddling will result from what the defendant does (for trespass to chattels).
Control: Exerting power over something.
Dominion: Asserting supreme power or authority over something.
Dispossess: To take physical control of the chattel without the consent of the person who has possession, but without exercising dominion over the chattel.
Intermeddle: Make physical contact with the chattel.
Causation: But for what the defendant did, the serious interference with the chattel would not have occurred, or the defendant was a substantial factor in producing the serious interference (for conversion). But for what the defendant did, the plaintiff would not have been dispossessed of the chattel or had it intermeddled with, or the defendant was a substantial factor in producing the dispossession or intermeddling (for trespass to chattel).

Major Defense and Counterargument Possibilities That Need to Be Explored

1. The property involved was not personal property (not a chattel).
2. The plaintiff was not in possession or entitled to immediate possession.
3. There was no intent to exercise dominion or control (for conversion), nor to dispossess or intermeddle (for trespass to chattels).
4. The interference was not serious enough.
5. The defendant's control over the chattel was trivial. There was no impairment. The plaintiff was not deprived of the use of the chattel for a substantial time.
6. The defendant did not cause the interference with the plaintiff's possession of the chattel.
7. The plaintiff consented to what the defendant did to the chattel and the defendant did not exceed that consent (on the defense of consent, see Chapter 23).
8. The interference with the plaintiff's property occurred while the defendant was defending the defendant's own property against the plaintiff (on the privilege of defense of property and other self-help privileges, see Chapter 23).
9. The interference with the plaintiff's property occurred while the defendant was recapturing the defendant's own property from the plaintiff (on the recapture of property and other self-help privileges, see Chapter 23).
10. The interference with the plaintiff's property occurred while the defendant was protecting person or property (on necessity and other self-help privileges, see Chapter 23).
11. The interference with the plaintiff's property occurred while the defendant was abating a nuisance (on abating a nuisance and other self-help privileges, see Chapters 19 and 23).
12. The plaintiff's suit against the government for conversion or trespass to chattels committed by a government employee may be barred by sovereign immunity (on sovereign immunity, see Chapter 23).
13. The plaintiff's suit against the government employee for conversion or trespass to chattels may be barred by public official immunity (on official immunity, see Chapter 23).
14. The plaintiff's suit against the charitable organization for conversion or trespass to chattels committed by someone working for the organization may be barred by charitable immunity (on charitable immunity, see Chapter 23).
15. The plaintiff failed to take reasonable steps to mitigate the harm caused when the defendant committed trespass to chattels; therefore, damages should not cover the aggravation of the harm caused by the plaintiff (on the doctrine of avoidable consequences, see Chapter 14).

Conversion and Trespass to Chattels Checklist Continued

Damages
In conversion, the plaintiff recovers the full fair market value of the chattel at the time and place of the conversion. In trespass to chattels, the plaintiff's recovery is limited to harm or injury caused the chattel, e.g., repair costs and cost of renting a substitute. If malice or hatred existed, punitive damages are also possible.

Relationship to Criminal Law
A number of crimes may also be involved in addition to these torts: theft or larceny, embezzlement, false pretenses, receiving stolen property, robbery, extortion, blackmail, burglary, etc.

Relationship to Other Torts
Misrepresentation: The defendant's interference with the chattel of plaintiff may have occurred through misrepresentation, so that this tort plus conversion or trespass to chattels are committed.

Negligence: If the plaintiff cannot establish that the interference with his or her property was intentional, he or she may be able to show negligence if there was unreasonable conduct by the defendant and actual harm to the property.

Federal Law
a. Under the Federal Tort Claims Act, the United States Government will be liable for claims arising out of conversion or trespass to chattels committed by one of its federal employees within the scope of employment (respondeat superior). (See Figure 23–7 in Chapter 23.)

b. There may be liability under the Civil Rights Act if the conversion or trespass to chattels was committed while the defendant was depriving the plaintiff of federal rights under color of law. (See Figure 23–8 in Chapter 23.)

Employer-Employee (Agency) Law
An employee who commits conversion or trespass to chattels is personally liable for this tort. His or her employer will *also* be liable for these torts if the conduct of the employee was within the scope of employment (respondeat superior). The employee must be furthering a business objective of the employer at the time. (On the factors that determine the scope of employment, see Figure 12–7 in Chapter 12.)

Paralegal Roles in Conversion or Trespass to Chattels Litigation
Fact finding (help the office collect facts relevant to prove the elements of conversion or trespass to chattels, the elements of available defenses, and extent of injuries or other damages):
• client interviewing
• field investigation
• online research (e.g., blue book value of a used car)

File management (help the office control the volume of paperwork in a conversion or trespass to chattels litigation):
• open client file
• enter case data in computer database
• maintain file documents

Litigation assistance (help the trial attorney prepare for a conversion or trespass to chattels trial and appeal, if needed):
• draft discovery requests
• draft answers to discovery requests
• draft pleadings
• digest and index discovery documents
• help prepare, order, and manage trial exhibits (visuals or demonstratives)
• prepare trial notebook
• draft notice of appeal
• order trial transcript
• cite check briefs
• perform legal research

Conversion and Trespass to Chattels Checklist Continued

Collection/enforcement (help the trial attorney for the judgment creditor to collect the damages award or enforce other court orders at the conclusion of the conversion or trespass to chattels case):
- draft postjudgment discovery requests
- field investigation to monitor compliance with judgment
- online research (e.g., location of defendant's business assets)

Research References for Conversion and Trespass to Chattels

Digests
In the digests of West, look for case summaries on these torts under key topics such as:

Conversion	Bailments
Trover and Conversion	Torts
Property	Damages

Corpus Juris Secundum
In this legal encyclopedia, see the discussion under topic headings such as:

Conversion	Bailments
Trover and Conversion	Torts
Property	Damages

American Jurisprudence 2d
In this legal encyclopedia, see the discussion under topic headings such as:

Conversion	Abandoned, Lost and Unclaimed Property
Property	Damages
Bailments	Torts

Legal Periodical Literature
There are two index systems to use to locate legal periodical literature on these torts:

INDEX TO LEGAL PERIODICALS AND BOOKS (ILP)	*CURRENT LEGAL INDEX (CLI)*
See literature in *ILP* under subject headings such as:	See literature in *CLI* under subject headings such as:
Conversion	Personal Property
Personal Property	Torts
Property	Property
Torts	Bailments
Damages	Intangible Property
Bailments	Damages
	Fraudulent Conveyances

Example of a legal periodical article you will find by using *ILP* or *CLI:*

Commercial Exploitation of DNA and the Tort of Conversion: A Physician May Not Destroy a Patient's Interest in Her Body-Matter by Aaron C. Lichtman, 34 New York Law School Law Review 531 (1989).

A.L.R., A.L.R.2d, A.L.R.3d, A.L.R.4th, A.L.R.5th, A.L.R. Fed.
Use the *ALR Index* to locate annotations on these torts. In this index, check subject headings such as:

Trover and Conversion	Property Damages
Conversion	Personal Property
Damages	Torts

Example of an annotation you can locate through these subject headings on these torts:

Punitive or Exemplary Damages for Conversion of Personality by One Other Than Chattel Mortgagee or Conditional Seller by E. LeFevre, 54 A.L.R.2d 1361 (1957).

Words and Phrases
In this multivolume legal dictionary, look up *conversion, trespass to chattels, chattels, dispossession, dominion, bona fide purchaser,* and every other word or phrase connected with

Conversion and Trespass to Chattels Checklist Continued

conversion and trespass to chattels discussed in this chapter. The dictionary will give you definitions of these words or phrases from court opinions.

CALR: Computer-Assisted Legal Research

Example of a query you could ask on WESTLAW or on LEXIS to try to find cases, statutes, or other legal materials on conversion and trespass to chattels: **conversion /p damages**

Example of search terms you could use on an Internet legal search engine such as LawCrawler (http://lawcrawler.findlaw.com) to find cases, statutes, or other legal materials on conversion and trespass to chattels: **conversion AND tort AND damages**

Example of search terms you could use on an Internet general search engine such as Alta Vista (http://www.altavista.com) to find cases, statutes, or other legal materials on conversion and trespass to chattels: **+conversion +tort +damages**

More Internet sites to check for materials on conversion, trespass to chattels, and other torts:
Jurist: (http://jurist.law.pitt.edu/sg_torts.htm)
LawGuru: (http://www.lawguru.com/search/lawsearch.html)
See also Tort Law Online at the end of Chapter 1.

DAMAGES

A successful plaintiff in an action for trespass to chattels can recover the cost of repairs or the cost of temporarily renting a replacement for the chattel. For major or aggravated interferences, the plaintiff can sue for conversion, for which the recovery is the full value of the chattel at the time it was converted. In effect, the party that interfered with the chattel is forced to buy it—even if this wrongdoer later offers to return the chattel in its original condition.

KIND OF INTERFERENCE

When is an interference serious enough for conversion? There is no absolute answer to this question that will cover every case. The court will consider a number of factors, no one of which is conclusive. The factors are outlined in Figure 8–1.

In general, neither **dispossession** (taking physical control of a chattel without consent but without exercising dominion over it) nor **intermeddling** (making physical contact with a chattel) are serious enough interferences for conversion. Both, however, would constitute trespass to chattels.

Dispossession

EXAMPLE: Dan takes Jim's book for an afternoon and reads it without permission. No damage is done to the book. It is returned. Dan never claims that he owned the book. Jim did not need the book while Dan had it.

* The extent and duration of the defendant's exercise of control or dominion over the chattel; the more substantial and lengthy the interference, the more likely it will constitute conversion.
* Whether the defendant intended to assert a right in the chattel that was inconsistent with the plaintiff's right of control.
* Whether the defendant acted in good faith or bad faith when interfering with the chattel.
* Whether the interference caused any damage or harm to the chattel.
* Whether the plaintiff suffered any inconvenience or expense as a result of the interference.

W. Page Keeton et al., *Prosser and Keeton on the Law of Torts* 90 (5th ed. 1984). *Restatement (Second) of Torts* §222A (1965).

FIGURE 8–1
Factors considered by a court to determine whether an interference with a chattel is serious enough for conversion.

Intermeddling

> **EXAMPLE:** Tom is sitting in the park with his new puppy. Paula comes over and starts petting it, even though Tom asks her to stop. The dog growls a little, but is not harmed.

In the intermeddling example, what if Paula accidently got a little ink on the white fur of the puppy? The case is still not serious enough to constitute conversion. In a trespass-to-chattels action, Tom would be limited to recovering any cost associated with cleaning the dog. Suppose, however, that the ink could not be removed or could be removed only by subjecting the dog to a painful chemical procedure. Now the interference may be serious enough to constitute the tort of conversion.

ASSIGNMENT

8.1

Has conversion or trespass to chattels been committed in any of the following cases?

a. After an argument, Susan places all of her boyfriend's belongings on the sidewalk in front of Susan's home. The boyfriend watches Susan do this. He sues her for converting his belongings.

b. Same facts as in *a*, except that the boyfriend does not learn about the removal of the belongings until he comes home from work on the day Susan placed them on the sidewalk.

c. George orders a very expensive meal at a restaurant where he is dining alone. He puts his silk jacket on the chair next to where he is sitting and goes to make a phone call in the hall. While away, Ralph, another patron, comes over to George's table. He tries on George's jacket in order to help decide whether he wants to buy one like it. He also pours a few drops of wine from George's glass into an empty glass Ralph brings over. Ralph wants to taste the wine in order to decide whether to order the same wine. George sues Ralph for converting his jacket and his meal.

d. Mary lies to her boyfriend, John, about her use of birth control. When she becomes pregnant, he sues her for converting his semen.

MISTAKE DEFENSE

It is not a defense that the defendant acted in good faith or made a reasonable **mistake,** although this is one of the overall factors that the court will take into consideration in determining whether the interference is serious enough for conversion.

> **EXAMPLE:** Lena steals Sam's rifle. She offers to sell the rifle to Ed, who has no idea where she got it. Ed buys it for $200. Lena disappears. When Sam finds out what happened, he demands that Ed return the rifle. Ed refuses. Sam then sues Ed for conversion.

Sam will win. It is no defense that Ed is a **bona fide purchaser** who bought the rifle thinking that Lena had the right to sell it. Ed intended to exercise total ownership and control over the gun when he bought it. This was in full contradiction to Sam's rights in the rifle. (A bona fide purchaser is someone who purchases property for value without notice of defects in the title of the seller to the property.)

ASSIGNMENT

8.2

Ted grows valuable and expensive orchids in his backyard. It is the end of the growing season. He has two orchids remaining from his most expensive variety.

He cuts one and places it in a basket in the yard next to the one still growing. Later that afternoon, Janice, one of Ted's houseguests, mistakenly thinks Ted is throwing away the orchid in the basket. She takes it from the basket and also cuts the one still growing. She puts them both in her suitcase. The next morning she wonders whether she made a mistake in taking the orchids without asking Ted. When Ted finds out what Janice did, he sues her for conversion. What result?

SUMMARY

The torts of conversion and trespass to chattels are designed to provide a remedy for intentional interferences with personal property. If the interference is serious, conversion is the appropriate remedy, requiring the wrongdoer to pay the plaintiff the full value of the chattel converted. Trespass to chattels covers less serious interferences. If the act constituting interference is intentional, it is no defense that the interference was an innocent mistake, as in the case of a bona fide purchaser.

KEY TERMS

chattel   79

conversion   79

trespass to chattels   79

dispossession   83

intermeddling   83

mistake   84

bona fide purchaser   84

Strict Liability

Chapter Outline

- Introduction
- Animals
- Strict Liability for Abnormally Dangerous Conditions or Activities

INTRODUCTION

As we saw in Chapter 1, there are three main categories of torts: intentional torts, negligence, and strict liability torts. **Strict liability** (sometimes referred to as **absolute liability** or **liability without fault**) means responsibility regardless of blameworthiness or fault. Persons who engage in certain kinds of activity will be liable or responsible for the harm that results even if they acted with the greatest of care to avoid the harm. The normal method of demonstrating blameworthiness or fault is for the plaintiff to show that the defendant's conduct fit within one of the intentional torts or was unreasonable (negligent). For some activities, however, the blameworthiness or fault of the defendant is irrelevant. As a matter of social policy, the law says that when designated activities cause harm, the defendant must pay—whether the defendant acted innocently, intentionally, or negligently. The same is true for harm that results from certain conditions that exist on the defendant's land.

In this chapter we will consider two categories of harm that lead to strict liability: harm caused by animals and harm caused by abnormally dangerous conditions or activities. In Chapter 16 on products liability, we will examine the separate tort called **strict liability in tort,** which covers harm caused by a defective product irrespective of the blameworthiness or fault of the manufacturer or distributor of the product.

One final point before we begin: there is some overlap among the three categories of torts studied in this book. For example, some of the intentional torts will lead to liability even though it may be difficult to find blameworthiness or fault in the defendant's conduct. Also, as we will see later, it is sometimes difficult to distinguish between negligence and the tort called strict liability in tort. Nevertheless, categorizing torts is useful as a starting point in studying tort law. Be prepared, however, to find an absence of rigid boundary lines among the various torts.

ANIMALS

The Centers for Disease Control and Prevention estimates that each year dogs bite 4.7 million people, 800,000 of whom require medical treatment. Half of all children are bitten by a dog before their twelfth birthday.[1] When a dog or other animal causes harm, the owner might be liable under several possible theories of recovery. The cause of action might be an intentional tort or negligence.

> **EXAMPLES:** Mary knows that her dog is aggressive around strangers. One day in the park, she guides her dog close to the leg of a stranger so that the dog will take a bite. The dog does so. Mary has committed a battery because she intended a harmful or offensive contact (see Chapter 3).
>
> Mary knows that her dog is aggressive around strangers. To prevent the dog from bothering anyone, she keeps the dog on a leash. One day in a crowded park, however, she carelessly drops the leash so that she can read a newspaper on the bench. A stranger walking by is bitten by the dog. Mary has committed negligence because her failure to use reasonable care caused harm (see Chapter 12).

What about strict liability? Can a pet owner be strictly liable for harm caused by an animal even if no intentional tort or negligence has been committed? The answer depends, in part, on whether the animal is wild or domestic.

Wild Animals

A **wild animal** is an animal in the state of nature, e.g., lion, bear, monkey. In most states, an owner (or keeper) of a wild animal will be strictly liable for any harm it causes whether or not the owner knew of the animal's dangerous propensities, irrespective of how well trained the animal may have been, and regardless of how much care the owner took to prevent harm to others by the animal.

Domestic Animals

A **domestic animal** is an animal that has been domesticated or habituated to live among humans, e.g., dog, cat, horse. An owner (or keeper) of a domestic animal will be strictly liable for the harm it causes if two elements can be established:

  i. owner has reason to know the animal has a specific propensity to cause harm, and
  ii. harm caused by the animal was due to that specific propensity.

> **EXAMPLE:** George knows that his dog, Fido, likes to bite joggers. Fido has never bothered anyone else. One day the dog bites Tom, a jogger. A few hours later, Fido knocks down Mary, a neighbor, while she is gardening.

In most states, George will be strictly liable to Tom since biting was a known propensity. There was no known propensity, however, for knocking people down. Therefore, there would be no strict liability to Mary. If she wants to recover, she must show that George was negligent in failing to prevent Fido from knocking her down or that he intended this result.

Occasionally, you will see the phrase, "every dog is entitled to one free bite." The implication of this statement is that an owner won't know about the propensity of the dog to bite until the dog has claimed its first human victim. Yet, this is not accurate. There might be other evidence of this propensity, e.g., the dog's inclination to lunge toward everyone with its mouth wide open. Another reason the first bite may not be

---

[1]Jane E. Brody, *Heeding the Warnings From Dangerous Dogs*, N.Y. Times, May 18, 1999, at D8.

"free" is that an owner might be subject to negligence liability for failing to control an obviously feisty and aggressive dog even if the dog has never bitten anyone.

A few states have passed special statutes that impose strict liability for harm caused by domestic animals with no known dangerous propensities. In effect, such statutes treat domestic animals the same as wild animals.

Sam knows that his dog bites other dogs. One day Sam's dog bites a stranger, the first time it has ever attacked a human. Is Sam subject to strict liability?

ASSIGNMENT

9.1

STRICT LIABILITY FOR ABNORMALLY DANGEROUS CONDITIONS OR ACTIVITIES

Next we examine those conditions or activities causing harm that can lead to strict liability. The tort is called **strict liability for abnormally dangerous conditions or activities** and sometimes, absolute liability for abnormally dangerous conditions or activities. It is important to keep in mind that the defendant is not necessarily home free if the plaintiff fails to establish that the condition or activity of the defendant qualifies for strict liability status. The plaintiff may still be able to win by showing that the defendant committed other torts such as trespass to land, nuisance, or negligence in maintaining the condition or engaging in the activity.

Most of the cases on strict liability for abnormally dangerous conditions or activities involve the way in which the defendant uses or abuses his or her land. It is also possible, however, to commit this tort while on someone else's land, e.g., transporting a large quantity of explosives over a neighbor's land or over a public highway.

 Strict Liability for Abnormally Dangerous Conditions or Activities Checklist

Definitions, Relationships, Paralegal Roles, and Research References

Category
Strict liability for abnormally dangerous conditions or activities is a strict liability tort (neither negligence nor intent must be shown).

Interest Protected by This Tort
The right to be free from harm caused by abnormally dangerous conditions or activities.

Elements of This Tort
i. Existence of an abnormally dangerous condition or activity
ii. Knowledge of the condition or activity
iii. Damages
iv. Causation

Definitions of Major Words/Phrases in the Elements
Abnormal: Unusual or non-natural for the area.
Dangerous: Creating a substantial likelihood of great harm to persons or property, which cannot be eliminated by the use of reasonable care by the defendant.
Proximate Cause: The defendant is the cause in fact of the harm that results. The kind of harm that results was foreseeable by the defendant, or should have been foreseeable. The plaintiff was within the class of people who were foreseeably endangered by the condition or activity.

Major Defenses and Counterargument Possibilities That Need to Be Explored
1. The condition or activity was not abnormally dangerous. (NOTE: The objective of the defendant is to try to force the plaintiff to prove negligence. This is accomplished if

Strict Liability for Abnormally Dangerous Conditions or Activities Checklist Continued

the plaintiff fails to show that the condition or activity was abnormally dangerous. Items 2 to 5 below try to establish that the condition or activity was not abnormally dangerous.)

2. The condition or activity was usual or natural for the environment in question.
3. The likelihood of serious harm from the condition or activity was small.
4. The danger in the condition or activity could have been eliminated by the use of reasonable care. (Defendant does not admit, however, that such care was not used.)
5. The value of the condition or activity to the community outweighed any possible danger.
6. A statute required or authorized the condition or activity.
7. The defendant was not aware of the condition or activity.
8. The defendant was not the cause in fact of the harm suffered by the plaintiff.
9. The kind of harm that resulted was not foreseeable.
10. The person injured was not a foreseeable plaintiff.
11. The plaintiff was aware of the danger, understood it, and unreasonably encountered it (assumption of the risk).
12. The plaintiff consented to what the defendant did (on the defense of consent, see Chapter 23).
13. The plaintiff's suit against the government for strict liability for abnormally dangerous conditions or activities committed by a government employee may be barred by sovereign immunity (on sovereign immunity, see Chapter 23).
14. The plaintiff's suit against the government employee for strict liability for abnormally dangerous conditions or activities may be barred by public official immunity (on official immunity, see Chapter 23).
15. The plaintiff's suit against the charitable organization for strict liability for abnormally dangerous conditions or activities committed by someone working for the organization may be barred by charitable immunity (on charitable immunity, see Chapter 23).
16. The plaintiff failed to take reasonable steps to mitigate the harm caused when the defendant committed strict liability for abnormally dangerous conditions or activities; therefore, damages should not cover the aggravation of the harm caused by the plaintiff (on the doctrine of avoidable consequences, see Chapter 14).

Damages
The plaintiff can recover compensatory damages for the harm caused by the defendant's condition or activity. Punitive damages may also be possible if the plaintiff can show that the defendant was malicious or reckless in allowing the harm to occur. (On the categories of damages, see Chapter 14.)

Relationship to Criminal Law
There may be a criminal statute that prohibits the defendant from maintaining the condition or engaging in the activity involved, e.g., a statute making it a crime to explode fireworks in public areas. The consequences of violating such a statute may include criminal penalties as well as civil liability for the strict liability tort under discussion in this chapter.

Other Torts and Related Actions
Negligence: If the condition or activity of the defendant does not qualify for strict liability status because the condition or activity is not abnormally dangerous, the plaintiff may be able to show that the defendant was negligent in connection with the condition or activity.

Nuisance: Nuisance should be considered when the condition or activity of the defendant interferes with the use and enjoyment of the plaintiff's land. In some states, there is liability for an absolute nuisance on the same facts that would constitute strict liability for an abnormally dangerous condition or activity.

Trespass to Land: This tort is used when there is an entry of a physical object on the land of the plaintiff due to the abnormally dangerous condition or activity of the defendant.

Wrongful Death: This action can be brought by the survivors of the plaintiff if death results from the abnormally dangerous condition or activity of the defendant.

**Strict Liability for Abnormally Dangerous
Conditions or Activities Checklist** Continued

Federal Law

Under the Federal Tort Claims Act, the United States Government will *not* be liable for a claim based on strict liability for abnormally dangerous conditions or activities committed by one of its federal employees. (See Figure 23–7 in Chapter 23.)

Employer-Employee (Agency) Law

An employee who commits strict liability for abnormally dangerous conditions or activities is personally liable for this tort. His or her employer will *also* be liable for this tort if the conduct of the employee was within the scope of employment (respondeat superior). The employee must be furthering a business objective of the employer at the time. (On the factors that determine the scope of employment, see Figure 12–7 in Chapter 12.)

Paralegal Roles in Litigation for Strict Liability for Abnormally Dangerous Conditions or Activities

Fact finding (help the office collect facts relevant to prove the elements of strict liability for abnormally dangerous conditions or activities, the elements of available defenses, and extent of injuries or other damages):
- client interviewing
- field investigation
- online research (e.g., records on weather conditions on the date of the accident)

File management (help the office control the volume of paperwork in a litigation of a case asserting strict liability for abnormally dangerous conditions or activities):
- open client file
- enter case data in computer database
- maintain file documents

Litigation assistance (help the trial attorney prepare for a trial and appeal, if needed):
- draft discovery requests
- draft answers to discovery requests
- draft pleadings
- digest and index discovery documents
- help prepare, order, and manage trial exhibits (visuals or demonstratives)
- prepare trial notebook
- draft notice of appeal
- order trial transcript
- cite check briefs
- perform legal research

Collection/enforcement (help the trial attorney for the judgment creditor to collect the damages award or to enforce other court orders at the conclusion of the case):
- draft postjudgment discovery requests
- field investigation to monitor compliance with judgment
- online research (e.g., location of defendant's business assets)

Research References for This Tort

Digests
In the digests of West, look for case summaries on this tort under key topics such as:

Explosives	Damages
Trespass	Torts
Waters and Water Courses	Death
	Nuisance

Corpus Juris Secundum
In this legal encyclopedia, see the discussion under topic headings such as:

Explosives	Damages
Trespass	Torts
Waters and Water Courses	Death
	Nuisance

Strict Liability for Abnormally Dangerous Conditions or Activities Checklist Continued

American Jurisprudence 2d
In this legal encyclopedia, see the discussion under topic headings such as:

Explosions and Explosives	Damages
Waters	Torts
Premises Liability	Death
Adjoining Landowners	Nuisance

Legal Periodical Literature
There are two main index systems to use to locate legal periodical literature on this tort:

INDEX TO LEGAL PERIODICALS AND BOOKS (ILP)	CURRENT LAW INDEX (CLI)
See literature in *ILP* under subject headings such as:	See literature in *CLI* under subject headings such as:
Water and Water Courses	Strict Liability
Liability without Fault	Explosives
Animals	Water
Fires and Fire Prevention	Damages
Trespass	Torts
Real Property	Real Property
Torts	Liability for Landslide Damages
Damages	Liability for Condition and
Adjoining Landowners	Use of Land

Example of a legal periodical article you will find by using *ILP* or *CLI*:

Common Carriers and Risk Distribution: Absolute Liability for Transporting Hazardous Materials by James R. Roberts, 67 Kentucky Law Journal 441 (1978–79).

A.L.R., A.L.R.2d, A.L.R.3d, A.L.R.4th, A.L.R.5th, A.L.R. Fed.
Use the *ALR Index* to locate annotations on this tort. In this index, check subject headings such as:

Absolute Liability	Torts
Floods and Flooding	Damages
Explosions and Explosives	Water

Example of an annotation you can locate through this index:

Liability for Property Damage caused by Vibrations, or the like, Without Blasting or Explosion by T. S. Tellier, 79 A.L.R.2d 966 (1961).

Words and Phrases
In this multivolume legal dictionary, look up *abnormally dangerous* and every other word or phrase connected with strict liability for abnormally dangerous conditions or activities discussed in this chapter. The dictionary will give you definitions of these words or phrases from court opinions.

CALR: Computer-Assisted Legal Research
Example of a query you could ask on WESTLAW to try to find cases or other legal materials on this tort: **"strict liability for abnormally dangerous activities" /p damages**

Example of a query you could ask on LEXIS to try to find cases or other legal materials on this tort: **strict liability for abnormally dangerous activities /p damages**

Example of search terms you could use on an Internet legal search engine such as LawCrawler (http://lawcrawler.findlaw.com) to find cases, statutes, or other legal materials on this tort: **"strict liability for abnormally dangerous activities"**

Example of search terms you could use on an Internet general search engine such as Alta Vista (http://www.altavista.com) to find cases, statutes, or other legal materials on this tort: **"strict liability for abnormally dangerous activities"**

More Internet sites to check for materials on strict liability for abnormally dangerous conditions or activities and other torts:
Jurist: (http://jurist.law.pitt.edu/sg_torts.htm)
LawGuru: (http://www.lawguru.com/search/lawsearch.html)
See also Tort Law Online at the end of Chapter 1.

Abnormally Dangerous Condition or Activity

The first element is the existence of an **abnormally dangerous condition or activity**. Some conditions or activities are so dangerous to persons or property that the defendant will be liable for the harm they cause even if the defendant neither intended the harm nor was negligent in producing the harm. It is not a defense for the defendant to show that he or she acted reasonably or used the greatest of care—strict liability will still be imposed.

A great deal of the law in this area stems from a famous English case, *Rylands v. Fletcher.*[2] The defendants built a reservoir on their land. The plaintiff owned a mine nearby. The mine was flooded when water from the defendant's reservoir broke through and reached the mine. The rule from this case, which was eventually accepted in most American states, is as follows:

If the defendant knows he or she is engaging in:

(a) a non-natural or abnormal use of land,
(b) that creates an increased danger to persons or property,

the defendant will be strictly liable for harm caused by this use. The plaintiff will not have to prove negligence.

In short, there is strict liability for abnormally dangerous conditions or activities. (As we will see later, however, there are foreseeability requirements that must also be met before a court will impose strict liability.)

The determination of what is abnormal or non-natural will, of course, depend on the environment. The following are examples that have been found to be abnormally dangerous:

- storing large quantities of inflammable liquids in an urban area
- blasting in a residential area
- extensive pile driving
- emitting noxious gases from a factory in a residential area

The activity or condition must be unusual for the area and present a serious threat of harm. The following are examples of cases that were *not* found to be abnormally dangerous because they did not meet both criteria:

- electric wiring in a business
- gasoline stored at a gas station underground
- a small amount of dynamite stored in a factory
- an oil well dug in a Texas field

Although damage caused by such activities may not be considered abnormally dangerous enough to qualify for strict liability status, a plaintiff may still be able to recover under other theories. If the defendant acted unreasonably, a negligence case is possible, perhaps with the help of res ipsa loquitur (see Chapter 12). Nuisance and trespass to land should also be explored (see Chapter 19).

---

[2]L.R. 3 H.L. 330 (1868).

Is airplane flying an abnormally dangerous activity? Suppose a plane crashes onto someone's land, causing substantial damage to people and property below. Strict liability? Years ago, many courts would say yes. As aviation has become more common and accepted, however, modern courts are inclined to say no. A plaintiff, therefore, must establish negligence or some other tort in order to recover.

Statutes often play a role in this area of strict liability. A statute, for example, might require or simply authorize a common carrier to transport dangerous substances. In such cases, strict liability is usually not applied when damage results from the activity. Liability will result only if negligence can be shown. On the other hand, there may be statutes that prohibit certain activity, e.g., blasting in certain areas or selling drugs to minors. It is sometimes unclear what civil consequences, if any, the legislature intended for a violation of such statutes. Research into the legislative history of the statute must be undertaken. A court might interpret the statute as calling for strict liability, negligence liability, or no civil liability at all for its violation.

The *Restatement of Torts* lists a number of factors that a court should analyze in determining whether something is abnormally dangerous:[3]

- the degree of risk of some harm to people, land, or chattels of others
- the likelihood that the harm that results from the activity will be great
- the inability to eliminate the risk by the exercise of reasonable care
- the extent to which the activity is not a matter of common usage
- the inappropriateness of the activity to the place where the activity is carried on
- the extent to which the value of the activity to the community is outweighed by its dangerous attributes

None of these factors is usually conclusive in deciding whether an activity is abnormally dangerous. The factors are simply aids for a court to determine the extent of the abnormality and the extent of the danger posed by the defendant.

In balancing these factors, if a court tips the scale against strict liability, it does not necessarily mean that the defendant has won the case. It simply means that the plaintiff must try to fit the facts of the case under the elements of other torts: negligence, nuisance, trespass to land, etc.

ASSIGNMENT

9.2

In each of the following situations, assume that the object or activity in question has resulted in damage or harm to someone. Do you think a court will impose strict liability? Why or why not?

a. Tom is moving his own barn. He places it on a huge truck platform and drives it on a public highway. It crashes into a bridge.

b. The XYZ Company has installed a large steam boiler in its factory. It **explodes.**

c. The large lake on Linda's land overflows into neighboring land after a thunderstorm.

d. From an army base in Florida, scientists send up a satellite. Unfortunately it lands in Newark, New Jersey.

e. Fred knows that he is HIV positive. Yet, he continues to have unprotected sex with others who are unaware of Fred's HIV status.

f. A bystander is shot when a handgun accidentally goes off during a robbery. The bystander sues the manufacturer of the handgun for engaging in an abnormally dangerous activity.

---

[3]*Restatement (Second) of Torts* § 520 (1965).

Knowledge of the Condition or Activity

A defendant will not be strictly liable for an abnormally dangerous condition or activity of which the defendant is unaware. The plaintiff must establish knowledge on the part of the defendant.

Causation: Cause in Fact and Proximate Cause

The harm that the plaintiff's person or property has suffered must have been caused by the defendant's abnormally dangerous condition or activity. The **cause-in-fact** tests are as follows:

- **but for** the defendant's conduct, the plaintiff would not have been harmed, or
- the defendant's conduct was a **substantial factor** in producing the harm suffered by the plaintiff

The second test is used when there is more than one cause factor involved.

Once cause in fact has been established, **proximate cause** must be explored. When we study proximate cause in Chapter 13, we will learn that the rules of proximate cause establish a cutoff point beyond which the defendant will not be liable for the harm he or she caused in fact. Proximate cause, therefore, is more of a policy question than a causation question.

The classic case raising the issue of proximate cause is the mink that was so frightened by the defendant's blasting some distance away that she killed her own offspring. Assume that blasting in the location was an abnormally dangerous activity and that the defendant was the cause in fact of the deaths. But was the defendant the proximate cause of this harm? Most courts would say no. Strict liability should not be extended this far. *The harm that results must be within the type of harm that was initially foreseeable.* A mink killing its kittens is not within the type of harm that is foreseeable from blasting. Similarly, *strict liability covers only those groups or classes of people that were within the foreseeable risk posed by the abnormally dangerous activity.* The owners of the mink were not within the class of persons that could be foreseeably harmed by blasting, unless, of course, the blasting occurred on a mink farm.

The proximate cause rules for strict liability are not as broad as the proximate cause rules for negligence (see Chapter 13). A court is more willing to find proximate cause in a negligence case than in a strict liability case involving abnormally dangerous activities. Unforeseeable **intervening causes** such as an **act of God** or an act of a third person are more likely to cut off liability in a strict liability case than in a negligence case. Courts are willing to limit the extent of liability in this way when there is an absence of fault in a defendant who is strictly liable. No such reluctance is shown toward defendants who are negligent or intentional wrongdoers. Suppose, for example, that the defendant maintains a lake that is abnormally dangerous. An unusual frost results in leakage, causing damage to neighboring land. In many courts, this act of God (the frost) would cut off the defendant's *strict liability,* whereas if the defendant had been careless in maintaining the lake, the act of God would probably not terminate *negligence* liability.

Defenses

Contributory negligence on the part of the plaintiff is not a defense to the tort of maintaining an abnormally dangerous condition or activity. This is so with all strict liability torts—the negligence of the plaintiff will not defeat liability. Suppose, for example, that Tom carelessly walks into an area where construction blasting is occurring. Tom fails to realize that blasting is going on, but if he had been exercising reasonable care for his own safety, he should have realized this. Tom is injured by the blasting. There is clear contributory negligence. This is not a defense, however, when the plaintiff is suing under the strict liability tort of maintaining an abnormally dangerous condition or activity.

If, however, the plaintiff knows of and understands the danger posed by the defendant and voluntarily proceeds to encounter it, then the plaintiff has assumed the risk of the danger. **Assumption of the risk** *is* a defense to a strict liability tort. To avoid permitting a defendant to use this defense as an unfair weapon against a plaintiff, however, the defendant must establish that the plaintiff's assumption of the risk was unreasonable. A plaintiff has a right to the reasonable use and enjoyment of his or her property. A defendant cannot encircle the plaintiff's land with a dangerous condition or activity and then assert assumption of the risk when the plaintiff uses his or her land and is injured because of the condition or activity. The defendant must show that this use was unreasonable, and courts are reluctant to make such a finding when the defendant has prevented the plaintiff from making ordinary and reasonable use of his or her property.

SUMMARY

Strict liability is the imposition of liability or responsibility for harm whether or not the person causing the harm displayed any fault or moral impropriety. In most states, an owner of a wild animal will be strictly liable for any harm it causes whether or not the owner knew of the animal's dangerous propensities and irrespective of how careful the owner was in trying to prevent any harm from occurring. In most states, an owner of a domestic animal will be strictly liable for the harm it causes if the owner had reason to know the animal had specific propensities to harm others, and the harm caused by the animal was due to that specific propensity.

A condition or activity is abnormal (for purposes of establishing strict liability for abnormally dangerous conditions or activities) if it is unusual or non-natural for the area. It is dangerous when it poses a substantial likelihood of great harm to persons or property that cannot be eliminated by the use of reasonable care by the defendant. If the abnormal condition or activity does not meet this definition of "dangerous," there can be no strict liability. In order to recover, the plaintiff must establish that the defendant created a nuisance, caused a trespass to land, or acted negligently with the condition or activity. For strict liability, the defendant must know that the condition or activity is dangerous, must be the cause in fact of the harm, and must be the proximate cause of the harm. For proximate cause, the harm that results must be within the type of harm that was initially foreseeable, and the plaintiff must be part of the group within the foreseeable risk posed by the abnormally dangerous condition or activity. Some consequences are so unforeseeable that the condition or activity of the defendant is not considered unusually dangerous for those consequences. Contributory negligence is not a defense, but unreasonable assumption of risk is.

KEY TERMS

strict liability   87

absolute liability   87

liability without fault   87

strict liability in tort   87

wild animal   88

domestic animal   88

strict liability for abnormally
dangerous conditions or
activities   89

abnormally dangerous condition
or activity   93

Rylands v. Fletcher   93

cause in fact   95

but for   95

substantial factor   95

proximate cause   95

intervening causes   95

act of God   95

contributory negligence   95

assumption of the risk   96

Negligence: A Summary

Chapter Outline

- Introduction
- Negligence and Breach of Duty
- Negligence and Insurance
- Shorthand Definition
- Negligence Checklist

INTRODUCTION

Negligence is the largest of the three major categories of torts (the other two being the intentional torts and the various kinds of strict liability). Negligence has been called a "catchall" tort in that it encompasses a wide variety of unreasonable actions and inactions that cause injury or other loss. This chapter is an overview of negligence. Elsewhere, more specific negligence topics will be treated. (See Figure 10–1.)

NEGLIGENCE AND BREACH OF DUTY

The word "negligence" is used in two different senses. It can mean the entire tort or only one of its elements. In this book, **negligence** means the entire tort that exists when all four elements are present: duty, breach of duty, proximate cause, and damages. You

FIGURE 10–1 Coverage of Negligence Topics.

Topic	Where Covered in This Book
Foreseeability	p. 13
Negligent Infliction of Emotional Distress	p. 75
Duty	p. 105
Breach of Duty	p. 115
Employer Liability	p. 138
Medical Malpractice	p. 144
Legal Malpractice	p. 149
Proximate Cause	p. 159
Damages	p. 175
Defenses	p. 187
Manufacturers and Retailers (products liability)	p. 199
Wrongful Death	p. 227
Owners and Occupiers of Land	p. 248

will also sometimes see the word negligence used in the narrower sense of **unreasonableness,** which is another way of phrasing the breach-of-duty element. Hence the statement, "he acted negligently" either means that one of the elements (**breach of duty**) has been established, or that the tort has been committed. In this book, we mean the latter.

NEGLIGENCE AND INSURANCE

It is commonly assumed by the public that if a driver hits a pedestrian on the street, the driver is responsible and must pay for the injury or other loss suffered by the pedestrian. This is not necessarily so. We must be careful to distinguish **insurance** law from negligence law. The injured party may be automatically compensated if the terms of an insurance policy so provide. For many insurance policies, all that is needed is a covered injury, a covered person, and causation. Much more is needed to trigger the law of negligence. You are not considered negligent simply because you cause an injury. The hallmark of negligence is **fault**—sometimes referred to as **culpability** or wrongfulness. The fault or wrong involved may be simple carelessness or momentary unreasonableness. But a lapse of some kind is required. We are *not* liable for every injury that we cause. We are liable under the law of negligence for those injuries we wrongfully cause in the sense that our conduct fell below a minimum standard of conduct when we caused the injury. One of our main objectives in the following chapters is to explore what this standard is. An important first step in achieving this objective is to avoid the trap of equating negligence with causation or with insurance.

SHORTHAND DEFINITION

A shorthand definition of the tort of negligence is *injury or other loss caused by unreasonable conduct.* In the vast majority of negligence cases that are litigated, the sole questions before the court are:

- Was the defendant's conduct unreasonable?
- Did this unreasonableness cause the plaintiff's injury or other loss?

In the next seven chapters, we will examine these questions along with a large number of others. As we do so, it is important that you not lose sight of the general definition of negligence as *injury or other loss caused by unreasonable conduct.* This definition will suffice for most negligence cases. While we must look at a maze of special rules in the law of negligence, there is a danger of thinking that the maze is the norm. It isn't.

NEGLIGENCE CHECKLIST

Before we begin a detailed study of the law of negligence, briefly examine the negligence checklist containing an overview of definitions, relationships, paralegal roles, and research references for this tort. You may want to refer back to this checklist while you are studying the next seven chapters that cover specific negligence issues.

 Negligence Checklist:

Definitions, Relationships, Paralegal Roles, and Research References

Category
Negligence is a category unto itself. It covers harm that is neither intentional nor the basis of strict liability.

Interest Protected by This Tort
The right to be free from injury or other loss to person or property caused by unreasonable conduct.

Negligence Checklist Continued

Elements of This Tort
i. Duty
ii. Breach of duty
iii. Proximate cause
iv. Damages

Definitions of Major Words/Phrases in the Elements

Duty: The obligation to use reasonable care to avoid risks of injuring the person or property of others (see Chapter 11).

Breach of duty: Unreasonable conduct (the foreseeability of an accident causing serious injury outweighed the burden or inconvenience on the defendant to take precautions against the injury, and the defendant failed to take those precautions) (see Chapter 12).

Proximate cause: The defendant is the cause in fact of the plaintiff's injury, the injury was the foreseeable consequence of the original risk, and there is no policy reason why the defendant should not be liable for what he or she caused in fact (see Chapter 13).

Damages: Actual harm or loss (see Chapter 14).

Major Defenses and Counterargument Possibilities That Need to Be Explored

1. The defendant owed the plaintiff no duty.
2. The injury was not foreseeable.
3. A serious injury was not foreseeable.
4. The burden or inconvenience on the defendant to avoid the injury outweighed the risk of the injury occurring. The burden or inconvenience of avoidance was substantial, whereas the risk of injury was minimal.
5. The activity of the defendant had significant social importance or utility, which justified his or her taking the risks of injury that might be caused by that activity.
6. The defendant was not the cause in fact of the plaintiff's injury. Under the two tests to determine cause in fact: (a) it cannot be said that "but for" what the defendant did or failed to do, the injury to the plaintiff would not have occurred; (b) the defendant was not a substantial factor in producing the plaintiff's injury.
7. The plaintiff's injury was not within the original risk created by the defendant. (There was no proximate cause.)
8. The plaintiff's injury was produced by a superseding intervening cause. (There was no proximate cause.)
9. The plaintiff's injury was produced by an intervening cause that was highly extraordinary. (There was no proximate cause.)
10. The plaintiff suffered no actual harm or loss due to the unreasonable conduct of the defendant. (There were no damages.)
11. The plaintiff was unreasonable in taking risks for his or her own safety and this helped cause the injury (contributory negligence).
12. The harm caused the plaintiff by his or her own negligence exceeded the minimum threshold established by the comparative negligence statute.
13. The plaintiff assumed the risk of his or her own injury.
14. The plaintiff failed to take reasonable steps to mitigate the harm caused by the defendant's negligence; therefore, damages should not cover the aggravation of the harm caused by the plaintiff (on the doctrine of avoidable consequences, see Chapter 14).
15. The plaintiff's suit against the government for negligence committed by a government employee may be barred by sovereign immunity (on sovereign immunity, see Chapter 23).
16. The plaintiff's suit against the government employee for negligence may be barred by public official immunity (on official immunity, see Chapter 23).
17. The plaintiff's suit against the charitable organization for negligence committed by someone working for the organization may be barred by charitable immunity (on charitable immunity, see Chapter 23).
18. The plaintiff's suit against a family member for negligence may be barred by intrafamily immunity (on intrafamily immunity, see Chapter 18).

Damages

Negligence requires proof of actual harm. Without it, the negligence case fails and no compensatory damages can be awarded. Nominal damages are not allowed in a negligence action. In general, punitive damages are not allowed for ordinary negligence. Recklessness or

Negligence Checklist Continued

malice of some kind is usually the basis for an award of punitive damages. (On the categories of damages, see Chapter 14.)

Relationship to Criminal Law

There are some crimes based on negligence, e.g., negligent homicide. More than ordinary negligence, however, is usually required. Negligence in criminal law requires at least recklessness.

Relationship to Other Torts

If you are not able to prove one of the intentional torts, explore the possibility of negligence. For example, if you cannot establish the tort of battery because you cannot prove that the defendant had the intent to cause a harmful or offensive contact, you may be able to establish the tort of negligence if you can prove that the harmful or offensive contact was caused by the defendant's unreasonable conduct. The same may be true of other intentional torts, such as conversion and false imprisonment. Whenever you are having difficulty establishing an intentional tort, determine whether the defendant created an unreasonable risk of the same injury occurring. If so, negligence may be an alternative cause of action. Finally, explore negligence as an alternative to strict liability torts.

Federal Law

a. Under the Federal Tort Claims Act, the United States Government will be liable for negligence committed by one of its federal employees within the scope of employment (respondeat superior) as long as the employee's conduct did not involve discretion at the planning level. (See Figure 23–7 in Chapter 23.)
b. There may be liability under the Civil Rights Act if the negligence was committed while the defendant was depriving the plaintiff of federal rights under color of law. (See Figure 23–8 in Chapter 23.)
c. Under the Consumer Product Safety Act, penalties can be imposed for violations of the rules of the Consumer Product Safety Commission (CPSC) concerning dangerous products on the market.

Employer-Employee (Agency) Law

An employee who commits negligence is personally liable for this tort. His or her employer will *also* be liable for negligence: (a) vicariously, if the conduct of the employee was within the scope of employment (respondeat superior), or (b) independently, if the employer was careless in hiring or supervising an incompetent employee who posed a risk of injuring others. (On the factors that determine the scope of employment, see Figure 12–7 in Chapter 12.)

Paralegal Roles in Negligence Litigation

Fact finding (help the office collect facts relevant to prove the elements of negligence, the elements of available defenses, and the extent of injuries or other damages):
• client interviewing
• field investigation
• online research (e.g., records on weather conditions on the date of the accident)

File management (help the office control the volume of paperwork in a negligence litigation):
• open client file
• enter case data in computer database
• maintain file documents

Litigation assistance (help the trial attorney prepare for a negligence trial and appeal, if needed):
• draft discovery requests
• draft answers to discovery requests
• draft pleadings
• digest and index discovery documents
• help prepare, order, and manage trial exhibits (visuals or demonstratives)
• prepare trial notebook
• draft notice of appeal
• order trial transcript
• cite check briefs
• perform legal research

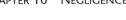

Negligence Checklist Continued

Collection/enforcement (help the trial attorney for the judgment creditor to collect the damages award or to enforce other court orders at the conclusion of the negligence case):
- draft postjudgment discovery requests
- field investigation to monitor compliance with judgment
- online research (e.g., location of defendant's business assets)

Research References for Negligence

Digests
In the digests of West, look for case summaries on negligence under key topics such as:

Negligence	Automobiles
Damages	Landlord and Tenant
Products Liability	Health and Environment
Master and Servant	Innkeepers
Physicians and Surgeons	Highways
Death	Nuisance
Animals	Contribution
Drugs and Narcotics	Carriers
Explosives	Telecommunications
Torts	

Corpus Juris Secundum
In this legal encyclopedia, see the discussions on negligence under topic headings such as:

Negligence	Landlord and Tenant
Damages	Health and Environment
Products Liability	Inns, Hotels and Eating Places
Master and Servant	Highways
Physicians and Surgeons	Nuisance
Death	Contribution
Animals	Carriers
Drugs and Narcotics	Telegraphs, Telephones,
Explosives	Radio and Television
Motor Vehicles	

American Jurisprudence 2d
In this legal encyclopedia, see the discussions on negligence under topic headings such as:

Negligence	Drugs, Narcotics and Poisons
Products Liability	Master and Servant
Premises Liability	Automobiles and Highway Traffic
Hospitals and Asylums	Occupations, Trades and Professions
Damages	Hotels, Motels and Restaurants
Contribution	Landlord and Tenant
Amusements and Exhibitions	Highways, Streets and Bridges
Animals	Physicians and Surgeons
Carriers	Health
Death	

Legal Periodical Literature
There are two index systems to use to locate legal periodical literature on negligence:

INDEX TO LEGAL PERIODICALS AND BOOKS (ILP)	**CURRENT LAW INDEX (CLI)**
See literature in *ILP* under subject headings such as:	See literature in *CLI* under subject headings such as:
Negligence	Negligence
Accidents	Automobiles
Act of God	Bailments
Automobile Insurance	Contribution
Contributory Negligence	Damages
Damages	Death by Wrongful Act
Highways and Streets	Exemplary Damages

Negligence Checklist Continued

Inns and Innkeepers	Drugs
Joint Tortfeasors	Employers' Liability
Landlord and Tenant	Food
Last Clear Chance	Hospitals
Master and Servant	Informed Consent
Motor Vehicles	Joint Tortfeasors
Nuisance	Landlord and Tenant
Products Liability	Liability for Condition and Use of Land
Personal Injuries	Malpractice
Proximate Cause	Products Liability
Physicians and Surgeons	Respondeat Superior
Res Ipsa Loquitur	Personal Injuries
Traffic Accidents	Physicians
Vicarious Liability	Tort Liability
Wrongful Death	

Example of a legal periodical article you will find on negligence by using *ILP* or *CLI:*

> *Emergency Room Negligence* by Steven E. Pegalis and Harvey F. Wachsman, 16 Trial 50 (May, 1980).

A.L.R., A.L.R.2d, A.L.R.3d, A.L.R.4th, A.L.R.5th, A.L.R. Fed.
Use the *ALR Index* to locate annotations on negligence. In this index, check subject headings such as:

Neglience	Landlord and Tenant
Aggravated Negligence	Products Liability
Attractive Nuisance	Rescue Doctrine
Comparative Negligence	Malpractice
Concurrent Negligence	Hospitals
Contributory Negligence or	Master and Servant
Assumption of Risk	Res Ipsa Loquitur
Corporate Officers, Directors	Mitigation or Aggravation
and Agents	of Damages
Governmental Immunity or Privilege	Federal Tort Claims Act
Gross Negligence	Health and Accident Insurance
Imputed Negligence and Liability	Policies and Provisions

Example of an annotation on negligence you can locate through the *ALR Index:*

> *Modern Development of Comparative Negligence Doctrine Having Applicability to Negligence Actions Generally* by Thomas R. Trenkner, 78 A.L.R.3d 339 (1977).

Words and Phrases
In this multivolume legal dictionary, look up *negligence, duty, breach of duty, proximate cause, damages, contributory negligence, comparative negligence, assumption of the risk,* and every other word or phrase connected with negligence discussed in the next seven chapters. The dictionary will give you definitions of these words or phrases from court opinions.

CALR: Computer-Assisted Legal Research
Example of a query you could ask on WESTLAW or on LEXIS to try to find cases, statutes, or other legal materials on negligence: **negligence/p damages**

Example of search terms you could use on an Internet legal search engine such as LawCrawler (http://lawcrawler.findlaw.com) to find cases, statutes, or other legal materials on negligence: **negligence AND tort**

Example of search terms you could use on an Internet general search engine such as Alta Vista (http://www.altavista.com) to find cases, statutes, or other legal materials on negligence: **+negligence tort**

More Internet sites to check for materials on negligence and other torts:
Jurist: (http://jurist.law.pitt.edu/sg_torts.htm)
LawGuru: (http://www.lawguru.com/search/lawsearch.html)
See also Tort Law Online at the end of Chapter 1.

SUMMARY

Negligence is the largest of the three major categories of torts. It covers injury or other loss caused by unreasonableness. (The other two categories are intentional torts and strict liability torts.) The broad meaning of negligence is the tort that has been committed when all four of its elements are established (duty, breach of duty, proximate cause, and damages). More narrowly, it refers to the second element of the tort: breach of duty. In the vast majority of negligence cases, defendants are liable for the injury or other loss they wrongfully cause. Insurance, on the other hand, provides compensation for every covered injury or loss caused by the insured. A shorthand definition of negligence is injury or other loss caused by unreasonable conduct.

KEY TERMS

negligence   97

unreasonableness   98

breach of duty   98

insurance   98

fault   98

culpability   98

Negligence: Element I: Duty

Chapter Outline

- General Rule on Duty
- Unforeseeable Plaintiff
- Nonfeasance and Special Relationships
- Gratuitous Undertaking
- Protection for the Good Samaritan

GENERAL RULE ON DUTY

What is a **duty?** In its broadest sense:

> A duty is an obligation or a requirement to conform to a standard of conduct prescribed by law.

From this broad definition, we come to a series of very specific interrelated questions:

- Who owes this duty?
- To whom is the duty owed?
- When does the duty arise?
- What is the standard of conduct to which there must be conformity?—i.e., duty to do what?

All of these questions can be answered by the **general rule on duty,** which is outlined at the beginning of Figure 11–1. This general rule will be adequate to cover the vast majority of automobile collision cases, on-the-job mishaps, and similar occurrences. The chart will also outline those circumstances that call for limitations on or modifications of the general rule on duty.

FIGURE 11–1 Duty in the law of negligence.

General Rule on Duty:

Whenever one's conduct creates a foreseeable risk of injury or damage to someone else's person or property, a duty of care arises to take reasonable precautions to prevent that injury or damage.

Exceptions and Special Circumstances:

1. The unforeseeable plaintiff, p. 106
   a. Zone-of-danger test of duty
   b. World-at-large test of duty
2. Nonfeasance and the special relationship, p. 108
3. Gratuitous undertaking, p. 112

We begin with a simple application of the general rule:

> **EXAMPLE:** You are driving down the road late at night. It is raining and the road is slippery.

These facts trigger the application of the general rule on duty. It is foreseeable that someone may be injured when you are driving under such conditions. Therefore, you owe a duty to take reasonable precautions to prevent such an injury—to slow down, turn on the headlights, watch extra carefully for pedestrians and other cars, keep a safe distance between your car and the car in front of you, etc. The more foreseeable the injury, the greater is the need for precautions.

Under the general rule, the duty is to use **reasonable care,** which will be discussed at length in the next chapter when we examine **breach of duty,** or unreasonableness. In the vast majority of cases, this duty is triggered by the **foreseeability** of injury or damage. We have already looked at foreseeability in tort law in Chapter 2, and we will examine it again when we discuss breach of duty and proximate cause. (A foreseeability analysis is needed to determine the applicability of three elements: duty, breach of duty, and proximate cause. In most cases, the foreseeability analysis is the same in all three elements. This is why foreseeability was treated separately in Chapter 2, with particular emphasis on the factors that go into the determination of foreseeability.)

For the remainder of this chapter, we will focus on those exceptions and special circumstances that have posed problems with the general rule on duty stated in Figure 11–1.

UNFORESEEABLE PLAINTIFF

Consider the sequence of events in Figure 11–2, based on the famous *Palsgraf* case.[1] A railroad conductor carelessly pushes a passenger onto a train. (We will call this passenger, Plaintiff #1.) This causes the passenger to drop an unmarked package, which explodes. The blast causes a scale to hit a bystander. (We will call this bystander, Plaintiff #2.)

Plaintiff #1 is a **foreseeable plaintiff** who will have no trouble suing the railroad for the negligence of its employee. A duty is clearly owed to the passenger. Since the employee carelessly pushed the passenger, some harm was foreseeable to the passenger's property or to the person of the passenger. What about the bystander, Plaintiff #2? At the time the employee pushed the passenger onto the train, no one could foresee danger to the bystander from the falling package. Plaintiff #2 is an **unforeseeable plaintiff.** An essential question in Plaintiff #2's negligence suit against the railroad is whether a *duty* was owed to this plaintiff. If not, then the first element of negligence cannot be established and hence the entire negligence cause of action will fall. How then do we determine whether a duty is owed to a person in Plaintiff #2's position? Two major tests have been proposed: the **Cardozo test,** or zone-of-danger test, and the **Andrews test,** or world-at-large test.[2] (See Figure 11–3.) States differ on which of these two tests is followed.

A number of points should be made about these two tests:

- The two tests focus only on the element of duty. All of the other elements of negligence must also be analyzed to determine whether the cause of action has been established.
- The Andrews test is broader than the Cardozo test. More plaintiffs can establish duty under the Andrews test because they do not have to be in the foreseeable zone of danger in order to be owed a duty. They only have to be in-

---

[1]*Palsgraf v. Long Island R.R.,* 248 N.Y. 339, 162 N.E. 99, 59 A.L.R. 1253 (1928). This is one of the most famous tort cases in American legal history.
[2]Cardozo wrote the majority opinion in the *Palsgraf* case (supra note 1); Andrews wrote the dissenting opinion.

FIGURE 11–2 Foreseeable and unforeseeable plaintiffs.

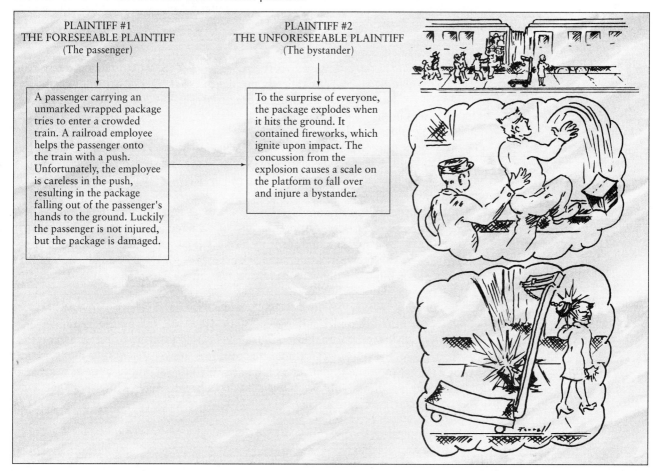

FIGURE 11–3 Negligence: When is a duty owed?

Zone-of-Danger Test (the Cardozo test)

A duty is owed to a specific person (plaintiff) in the **zone of danger,** as determined by the test of foreseeability.

World-at-Large Test (the Andrews test)

A duty is owed to anyone in the **world at large** (any plaintiff) IF:
1. the plaintiff (who sues) suffers injury as a result of
2. unreasonable conduct of the defendant toward anyone, whether or not the plaintiff who sues was in the zone of danger. This plaintiff does not have to have been in the zone of danger as long as *someone* (in the world at large) was in this zone because of the action or inaction of the defendant.

jured as a result of the defendant's unreasonable conduct that created, and placed *someone* in, the zone of danger.

- A choice between the two tests must be made when the facts involve a chain of events and an unanticipated person—the unforeseeable plaintiff. The two tests give two different standards on whether such a person is owed a duty. If, however, the facts do not involve a chain of events, then the great likelihood is that both tests would produce the *same* result on whether a duty is owed (i.e., it would make no difference in such cases which test is used).

Let us now apply the two different tests to the fact situation in Figure 11–2 involving the passenger whose package was damaged and the bystander on whom the scale fell. What would happen in a state that has adopted the zone-of-danger (Cardozo) test? How does this compare with the outcome in a state that has adopted the world-at-large (Andrews) test?

1. Zone-of-danger state:
   Would a duty be owed to the passenger? YES, as we have already seen. When the employee carelessly pushed the passenger, it was foreseeable that some injury or damage would result to this passenger. Hence, the passenger was in the zone of danger.
   Would a duty be owed to the bystander? NO. Pushing the passenger created no foreseeable risk to a bystander since there was no indication to the employee that there were fireworks or any other dangerous object in the passenger's unmarked package. The bystander was outside the zone of danger.

2. World-at-large state:
   Would a duty be owed to the passenger? YES. The two-part test has been met: the passenger suffered injury or damage (to the package) as a result of unreasonable conduct (the careless push) directed at someone (here, the passenger). Although it is not necessary for the passenger to have been in the zone of danger under this test, in fact, the passenger was within this zone.
   Would a duty be owed to the bystander? YES. The two-part test has been met: the bystander suffered an injury (the scale fell on the bystander) as a result of unreasonable conduct (the careless push) directed at someone (here, the passenger). Under this test, it is not necessary that the bystander be in the zone of danger as long as someone was in this zone as a result of the defendant's unreasonable conduct. The passenger is the "someone" who was in the zone of danger.

ASSIGNMENT

11.1

Helen and Grace are on a subway train on the way home from an office where they work together. Both are standing near one of the doors of the crowded train. Suddenly, the door opens while the train is moving and Helen falls out. Moments later, the train stops when the driver realizes what has happened. (Assume that the reason the door opened was negligent maintenance by the subway.) Grace watches in horror as Helen falls out the door. When the train stops, Grace immediately climbs down through the open door onto the tracks in order to try to help Helen. As Grace searches in the dark, she slips on a live rail and dies from electrocution. Luckily, Helen finds her way to safety with only minor injury. Helen and Grace's estate now bring separate negligence actions against the subway. Focus solely on the issue of duty:

a. In a zone-of-danger (Cardozo) state, did the subway owe a duty to Helen? Explain. To Grace? Explain.

b. In a world-at-large (Andrews) state, did the subway owe a duty to Helen? Explain. To Grace? Explain.

NONFEASANCE AND SPECIAL RELATIONSHIPS

Most negligence liability is based on **affirmative conduct** that is improper or unreasonable. This is called **misfeasance**. With limited exceptions, negligence liability cannot be based on a mere omission or failure to act, called **nonfea-**

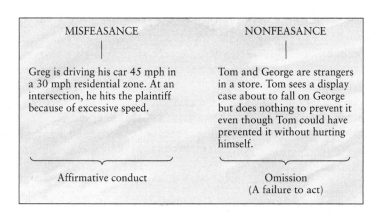

FIGURE 11–4
Misfeasance and nonfeasance.

sance.[3] Only if a **special relationship** existed between the plaintiff and defendant will nonfeasance by the defendant lead to negligence. Compare the two situations in Figure 11–4.

When Greg (in Figure 11–4) is sued by the plaintiff for negligence in the first situation, there will not be a problem establishing the existence of a duty. In such cases of misfeasance, there is almost never a duty problem. Affirmative conduct by Greg (his driving) created a risk of foreseeable injury to the plaintiff. It is very easy to establish the existence of a duty when affirmative conduct (alone or in combination with inaction) creates such a risk. The vast majority of negligence cases fall into the misfeasance category.

Now let us focus on the second hypothetical in Figure 11–4, involving Tom and George. Here we have *non*feasance. There was no affirmative conduct by Tom. He did nothing to create or increase the risk of injury to George. Rather, there was an omission, a failure to act. In most states, there is no duty in such situations to exercise any kind of care unless a special relationship exists between the parties. These special relationships will be outlined later in Figure 11–6.

In most cases involving strangers such as Tom and George, there is no such special relationship, and hence no duty to act with reasonable care. It is surprising to many to learn that *you have no duty to assist someone simply because it is possible for you to give assistance without harming yourself.* Nor does the mere foreseeability of injury give rise to a duty to give aid. According to the American Law Institute:

> The fact that the actor realizes or should realize that action on his part is necessary for another's aid or protection does not of itself impose upon him a duty to take such action.[4]

The classic example is the stranger who refuses to lift a finger to save the life of a drowning victim even though the stranger would be under no jeopardy in making the effort. There is *no* requirement in our law to be a **Good Samaritan.** In fact, if someone voluntarily decides to be a Good Samaritan and renders assistance, even though there was no initial duty to do so, the Good Samaritan can be sued for negligence if he or she fails to use reasonable care in rendering this free assistance! Although special statutory protection for the Good Samaritan has recently been enacted, the fear of being sued continues to discourage many potential Good Samaritans from rendering assistance. (We will discuss this area of the law later in the section on Gratuitous Undertaking.)

Most accidents involve *both* conduct and omissions; for example, while driving on the highway (affirmative conduct), the defendant failed to slow down at the intersection and failed to use the horn to warn the inattentive plaintiff (omissions). This

---

[3]Do not confuse the following three words. *Nonfeasance* is the omission of an act, the failure to act. *Misfeasance* is improper or unreasonable action. **Malfeasance** is wrongful or illegal actions by a public official.

[4]*Restatement (Second) of Torts* § 314 (1965).

example would be considered a *mis*feasance case of negligence, even though there were components of *non*feasance in it. Generally, if there was *some* affirmative conduct that helped cause the injury, you will not need to worry about the existence or nonexistence of a special relationship even though omissions were involved. The nonfeasance case usually arises when all the defendant "did" was to "decide" to do nothing to help the plaintiff. Here the special relationship will be critical. Without it, the plaintiff's negligence case falls because there is no duty to act.

In addition to the presence of a special relationship, the defendant's duty depends on the foreseeability of injury and the opportunity to do something about it, as diagrammed in Figure 11–5.

FIGURE 11–5
Duty in nonfeasance cases.

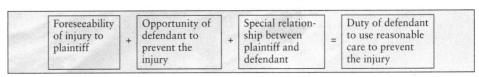

| Foreseeability of injury to plaintiff | + | Opportunity of defendant to prevent the injury | + | Special relationship between plaintiff and defendant | = | Duty of defendant to use reasonable care to prevent the injury |

The duty is *not* to prevent the injury. The duty arising from the special relationship is simply to use *reasonable care* to avoid the injury. The duty does not guarantee anything. Here are some examples of what reasonable care might entail:

- taking reasonable steps in advance to try to make the area safe
- taking reasonable steps to try to prevent third persons under the defendant's control from injuring the plaintiff
- taking reasonable steps immediately after the injury to try to prevent aggravation of the injury

What are the special relationships? The main ones are outlined in Figure 11–6.

A good deal of controversy has recently centered around the problem of controlling the conduct of third parties who are not part of the special relationship itself.

EXAMPLE: Tom is a patient of Dr. Edward Smith, a therapist. During a session, Tom tells Dr. Smith that he is going to kill his girlfriend. The latter is not a patient of Dr. Smith. The next day, Tom carries out his threat and kills his girlfriend.

The girlfriend's estate now brings a negligence action against Dr. Smith. Again, we have a nonfeasance problem. We have omissions: Dr. Smith did not warn the girlfriend of Tom's threat, he did not tell the police of the threat, he did not tell the girlfriend's family about the threat, etc. The question is whether Dr. Smith owed a *duty* to the girlfriend. He engaged in no affirmative conduct toward the girlfriend that placed her in danger or that increased the danger she was in because of Tom. Hence, we do not have misfeasance. There was no special relationship between Dr. Smith and the girlfriend. The traditional result, therefore, in such situations is that there is no duty and hence no liability for negligence. It should be noted, however, that not all states follow this traditional rule. Some states, and the *Restatement*,[5] will say that a duty of reasonable care *would* be owed by the doctor to the girlfriend in such a case.

---

[5]*Restatement (Second) of Torts* § 315 (1965).

ASSIGNMENT
11.2

Dr. George Donovan is treating an AIDS patient, Kevin Smith. Kevin tells Dr. Donovan that he no longer uses protection in his sexual relations with his roommate, whom Dr. Donovan has never met, and with Paul Grondon, who is also a patient of Dr. Donovan. By remaining silent about Kevin's sexual practices, could Dr. Donovan be sued for negligence by anyone who contracts AIDS from Kevin?

Principle

In nonfeasance cases, there is no duty to use reasonable care (and hence no negligence) unless the plaintiff fits within one of the following categories of special relationships. If none of the relationships exist, there is no duty to act, and hence omissions (nonfeasance) by the defendant cannot constitute negligence. This applies only to nonfeasance cases. If the defendant has engaged in affirmative conduct, there is usually a duty to use reasonable care whether or not a special relationship exists between plaintiff and defendant.

Special Relationships

1. Common Carrier/Passenger

Example: A passenger on a bus becomes ill or is in danger because of what another passenger is doing. The bus driver has a duty to use reasonable care to help the passenger in trouble even though the driver did not cause the trouble. This duty arises because of the special relationship the law imposes between a bus company or other common carrier and a passenger.

2. Innkeeper/Guest

Example: A hotel guest becomes ill or is injured on the premises. Hotel employees have a duty to use reasonable care to help the guest regardless of who caused the difficulty. This duty arises because of the special relationship the law imposes between a hotel or other innkeeper and a guest.

3. Employer/Employee

Example: An employee is injured on the job. The employer has a duty to use reasonable care to help the employee no matter who caused the injury. This duty arises because of the special relationship the law imposes between employer and employee. (See Chapter 24 on the system of workers' compensation that covers such injuries.)

4. Possessor of Land/Invitee

Example: A customer in a department store becomes ill or is in danger because of what another customer is doing. A store employee has a duty to use reasonable care to help the customer in trouble even though the store did not cause the trouble. This duty arises because of the special relationship the law imposes between owners or other possessors of land such as a department store and invitees on the land such as customers. (For more on duties owed invitees, see Chapter 19.)

5. Parent/Child

Example: A child falls off a chair at home while playing and is in pain on the floor. A parent has a duty to use reasonable care to aid the injured child even if the fall was not the fault of the parent. This duty arises because of the special relationship the law imposes between parents and their children. (On whether a child can sue his or her parent in tort, see intrafamily tort immunity in Chapter 18.)

6. School/Student

Example: One student injures another in a violent attack during a gym class. A school employee has a duty to use reasonable care to aid the injured student even if no school employee was at fault in causing the injury. This duty arises because of the special relationship the law imposes between a school and its students.

7. Jail or Prison/Inmate

Example: An inmate becomes sick in jail or prison. Employees at the institution have a duty to use reasonable care to aid the inmate even if the institution was not at fault in causing the sickness. This duty arises because of the special relationship the law imposes between jails or prisons and their inmates.

FIGURE 11–6
Special relationships that create a duty to use reasonable care in nonfeasance cases.

GRATUITOUS UNDERTAKING

Question: If you do something that you do not have to do, is there a duty to do it with reasonable care?

An **undertaking** is simply doing something. The undertaking is **gratuitous** if there was no obligation to do it—the defendant did it for free. Many undertakings are not for free. Rather, they result from "payment" of one kind or another. In the law of contracts, this payment is often referred to as **consideration**. A homeowner may enter a contract with an electrician to re-wire a house for a set fee. The work of the electrician on the wiring is an undertaking supported by consideration. There is no duty problem here. The electrician has the duty to perform the undertaking (the re-wiring) with reasonable care. Suppose, however, that the undertaking is *not* supported by consideration. Suppose that the undertaking is gratuitous.

EXAMPLE:

- An electrician agrees to re-wire a house for $3,000. While doing this job, he discovers a broken water valve in the bathroom. On his own, as a goodwill gesture, the electrician decides to fix the valve. Because of his inexperience with plumbing, the electrician causes additional damage to the pipes. Working on the pipes was a gratuitous undertaking. Did the electrician have a *duty* to use reasonable care in trying to fix the water valve?

- Phil is an off-duty lifeguard driving by a lake in another state. He sees a small, unattended child drowning close to the shore. Phil stops his car and decides to help. While Phil is carrying the child out of the water, the child's arm is broken due to Phil's carelessness in holding the child. Phil did not have a duty to come to the aid of the child because no special relationship existed between them. Phil's act of help was a gratuitous undertaking. Did Phil owe a *duty* to use reasonable care in helping the child?

The answer to both questions is *yes*. Even though there may be no duty to do anything, if you decide to do something, you have the duty to do it reasonably. The duty arises from a gratuitous undertaking. The defendants (the electrician and Phil in the preceding examples) are said to have assumed the duty on their own.

A final dimension of this problem must be considered. Suppose a defendant, again someone who has no special relationship with plaintiff, makes a gratuitous **promise** to the plaintiff.

EXAMPLE:
Richard is injured on the road. A passerby sees Richard and says, "Don't do anything. Lie still. I'll get help." Soon another stranger comes by and asks Richard if he needs any help. He says, "No, someone has just gone for help." In fact, the original passerby did nothing, thinking (foolishly) that someone else would probably help Richard.

Did the original passerby owe Richard a *duty* to perform his gratuitous promise with reasonable care? The traditional answer has been no. More modern cases, however, are beginning to find that a duty does exist as long as there has been **reliance** by plaintiff on the defendant's promise. Such was clearly the case with Richard, who did not seek further help because of the first passerby's promise. The promise increased the risk to Richard since it discouraged him from seeking further help.

ASSIGNMENT

11.3

a. ABC Realty Company leases space to Jones, who uses it as a grocery store. The lease agreement provides that all repairs and maintenance are the responsibility of Jones. One day, an officer of the ABC Realty Company tells

Jones that the company is thinking about installing smoke detectors to re-place the rusty sprinkler system. Two days later, a customer is injured in Jones's store due to a fire. The sprinkler system did not work and smoke de-tectors had not been installed. Did ABC Realty Company owe a duty of rea-sonable care to the customer?

b. The B & O Railroad (RR) has a track that crosses a county street. For years, the RR stationed one of its employees at this crossing in order to warn oncoming traffic using the county street of an approaching train. There is no law that requires the RR to keep this employee at this crossing. You may assume that if the RR had never placed an employee at this crossing, a claim of negligence against the RR would not be successful. In fact, however, the RR had an em-ployee at this crossing for years. As a train approached, the employee stepped out onto the county street and warned all traffic to stop. The employee lived in the area, and hence knew many of the automobile drivers that used the crossing. For the last three years, the RR had been experiencing declining business and never had more than two trains crossing the county street on any given day. The poor business also led to employee layoffs. On December 3rd, the employee who had worked the county street crossing was laid off. She was not replaced. Hence, no RR employee now works at the county street crossing. In the view of the RR, the sound of an oncoming train would be warning enough to cars approaching the county street. On December 6th of the same year, Peter Blanchard was driving his truck on the county street in question. He was making a delivery from a neighboring state. He crashed into one of the RR trains at the point where the county street and the RR track meet. At all times Peter was driving very carefully. It was a rainy night, and hence he did not hear the oncoming train. You may assume that Peter will be able to establish that the accident would not have happened if the RR em-ployee (who was laid off on 12/3) had been on duty at the time of the acci-dent. Peter Blanchard brings a negligence action against the B & O RR for its failure to have the employee present to warn traffic of oncoming trains at the crossing. Discuss the element of duty.

c. Rich is driving down the road carefully. Suddenly a storm begins. Visibility is very poor. Rich unavoidably hits a pedestrian, who suffers a broken leg. Rich gets out of the car and runs toward the pedestrian. When Rich sees the injury, he panics. He does not know what to do. Hours go by without Rich doing anything. The pedestrian dies. Did Rich owe the pedestrian a duty? Give an argument that he did. Give an argument that he did not.

PROTECTION FOR THE GOOD SAMARITAN

The Good Samaritan rules do not encourage people to come to the aid of their fel-low citizens. "Try to do a good deed for someone and you end up being sued!" Some studies show that one in six potential volunteers refuses to become involved because of a fear of a lawsuit in the event that a mistake is made while trying to render aid. Even if the Good Samaritan wins the lawsuit, the embarrassment, time lost, and ex-pense of defending oneself in court are enough to make many would-be rescuers con-clude that the wiser course is to "mind my own business" rather than try to help a person in distress.

To combat this uncharitable inclination, a few states have passed laws *requiring* a citizen to become a Good Samaritan in emergency situations. Here is an example of this extreme approach:

Minnesota Statutes Annotated § 604A.01

Duty to assist. A person at the scene of an emergency who knows that another person is exposed to or has suffered grave physical harm shall, to the extent that the person can do so without danger or peril to self or others, give reasonable assistance to the exposed person. Reasonable assistance may include obtaining or attempting to obtain aid from law enforcement or medical personnel. A person who violates this subdivision is guilty of a petty misdemeanor.

Most states do not go this far. It is more common for a state to encourage rescue efforts by relieving Good Samaritans of civil liability for negligence in rendering emergency care or assistance. In such states, if a Good Samaritan makes a careless mistake, there is no negligence liability. In 1997, Congress passed the Volunteer Protection Act, which provides that "no volunteer of a nonprofit organization or governmental entity shall be liable for harm caused by an act or omission of the volunteer." There are exceptions, however, to this limitation of liability. For example, the volunteer *can* be liable for harm "caused by willful or criminal misconduct, gross negligence, reckless misconduct, or a conscious, flagrant indifference to the rights or safety of the individual harmed by the volunteer." (42 U.S.C. § 14503). This federal act applies to every state unless the state already provides protection for the volunteer or unless the state elects not to have the act apply. If a state "opts out" of the act and does not have its own program of protection, the old rules apply—a Good Samaritan can be sued for negligence in such states.

SUMMARY

Whenever one's conduct creates a foreseeable risk of injury or damage to someone else's person or property, a duty of reasonable care arises to take precautions to prevent that injury or damage. Under the Cardozo test, a duty is owed to a specific person who is foreseeably in the zone of danger. Under the Andrews test, a duty is owed to someone who suffers injury as a result of the defendant's unreasonable conduct toward anyone, even if the person injured was not in the zone of danger. Nonfeasance alone does not create a duty unless there is a special relationship between the parties. Among the special relationships are common carrier and passenger, innkeeper and guest, employer and employee, etc. If the defendant undertakes a task, he or she assumes a duty to perform it with reasonable care even though there was no initial duty to undertake it and even though the undertaking was gratuitous. If the defendant promises to undertake a task, he or she assumes a duty to perform it with reasonable care if the plaintiff relies on the promise, even though there was no initial duty to undertake it and even though the promise was gratuitous. Many states have laws that limit the liability of the Good Samaritan for simple negligence.

KEY TERMS

duty 105
general rule on duty 105
reasonable care 106
breach of duty 106
foreseeability 106
foreseeable plaintiff 106
unforeseeable plaintiff 106
Cardozo test 106

Andrews test 106
zone of danger 107
world at large 107
affirmative conduct 108
misfeasance 108
nonfeasance 108
malfeasance 109
special relationship 109

Good Samaritan 109
undertaking 112
gratuitous 112
consideration 112
promise 112
reliance 112

Negligence: Element II: Breach of Duty (Unreasonableness)

Chapter Outline

- Standard of Care: Reasonableness
- Breach-of-Duty (Unreasonableness) Equation
- Objective or Subjective Standard?
- Res Ipsa Loquitur
- Custom and Usage
- Violation of a Statute
- Compliance with a Statute
- Gross Negligence (Unreasonableness) and Willful, Wanton, and Reckless Conduct
- Vicarious Liability
- Medical Malpractice
- Legal Malpractice

STANDARD OF CARE: REASONABLENESS

In Chapter 11, we studied the first element of negligence: duty. In the vast majority of cases, the duty is to use **reasonable care** to avoid injuring others, both bodily injury and property damage. Now we begin our examination of the second element of negligence: **breach of duty**. A breach of duty exists if the defendant engages in **unreasonable** conduct. When can we say that someone has acted unreasonably? One of the difficulties of tort law is to define what we mean by reasonableness as the **standard of care** by which to measure the breach of duty that leads to negligence liability. This difficulty will be our challenge in this chapter.

Comparative Standard

To establish a breach of duty by showing unreasonable conduct on the part of the defendant in a negligence case, five steps are necessary:

> **Step 1:** State the injury the plaintiff claims to have suffered because of the defendant.
>
> **Step 2:** Identify the specific acts or omissions of the defendant about which the plaintiff is complaining.

Step 3: Turn back the clock in your mind to the time just before the acts and omissions identified in step 2. Ask yourself what a reasonable person would have done under the same or similar circumstances *at that time.* (You answer this question by using your common sense of what a reasonable person would have done and, most important, by reading what court opinions have said a reasonable person would have done in such circumstances.)

Step 4: Compare the specific acts and omissions of the defendant identified in step 2 with what you said a reasonable person would have done in step 3.

Step 5: Reach your conclusion:

a. If the comparison in step 4 tells you that the defendant did exactly what a reasonable person would have done (or that there is a substantial similarity), then you can conclude that the defendant acted reasonably, and hence there was no breach of duty.

b. If the comparison in step 4 tells you that a reasonable person would have done the opposite of what the defendant did (or would have acted substantially differently from the defendant), then you can conclude that the defendant acted unreasonably, and hence there was a breach of duty.

In flowchart form, the comparative process is outlined in Figure 12–1.

Examine the following excerpt from a memorandum of law that discusses the reasonableness of a truck driver who caused an accident on the road. Assume that one of the arguments against the truck driver was that he obviously acted unreasonably when he took his eyes off the road just before the accident. Here is the response of the truck driver. Excerpt B is a rewrite of Excerpt A.

Excerpt A:

The truck driver took his eyes off the road to look at his instrument panel and it was at this point that the truck collided with the other car. The driver did nothing unreasonable in taking his eyes off the road for a moment.

FIGURE 12–1
Reasonableness by comparison.

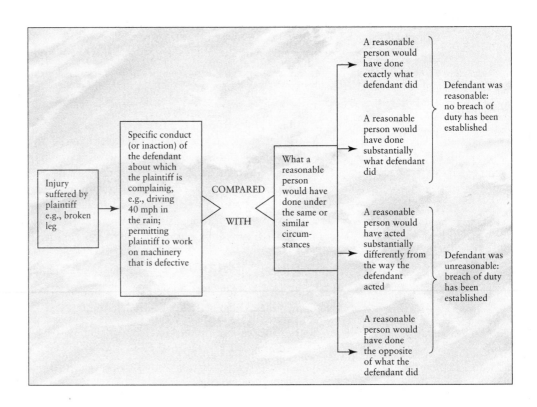

Excerpt B:

> The truck driver took his eyes off the road to look at his instrument panel and it was at this point that the truck collided with the other car. It is not uncommon for truck drivers to take their eyes off the road. Reasonable drivers would not keep their eyes on the road at all times. For example, drivers glance at their gas gauge, their rear view mirror, etc. Trucks are designed with instrument panels that must be checked while the truck is moving. Drivers can't pull over every time they need to look away from the road. Hence, reasonable drivers must take their eyes off the road to look at their instrument panel, if only momentarily. It cannot be said, therefore, that the driver in this case was unreasonable simply because he took his eyes off the road momentarily.

Excerpt A does not demonstrate an understanding of the comparative nature of reasonableness. There is no comparison between what the truck driver did and what a reasonable truck driver would have done. All we have is a *conclusory* statement that he acted reasonably. The rewrite in Excerpt B, on the other hand, shows a very good grasp of the comparative nature of reasonableness. A major focus of the excerpt is on what a reasonable truck driver would have done under the same circumstances. This is compared to what the truck driver in this case actually did.

Reasonableness versus Perfection

What is a **reasonable person?** Unfortunately, it is easier to define what a reasonable person is *not* than to say definitively what one is. First, let us look at the traditional definition:

> A reasonable person is an ordinary, prudent person who uses reasonable care to avoid injuring others.

This definition, although commonly used, is not very satisfactory. We are still left with the questions of what is "ordinary," what is "prudent," what is "reasonable care." We will focus on these questions in great detail later. For now, we need to confront the major myth that the reasonable person is a perfect person, or more narrowly, that a reasonable person does not injure other people. Figure 12–2 gives an overview of some of the basic differences among the perfect person, the reasonable person, and the unreasonable person.

BREACH-OF-DUTY (UNREASONABLENESS) EQUATION

To avoid injuring others, the reasonable person tries to avoid the dangers or risks of injury. How is this done? What mental process is used to decide what dangers to take precautions against? The reasonable person applies the **breach-of-duty equation** in Figure 12–3.

If the danger of a serious accident outweighs the burden or inconvenience of taking precautions to avoid the accident, the reasonable person would take those precautions. The failure of the defendant to do so would mean that the defendant was unreasonable and had committed a breach of duty in the law of negligence. If, on the other hand, the danger of a serious accident is so slight that the danger would not outweigh the relatively high burden or inconvenience of the precautions that would be needed to avoid the accident, then the reasonable person would *not* take these precautions. The failure of the defendant, therefore, to take these precautions would not amount to a breach of duty. The defendant is not deemed to be unreasonable even though the precautions would have prevented the accident the defendant caused.

FIGURE 12–2 Perfect/
reasonable/unreasonable
persons.

Misleading

Perfect Person	Reasonable Person	Unreasonable Person
1. Never causes an accident.	**1.** Does cause accidents, but they are never due to carelessness.	**1.** Causes accidents due to carelessness.
2. Never makes a mistake leading to an accident.	**2.** Does make mistakes leading to accidents, but the mistakes are never careless.	**2.** Makes careless mistakes leading to accidents.
3. Reacts perfectly in an emergency in order to prevent accidents.	**3.** Reacts as cautiously as possible in an emergency, but can still make a mistake in an emergency that causes an accident. These mistakes, however, are not careless.	**3.** Reacts carelessly in an emergency, causing accidents.
4. Has the right knowledge and experience needed to avoid accidents.	**4a.** Has the knowledge and experience common to everyone, and uses them to help avoid accidents.	**4a.** Does not have or fails to use the knowledge and experience common to everyone to help avoid accidents.
	b. When more expert knowledge and experience are available, the reasonable person uses them to help avoid accidents. **Note:** even with the use of common or expert knowledge and experience, accidents can happen, but they are not due to carelessness.	**b.** When more expert knowledge and experience are available, the unreasonable person does not adequately use them to help prevent accidents.
5. Will undergo any inconvenience or burden to avoid an accident.	**5.** Will undergo only reasonable inconvenience or burden to avoid an accident.	**5.** Refuses to undergo even reasonable inconvenience or burden to avoid an accident.

FIGURE 12–3
Breach-of-duty equation.

Foreseeability of the danger of an accident occurring ——————— Foreseeability of the kind of injury or damage that will result if an accident occurs	balanced against	The burden or inconvenience on the defendant of taking precautions to avoid the accident ——————— The importance or social utility of what the defendant was trying to do before the accident

To better understand the breach-of-duty equation, we need to explore the following topics:

- danger/caution hypothesis
- foreseeability
- burden or inconvenience
- importance or social utility

Danger/Caution Hypothesis

A **hypothesis** is a theory or assumption. For every fact or group of facts, it is possible to state a hypothesis about the amount of danger that is present and the amount of caution that is needed to offset or eliminate the danger. The overriding principle is as follows: THE GREATER THE DANGER, THE GREATER THE CAUTION NEEDED. Here are some examples:

Facts: A sharp knife is on a table in a day care center.

Danger hypothesis: Knives are very attractive to children; knives are often easy for children to pick up; children do not appreciate the danger of knives; knives can seriously injure parts of the body with minimal force. Therefore, a sharp knife on a table in a day care center presents a VERY GREAT DANGER of SERIOUS injury to one of the children.

Caution: Given the high risk of potential danger, a GREAT DEAL of CAUTION is needed to avoid an injury from the knife. Precautions include removing the knife from the room or locking it away so that it is not reachable by any of the children.

————————————

Facts: A sharp knife is on a table in a factory.

Danger hypothesis: Factories are places for adults; adults know how to handle sharp knives, especially if the knife is used in a factory where the workers are skilled. Therefore, a sharp knife on a table in a factory poses ALMOST NO DANGER of injury to anyone.

Caution: Given the minimal and almost nonexistent danger posed by the knife, VERY LITTLE CAUTION is needed to avoid an injury from the knife.

ASSIGNMENT

12.1

Analyze the following fact situations. Assess the danger/caution hypothesis for each fact situation. Identify all possible dangers in each. How likely is each danger to lead to an injury? What kind of injury? In the light of your assessment of each danger, state how much caution is needed to avoid the injury. What precautions need to be taken?

a. A sign on a busy three-lane street says, "USE TWO LANES GOING NORTH FROM 6 A.M. to 9:30 A.M. AND FROM 4:30 P.M. to 6:30 P.M. EXCEPT HOLIDAYS AND WEEKENDS. USE ONE LANE AT ALL OTHER TIMES."

b. Mary owns a motorcycle. Her friend, Leo, does not know how to drive it. Mary lets Leo drive the motorcycle while Mary is sitting right behind him, giving instructions as they drive in an empty lot.

c. The XYZ Chemical Company manufactures a new floor cleaner. On the label of the bottle containing the cleaner, there are very bright colors and a cartoon of a happy person cleaning the floor. The ingredients are listed on the label, plus a warning to keep the liquid away from eyes.

Of course, it can be argued that there is danger lurking in everything. It is possible to conceive of a set of acts in which any object (e.g., a tissue) could be used to injure someone in some way. This is not the kind of danger we are talking about in negligence law. It is not a breach of duty to fail to take precautions against every conceivable danger. Reasonableness does not require excessive caution.

How do we decide the amount of caution that *is* reasonable in a given set of circumstances? The answer depends on carefully weighing the elements of the breach-of-duty equation in Figure 12–3.

- **The FORESEEABILITY of an accident occurring.**
  The more foreseeable the accident is, the more caution a reasonable person would take to try to prevent the accident.
- **The FORESEEABILITY of the kind of injury or damage that would result from the accident if it occurs.**
  The more serious the kind of injury or damage that is foreseeable, the more caution a reasonable person would take to prevent the accident.
- **The BURDEN or INCONVENIENCE that would be involved in taking the precautions necessary to avoid the accident.**
  The greater the burden or inconvenience, the less likely a reasonable person would take the precautions to avoid the accident.
- **The IMPORTANCE or SOCIAL UTILITY of what the defendant was trying to do before the accident.**
  The more important or socially useful it is, the more likely a reasonable person would take risks in carrying it out.

Foreseeability

In Chapter 2 we took a detailed look at foreseeability and the methods by which it is determined. Review the foreseeability-determination formula in that chapter (see Figure 2–2). Our concern here is the foreseeability of the danger of an accident occurring (e.g., a customer slipping on a wet floor, a worker dropping a case of dynamite, an electric switch malfunctioning) and the danger of a particular kind of injury or damage occurring (e.g., death, crop destruction). As indicated in the formula in Figure 2–2, there are eight interrelated topics to be assessed:

- area analysis
- activity analysis
- people analysis
- preparation analysis
- assumptions about human nature
- historical data
- specific sensory data
- common sense

Assessing all of these topics will tell us what dangers a reasonable person would have foreseen. Once we know what a reasonable person would have foreseen, we know what the defendant *should* have foreseen.

Recall that we do not simply want to know *whether* the danger is foreseeable. The critical question is *how foreseeable* are the dangers. Review the foreseeability spectrum in Figure 2–1 in Chapter 2. Are we talking about a danger that is only a slight possibility? A slight probability? A highly unusual danger? A certainty?

Burden or Inconvenience

Next, we examine the *burden or inconvenience* that would have to be borne in order to avoid the danger. Our focus at this point is not *who* should bear the burden or inconvenience, but *what* precisely *is* this burden or inconvenience. Suppose that the danger under discussion is a customer falling on a wet floor in a supermarket on a rainy day, and that the kind of injury posed by this danger is a broken or bruised limb. After going through the foreseeability-determination formula, assume we conclude that both dangers are fairly probable. Now let us focus on the burden or inconvenience on the supermarket of eliminating the danger. Burdens or inconveniences fall into the interrelated categories of cost, time, and effectiveness:

- Costs
  How much money would have been needed to take the steps needed to prevent the accident from happening? The cost of a sign saying, "CAUTION,

WET FLOOR"? The cost of an employee whose job on a rainy day is to mop the floor all day long? Every hour? The cost of a rug to absorb the water? The cost of closing the store on rainy days? Etc.

- **Time**
  How much time would have been lost in having the sign painted? How much time would have been lost in having an employee mop up all day? Every hour? Etc.

- **Effectiveness**
  By effectiveness, we do not mean the effectiveness of the precautions in preventing the accident. Rather, the question is what impact any of the precautions would have had on the overall effectiveness of what the defendant was doing. If the precautions had been taken, how would they have affected the defendant's operation or activity? Going through the modest trouble of making and using a "WET FLOOR" sign would certainly not alter the effectiveness of the supermarket's business very much. Closing every day that it rains, however, would substantially disrupt the effectiveness of the supermarket's business. Indeed, this burden might amount to having to go out of business.

Importance or Social Utility

Finally, we examine the *importance or social utility* of what the defendant was trying to do before the accident occurred. Was the defendant driving to work? Watching a football game? Playing a practical joke? Skydiving for fun? Trying to cure cancer? Saving a child from a fire? The more beneficial or socially useful the activity, the more likely it is that a reasonable person would take risks to accomplish the goals involved. This does not mean that a reasonable person would never take any risks of injury if engaged in a mundane or frivolous task. It simply means that reasonable persons would take fewer risks of injuring someone else (or themselves) while engaged in such tasks than they would in tasks that we would all agree are more important and socially beneficial.

The reasonable person, therefore, will juggle all four components of the equation in order to decide what risks should be taken and what precautions should be taken to avoid an accident. The foreseeability of an accident, the foreseeability of the kind of injury or damage, the burden or inconvenience of the precautions, and the importance or social utility of the defendant's conduct must all be properly assessed. *Defendants will be found to have breached their duty if these factors were not assessed in the same or in substantially the same manner as a reasonable person would have assessed them.* This weighing or balancing of risks and benefits through the breach-of-duty equation is known as a **risk-benefit analysis** (also called a cost-benefit analysis or a **risk-utility analysis**).

Cynics charge that some manufacturers go through a drastically different kind of risk-benefit analysis when they decide whether to add a safety feature to a product.

> **EXAMPLE:** The XYZ Motor Company places the gas tank in the rear of its cars. Since rear-end collisions are common, this location of the tank increases the risk of fire explosion from such collisions when the tank is hit. A number of such explosions in fact occur, leading to judgments against XYZ. As the company prepares for next year's models, it must decide whether to keep the gas tank in the rear or to locate it in a place less likely to lead to such fire explosions. An XYZ engineer writes a memo that calculates how much future lawsuits might cost per vehicle if the tank is kept in the rear. To reach this figure, the cost of anticipated lawsuits is divided by the number of vehicles expected to be sold. This calculation leads to the conclusion that the litigation cost of keeping the

tank in the rear would be only a few dollars per vehicle. Since this cost is less than what the company would have to spend to move the tank, the company decides to keep the tank in the rear for its new models.

Can you imagine how excited a personal-injury attorney would be to obtain a copy of such a memo? Ecstatic would be the more likely reaction. This is precisely what happened in 1999 when a California jury awarded $4.9 billion to six people who were severely burned when their General Motors car was rammed from behind by another vehicle. The verdict consisted of $107.6 million in compensatory damages and $4.8 billion in punitive damages. (The trial judge reduced the punitive damages to $1.09 billion, but allowed the compensatory award to stand. G.M. then announced that it would file an appeal.) The burns were caused by the explosion of the gas tank in the rear of the car in which the six plaintiffs were riding. Their attorney was able to introduce into evidence a "smoking-gun" memo written by Edward Ivey, a G.M. engineer. The memo estimated that the company would have to pay out $200,000 for each fatality caused by the placement of the gas tank. Based on the number of cars on the road, "Mr. Ivey came up with an estimate of the cost to G.M. of $2.40 per vehicle."[1] Other evidence showed that the cost of redesigning the car to prevent this kind of accident would have been $8.59 per vehicle. Although there was some controversy at the trial over what role the Ivey memo had in the design decisions of G.M., there was little doubt that the memo had a major impact on the decision of the jury. G.M. refused to spend $8.59 to prevent the kind of tragedy that occurred. The plaintiffs' attorney told the jury that under a risk-benefit analysis, G.M. felt it was cheaper to pay $2.40 to litigate and settle the cases arising from the anticipated fatalities.

This is *not* the kind of analysis a reasonable manufacturer would make in applying the breach-of-duty equation in Figure 12–3. As we will see in Chapter 16 on products liability, a company should not make safety decisions solely on the basis of the cost of litigation. The question should not be how much will a death or maiming cost the company through verdicts and settlements. In light of the value of the product, the question should be how likely (foreseeable) is severe injury and what burdens would have to be undertaken to add a safety feature that would prevent the injury. If the burdens are relatively low and the risk of severe injury is high, a reasonable manufacturer would add the safety feature. This is very different from concluding that it would be cheaper to pay injured plaintiffs than to fix the problem by redesigning the product.

OBJECTIVE OR SUBJECTIVE STANDARD?

It is important that you understand the distinction between a **subjective standard** and an **objective standard.** By "standard" we mean the method by which something is assessed or measured.

A subjective standard is being used when something is measured solely by what one individual (e.g., the defendant) actually did, knew, believed, or understood. When Bob says, "that car is attractive," he is probably using a subjective standard: attractiveness *to Bob.* An objective standard is being used when something is defined or resolved solely by comparing one person to one or more other persons. When Bob says, "Jane is an excellent athlete," he is probably using an objective standard. Jane is excellent because she performs as well as or better than *other* athletes. The quality of her athletic skills is determined by comparing her to other athletes—an objective standard.

We said earlier that reasonableness was a comparative standard: we compared what the defendant did to what a reasonable person would have done. This suggests that reasonableness is an objective standard. In the main, this is so. To at least some extent, however, reasonableness is also a subjective standard, as we shall see.

There is, of course, no actual human being who holds the title of "reasonable person." The concept of the reasonable person (sometimes called the "reasonable

---

[1]Andrew Pollack, *Paper Trail Haunts G.M. After It Loses Injury Suit: An Old Memo Hinted at the Price of Safety,* N.Y. Times, July 12, 1999, at A12.

man") was invented in order to provide juries with guidance in trying to determine whether conduct that unintentionally caused injury was wrongful and hence negligent.[2] We now take a closer look at who this reasonable person is. We know that the reasonable person is not perfect. The reasonable person can and does cause accidents. Such accidents, however, are never due to carelessness or imprudent behavior. (See Figure 12–2.) What else do we know about this person? We examine first the physical characteristics and then the mental characteristics of the reasonable person.

Physical Characteristics

The reasonable person has the same physical strengths and weaknesses as the defendant. Hence, if a blind man causes an accident and is sued, the blind man's conduct will be measured against what a reasonable *blind* person would have done under the same or similar circumstances.

> **EXAMPLE:** Fred is blind. While walking down the corridor, he bumps into the plaintiff who falls and is injured. Fred was not using his cane at the time.

Assume that if Fred did not have a sight handicap, the accident would not have happened. This does not necessarily mean that Fred was negligent. The question is not how a reasonable person with no physical disabilities would have acted. The question is how a reasonable person who is blind would have acted. Phrased another way, how would a reasonable person have acted under the circumstances when one of those circumstances is his or her blindness? It may be that Fred was not acting unreasonably in walking without a cane. Suppose, for example, that he was taking a short walk in an area he was very familiar with and that he had other means of sensing objects around him. A reasonable person who is blind, therefore, might not use a cane in such a case. Note that as to physical characteristics, the standard is both objective (the reasonable person) and subjective (a reasonable person with the same physical characteristics as the defendant).

Sometimes a physical handicap may require greater precautions than those expected of a person without such infirmities.

> **EXAMPLE:** Mary has two broken legs. Yet she continues to drive. While driving one day on the freeway, she causes an accident.

If Mary is sued for negligence, the question will not be whether she was driving as best she could. This would be a totally subjective standard. Rather, the issue will be what the reasonable person with two broken legs would have done. It may be that such a person would not have driven on the freeway or would drive only cars that are specially equipped for handicapped drivers. If Mary failed to use such precautions, she acted unreasonably.

Suppose, however, that the defendant had physical capacities *beyond* that of most people, e.g., superior vision, quicker reflexes. The test of reasonableness for this defendant is what a reasonable person *with these same physical strengths* would have done.

---

[2]If the defendant *intended* the contact or the injury that the plaintiff suffered, then we are not talking about negligence as the cause of action. The plaintiff may be able to use one of the intentional torts, e.g., battery. Intentional conduct may even lead to prosecution for a crime (e.g., criminal trespass, manslaughter).

ASSIGNMENT 12.2

Fred is blind. While lighting a cigarette, he causes a fire because he did not know that he was in an area containing flammable materials. He could not see a sign that read, "Warning: Highly Flammable Vapors. No Smoking." Was Fred negligent?

Mental Characteristics (When the Defendant Is an Adult)

Here we are talking about knowledge, intelligence, and overall mental ability that comes from experience and learning. In this regard, the reasonable person is neither exceptionally bright, nor of low intelligence. The reasonable person has the basic knowledge and intelligence needed in everyday life to handle the common occurrences of living. For example, a reasonable person would know that an exposed electrical wire can be very dangerous, but is not expected to know how to repair wire cables. A reasonable person would know that a child in a large body of water can drown, but is not expected to know how to perform complicated medical procedures on a drowning victim.

Suppose that the defendant has a mental illness or deficiency that prevents him or her from knowing that electricity is dangerous or that water can drown people. Is this defendant still held to the standard of the reasonable person who has no such illness or deficiency? Yes. Such defendants are therefore held to a standard that they cannot meet. The standard as to mental characteristics is very objective. For physical handicaps, discussed earlier, the test is what the reasonable person *with defendant's physical handicap* would have done. For mental disabilities in an adult, the test is what a reasonable person *without defendant's mental disabilities* would have done.

Suppose, however, that the defendant has mental strengths beyond that expected of everyone. For example, the defendant may be a doctor, an electrician, a police officer, etc. When this individual causes an injury, the standard of performance will be the reasonable person *with this special knowledge or skill*. Hence, the standard is subjective in the sense that we are talking about the special knowledge or skill *of the defendant,* but is objective in that we are comparing the defendant's conduct with that *of a reasonable person* with that knowledge or skill.

The special problems involving a doctor's skills (medical malpractice) and an attorney's skills (legal malpractice) will be discussed at the end of the chapter.

Mental Characteristics (When the Defendant Is a Child)

An exception is made when the defendant is a child. When assessing breach of duty by a child, the standard is substantially subjective: What would a reasonable child of the age and intelligence of the defendant have done under the same or similar circumstances? Finally, however, there is an exception to this exception. When the child is engaging in an adult activity, such as driving a car, the child will be held to the standard of a reasonable *adult.*

RES IPSA LOQUITUR

Res ipsa loquitur (RIL) means "the event or thing speaks for itself." It is a doctrine used by a plaintiff having trouble proving the defendant's breach of duty—the defendant's unreasonableness. RIL is an evidentiary tool designed to give the plaintiff a break in certain kinds of situations.

> **EXAMPLE:** Plaintiff sues the owner of a building for negligence after being injured in an elevator that suddenly crashed to the basement from the second floor. The *only* evidence plaintiff is able to introduce is the fact of being in the elevator when it collapsed.

Without the aid of res ipsa, the plaintiff would lose because of the failure to establish the second element of negligence—breach of duty. Where is the specific evidence that the building owner was unreasonable in the maintenance of the elevator? There is none. All we know is that the accident happened. If res ipsa applies in such a case, the jury will be allowed to draw an inference of unreasonableness. In effect, res ipsa simply allows the plaintiff to get his or her case to the jury. It does not mean that the plaintiff has won the case.

What are the elements of a res ipsa case, in which the inference of unreasonableness can be drawn simply by reason of the fact that the accident happened? What

Traditional Statement of the Elements	Statement of the Elements as Applied
1. The event must be of a kind that ordinarily does not occur in the absence of someone's negligence.	**1.** It must be more likely than not that the accident was due to someone's unreasonableness.
2. The event must be caused by an agency or instrumentality within the exclusive control of the defendant.	**2a.** It must be more likely than not that the accident was due to the *defendant's* unreasonableness.
	b. The possibility, if any, that the unreasonableness of others caused the accident must be adequately eliminated.
3. The event must not have been due to any voluntary action or contribution on the part of the plaintiff.	**3.** Plaintiff must not be a responsible cause of the accident.

FIGURE 12–4 Elements of a res ipsa loquitur case.

does the plaintiff have to prove in order to get the case to the jury and require the latter to consider (but not necessarily accept) the inference of the defendant's unreasonableness? The three basic elements that must be established by the plaintiff are outlined in Figure 12–4.

More Likely Than Not Due to Someone's Unreasonableness

> **Example:** Tom is driving his car down the street. Suddenly, his front tire blows out. His car runs into plaintiff's car. Plaintiff sues Tom for negligence. The only evidence of unreasonableness introduced by the plaintiff is the fact of the tire blow out. Is this a res ipsa case?

No. The first element of a res ipsa case has not been satisfied. The most likely explanation of the tire blow out is *not* someone's unreasonableness. An equally likely explanation is that Tom unknowingly and quite innocently ran over a nail or other sharp object. To be sure, Tom's unreasonableness is a *possible* explanation. A mere possibility of unreasonableness, however, is not enough for the first element of a res ipsa case.

Compare the tire blow out case with the elevator case mentioned earlier. Can it be said that it is more likely than not that the explanation for an elevator falling from the second floor is someone's unreasonableness? The answer in this case is yes. One might indeed go so far as to say that it is highly likely that someone was unreasonable. Here are some of the arguments that could be made in support of this conclusion:

- It is commonly known that elevators require frequent inspections.
- If the inspections are adequate, they should reveal defects.
- A falling elevator can cause severe damage to passengers.
- Given the severity of the potential damage, one would expect very careful maintenance by those in charge of the operation and safety of the elevator; when an elevator falls, the likelihood is that this kind of care was not given.
- Elevators have been in existence for a long time; they are not mysterious machines we know very little about; hence, we cannot say that the mishap was probably due to some unknown factor.
- There is safety equipment on an elevator system; if this equipment were being maintained properly (reasonably), it is unlikely that the collapse would occur.

The plaintiff does not have to prove that the *only* explanation for the accident was someone's unreasonableness. The plaintiff does not have to prove that no other cause is possible. The test for this first element is whether unreasonableness by someone is *more likely than not* the explanation. Hence, a defendant does not defeat a res ipsa case simply by showing that it is *possible* that the accident was *not* due to unreasonableness.

ASSIGNMENT

12.3

Examine the following list of accidents. How likely is it that each accident was due to someone's unreasonableness? Where on the "spectrum of likelihood" does each accident fall? Give reasons for your answer. If more than one answer is possible, explain all the answers. In each case you can assume that the person injured is trying to get to the jury on a res ipsa theory. Assume that the only evidence available is the fact of the accident.

a. A passenger is injured when an airplane explodes on the runway before takeoff.

b. Electricity leaks from a wire and injures a child.

c. A small insect is found in a can of soup, injuring a consumer.

d. A large nail is found in a can of soup, injuring a consumer.

e. Two cars collide on the street, injuring a pedestrian.

f. A car collides into a parked car, damaging the latter.

g. A bottle of soda explodes, injuring a customer.

h. Cattle stray onto a road, damaging a parked car.

More Likely Than Not Due to Defendant's Unreasonableness

When the first element of res ipsa is established, we know that the accident was more likely than not due to *someone's* unreasonableness. In a lawsuit, of course, you do not sue a vague someone—you must sue the *defendant*. The second element of res ipsa requires the plaintiff to show that it is more likely than not that the accident was caused by the unreasonableness *of the defendant*. If the unreasonableness of the defendant is a mere possibility, or if there is a 50/50 possibility that the accident was due to the unreasonableness of someone other than the defendant, then the second element of res ipsa has not been established.

> **EXAMPLE:** Mary is a passenger on XYZ Airlines, which manufactures and flies its own commercial planes. While Mary's plane is flying over the ocean, it disappears. Mary's estate sues XYZ for negligence and tries to get its case to the jury on a res ipsa theory. The only evidence of unreasonableness offered by the estate is the fact that the plane disappeared.

Can it be said that it is more likely than not that the defendant's (XYZ's) unreasonableness caused the disappearance of the plane, e.g., due to a defectively built or maintained plane? It is surely *possible* that other causes created the disappearance (e.g., a sudden violent storm that could not have been anticipated, a bomb concealed in luggage that could not be detected by current equipment, another passenger who went insane). It is possible that there was no unreasonableness by the defendant, XYZ Airlines. Yet, a jury could still conclude that the defendant's unreasonableness was more likely than not the cause of the accident leading to the disappearance. XYZ Airlines apparently had exclusive control of the plane—it built and operated the plane. Airplane travel is very common in our society. Crashes are thoroughly investigated and the results usually point to some defect in the design, construction, or operation of the plane—or at least one could reasonably argue this position. Given XYZ's exclusive control, a jury could, therefore, conclude that the disappearance was due to XYZ's unreasonableness in some respect.

Two other major issues need to be considered in connection with the second element of res ipsa: 1. What if the defendant was not in exclusive control of what caused the accident? 2. What if more than one person is sued and not all of them could have caused the accident?

1. What if the defendant was not in exclusive control of what caused the accident? In spite of the traditional way in which the second element of res ipsa is commonly phrased (see first column of Figure 12–4), it is *not* always necessary for the defendant to be in exclusive control of what caused the accident. Exclusive control is simply *one* of the ways to prove that the unreasonableness causing the accident was that of the defendant. Assume that a soda bottle explodes in the plaintiff's hands. At the time of this accident, the bottle may no longer be in the exclusive control of the manufacturer. Yet, res ipsa loquitur is still possible in negligence suits of this kind.[3] It is true that before the bottle reached the consumer, it passed through several hands in addition to the manufacturer. A trucking company, for example, as well as one or more distributor/retailers may have made some contact with the bottle. It is admittedly difficult for the consumer to use res ipsa to show that it was the manufacturer's unreasonableness that was responsible for the explosion of the bottle. The law, however, tends to be somewhat lenient on plaintiffs in such cases, knowing the tremendous problem of proof that they have. The second element of res ipsa can still apply if the plaintiff submits enough evidence to enable a jury to conclude that the explosion was *probably not* due to anyone else in the chain of distribution between the manufacturer and consumer. Examples of such evidence include:

- evidence of careful handling of the bottle once it left the manufacturer, or the absence of evidence of careless handling during this time
- no evidence the bottle was dropped once it left the manufacturer
- no evidence of cracks on the bottle
- no improper storage indicated

Such evidence, although fairly weak in itself, is usually sufficient to permit a jury to rationally eliminate other potential causes so as to conclude that it is more likely than not that the unreasonableness of the defendant (here, the manufacturer) caused the bottle to explode. If, of course, there is strong specific evidence to the contrary (e.g., evidence of vandalism or dropping since it left the hands of the manufacturer), the plaintiff will have great difficulty establishing the second element of res ipsa.

---

[3]Additional theories of liability against the manufacturer include strict liability in tort and breach of warranty. See Chapter 16.

ASSIGNMENT

12.4

In the following two cases, has the second element of res ipsa loquitur been established? Be sure to include a discussion of possible explanations in each case. What further evidence would you try to obtain in both cases?

a. Richard is a customer in Karen's supermarket. He slips on a ripe, yellow banana peel and is injured.

b. Richard is a customer in Karen's supermarket. He slips on a black, moldy banana peel and is injured.

---

2. What if more than one person is sued and not all of them could have caused the accident? The classic res ipsa case involving multiple defendants is *Ybarra v. Spangard*,[4] in which a patient received an injury while unconscious. The patient sued all the doctors, nurses, and other hospital employees involved. Since the plaintiff was unconscious at the time of the injury, there was no way for the plaintiff to give direct testimony about which of the defendants was or was not responsible. No other evidence was available. Hence, according to our test on the second element of res ipsa, the plaintiff cannot show it is more likely than not that the unreasonableness of any of the individual defendants caused the injury. Remarkably, however, the court in *Ybarra* allowed the application of res ipsa loquitur against all of the defendants. This had the practical effect of forcing these defendants to decide among themselves who was responsible. Failing to do this, **joint and several liability** would result. This means each defendant is liable for all the damages suffered by the plaintiff, who can sue any or all of the defendants until 100 percent of the damages are recovered. (An individual defendant who is joint and severally liable cannot force the plaintiff to collect part of the damages from the other defendants.)

Not all states follow the *Ybarra* case. Many would deny the application of res ipsa in such cases because of the difficulty of establishing the second element of res ipsa. The unusual ruling in *Ybarra* may have been due to a special duty of care that medical personnel owe patients and to the fact that in *Ybarra* there was a preexisting relationship among all the defendants.[5]

Plaintiff Is Not a Responsible Cause of the Accident

The final element of res ipsa the plaintiff must establish is that the plaintiff was not the responsible cause of the accident. In the vast majority of cases, this means little more than plaintiff's showing that there was no contributory negligence (or more accurately, showing that the plaintiff's own unreasonableness, if any, did not cause the accident). In the bottle explosion case, for example, the plaintiff must show that there is no evidence he or she mishandled or dropped the bottle while holding it.

CUSTOM AND USAGE

Often in a negligence case the plaintiff alleges that the defendant failed to take specific precautionary steps and that this failure led to the plaintiff's injury. For example:

- the failure to place a safety guard on a bicycle wheel
- the failure to build a fence alongside a railroad track
- the failure to place a rubber mat in front of a store
- the failure to have two-way radios in tugboats
- the failure to perform a medical test to detect a certain disease

---

[4]25 Cal. 2d 486, 154 P.2d 687 (1944).
[5]W. Page Keeton et al., *Prosser and Keeton on the Law of Torts* 252 (5th ed. 1984).

A common response of the defendant in these cases is that no one else in the field takes these steps. The defendant is saying: "a reasonable person in my position would not have taken these steps; it is the custom in the field to act the way I acted." Hence, the question becomes: When is it reasonable to do what everyone else is doing or to fail to do something when everyone else fails to do it as well?

What is reasonable depends on a wide variety of circumstances. One of these circumstances is what others are doing. It may be unreasonable, for example, to expect a defendant to take a very expensive precaution that no other person in the defendant's position has ever taken and that is designed to avoid the small risk of very minor injury. On the other hand, it may be that an entire industry or profession is being unreasonable in failing to take a certain precautionary step. They may be acting unreasonably in spite of the fact that everyone is acting in the same way. To let them off the hook would provide little incentive to raise their standards.

Recall the breach-of-duty equation: The foreseeability of injury must be balanced against the extent of the burden or inconvenience of taking precautions against the injury occurring. (See Figure 12–3.) The more foreseeable the danger of serious injury, the more reasonable it is for the defendant to bear the burden or inconvenience of trying to prevent the injury. This principle helps us assess the impact of **custom and usage.**

We need to ask *why* the business or profession acted or failed to act in a certain way. Suppose a company manufactures a product, but does not add a device that would protect the public against a particular kind of injury. Suppose further that this is the custom in the industry—no manufacturer adds the device. Why isn't the device added? Because the injury is very rare? If so, this is relevant to the foreseeability of danger in the breach-of-duty equation. Because of the cost of adding the device? Would the price to the consumer be so high that only the wealthy could afford the product with the device? Because of a loss of effectiveness? If the device were added, would the product be significantly less effective in its primary function? These questions are relevant to the burden/inconvenience component of the breach-of-duty equation.

In short, the most you can say is that custom and usage is *a* relevant factor in the law of negligence, but it almost never settles the question of what is reasonableness or unreasonableness.

VIOLATION OF A STATUTE

In a negligence case, the plaintiff will often include an allegation that the defendant violated a statute.

> **EXAMPLE:** Ron Davis carelessly drives his truck onto Ed Packard's land. Davis crashes into a lamppost. The impact causes a gasoline storage tank on the truck to flip over, spilling the contents on the ground. A spontaneous fire breaks out, causing extensive damage. Packard sues Davis for negligence. The complaint alleges that Davis was driving his truck carelessly (unreasonably) and that Davis violated a statute, § 200 of the state statutory code. This section prohibits the transportation of gasoline in the kind of storage container Davis was using.

What is the effect of the statute on the negligence claim? Does the violation of § 200 make it easier for Packard to establish breach of duty? How, if at all, is the violation relevant? We know that the standard of care in a negligence case is reasonableness as measured by the breach-of-duty equation of Figure 12–3. If the defendant violates a statute, does this violation, in effect, become the standard of care that determines the defendant's reasonableness? Can we conclude that the defendant was unreasonable *solely because* he or she violated the statute? Unfortunately, most statutes say nothing explicit about how a violation might be relevant to a negligence suit such as Packard's.

The statute may impose a fine or other criminal penalties for a violation, but say nothing about whether the violation allows a victim to bring a tort action such as negligence. When the statute is silent on this point, we need a method of analyzing how a statutory violation might affect the standard of care in a negligence case.

In addition to statutes, there may also be an allegation that the defendant violated a local ordinance (e.g., a traffic ordinance) or an administrative regulation (e.g., an on-the-job safety regulation). Although the following discussion will focus on statutes, the same method of analysis can be used when the negligence case includes alleged violations of ordinances or administrative regulations.

There is an eight-part analysis you need to use to determine how to handle an alleged violation of a statute in a negligence case:

1. State what the defendant did or failed to do that the plaintiff claims was a breach of duty (unreasonableness).
2. State whether a statute might be involved. (The plaintiff's complaint may allege a violation of a statute. Your own legal research may uncover such statutes.)
3. If so, determine whether the statute was violated.
4. If so, determine whether the violation was excused.
5. If not, determine whether the violation of the statute caused the accident.
6. If so, determine whether the plaintiff was within the class of persons the statute was intended to protect.
7. If so, determine whether the statute was intended to avoid the kind of harm the plaintiff suffered.
8. If so, determine whether your state considers the violation to be negligence per se, a presumption of negligence, or simply some evidence of negligence.

In most states, when an unexcused violation of a statute causes harm to a person, the violation will constitute negligence per se (or unreasonableness per se) if the statute was intended to cover this class of victim and this kind of harm. Let us go through the steps to see how we reach this conclusion.

At the end of this section you will find a flowchart (Figure 12–5) on how these eight steps fit together.

It is important to keep in mind that a plaintiff's failure to establish the statute as the standard of care does *not* mean that the defendant wins the case. What the defendant did or failed to do may be found by a court to have been unreasonable *independent* of any statute. A given accident may involve hundreds or thousands of facts, only a small portion of which may be relevant to a particular statute. Suppose a statute requires farmers to place a fence around certain kinds of animals. No fence is erected and the plaintiff is injured by one of the farmer's animals. It may be that after we go through the eight-part analysis, we will come to the conclusion that a court would *not* adopt the statute as the standard of reasonable conduct. This would eliminate the statute from the case. It is *still* possible, however, that the court will find that the defendant acted unreasonably in failing to build the fence. If so, it will not be due to the violation of the statute; it will be due to the court's application of the breach-of-duty equation in which the absence of a fence is but one of the factors that enter into the balancing required by the equation (see Figure 12–3).

We now take a closer look at the steps used to analyze the impact of a statute in a negligence case. Assume that we have identified what the defendant allegedly did or failed to do (step 1) and have found a statute that might be applicable (step 2). The following discussion covers steps 3–8 of the eight-step process:

Was the Statute Violated?

EXAMPLE: Tom is driving his motorcycle 30 mph downtown when he crashes into the car of the plaintiff, who sues Tom for negligence. There is a statute in the state (§ 100) that says, "No motor vehicle can travel more than 25 mph in a thickly settled district."

The first step of our analysis is to identify what the defendant did or failed to do that allegedly was unreasonable. (While driving 30 mph downtown, Tom hit the plaintiff's car.) The second step is to identify any statutes that might apply to the case. (Section 100 provides that "No motor vehicle can travel more than 25 mph in a thickly settled district.") Next we ask whether this statute was violated.

One of the components or elements of § 100 is "motor vehicle." Is a motorcycle a "motor vehicle" under the statute? It depends on how broadly or narrowly we can define "motor vehicle." Another element of § 100 is "thickly settled district." Tom was downtown at the time of the crash. The phrase "thickly settled district" needs to be defined in order to determine whether downtown is within such a district. These definition questions are answered by finding the **legislative intent** of § 100. What was the intent of the legislature when it enacted § 100? What was the purpose of this statute? Answering these questions through legal research (particularly by trying to find court opinions that have interpreted § 100 in the past) will help us find the definitions we need. Our conclusion might be that "motor vehicles" are those vehicles with four or more wheels and that "thickly settled district" refers to residential areas, not to downtown. If so, then Tom did not violate § 100.

This does not mean, however, that the plaintiff loses the case for failure to convince the court that the defendant violated a particular statute. Independent of the statute, the plaintiff may be able to show that the defendant was driving unreasonably, given the totality of the circumstances. In our motorcycle case, the plaintiff will argue that going 30 mph was unreasonable in light of all of the circumstances such as the road conditions, the level of traffic, the position of the plaintiff's car, etc. The statute—§ 100—may be out of the case, but the plaintiff may still be able to show that Tom was negligent.

Was the Violation Excused?

It is not enough to show that the defendant violated a statute. If the violation was excused, it cannot be used to show that the defendant was unreasonable.

> **EXAMPLE:** John causes an accident while driving at night. His car crashes into the plaintiff's car. John's front lights suddenly went out and he could not see the plaintiff's car in front of him. The plaintiff sues John for negligence.

Assume that there is a statute that requires headlights to be on at night. Clearly, John has violated this statute. But his violation was probably excused, particularly if he had no warning that the lights might be defective. This takes the violation out of the negligence case. When we ask whether the violation of a statute constitutes proof of the defendant's unreasonableness, we are referring to unexcused violations.

Did the Violation Cause the Accident?

There was a time when all American males of a certain age were required by statute to carry a draft card on their person. Suppose such a person injures someone in a car accident while he is not carrying his draft card. The defendant has clearly violated the draft card statute. But this is not relevant to the accident. Not having a draft card certainly did not cause the car accident.

Use the but-for test or the substantial-factor test to determine whether the violation of the statute caused the accident. (These tests are covered in Chapter 13.) If there had been no violation (i.e., "but for" the violation), would the accident still have occurred? If so, then the violation did not cause the accident. When more than one possible cause exists, the test is whether the violation was a substantial factor (along with other factors) in producing the accident. If not, then the violation did not cause the accident.

Licensing statutes often raise causation questions:

- You are in a traffic accident at a time when your driver's license has expired.
- You are a doctor whose license has been suspended and you are sued for a medical injury you caused while you were without a license.
- You are a contractor who fails to obtain the required permit to build a house; you are sued when the house collapses and injures someone.

In most license cases such as these, it cannot be said that the violation caused the harm. You may have had the same mishap if you had had the driver's license, doctor's license, or building permit. It is very weak to argue that because you did not have the license, you probably were incompetent in what you were doing. Competence is determined by a host of other factors, e.g., age, prior experience, training. It cannot be said that simply because you did not have a license, you acted unreasonably in doing what you did. Competent doctors, for example, do not automatically become incompetent the day after their medical licenses expire.

Assume that a statute requires handrails on the stairs of every restaurant facility. A customer at a restaurant slips and falls on the stairs where there are no handrails. There appears to be a clear violation of the statute. But did the violation *cause* the fall? The answer appears to be yes. Of course, we need to know more facts in order to determine whether the fall would have occurred even if there were handrails, or if their absence was a substantial factor in the fall. For example, how quickly did the accident happen? How wide were the steps, and where was the plaintiff at the time of the fall? If the plaintiff fell in the center of very wide steps, it may have been impossible to have reached handrails if they were available.

Is Plaintiff Within the Class of Persons Protected by the Statute?

It is not enough that the plaintiff establishes a violation of a statute, which is the cause of the injury suffered by the plaintiff. More analysis of the statute is needed to determine whether the plaintiff is the kind of person the statute was designed to protect.

Suppose that you have a statute requiring factories to have certain safety devices on machines. A factory violates the statute by not installing these devices. One day a salesperson happens to be in the factory and is injured while walking past one of the machines. Assume that there is no difficulty establishing causation. The salesperson can prove that "but for" the failure to have the safety device, the accident would not have occurred. The question then becomes: Who was the statute designed to protect? Only factory employees? If so, the breach of statute cannot be the basis of the salesperson's claim that the factory was unreasonable (negligent). Was it designed to protect *anyone* who is in the factory on business? If so, the salesperson can use the statute.

ASSIGNMENT

12.5

a. A statute requires department stores to report all accidents occurring on elevators to a city agency. Over the years, the XYZ department store has never reported accidents on some of its elevators. Recently, a customer was injured on one of the XYZ elevators. The customer sues the XYZ store for negligence. The customer bases the entire breach-of-duty claim on the violation of the statute. Discuss causation.

b. A statute requires all vacant lots to be fenced at all times. Tom owns a vacant lot in the city, which has no fence. One day a stranger cuts through Tom's lot and injures himself by falling into a hole that is very difficult to see. The stranger sues Tom for negligence. What breach-of-duty argument will the stranger make based on the statute? What will Tom's response be?

Was the Statute Intended to Avoid this Kind of Harm?

Closely related to the class-of-plaintiff problem just discussed is the question of whether the statute was meant to cover the kind of harm or injury the plaintiff suffered.

> **EXAMPLES:**
>
> - A statute requires all traffic to drive under 55 mph on the highways. Defendant crashes into plaintiff while defendant is driving 65 mph. *Is the purpose of statute* to:
>   a. Save lives?
>   b. Save gas?
>
> - A statute requires employers to have sprinkler systems in good repair at all times. One day the sprinkler system at a plant malfunctions. It is activated even though no fire exists. The entire plant is flooded. An employee, who is laid off because of the flood, sues the employer for lost wages due to the breach of the statute. *Is the purpose of statute* to:
>   a. Avoid personal injuries in case of fire?
>   b. Avoid economic loss due to flooding?
>
> - A statute requires that all commercial poison be stored in properly designated containers. A business fails to use the right containers. One day the box containing the poison explodes because it was stored too close to heat. The explosion would not have occurred if the correct containers had been used. A customer is injured by the explosion. *Is the purpose of statute* to:
>   a. Prevent people (or animals) from being poisoned?
>   b. Prevent explosions?

If the statute was not intended to cover the kind of harm that resulted, the plaintiff cannot use the breach of the statute as the basis of the breach-of-duty argument. As we said before, however, even if the statute was not intended to cover what happened, plaintiff should still try to establish unreasonableness as if the statute did not exist. In the poison example, even if the statute was not intended to cover explosions, a court could still find that the defendant was unreasonable in the method used to store the poison if, according to the breach-of-duty equation, the danger of explosion was highly foreseeable and the burden or inconvenience on the defendant of preventing this danger by proper storage was minimal.

Does the Violation of the Statute, in and of Itself, Constitute a Breach of Duty?

Finally, we come to the point of assessing the consequences of our analysis. Assume that you work for a law firm that represents the plaintiff in a negligence case. You have gone through all the hurdles and are able to show that:

- The defendant violated a statute.
- The violation was not excused.
- The violation caused the plaintiff's injury.
- The plaintiff is within the class of persons the statute was intended to protect.
- The injury suffered by the plaintiff was the kind of harm the statute was designed to include.

Does this mean that the plaintiff wins the case? Not quite. More analysis is needed. We need to determine whether the violation means that the defendant was unreasonable and, therefore, committed a breach of duty. Can we say that the defendant acted unreasonably *solely because* of the violation? In other words, if the plaintiff offers no evidence other than the violation, has the plaintiff established breach of duty?

We need to do legal research to answer this question. There are different ways that states treat a violation of a statute in a negligence case. Here are the three options:

Negligence (Unreasonableness) Per Se The violation of the statute may be **negligence per se** (or unreasonableness per se). This means that the jury *must* find that the defendant acted unreasonably. The plaintiff does not have to introduce any evidence of unreasonableness other than the violation of the statute. The defendant will not be allowed to offer evidence that he or she acted reasonably in spite of the violation. (Negligence per se is also referred to as negligence *as a matter of law.*)

Presumption of Negligence (of Unreasonableness) The violation of the statute may amount to a **presumption** of negligence (of unreasonableness). This means that the jury must find that the defendant acted unreasonably *unless* the defendant offers convincing evidence that he or she acted reasonably in spite of the violation. (A presumption is an assumption of fact that can be drawn when another fact or set of facts is established. The presumption is *rebuttable* if a party is allowed to introduce evidence that the assumption is false.)

Evidence of Negligence (of Unreasonableness) The violation of the statute may simply amount to some evidence of negligence (of unreasonableness). The jury is free to reject this evidence if it does not find it convincing enough. The defendant can offer evidence that he or she acted reasonably in spite of the violation.

Most states choose the first option: a violation of a statute is negligence per se (unreasonableness per se). There are some states, however, that do not go this far. They will treat the violation as a presumption or simply as some evidence of negligence (of unreasonableness). Again, you need to do legal research to determine which option your state will use.

Figure 12–5 presents an overview of the eight-part analytical process we have been examining to determine whether a violation of a statute, in and of itself, constitutes a breach of duty.

COMPLIANCE WITH A STATUTE

Thus far we have seen that just because a defendant has *violated* a statute, it does not necessarily mean the defendant was unreasonable. We now look at the converse problem. If a defendant can show *compliance* with a statute, does it necessarily mean he or she acted reasonably at the time the accident occurred? *No*, but compliance can be strong evidence of reasonableness.

Suppose, for example, that a safety statute requires railroad companies to place flashing red lights at all points where tracks cross public highways. The fact that the railroad complies with this statute and has the lights in place does not guarantee that a court will find that the railroad acted reasonably. Suppose an accident occurs at a corner where the lights are working, but it is clear that much more is needed by the railroad to prevent injuries because of the large number of accidents in the past at this same intersection. In such a case, the statute amounts only to the *minimum* conduct expected of the railroad. Reasonableness may have called for additional precautions, e.g., a swing gate, an alarm, or an attendant on duty at the intersection during times of heavy traffic. The railroad is not off the hook simply by showing compliance with the statute. Similarly, a motorist traveling 30 mph who causes an accident cannot claim that he or she was driving at a reasonable speed simply because he or she was well within the speed limit of 45 mph. Compliance is evidence of reasonableness, but it is not conclusive.

To summarize, the statute merely sets the minimum standard of conduct, but reasonableness under the circumstances might call for more than what the statute requires.

FIGURE 12–5   How to determine whether the violation of a statute will become the standard of care in a negligence action.

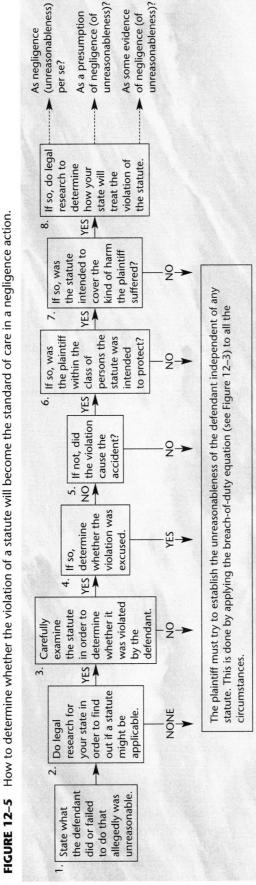

GROSS NEGLIGENCE (UNREASONABLENESS) AND WILLFUL, WANTON, AND RECKLESS CONDUCT

Some states have statutes that cover special negligence cases, such as that of a *guest* injured in an automobile.

> **EXAMPLE:** Mary is on her way to the post office. Her neighbor asks Mary if he could have a ride, since he also needs to go to the post office. Mary agrees. On the way, Mary negligently hits a tree. The neighbor is injured and sues Mary for negligence.

The neighbor is a guest in Mary's car—he did not pay for the ride and there is no indication that Mary derived any benefit from the neighbor's presence in the car other than social companionship. There are **guest statutes** in many states that make it difficult for guests to sue their automobile hosts. Such statutes require guests to prove a greater degree of negligence (unreasonableness) than in non-guest/host suits. **Ordinary negligence** (unreasonableness) is not enough. The following are some of the terms used in guest statutes to describe the degree of negligence (unreasonableness) a guest must prove:

Gross Negligence (Gross Unreasonableness)
The failure to use even a small amount of care to avoid foreseeable harm.

Willful, Wanton, and Reckless Conduct
Having knowledge that harm will probably result from one's actions or inactions (harm is *very* foreseeable).

In our tree case involving Mary and the neighbor, if Mary simply failed to do what an ordinary, reasonable person would have done to avoid the tree, the neighbor would lose his negligence action in a state that imposes standards such as those just listed. To be grossly negligent or reckless, Mary would have had to be drunk at the time, or be traveling 60 mph in a 20 mph zone before hitting the tree.

As we shall see later, gross negligence (unreasonableness) or willful, wanton, and reckless conduct will often be the basis for awarding punitive damages in a negligence case.

ASSIGNMENT

12.6

Matthew is driving from one city to another in your state. The distance is 50 miles. His best friend, George, asks Matthew if he could drive him to a point midway between the two cities. Matthew is delighted to do him this favor, since he enjoys his company very much. When they reach the point where George is to get off, the latter gives Matthew $5 as a contribution toward the cost of gas. As George is getting out, Matthew sneezes and steps on the accelerator by mistake, injuring George. George sues Matthew for negligence. Discuss George's chances of winning this case.

VICARIOUS LIABILITY

"Vicarious" means taking the place of another. Vicarious negligence, or more accurately, vicarious unreasonableness, means that one person will be found to be unreasonable solely because someone else is unreasonable. The unreasonableness of one person will be thrust upon or imputed to another person. Other terms used to mean the same thing include **vicarious liability** and **imputed negligence**. Again, since we are discussing only one element of negligence—breach of duty—it is more accurate to say: imputed unreasonableness. The unreasonableness of one person is charged or "credited" to another person, even though the latter did nothing wrong or unreasonable. The three types of vicarious unreasonableness we will consider are outlined in Figure 12–6. Vicarious liability is not automatic in the three situations of Figure 12–6. As we shall see, there are tests that must be applied before this liability can be imposed.

Two major points need to be kept in mind as we explore each of the three forms of vicarious unreasonableness. The first deals with who can be sued, and the second deals with the distinction between vicarious liability and independent liability:

Who Can Be Sued?

You will note in the three examples of Figure 12–6 that Sara, Joe, and Jessica were the defendants in the three negligence actions. What about the other three who, as the drivers, were more directly responsible for the accidents: Mary, Ed, and Bob? Can they also be sued for negligence? Yes. *Joint and several liability* exists. If a person is jointly and severally liable, he or she is individually responsible for 100 percent of the damages suffered by the plaintiff. The plaintiff can sue all of these persons together or can sue any one or more of them until 100 percent of his or her damages are recovered. An individual defendant cannot force the plaintiff to collect part of the damages from other persons. (If a defendant is upset about paying all of the damages, he or she can seek **contribution** from the others in a separate action where the plaintiff is not a party.) Since all of the individuals in Figure 12–6 are jointly and severally liable, here are the actions that are possible:

Plaintiff v. Sara *or*	Plaintiff v. Joe *or*	Plaintiff v. Jessica *or*
Plaintiff v. Mary *or*	Plaintiff v. Ed *or*	Plaintiff v. Bob *or*
Plaintiff v. Sara and Mary	Plaintiff v. Joe and Ed	Plaintiff v. Jessica and Bob

Mary, Ed, and Bob are not off the hook simply because Sara, Joe, and Jessica are vicariously liable. Why then would the plaintiffs want to bring an action against Sara, Joe, and Jessica? The practical answer is the **deep pocket** reality: a plaintiff wants to

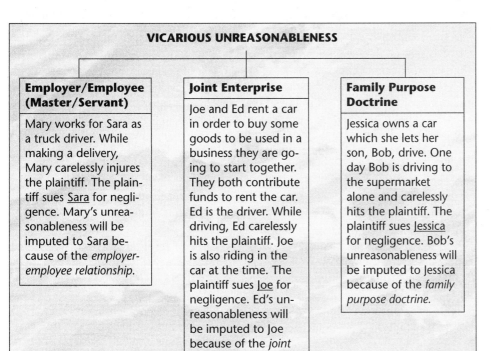

FIGURE 12–6 Vicarious unreasonableness.

VICARIOUS UNREASONABLENESS

Employer/Employee (Master/Servant)

Mary works for Sara as a truck driver. While making a delivery, Mary carelessly injures the plaintiff. The plaintiff sues <u>Sara</u> for negligence. Mary's unreasonableness will be imputed to Sara because of the *employer-employee relationship*.

Joint Enterprise

Joe and Ed rent a car in order to buy some goods to be used in a business they are going to start together. They both contribute funds to rent the car. Ed is the driver. While driving, Ed carelessly hits the plaintiff. Joe is also riding in the car at the time. The plaintiff sues <u>Joe</u> for negligence. Ed's unreasonableness will be imputed to Joe because of the *joint enterprise*.

Family Purpose Doctrine

Jessica owns a car which she lets her son, Bob, drive. One day Bob is driving to the supermarket alone and carelessly hits the plaintiff. The plaintiff sues <u>Jessica</u> for negligence. Bob's unreasonableness will be imputed to Jessica because of the *family purpose doctrine*.

go after the party with the deepest pocket, i.e., the one who probably has the financial resources from which a negligence judgment can be satisfied. If vicarious liability exists, the deep pocket strategy can be used. But again, this does not mean that the other parties cannot also be sued, or that both parties cannot be sued together.

Vicarious Liability and Independent Liability

In the three examples in Figure 12–6, there is no indication that the parties vicariously liable (Sara, Joe, and Jessica) did anything wrong, careless, or unreasonable themselves. They were not individually at fault. Suppose, however, that they were, as in the following scenarios.

Employer/Employee Case
- Sara knew that Mary was a poor driver, but let her drive anyway.
- Sara instructed Mary to make the delivery as fast as she could, even if it meant breaking the speed law.
- Sara never bothered to check to determine whether her drivers were properly trained.

Joint Enterprise Case
- Joe knew that Ed was a poor driver, but let him drive anyway.
- The accident happened because Joe carelessly distracted Ed.
- Joe knew that the car was defective; this defect contributed to the accident.

Family Purpose Doctrine Case
- Jessica knew that Bob was a poor driver, but let him drive anyway.
- Jessica instructed Bob to get to the supermarket and back as soon as possible, even if it meant breaking the speed law.
- Jessica knew that the car was defective; this defect contributed to the accident.

Now we have *individual* fault on the part of the parties who were not driving. Sara, Joe, and Jessica may be liable for their own negligence as well as vicariously liable.

In the discussion that follows, we will assume that the defendants are not independently liable because of any unreasonableness of their own. Our focus is on vicarious liability only. You should always keep in mind, however, the distinction between vicarious and **independent liability,** because in any given case a defendant may be legitimately faced with both theories of liability.

Employer/Employee Vicarious liability because of the **employer/employee relationship** (sometimes referred to as the **master/servant relationship**) is often given the Latin name, **respondeat superior,** meaning "look to the man higher up." The underlying principle has been phrased as follows: "He who does a thing through another does it himself."[6] The employer/employee relationship is one example of a broader category of relationships called **principal/agent.** Generally, an *agent* is someone who agrees to do something on behalf of another. A *principal* is the person on whose behalf the agent is acting and who has some authority or control over the agent while so acting.

Our study of the vicarious liability of an employer shall center on two questions: 1. When is an employee acting within the scope of employment so that the employer is vicariously liable? and 2. When is defendant vicariously liable for the negligence of his or her independent contractor?[7]

1. When is an employee acting within the scope of employment? The overriding principle is that the employer is vicariously liable for the torts of his or her employee if the latter was acting within the **scope of employment** at the time. A great deal of

---

[6]W. Page Keeton et al., *Prosser and Keeton on the Law of Torts* 499 (5th ed. 1984).

[7]The distinction between an employee and an independent contractor is also important for federal tax purposes. Social security and withholding taxes, for example, must be deducted from payments to employees, but not to independent contractors. The Internal Revenue Service has its own tests to determine when a worker is an employee. Employers can be fined for attempting to treat employees as independent contractors.

litigation has resulted from trying to define the phrase "scope of employment." (As we shall see in Chapter 24, the comparable phrase in the law of workers' compensation is, "arising out of and in the course of employment.")

There is no absolute definition of scope of employment. A working definition is as follows:

> Scope of employment is that which is foreseeably done by the employee for the employer under the employer's specific or general control.

Scope of employment is not determined by what the employer has authorized the employee to do, although authorization is one factor a court will consider. Suppose that a boss tells her hardware clerk not to allow a customer to operate the automatic paint mixer. The employee violates this instruction, resulting in an injury to a customer. This violation does not mean respondeat superior will not apply. The boss will still be vicariously liable for the negligence of her employee if the latter was acting for the boss, under the latter's control, and if what the employee did should have been foreseeable to the boss because of prior conduct of the employee and the nature of the work.

A major concern of the courts has been the so-called **frolic and detour** of an employee. There is no vicarious liability if the negligent act of the employee was committed while he or she was on a frolic and detour of his or her own.

> **EXAMPLE:** Bill is an employee of a delivery company. One morning while making a delivery for the company, he drives the company truck 25 miles out of the way to spend three hours with his girlfriend. While driving out of the girlfriend's drive in order to return to work, Bill rams the company truck into the plaintiff's fence.

It is highly unlikely that the plaintiff can win a negligence action against the employer; the accident was not within the scope of employment—the employee was on a frolic and detour of his own. The plaintiff will be limited to a suit against the employee (Bill). A major characteristic of a frolic and detour is that the employee is acting for his or her personal objectives rather than acting primarily for the employer's business.

There is a large gray area where courts have had difficulty determining what is within the scope of employment. A number of factors are considered in identifying this scope. The factors are outlined in the scope of employment checklist in Figure 12–7. No single factor is determinative; a court will weigh them all. Although our emphasis has been on negligence liability (vicarious unreasonableness), the factors in the checklist would also be used by a court to determine whether the employer would be liable for any intentional torts committed by the employee, such as battery, fraud, or false imprisonment.

ASSIGNMENT

12.7

Apply the scope of employment checklist of factors in Figure 12–7 to determine whether the employees in the following situations were acting within the scope of their employment at the time of the accident. Identify further fact investigation you may need. In each instance, the plaintiff is suing the employer on a respondeat superior theory.

a. The ashes from the employee's cigarette fall onto the plaintiff's fur coat, causing substantial damage. The plaintiff sues for negligence.

b. While making a delivery in a company truck, the employee travels five miles out of the way to visit his ailing mother. He stays three hours. On his way back to the company plant to return the truck, he injures plaintiff in a traffic accident. The plaintiff sues for negligence.

c. The employee is a door-to-door salesperson. At one house, the employee gets into an argument with the plaintiff, who owns the house. The plaintiff calls the employee "stupid." The employee hits the plaintiff, who now sues for battery.

A "yes" answer to any of the following interrelated questions would help support a conclusion that the employee did act within the scope of employment. A "no" answer helps support the conclusion that the act was outside this scope. A single yes or no answer is rarely conclusive. A court will weigh all of the factors before deciding what was within or outside of the scope of employment. The "conduct" referred to in the following eight categories of questions is what the employee did that accidently resulted in the plaintiff's injury, which is now the basis of the plaintiff's negligence suit against the employer.

1. Authorization
   Was the employee's conduct substantially within what the employer authorized the employee to do?
2. Purpose
   Was the employee acting to pursue the business interests of the employer? If the employee also had personal objectives in what was done, can it nevertheless be said that the employee was acting *primarily* to pursue the business interests of the employer?
3. Normalcy
   Was the employee's conduct common or usual in the job being performed?
4. Foreseeability
   Was the conduct of the employee foreseeable to the employer?
5. Time
   Was the employee's conduct undertaken substantially within the time of work for the employer?
6. Place
   Was the employee's conduct undertaken substantially within the place or locale authorized by the employer for such conduct?
7. Special Obligation
   Was the employer engaged in the kind of business on which the courts have historically placed a special obligation for the protection of its customers, e.g., common carriers, innkeepers?
8. Common Sense
   As a matter of common sense, can we say that the employee's conduct was within the scope of employment?

2. **When is the defendant vicariously liable for the negligence of his or her independent contractor?** Different rules apply when the defendant hires an **independent contractor**. The distinction between an employee and an independent contractor is not always easy to draw. Some of the significant points of difference include:

- The person doing the hiring has less control over the independent contractor than over the employee.
- The independent contractor has a great deal more discretion over the way the job is done than an employee.
- The employee is on the payroll of the employer, whereas the independent contractor is hired primarily to produce a certain product or result without being on the payroll.

For example, compare the following two ways in which a business hires an accountant:

- Gabe's Fine Furniture, Inc. pays an accountant an annual fee of $500 to prepare its federal and state tax returns. The accountant comes to Gabe's business about four times a year to collect data from the company's financial books. The data is used for the tax returns.
- Ace Trucking Co. pays an accountant $1,538.46 every two weeks ($40,000 a year) to keep its books, pay accounts receivable, prepare the payroll, prepare tax returns, and perform other accountancy tasks in the financial office of the company.

Gabe's accountant is an independent contractor, whereas Ace's accountant is an employee. The latter is on staff and is subject to as much supervision as the company's management decides to provide. Gabe's accountant, on the other hand, probably performs his or her task with relatively little supervision from anyone at the furniture company. Another example would be a company that pays an attorney a fee to bring a lawsuit or to handle some other specific legal problem. This attorney is an independent contractor. If, however, the company has attorneys on its permanent payroll staff, the attorney is an employee. (Employed attorneys are called *in-house attorneys,* whereas independent contractor attorneys are referred to as *outside counsel.*)

The general rule is that the person who hires independent contractors is *not* liable for their torts. (See Figure 12–8.) If you are injured by an independent contractor, your only recourse is to sue the independent contractor. Under this general rule, respondeat superior does not apply. There are, however, two major exceptions. Vicarious liability will continue to apply when someone is injured while the independent contractor is performing:

- a **non-delegable duty** (e.g., a city's duty to keep its streets in repair) or
- an **inherently dangerous** task (e.g., transporting dynamite).

(See other examples in Figure 12–8.) While performing work in either category, the independent contractor is treated as an employee for purposes of vicarious liability.

General Rule

A defendant is *not* vicariously liable for the torts of his or her independent contractor. If the independent contractor injures someone while working for the defendant, the victim is limited to suing the independent contractor.

Exceptions

There are two circumstances in which a defendant *will* be liable for the torts committed by his or her independent contractor:

1. the independent contractor is performing certain non-delegable duties of the defendant (e.g., a city's duty to keep its streets in repair, a landlord's duty to keep the leased premises safe for business visitors, a duty of a common carrier to transport passengers safely, and other special duties imposed by statute or regulation), or
2. the independent contractor is performing inherently dangerous work for the defendant (e.g., transporting dynamite, keeping vicious animals, conducting fireworks exhibitions).[8]

FIGURE 12–8 Liability for torts of independent contractors.

Recall the distinction made earlier between vicarious liability and independent liability. Assume that a defendant is careless in selecting an independent contractor such as by hiring someone who is obviously incompetent to perform a job that could injure someone. The defendant might be subject to independent liability for what is called **negligent hiring** to anyone injured by the independent contractor. The same is true if the person hired is an employee, although for employees the basis of the employer's liability would be both vicarious liability and independent liability.

ASSIGNMENT

12.8

a. A business hires a construction company to erect a commercial building. While one of the company's executives is driving back from the job site in her car, she carelessly hits Tom's car.

---

[8]Some of these activities may also impose strict liability. See Chapter 9.

b. A month later, the company is transporting a gigantic derrick along a small county road on the back of a massive trailer. An accident occurs when the derrick falls off the trailer and damages Mary's barn.

In each case, who can sue whom and on what theories? Be sure to discuss vicarious liability, if applicable.

Joint Enterprise   We come now to the second example of vicarious unreasonableness listed in Figure 12–6—the **joint enterprise**. For parties to be engaged in a joint enterprise, the following elements must be present:

1. an express or implied agreement to participate in the enterprise together
2. a common purpose (usually financial or business-related)
3. a mutual right to control the enterprise

In a few states, the agreement can be to go to a picnic or to the zoo. In most states, however, the common purpose must be financial or business-related.

The third element has caused the courts the most difficulty. How, for example, do you establish that two people riding in a car for a common business purpose have the same (mutual) right to control the direction and operation of the car?

Mutuality of the right of control is not established simply because both are riding together for a business purpose. There must be more concrete indications that the passenger has the same right to control the direction and operation of the car as the driver. Such indications would include: they rented the car with their joint funds; both own the car; they share expenses on the maintenance of the car; both have driven the car in the past; on this trip, they alternate the driving; the passenger is reading the road map and giving route instructions to the driver, etc. The court must be able to find that there was a clear understanding between the parties that both had an equal say in the operation of the car, even if only one party did all the driving at the time the car had the accident injuring the plaintiff. Taking all the factors into consideration, the question is whether it would have been odd, unusual, or presumptuous for the passenger to have exercised the same authority as the driver in the operation of the car. If so, there probably was no joint control.

Once a joint enterprise is established, vicarious liability comes into play. In automobile cases, the passenger is vicariously unreasonable if the driver's unreasonableness caused the accident. In a sense, the joint enterprise is treated as a partnership in which one partner becomes personally liable for the acts of all the other partners. Most joint enterprises, however, are usually more limited in their duration and less structured than the traditional partnership.

ASSIGNMENT 12.9

a. Husband and wife are in a car on their way to sign up for a motel training course in which couples are taught the motel business. The car is in both names. The wife is driving. An accident occurs. The third party sues the husband for negligence. How would you determine if there is a joint enterprise?

b. Dr. Jones and Dr. Smith practice medicine separately; they are not partners. During times of vacation, however, they cover for each other's patients. While Dr. Smith is on vacation, Dr. Jones sees one of Dr. Smith's patients. The patient suffers an injury because of negligent treatment by Dr. Jones. Assume that Dr. Jones, unlike Dr. Smith, has no liability insurance and almost no assets. Dr. Smith, therefore, is the "deep pocket." Vicarious liability? Can the patient sue Dr. Smith for the negligence of Dr. Jones? Assume that Dr. Smith had no reason to suspect that Dr. Jones would ever commit negligence.

Once a joint enterprise is established, there can *also* be **imputed contributory negligence.** Compare the following two cases:

Case I (Imputed Negligence) Dan and Paul are engaged in a joint enterprise. They are in a truck on a highway. Dan is driving and Paul is a passenger. Dan carelessly crashes into Mary's car. Mary sues Paul for negligence (Mary v. Paul). Because of the joint enterprise, the negligence (unreasonableness) of Dan is imposed upon (i.e., imputed to) Paul.

Case II (Imputed Contributory Negligence) Same accident as in Case I except that this time Paul sues Mary for negligence (Paul v. Mary), claiming that her negligence caused the crash with Dan. Mary's defense is that Dan's negligence caused the accident and his contributory negligence should be imposed upon (i.e., imputed to) Paul because of the joint enterprise between them.

The same principle of imputed contributory negligence will apply in the employer-employee relationship discussed earlier. If the employer sues a third party for damages suffered by the employer arising out of an accident in which the employee was also negligent, the contributory negligence of the employee will be imputed to the employer in the employer's negligence action against the third party. For more on contributory negligence, see Chapter 15.

Family Purpose Doctrine The final form of vicarious unreasonableness mentioned in Figure 12–6 is based on the **family purpose doctrine.** It makes a nondriver vicariously liable for an accident caused by a driver. Not all states have adopted the family purpose doctrine, and those that have, do not all agree on its elements. In general, the elements are as follows:

- Defendant must own the car, or have an ownership interest in it (e.g., co-owner), or control the use of the car.
- Defendant must make the car available for family use rather than for the defendant's business. (In some states, the defendant must make it available for general family use rather than just for a particular occasion.)
- The driver must be a member of the defendant's immediate household.
- The driver must be using the car for a family purpose at the time of the accident.
- The driver must have had the defendant's express or implied consent to be using the car at the time of the accident.

The defendant does not have to be the traditional head of the household and does not have to be in the car at the time of the accident. Again, individual states, by case law or by statute, may impose different elements to the doctrine or may reject it entirely.

Parent and Child The traditional rule is that parents are not vicariously liable for the torts committed by their children. If a child commits negligence (or an intentional tort), the child is personally liable. The parent might be individually (not vicariously) liable for his or her own negligence in failing to use available opportunities to control a child with known **dangerous propensities** or for actually participating in the unreasonable conduct of the child. Similarly, there can be individual liability for **negligent entrustment** whenever a person carelessly allows someone such as a child to use a vehicle, tool, or any other object that poses an unreasonable risk of harm to others. This kind of liability is quite separate from the parent being vicariously liable simply because he or she is the parent of a child who commits a tort.

In some states, however, there are statutes that *do* impose vicarious liability on parents for the torts of their child, but only up to a limited dollar amount, e.g., $3,000. (See also Chapter 18 on torts against and within the family.)

MEDICAL MALPRACTICE

Medical malpractice is often one of the major areas of a tort practice. It consists of professional misconduct or wrongdoing by medical practitioners such as doctors. A crusading personal injury attorney would say that there are many medical malpractice claims because there are many victims of medical incompetence. "Findings from several studies of large numbers of hospitalized patients indicate that each year a million or more people are injured and as many as 100,000 die as a result of errors in their care. This makes medical care one of the leading causes of death, accounting for more lost lives than automobile accidents, breast cancer or AIDS."[9] A cynic, on the other hand, would say the main reason medical malpractice is a large part of the practice of many attorneys is simply that doctors and hospitals are deep pockets—defendants who have resources (i.e., personal wealth and liability insurance) with which to pay a judgment.

According to a 1998 report of the Physician Insurers Association of America, just over 31 percent of all medical malpractice claims made between 1985 and 1998 resulted in a payout through settlement or litigation. (Almost a fourth of these payouts were OB-GYN claims.) When a payout did result, the average amount was $154,910. Payments of a million dollars or more rose from 8 percent of the claims in 1985 to 20 percent in 1997. The conditions leading to the largest number of medical malpractice claims are listed in Figure 12–9.[10]

Physician-Patient Relationship

A **physician-patient relationship** arises when a doctor undertakes to render medical services in response to an express or implied request for services by the patient or by the patient's guardian. The relationship does not come into existence simply because the doctor provides emergency medical care to an injured person. Yet, in providing such services, the doctor must use reasonable care.[11]

A doctor is not required to accept every patient. Once the physician-patient relationship exists, however, the doctor cannot withdraw at will. He or she must give reasonable notice of withdrawal so that the patient has an opportunity to find alternative treatment. On the other hand, the patient can end the relationship at any time by firing the doctor for any reason, but will remain responsible for the agreed-upon fee up to the time of termination.

Warranty

Normally a doctor does not warrant or promise a particular cure or other result. If such a **warranty** or promise is given, the patient has a breach-of-warranty or breach-of-contract action against the doctor if the result or cure is not produced. Although doctors are understandably reluctant to give express guarantees, they sometimes use language to their patients that a court will interpret as a guarantee. Suppose, for example, that a doctor makes the following statements to a patient about an operation:

"The operation will take care of all your troubles."

"You'll be able to return to work in approximately three or four weeks at the most."

---

[9]*Concerning Patient Safety and Medical Errors,* Statement of Harvard Professor Lucian Leape, M.D., before the Subcommittee on Labor, Health and Human Services, and Education, U.S. Senate, January 25, 2000 (http://www.apa.org/ppo/science/leape.html).

[10]Physician Insurers Association of America, *Risk Management Review of Malpractice* in *Special Section: Medical Malpractice Statistics,* 15 No. 11 Med. Malpractice L. & Strategy § 1 (Leader Publications, Sept. 1998) (WESTLAW cite in HTH-TP database: 15 No. 11 MED-MALLST S1). See also http://www.phyins.org.

[11]Office of the General Counsel, American Medical Association, *Medicolegal Forms with Legal Analysis* 1 (1973).

Condition Leading to Claim	Number of Claims	Average Payout
Brain-damaged infant	3,466	$477,968
Breast cancer	3,337	205,851
Pregnancy	2,417	127,959
Acute myocardial infarction	2,202	188,281
Displacement of intervertebral disc	2,087	185,484
Cancer of lung or bronchus	1,806	148,907
Fracture of femur	1,522	94,491
Appendicitis	1,519	89,885
Cataracts	1,459	108,267
Colorectal cancer	1,457	199,235
Back disorders	1,430	147,881
Abdominal/pelvic symptoms	1,355	130,871
Sterilization	1,341	53,634
Elective plastic surgery	1,216	59,629
Coronary atherosclerosis	1,199	161,352

FIGURE 12–9 Largest medical malpractice claims (1985–1998).

Such language could be interpreted as a promise to cure. If the patient is not cured, a breach-of-contract action may be successful against the doctor *even if the doctor was not negligent in performing the operation.*

A mere opinion by a doctor on the probable results of treatment is not a promise. It is sometimes very difficult, however, to distinguish between a prediction of probabilities and a promise.

Negligence

Doctors are not liable for every mistake they make that causes injury. There is no **strict liability,** or liability without fault, for the services of doctors, attorneys, or other professionals. Plaintiffs must show that their injury was wrongfully caused.

The main category of wrongful conduct in this area is **negligence,** which is harm caused by the failure to use reasonable care (see Chapter 10). Because doctors have specialized skill and knowledge, they are measured by what a reasonable doctor would have done with that specialized skill and knowledge. Simply stated, the standard is as follows:

A doctor must use the skill and learning commonly possessed by members of the profession in good standing.[12]

There is considerable controversy, however, as to whether this standard is to be gauged from a national or from a local perspective:

national standard: A doctor is required to have and use the equipment, knowledge, and experience that doctors have and use nationally.

local standard: A doctor is required to have and use the equipment, knowledge, and experience that doctors have and use locally or in localities similar to the community where the defendant-doctor practices.

In assessing reasonable care, one of the considerations of the court will be how other doctors commonly practice. What is the **custom** of sound medical practice for treating a particular ailment? To help a jury answer this question, expert witnesses are called, typically other doctors. If a state has adopted a national standard, an expert from anywhere in the country can testify. If, however, the state has adopted a local standard, a doctor from a big medical facility will not be allowed to give testimony on sound medical practice if the doctor being sued for malpractice is from a small rural town.

---

[12]W. Page Keeton et al., *Prosser and Keeton on the Law of Torts* 187 (5th ed. 1984).

States that impose a local standard take the position that a doctor in a small community with limited resources should not be held to the standard of a doctor practicing in a large metropolitan area with access to state-of-the-art facilities and close to unlimited resources. Some doctors will understandably refuse to practice in rural areas of the country if they know that their mistakes will be judged by a standard they cannot meet because of the limited resources available to them.

There are strong arguments, however, in favor of a national standard, which a number of states impose. A national standard will tend to increase the quality of care a patient receives. Also a national standard is more likely to overcome a **conspiracy of silence,** which is the reluctance or refusal of one member of a group to testify against another member. In small communities where most doctors know each other and refer business to each other, an injured patient may find it difficult, if not impossible, to find a doctor willing to testify against another doctor. A national standard, on the other hand, would allow doctors from outside the community to testify. They arguably would be more willing to do so since they would not have the close personal and professional ties that doctors in the same small community have. Another argument in favor of a national standard is the fact that medical training for all doctors has become more standardized at a high level of skill. Furthermore, doctors everywhere are close to having equal access to the most current medical science through the Internet and other online resources.

Regardless of whether a state uses a local or a national standard, there still may be disagreement over the treatment that should be given in a given case. Schools of thought exist, as in any area. If there is more than one recognized method of diagnosis or treatment, and no one of them is used exclusively and uniformly by all practitioners in good standing, doctors, in the exercise of their best judgment, can select one of the approved methods. Negligence is not established simply because it turns out to be the wrong selection or because other doctors would have used other methods. Again, the test is reasonableness. If more than one approach is reasonable, doctors will not be liable if they make a mistake as long as diligence and good judgment were otherwise used in the method selected and applied.

Informed Consent

Doctors can commit a **battery** if they make physical contact with a part of the patient's body without consent or beyond the consent provided by the patient. Most cases, however, are decided under a negligence theory. The patient argues that there was no **informed consent** in that the doctor negligently failed to inform the patient of the risks involved in what was to be done. This failure allegedly prevented the patient from being able to make an intelligent decision on whether to seek the operation or treatment. The problem is serious. A recent study conducted by doctors reached the startling conclusion that only 1 of 10 patient decisions are based on informed consent. Patients were simply not told enough. In effect, something was missing from the doctor-patient discussions 90 percent of the time![13]

How much information on the benefits and risks of a proposed treatment must a doctor provide a patient? To tell the patient everything might take hours of explanation and reams of printed information. States differ on what a patient must be told in order for his or her consent to be informed. Here are the two most commonly used tests:

> **reasonable patient standard:** A doctor must disclose information on the risks and benefits of a proposed treatment that a reasonable patient with the plaintiff's condition would wish to know. In a state that adopts this standard, no expert

---

[13]Clarence H. Braddock, et al., *Informed Decision Making in Outpatient Practice,* 282 Journal of the American Medical Association 2313 (December 22/29, 1999). *Study Shows Doctors are Lax in Giving Information to Patients,* N.Y. Times Nat'l Ed., Dec. 22, 1999, at A16.

witnesses would be needed on this issue since jurors are capable of concluding what a reasonable patient would want to know.

reasonable doctor standard: A doctor must follow the standards of the profession as to how much information on the risks and benefits of a proposed treatment would be disclosed to a patient in the plaintiff's condition. In a state that adopts this standard, expert witnesses would be needed to help the jury decide the standard practice of disclosure by doctors.

If a case is litigated, the two tests could lead to different results. It is possible for a reasonable doctor to withhold information that a reasonable patient would have wanted to know. When this occurs, the patient would lose in a state that has adopted the reasonable doctor standard.[14]

Consent forms are often used by doctors and hospitals as a way of providing information and avoiding liability. At times, however, these forms are inadequate. Suppose that a woman consents to a simple appendectomy. The surgeon, however, performs a total hysterectomy as a precautionary measure, because he feels that it would be a sound medical procedure even though no emergency existed. Before the operation, the woman signed the following statement:

"I hereby authorize the physician in charge to administer such treatment as found necessary to perform this operation which is advisable in the treatment of this patient."

A court would probably find this consent form to be invalid. It is very ambiguous. It does not designate the nature of the operation and therefore does not state what is being consented to. It is close to a blanket authorization to do whatever the doctor thinks is wise.

Suppose that the condition of the patient is such that it would be dangerous to inform him or her of all the details of a proposed treatment. Or suppose that the doctor discovers an unanticipated emergency after the patient is under anesthesia and an incision has been made. How is consent to be handled in these situations? A court will examine all of the circumstances in order to determine whether it was reasonable for the doctor not to obtain consent or even to ask for it. The factors to be considered include: the seriousness of the patient's condition, the patient's emotional stability, the availability of time, the extent of the emergency, the practice in the medical community in such cases. A court might conclude that it was reasonable for the doctor to proceed without consent.

Reform

In the 1980s, the country faced what was called a medical malpractice crisis; some feel that the crisis is still with us. One way to gauge whether this is so is to look at the cost of liability insurance that doctors and hospitals buy to protect themselves against medical malpractice suits. In 1960, doctors and hospitals paid under $100 million for liability insurance. In the late 1990s, they were paying nearly $10 billion annually, an increase of about 10,000 percent.[15] In some areas of the country, doctors have withdrawn from certain high-risk kinds of practice (e.g., delivering babies) because of the frequency of litigation and the high cost of malpractice insurance associated with those areas of practice.

Many blame the legal system for a large part of the skyrocketing cost of health care. Doctors, for example, allegedly order expensive tests solely to make them "look good" in court in the event of a later malpractice suit by a patient. This is known as the practice of **defensive medicine**—the ordering of precautionary tests and procedures intended primarily to shield doctors from possible lawsuits. Studies have

[14]Kenneth S. Abraham, *The Forms and Functions of Tort Law* 77 (1997).
[15]Id. at 70.

shown that liability premiums and defensive medical measures are a significant part of the cost of every visit to a doctor or medical facility.[16]

Insurance companies are particularly angry about the system of compensating attorneys through the **percentage fee.** This kind of fee gives attorneys a percentage of any payout through settlement or litigation their clients obtain. The large amount of the percentage (e.g., 30–40 percent) arguably causes attorneys to be excessively aggressive in pursuing litigation for their clients. Attorneys, on the other hand, deny that there is a malpractice insurance crisis, arguing that if there is a problem, it is due primarily to greedy insurance companies and incompetent doctors and hospitals.

The turmoil has led to reform proposals in every state. There is a great diversity in the kinds of reforms that different states have enacted or considered. Here are some examples:

- Limiting damage awards (**damage caps**). The state would limit the amount of damages that can be awarded in a medical malpractice lawsuit. Typically, a state might limit the amount of a plaintiff's non-economic damages, such as pain and suffering, to between $250,000 and $500,000.
- Limiting attorney fees (**fee caps**). A state might limit the percentage of the recovery a plaintiff's attorney can receive as a fee.
- Allowing **collateral source** offsets. A collateral source is an amount of money an injured party receives independent of the tortfeasor (see Chapter 14). An example would be payments an injured plaintiff pedestrian receives from a medical insurance policy provided by an employer. Under the traditional rule, a tortfeasor cannot seek the reduction of damages by amounts received from collateral sources. Juries are not even allowed to be told that collateral sources exist. There are some states, however, that have changed this rule and now permit amounts received from some collateral sources to be deducted from (offset by) the total damages caused by the tortfeasor.
- Requiring cooling-off periods. To encourage negotiation and settlement between the parties, some states enforce a cooling-off period (e.g., ninety days) during which litigation cannot begin. A malpractice claimant must give the doctor or hospital a formal notice of intent to file a suit. During the cooling-off period, the **statute of limitations** does not run—it is **tolled**—so that the plaintiff is not placed at a disadvantage by waiting to file. The statute of limitations is a law that designates a time period within which a lawsuit must be commenced or it can never be brought.
- Requiring **alternative dispute resolution** (ADR). A state may require the parties to attempt to resolve their dispute by using alternative dispute resolution before being allowed to litigate in court. ADR can take a number of formats. The state might have a system of **screening panels** that try to weed out frivolous cases before they are brought to court for trial. A panel could consist of a group of neutral attorneys and physicians who examine the evidence, consult with medical experts, and decide whether the patient was a victim of negligence. The panel may encourage settlement or dismissal of the claim. More traditional forms of ADR are mediation and arbitration. In **mediation,** parties bring their dispute before a neutral third party—the mediator—who hears the arguments from both sides and encourages the parties to resolve the matter on their own. The mediator does not render a decision. In **arbitration,** on the other hand, the parties bring their dispute before a neutral third party—the arbitrator—who hears the arguments from both sides and renders a decision. None of these ADR proceedings are binding. They are simply steps the parties are required to try before they are allowed to bring their medical malpractice case before a court.
- Providing more information about doctors. To keep track of (and to help weed out) incompetent or unprofessional doctors, particularly those who

---

[16]Physician Insurers Association of America, supra note 10.

move from one state to another, a **National Practitioner Data Bank** was created to collect information about doctors who had been defendants in malpractice cases and who had paid claimants through settlement or litigation. A hospital is required to check the information in the Data Bank whenever a doctor seeks appointment or reappointment to its medical staff.

- Adopting the **English rule.** To discourage the filing of frivolous malpractice lawsuits, one state has adopted the English rule under which the party who loses the trial must pay both parties' attorney fees and other legal expenses. With some exceptions, most of our courts follow the American rule under which each side pays its own legal expenses.
- Imposing limited **no-fault systems** of medical malpractice. Under no-fault, a victim of medical incompetence (malpractice) receives compensation from insurance whether or not negligence or fault can be proven. In the few states that have experimented with no-fault, it is applied in only limited kinds of cases such as those involving brain-damaged newborns.
- Considering **enterprise liability.** One of the most radical proposals is called enterprise liability. It would allow injured patients to sue either the hospital where they were treated or the health plans to which doctors and other providers subscribe. Individual doctors would no longer be subject to malpractice lawsuits. One variation on this proposal would permit courts to hold health plans strictly liable for all medical injuries suffered by their beneficiaries, regardless of whether the injury was a result of negligent care. The more traditional enterprise liability proposal, however, would require a determination of negligence before a hospital's managed care organization would be held liable for a patient's injury. Enterprise liability has not been enacted to date.[17]

The turmoil—along with proposals for further change and reform—continues today.

LEGAL MALPRACTICE

Legal malpractice refers to professional misconduct or wrongdoing by attorneys, primarily negligence. As we have seen, negligence is the failure to use reasonable care (see Chapter 10). Because attorneys have specialized skill and knowledge, they are measured by what a reasonable attorney would have done with that skill and knowledge. Attorneys, like doctors, must use the skill and learning commonly possessed by members of the profession in good standing. Liability for negligence will not automatically result when an attorney makes a mistake or loses the case. Unless the attorney specifically guarantees a result, the standard of care will be reasonableness, not warranty. Expressed in greater detail, the standard is as follows:[18]

> Ordinarily when an attorney engages in the practice of the law and contracts to prosecute an action in behalf of his client, he impliedly represents that (1) he possesses the requisite degree of learning, skill, and ability necessary to the practice of his profession and which others similarly situated ordinarily possess; (2) he will exert his best judgment in the prosecution of the litigation entrusted to him; and (3) he will exercise reasonable and ordinary care and diligence in the use of his skill and in the application of his knowledge to his client's cause.
>
> An attorney who acts in good faith and in an honest belief that his advice and acts are well founded and in the best interest of his client is not answerable for a mere error of judgment or for a mistake in a point of law which has not been settled by the court of last resort in his State and on which reasonable doubt may be entertained by well-informed lawyers.

---

[17]Risa B. Greene, *Federal Legislative Proposals for Medical Malpractice Reform: Treating the Symptoms or Effecting a Cure?* 4 Cornell Journal of Law and Public Policy 563 (Spring, 1995).
[18]*Hodges v. Carter,* 239 N.C. 517, 519–20, 80 S.E.2d 144, 145–46 (1954).

FIGURE 12–10
Professional liability claims against law firms by error group.

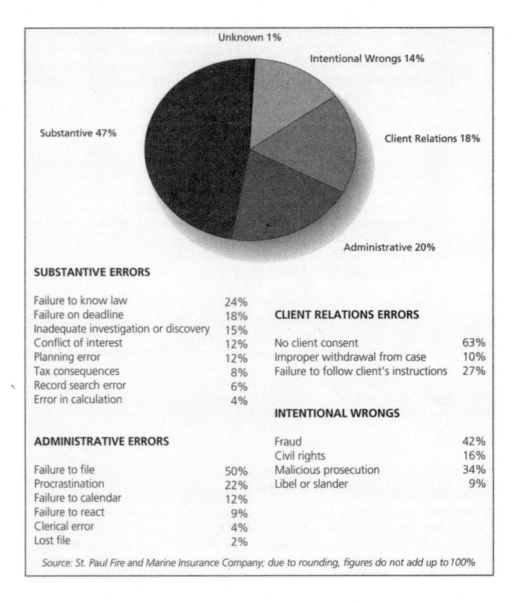

SUBSTANTIVE ERRORS

Failure to know law	24%
Failure on deadline	18%
Inadequate investigation or discovery	15%
Conflict of interest	12%
Planning error	12%
Tax consequences	8%
Record search error	6%
Error in calculation	4%

CLIENT RELATIONS ERRORS

No client consent	63%
Improper withdrawal from case	10%
Failure to follow client's instructions	27%

INTENTIONAL WRONGS

Fraud	42%
Civil rights	16%
Malicious prosecution	34%
Libel or slander	9%

ADMINISTRATIVE ERRORS

Failure to file	50%
Procrastination	22%
Failure to calendar	12%
Failure to react	9%
Clerical error	4%
Lost file	2%

Source: St. Paul Fire and Marine Insurance Company; due to rounding, figures do not add up to 100%

Conversely, he is answerable in damages for any loss to his client which proximately results from a want of that degree of knowledge and skill ordinarily possessed by others of his profession similarly situated, or from the omission to use reasonable care and diligence, or from the failure to exercise in good faith his best judgment in attending to the litigation committed to his care.

If attorneys hold themselves out to the public as specialists in a particular area of the law (e.g., criminal law or patent law), the standard of competence is not the general practitioner handling such a case, but the specialist in good standing using the skill and knowledge normally possessed by such specialists. The *Restatement of Torts 2d* phrases the standard this way:[19]

Special representation. An actor undertaking to render services may represent that he has superior skill or knowledge, beyond that common to his profession or trade. In that event he incurs an obligation to the person to whom he makes such a representation, to have, and to exercise, the skill and knowledge which he represents himself to have.

---

[19]*Restatement (Second) of Torts* § 299A, comment d (1965).

One way to gauge the kinds of malpractice with which attorneys have been charged is to examine the claims handled by insurance companies that sell liability insurance to attorneys. See Figure 12–10 for the breakdown in the categories of substantive errors, administrative errors, client relations errors, and intentional wrongs committed by attorneys.

Mistakes

A distinction should be made between:

- a reasonable mistake that could have been made by any attorney in good standing using the skill and knowledge normally possessed by attorneys, and
- an unreasonable mistake that would not have been made by an attorney in good standing using the skill and knowledge normally possessed by attorneys.

Only the latter kinds of mistakes will lead to liability for negligence. (See Figure 12–11.) The test is not whether the average attorney would have made the mistake. The focus is on the attorney in good standing using the knowledge and skill normally possessed by attorneys.[20]

FIGURE 12–11 Mistakes of attorneys.

Kind of Mistake	Examples	Negligence Consequences
1. Technical/mechanical mistake *not* involving the exercise of judgment.	• Attorney forgets to file an action and client is thereby barred by the statute of limitations. • Attorney forgets to appear in court and client thereby has a default judgment entered against him or her.	It is relatively easy for a client to win a negligence action against an attorney based on this kind of mistake. (See, however, the discussion on causation.)
2. Tactical mistake involving the exercise of judgment and discretion in a relatively uncomplicated area of the law.	• Attorney decides not to call a certain witness who would have been able to provide valuable testimony. • Attorney does not object to the introduction of certain evidence at trial from the other side and thereby waives the right to object on appeal.	It is difficult for a client to win a negligence action against an attorney based on this kind of mistake unless what the attorney did or failed to do was blatantly contrary to what would be considered good or competent practice. (See discussion on causation.)
3. Tactical mistake involving the exercise of judgment and discretion in a complicated area of the law.	• Attorney fails to challenge the constitutionality of a guest statute. • Attorney calls an expert witness on a design defect in a products liability case and the witness gives very damaging testimony to the attorney's own case.	It is almost impossible for a client to win a negligence action against an attorney based on this kind of mistake. This is so not only because of the complexity of the area of the law, but also because of the difficulty of proving causation, i.e., that the mistake caused the client any harm. (See discussion on causation.)

---

[20]*Restatement (Second) of Torts* § 229A, comment e (1965).

It is important to keep in mind that the attorney is the agent of the client. While the attorney is representing the client (within the scope of the attorney's "employment"), the client is bound by what the attorney does. This includes both successes and mistakes. Hence, if the attorney makes a mistake and the client loses the case as a result, the recourse of the client is to sue the attorney and try to establish that an unreasonable mistake was made that would not have been made by an attorney in good standing using the skill and knowledge normally possessed by attorneys.[21]

There are three basic interrelated errors in the way an attorney practices law that often lead to successful negligence actions against the attorney. Errors in practicing law that can make an attorney vulnerable include:

- **Taking Too Many Cases**
  There are strong temptations to keep adding new cases to the attorney's case-load. Although one might admire "busy" attorneys, the danger exists that they have more than they can competently handle.
- **Failure to Do More Than Minimal Legal Research**
  Legal research can be difficult and time-consuming. It is much easier "to practice out of one's hip pocket." Courts, however, have warned attorneys that the failure to do needed legal research is a strong indication of incompetence.
- **Failure to Consult and/or Associate with More Experienced Attorneys**
  The tendency in legal practice is for an attorney to concentrate on certain kinds of cases—to specialize. Even many general practitioners will emphasize one or two categories of cases in their practice. What happens when the client with a new kind of case walks into the office? If the case is taken and the attorney does *not* have enough time to learn the theory and practicalities of a new area of the law, it is strong evidence of incompetence if the attorney fails to consult with attorneys who are experienced in that area of the law, and perhaps, with the client's consent, to work with such an attorney on the case.

Causation

To win a negligence case against an attorney, it is not enough to establish that the attorney made an unreasonable mistake; causation must also be proven. For certain kinds of attorney errors, a **trial within a trial** must occur.

> **EXAMPLE:** George hires John Taylor, Esq. to represent him in a products liability case against XYZ Motor Company. The car George bought from XYZ exploded, causing $100,000 in injuries to George. John Taylor is so tied up with other cases that he neglects to file the action within the statute-of-limitations period. Hence, George can no longer sue XYZ Motor Company; the action is barred. George now sues John Taylor for negligence (malpractice) in letting the statute of limitations run. Assume that the error of John Taylor was quite unreasonable. What can George recover from John Taylor? $100,000? Is that what he lost? Did John Taylor *cause* $100,000 in damages? The answer is yes—but only if George can establish:
>
> 1. that he would have won his case against XYZ Motor Company, and,
> 2. that the recovery from XYZ would have been at least $100,000.
>
> In George's negligence suit against John Taylor, George must establish that he would have won the $100,000 suit against the XYZ Motor Company if the suit had not been barred by the statute of limitations. This, then, is the suit within the suit, or the trial within a trial.

---

[21]Depending on the kind of mistake the attorney made, some courts might permit the client to "undo" the error by correcting it, e.g., permit a client to file a document even though the client's attorney had negligently allowed the deadline for its filing to pass. It is rare, however, that the courts will be this accommodating. A client will have to live with the mistakes of his or her attorney and seek relief solely by suing the attorney for negligence. See R. Mallen & V. Levit, *Legal Malpractice* 45ff (1977).

The difficulty of establishing causation can be further complicated: Suppose XYZ Motor Company is bankrupt. Even if George could have won a $100,000 judgment against XYZ, he would have been able to collect nothing or very little. Hence, it cannot be said that John Taylor's negligence in waiting too long to file the action caused George a $100,000 loss. In such circumstances, George would have to prove (in his action against John Taylor) that there would have been something to collect from XYZ Motor Company.

Indemnity

Indemnity is the right to have another person pay you the full amount you were forced to pay. In tort law, when one party is liable to a plaintiff solely because of what someone else has done (e.g., employer is liable because of what employee did), the party who is liable, and who pays as a result of the liability, can often receive indemnity from the person whose action produced the liability. Assume that an attorney is representing a *defendant* in a suit brought against the latter. Assume further that the defendant loses the suit and must pay the judgment solely because of the negligence of the attorney. In some states, the defendant can ask a court to force the attorney to *indemnify* him or her based upon the above definition of indemnity.[22]

Karen Smith, Esq. represents Jim Noonan in the preparation of a will. It was Jim's intent that his friend Ralph Skidmore receive a bequest of $10,000. Karen Smith drafts the will. After Jim dies, it is discovered that Karen Smith made a mistake in drafting the will that resulted in Ralph receiving nothing.	**ASSIGNMENT** **12.10**

a. Make an argument that Karen Smith did not *cause a* $10,000 loss to Ralph. Assume that Jim died at the age of 35, one year after the will was drafted, and that his death was a surprise to everyone—including Jim.

b. Are there any other problems that might prevent Ralph from being able to bring a negligence action against Karen Smith?

Paralegals

Two questions should be kept in mind. First, when are paralegal employees *personally liable* for their torts? Second, when are employers *vicariously liable* for the torts of their paralegal employees? (As we saw earlier in the chapter, **vicarious liability** simply means being liable because of what someone else has done or failed to do.) The short answer to the first question is: *always.* The short answer to the second question is: *when the wrongdoing by the paralegal was within the scope of employment.*

Several different kinds of wrongdoing are possible. The paralegal might commit:

- the tort of negligence
- an intentional tort, such as battery
- an act that is both a crime (such as embezzlement) *and* an intentional tort (such as conversion)

A client who is injured by any of these torts can sue the paralegal in the same manner that a patient in a hospital can sue a nurse. Paralegals are not relieved of liability simply because they work for, and function under the supervision of, an attorney. Every citizen is *personally* liable for the torts he or she commits. The same is true of the crimes they commit.

Next we turn to the employers of paralegals. Are they *also* liable for wrongdoing committed by their paralegals? Assume that the supervising attorneys did nothing

---

[15]R. Mallen & V. Levit, *Legal Malpractice* 124 (1977).

wrong themselves. For example, the attorney did not commit the tort or crime as an active participant with the paralegal, or the attorney was not careless in selecting and training the paralegal. Our question is: Can an attorney be liable to a client solely because of the wrongdoing of a paralegal? As we noted, such *vicarious liability* exists when one person is liable solely because of what someone else has done or failed to do. The answer to our question is found in the doctrine of respondeat superior, which makes employers responsible for the torts of their employees or agents when the wrongdoing occurs within the scope of employment.[23]

Hence, if a paralegal commits a tort within the scope of employment, the client can sue the paralegal or the attorney, or both. This does not mean that the client recovers twice; there can be only one recovery. The client is simply given a choice in bringing the suit. In most cases, the primary target of the client will be the employer, who is the so-called deep pocket, the one who has resources from which a judgment can be satisfied.

Finally, we need to examine what is meant by "scope of employment." Not every wrongdoing of a paralegal is within the scope of employment simply because it is employment related. The test is as follows: Paralegals act within the scope of employment when they are furthering the business of their employer, which for our purposes is the practice of law. (See Figure 12–7 for more on scope of employment.) Slandering a client for failure to pay a law firm bill certainly furthers the business of the law firm. But the opposite is probably true when a paralegal has an argument with a client over a football game and punches the client during their accidental evening meeting at a bar. In the latter example, the client could not sue the paralegal's employer for the intentional tort of battery under the doctrine of respondeat superior, because the battery was not committed while furthering the business of the employer. Only the paralegal would be liable for the tort under such circumstances.

When a paralegal commits negligence within the scope of employment, the attorney becomes as fully responsible for what the paralegal did as if the attorney had personally committed the negligence. The work product of the paralegal blends into the work product of the attorney. Clients hiring a law firm are led to believe that the services to be received would be of professional quality, regardless of what tasks might be delegated to employees within the firm. Hence, when a client is harmed by a negligent mistake committed by a paralegal and brings a negligence action against the attorney, negligence will be measured by what a reasonable attorney would have done, not by what a reasonable paralegal would have done.

ASSIGNMENT **12.11**	Mary Smith is a paralegal at the XYZ law firm. One of her tasks is to file a document in court. She negligently fails to do so. As a result, the client loses the case through a default judgment entered against the client. What options are available to the client?

There have not been many tort cases in which paralegals have been sued for wrongdoing in a law office. Yet as paralegals become more prominent in the practice of law, more are expected to be named as defendants. Michael Martz, General Counsel of the Mississippi Bar Association, makes the unsettling point that the prominence of paralegalism means there will be more suits against them. "As paralegals become more and more professional and proficient, they . . . will become better targets for

---

[23]We are talking here of vicarious *civil* liability, or more specifically, the tort liability of employers because of the torts committed by their employees. Employers are not subject to vicarious *criminal* liability. If a paralegal commits a crime on the job, only the paralegal goes to jail (unless the employer actually participated in the crime).

disgruntled clients looking for someone to sue."[24] The most common kinds of cases involving paralegals have occurred when the paralegal was a notary and improperly notarized signatures under pressure from the supervising attorney.

SUMMARY

In most negligence cases, the standard of care is reasonableness, which is determined by assessing the totality of circumstances. The defendant has breached this standard if his or her acts and omissions are substantially different from those of a reasonable person under the same or similar circumstances. Reasonableness is determined by comparing what this person would have done to what the defendant did or failed to do. A reasonable person is someone who can make mistakes and cause injury, but never due to carelessness. If the danger of a foreseeably serious accident outweighed the burden or inconvenience of taking precautions to avoid the accident, the reasonable person would take those precautions. In assessing a burden or inconvenience, the court will consider cost, time, and effectiveness. The more important or socially useful the activity, the more likely it is that a reasonable person would take the risks involved in the activity.

Physically, a reasonable person has the same strengths and weaknesses as the defendant. Mentally, the reasonable person has the basic knowledge and intelligence needed in everyday life, even if the defendant does not. If the defendant has more than the minimum (e.g., has professional) knowledge and skills, then the reasonable person is deemed to have the same knowledge and skills. If the defendant is a child, the standard is a reasonable child of the age and intelligence of the defendant, unless the defendant was engaging in an adult activity, in which case the standard is the reasonable adult.

Res ipsa loquitur allows a jury to infer unreasonableness simply by reason of the fact that the accident happened, even if there is no direct or specific evidence of unreasonableness. It must be more likely than not that the accident was due to someone's unreasonableness—the defendant's—and the plaintiff must not be a responsible cause of the accident.

Custom and usage (what others in the business or industry are doing) is one of the factors a court will consider in assessing reasonableness. Following custom and usage does not necessarily make a defendant reasonable. Under the breach-of-duty equation, a defendant may be required to do more than what everyone else is doing.

If the defendant has violated a statute, the unexcused violation might be considered negligence per se, create a presumption of negligence, or simply be some evidence of negligence. We need to ask if the violation caused the accident, if the plaintiff is within the class of persons protected by the statute, and if the plaintiff has suffered the kind of harm the statute was intended to avoid. Conversely, the defendant's compliance with a statute does not automatically establish reasonableness. Compliance may merely constitute some evidence of reasonableness. Reasonable care under the circumstances may call for more than the minimum requirements imposed by the statute.

Guest statutes often refuse to impose liability on hosts unless the latter have committed gross negligence or have been willful, wanton, or reckless. Under the doctrine of respondeat superior, employers are vicariously liable for the negligence committed by their employees within the scope of employment. There is no vicarious liability for the negligence committed by independent contractors unless the latter are performing non-delegable duties or inherently dangerous work. Participants in a joint enterprise are vicariously liable for the negligence committed by

---

[24]Michael Martz, *Ethics, Does a Paralegal Need Insurance?* The Assistant, p. 13 (Mississippi Ass'n of Legal Assistants, Fall 1993).

each other in furtherance of the objective of the enterprise. Under the family purpose doctrine, the owner of a car who makes it available for family (nonbusiness) use will be vicariously liable for the negligence of a driver in the owner's immediate household who was using the car for a family purpose at the time of the accident with the express or implied consent of the owner. Unless modified by statute, parents are not vicariously liable for the torts of their children.

A physician-patient relationship arises when a doctor undertakes to render medical services in response to an express or implied request for services by the patient or by the patient's guardian. Doctors are not liable for breach of contract unless they guarantee a result. Nor is there strict liability. They are held to the standard of negligence: A doctor must use the skill and learning commonly possessed by members of the profession in good standing. States disagree on whether this standard of care is judged from a national or a local perspective. The failure of a doctor to provide informed consent on the treatment proposed may lead to a battery claim, although more often the claim is negligence. The amount of disclosure a doctor must provide is determined by a reasonable patient standard or by a reasonable doctor standard. Consent forms must not be so ambiguous as to amount to a blanket authorization of whatever the doctor thinks is wise to do.

Critics say that medical malpractice law causes doctors to practice defensive medicine, increasing the cost and unavailability of coverage. Proposals for reform have included damage caps, fee caps (particularly on the contingent fee), collateral source offsets, cooling-off periods, alternative dispute resolution, a National Practitioner Data Bank, the English rule, limited no-fault systems, and enterprise liability.

To determine an attorney's negligence liability, the standard of care is the skill and knowledge commonly possessed by attorneys in good standing. Every mistake made by an attorney will not necessarily lead to negligence liability. It must be an unreasonable mistake that actually causes the client a loss. If a paralegal commits a tort, such as negligence, he or she is personally liable to the defendant. Under the theory of respondeat superior, the supervising attorney is also liable for the wrong committed by the paralegal if it occurred within the scope of employment. When a client sues a law firm because of harm caused by paralegal negligence, the firm is held to the standard of what a reasonable attorney should have done, not what a reasonable paralegal should have done.

KEY TERMS

Negligence: Element III: Proximate Cause

Chapter Outline

- Introduction
- Cause in Fact
- Cut-Off Test of Proximate Cause
- Overview of Steps Needed to Analyze Proximate Cause

INTRODUCTION

Proximate cause[1] involves two separate questions, only one of which deals with causation. The two questions are:

1. The causation question (*cause in fact*):
   Did the defendant cause the plaintiff's injury?
2. The policy question (a *cut-off test*):
   At what point will the law refuse to hold the defendant responsible for the injury or injuries that he or she has in fact caused?

In the vast majority of negligence cases, the policy question does not need to be considered. Defendant breaks plaintiff's leg in an automobile accident in which the defendant is driving at an excessive rate of speed. We do not need a cut-off test once we establish that the defendant in fact caused plaintiff's leg injury. There is no reason to refuse to hold the defendant responsible. The defendant is the proximate cause of the leg injury in this case. The two-fold questions of proximate cause become critical in two main situations:

- when the injury suffered by the plaintiff appears to be unusual or unexpected, *or*
- when other causes join the defendant in a chain-type sequence

Assume that Sam unreasonably drives his car down the street at an excessive rate of speed and hits the plaintiff, breaking the latter's leg. While the plaintiff is lying in the road, a second car runs over the plaintiff's arm, and disappears. When the ambulance finally arrives and takes the plaintiff to the hospital, a nurse carelessly treats the

---

[1]Sometimes referred to as **legal cause.**

plaintiff, causing injury to the plaintiff's knee. Assume that *only* Sam is sued for negligence. The proximate cause issue is two-fold:

1. **Cause in Fact:**
   a. Did Sam cause the original leg injury by hitting the plaintiff?
   b. Did Sam cause the arm injury when the second car ran over the plaintiff's arm?
   c. Did Sam cause the knee injury that resulted from the nurse's carelessness?
2. **Policy (cut-off):**
   Should Sam be responsible for *all* the injury or injuries that he has in fact caused? Should Sam be liable for what the nurse did and for what the second car did, as well as for what he directly did himself when he hit the plaintiff? Did Sam proximately cause the arm and knee injuries as well as the original leg injury?

The tests of proximate cause, outlined in Figure 13–1, will answer all of these questions. We need to examine these tests as well as some important modifications or exceptions to them.

CAUSE IN FACT

The **but-for test** and the **substantial factor test** are alternative tests that courts often use to determine whether the defendant was the cause in fact of the plaintiff's injury. As we shall see, the substantial factor test is fully adequate and often easier for a plaintiff to establish. It is important, however, that you understand both tests.

The but-for test asks the following question: Would the plaintiff have been injured but for what the defendant did or failed to do? Under this test, if the plaintiff would have been injured regardless of what the defendant did or failed to do, the defendant did not cause the injury.

> **EXAMPLES:**
>
> - Dwayne is an ambulance driver. One day he gets a call from the plaintiff's home for an ambulance to take the plaintiff to the hospital. Dwayne takes the call at 9:00 A.M. Because of Dwayne's careless driving, he arrives at the plaintiff's home 45 minutes later than he would have arrived if he had not been careless. When he does arrive, the plaintiff is already dead. According to the coroner's report, the plaintiff died at 9:01 a.m. Dwayne was not the cause in fact of the death. Dwayne was careless and unreasonable in driving to the plaintiff, but the plaintiff would have died even if Dwayne had driven with great caution and skill. But for what Dwayne did or failed to do, the plaintiff would still have been dead when he arrived to take her to the hospital. Hence, there was not cause in fact.
> - Mary is a doctor whose license to practice medicine has been suspended for a year because of the illegal prescription of drugs to several

FIGURE 13–1 The tests of proximate cause.

1. The Cause-in-Fact Tests
a. But-for test[2] (used when there is only one alleged cause): Is it more likely than not that but for the defendant's unreasonable acts or omissions, the injury would not have been suffered by the plaintiff?
b. Substantial factor test (used when there is more than one alleged cause): Is it more likely than not that the defendant's unreasonable acts or omissions had a significant role in producing the injury suffered by the plaintiff?
2. The Cut-off Test: Is the injury suffered by the plaintiff the *foreseeable consequence* of the *original risk* created by the defendant's unreasonable acts or omissions?

[2]Also referred to as the **sine qua non test.**

patients. In secret, however, Mary continues her practice. During this time, she performs a routine operation on George. George suffers serious complications following the operation and dies. His estate sues Mary for negligence. At the trial there is no evidence that Mary was careless or unreasonable in performing the operation. The estate introduces evidence that Mary performed the operation while her license was suspended. The lack of a license, however, was not the cause in fact of George's death. Even if Mary had had a license, the death would still have occurred. But for Mary's not having a license, it cannot be said that George would not have died. There was no evidence that Mary did not use adequate professional skill in performing the operation. It may be that a separate criminal proceeding can be brought against Mary for practicing without a license, but the estate loses its negligence action for failure to establish cause in fact.

- Sam carelessly drives his car into Fred's barn. But for the way Sam drove, the damage to the barn would not have occurred. Sam, therefore, is the cause in fact of the damage to Fred's property.

The but-for test is sufficient for most tort cases on the issue of causation. This includes negligence cases as well as those charging intentional torts or strict liability torts. There is, however, an alternative test: the defendant will be considered the cause in fact of the plaintiff's injury if the defendant was *a substantial factor* in producing the injury. Every time you establish cause in fact by the but-for test, you certainly have established that the defendant was a substantial factor. But the converse is not necessarily true:

EXAMPLE: Helen and Jane carelessly shoot their hunting guns at the same time through some bushes, trying to hit an animal. Both bullets, however, hit plaintiff, who is killed instantly. Either bullet would have killed the plaintiff. Here, the but-for test leads to a bizarre result. Helen says, correctly, that but for her bullet, the plaintiff would have died anyway. Jane says, correctly, that but for her bullet, the plaintiff would have died anyway. Hence, both use the but-for test to show that she individually was not the cause in fact of the plaintiff's death.

The plaintiff's estate would not be able to win a negligence action against anyone if the but-for test were the only test to determine cause in fact in such a case. Hence the need for an alternative test. If either Helen or Jane was *a substantial factor* in producing the death, then either one is the cause in fact of the death. When two people fire a bullet at a person who is killed by the impacts, the law will say that they are both substantial factors in producing the death. In this case, therefore, the substantial factor test leads to the establishment of cause in fact, even though the but-for test would not do so.

It is usually easier for a plaintiff to establish cause in fact by the substantial factor test than by the but-for test, but in most cases, both tests will lead to the same result. In tort law, it is sufficient if the plaintiff proves cause in fact by the broader substantial factor test. *In analyzing any tort problem on the issue of cause in fact, you should apply both tests, but always keep in mind that the substantial factor test will be sufficient.* Plaintiffs will have a stronger case if they can show cause in fact by the but-for test. Hence, you should determine whether this can be done on the facts before you. If not, move on to the substantial factor test, particularly when more than one cause has contributed to the plaintiff's injury.

Note that the substantial factor test requires only that the defendant be *a* substantial factor. It is not necessary that the defendant be the *sole* or *only* cause of the plaintiff's injury in order to be the cause in fact of the injury. It is not even necessary to show that the defendant was the dominant factor in producing the injury. Being *a* substantial factor is enough.

Phrasing the causation means asking the question by using important facts along with the legal test for causation. For example, "But for the defendant's excessive speed on a slippery road at night, would the plaintiff's car have been struck by the defendant's car?" Re-read the fact situation at the beginning of this chapter about Sam and the plaintiff whose leg, arm, and knee were injured.

a. For each of these injuries, phrase the cause-in-fact question using the but-for test (one question per injury).

b. For each of these injuries, phrase the cause-in-fact question using the substantial factor test (one question per injury).

You do not have to answer the questions; simply phrase them

Evidence of Causation

What do we mean when we say that there is evidence of causation—whether we are using the but-for test or the substantial factor test? How does one establish a connection between cause and effect? For the vast majority of cases, our most sophisticated tool in assessing causation is common sense based upon everyday experience. Our common sense depends heavily on the factors of *time, space,* and *history.* These factors present us with some fundamental hypotheses about life and human nature.

Time: When did the injury occur? After the defendant's acts or omissions? The shorter the time between the plaintiff's injury and the acts or omissions of the defendant, the more convinced we are that those acts or omissions caused the injury. The more time that elapses between the defendant's acts or omissions and the injury of the plaintiff, the more skeptical we are that those acts or omissions caused the injury.

EXAMPLES:

- Tom becomes sick seconds after drinking a beer. Common sense tells us that drinking the beer may have caused the sickness since the two events (drinking and sickness) came so close together. We would be less inclined to reach this conclusion, however, if Tom's sickness occurred two weeks later.
- Mary and Claire belong to the same social club. Mary has a pet-walking business in which all of her clients are members of the club. (Every morning, an employee of Mary's business goes to the homes of clients to get their pets for walks.) Her business drops by 80 percent within one week after Claire tells many other club members that Mary is incompetent. Common sense tells us that Claire's derogatory statement may have caused some or all of Mary's decline in business, since the decline occurred so soon after Claire made the statement. We would be less inclined to reach this conclusion if the decline occurred a year later.

In the first example, notice that we did not say that the beer caused the sickness because the sickness occurred seconds after drinking it. Nor did we say that the beer could not have caused the sickness if it occurred two weeks later. Rarely can such definitive conclusions be made on the basis of time evidence alone. All we can say is that our common sense suggests these conclusions, although we are willing to look at any other evidence that may suggest different conclusions. In the second example, we did not say that the derogatory statement caused the decline in business because the decline occurred one week after the derogatory statement was made. Nor did we say that the statement could not have caused the decline if it occurred a year later. All we can say is that time evidence is one of the relevant pieces of information that we need to consider.

Space: Did the injury occur in the same area or vicinity where the defendant acted or failed to act? The closer we can pinpoint the defendant's acts or omissions to the area or vicinity of the plaintiff's injury, the more convinced we are that those acts or omissions caused the injury. The greater the distance between the area or vicinity of the injury and the area or vicinity of the defendant's acts or omissions, the more skeptical we are that those acts or omissions caused the injury.

EXAMPLES:

- One of Bob's jobs at a printing plant is to pour a certain ink, which has a heavy odor, into the presses. Bob develops a respiratory problem. He says that the problem is due to breathing the ink fumes. Common sense tells us that the ink fumes may have caused the respiratory problem since he worked so close to the ink. We would be less inclined to reach this conclusion, however, if Bob worked 500 yards away from the presses that use the ink.

- Lena is a department store clerk where she is in charge of one of the five cosmetics counters. Occasionally she works at the other four counters. The store suspects that she is stealing cosmetics (which would constitute the crime of larceny and the tort of conversion). All of the missing cosmetics were at Lena's main counter and at those counters where she occasionally has worked. Common sense tells us that Lena may have taken the cosmetics since she was physically present at those counters where the goods were missing. We would be less inclined to reach this conclusion, however, if Lena never worked at the counters that experienced the missing cosmetics.

These observations about time and space evidence are simply hypotheses or assumptions about life and human nature. They are nothing more than points of departure in our search for causation. We must never close our mind to evidence that may point to other conclusions. Some illnesses, for example, may not appear until months or years after an accident, yet we can still be convinced that one caused the other. So, too, we can be convinced that actions taken in New York can lead to damage or injury in California. There is nothing ironclad about the hypotheses. Just as we can be convinced that the defendant has caused an injury that is far removed in time and space from what the defendant did or failed to do, so too, cases may arise in which we can be convinced that the defendant did not cause an injury that occurred immediately after the defendant's acts or omissions. The facts of each individual case must be carefully scrutinized. The predisposition of our common sense, however, tells us to begin this scrutiny with the hypotheses on time and space.

Assume that for years a railroad has stationed a guard at a point where the track crosses a highway. One day, the railroad removes the guard. Two days later, a train crashes into a car at the intersection. Was the absence of the guard the cause in fact of the injury? Was the absence of the guard a substantial factor in producing the injury? Among the evidence to be introduced by the plaintiff's attorney are time and space evidence. The attorney will present evidence to show that the crash occurred soon after the guard was removed (time) and that the crash occurred at the very intersection where the guard was once stationed (space). Common sense tells us, according to this attorney, that the accident would not have happened if the guard had been there, or at the very least, that the absence of the guard was a substantial factor in producing the crash. Time-and-space evidence is critical on the issue of causation, but not necessarily determinative. Other evidence might show that the job function of the guard was not to try to prevent the kind of collision that occurred and that even if the guard had been present, the collision would have occurred anyway. Again, the time and space evidence is but a point of departure.

Another important source of causation evidence is *history*. Here again, a basic hypothesis is in play.

History: In the past, have the same or similar acts or omissions by the defendant or people like the defendant produced this kind of injury? The more often this kind of injury has resulted from such acts or omissions in the past, the more convinced we are that the acts or omissions of the defendant caused the injury. If this kind of injury has never or has rarely been produced by such acts or omissions, we are more skeptical that the defendant's acts or omissions caused the injury.

Of course, just because something has happened in the past does not necessarily mean that it happened in this particular case. The predisposition of our common sense, however, tells us that history does tend to repeat itself. Hence, our common sense leads us to inquire about the past. In the railroad crossing case, for example, the plaintiff's attorney may try to introduce evidence that collisions between trains and cars never occurred when the guard was on duty, as a way of proving that it is more likely than not that the absence of the guard caused the collision.

Hence, evidence of time, space, and history is critical in beginning to collect evidence of causation in fact. We are drawn to search out such evidence on the basis of some basic hypotheses about time, space, and history. Such evidence will not always be conclusive—either way—on the issue of causation in fact. All of the facts and circumstances of a given case must be examined. Start your examination, however, with the evidence of time, space, and history.

ASSIGNMENT	
13.2	Re-read the fact situation at the beginning of this chapter about the plaintiff whose leg, arm, and knee were injured. Was Sam the cause in fact of each of these injuries? (Sam is the driver who initially hit the plaintiff while driving at an excessive rate of speed.)

Weight of the Evidence

Let us shift our focus for a moment away from the tests for causation in fact (but-for and substantial factor) to the **standard of proof** needed to establish causation in fact. (See Figure 13-2.) By standard of proof we mean how convincing the evidence of something must be before a fact finder can accept it as true. (The fact finder is the jury or, if there is no jury, the judge.) The amount and believability of evidence is referred to as the **weight of the evidence.** The standard of proof, therefore, can be phrased as the "weight" that evidence of something must have before a fact finder can accept it as true. Here our focus is on how convincing the plaintiff's evidence must be that the defendant was a cause in fact of the plaintiff's injury. There are several different "weights" that evidence can have. Evidence of something can be overwhelming, highly likely, more likely than not, fifty/fifty, possible, etc. In most tort cases, the minimum standard of proof that must be met is **preponderance of the evidence.** Under this standard, a party must prove that its version of a fact is more likely true than not. This preponderance-of-the-evidence standard ("more likely than not") is the minimum degree of believability (the minimum weight) that a plaintiff's evidence must have in order for a fact finder to be able to accept the plaintiff's version of who was the cause in fact of his or her injury. Using the two tests for cause in fact, the standard would be expressed as follows:

> Plaintiff must produce evidence that is convincing enough for a fact finder to conclude it is *more likely than not* that the defendant was a substantial factor in producing the injury, *or*

> Plaintiff must produce evidence that is convincing enough for a fact finder to conclude it is *more likely than not* that but for what the defendant did, the plaintiff's injury would not have occurred.

FIGURE 13–2
To prove causation, attorneys often hire consultants to help explain why and how things went wrong. If they are engineers or scientists, they are sometimes called forensic engineers or scientists. Exponent, Inc. is a company consisting of these individuals. One of the cases for which they were hired involved the death of 113 people at the Hyatt Regency Hotel in Kansas City. An estimated 2,000 people had gathered in the lobby area to enjoy a tea dance. Suddenly, the two walkways that spanned the lobby collapsed. Forensic engineers from Exponent, Inc. sifted through the wreckage for four days. Speculation that the accident had been the result of "harmonic vibrations" caused by dancers on the walkway were disproved by mathematical models of walkways and by the sequence of events. Combined testing, materials, and stress analysis led the engineers to testify that the collapse had occurred when a bolt end on a rod that attached the walkways to the ceiling had pulled through a walkway beam.

Photo courtesy of Exponent, Inc.

A mere *possibility* that the defendant was a substantial factor in producing the injury is not enough. (Or a mere possibility that but for what the defendant did, the plaintiff would not have been injured is not enough.) Anything is possible. A fifty/fifty possibility is also not enough. In mathematical terms, believability must be *at least* greater than 50 percent. This is what is meant by the more-likely-than-not standard. (See Figure 13–3.)

CUT-OFF TEST OF PROXIMATE CAUSE

As we said at the beginning of this chapter, there are two dimensions of proximate cause: a cause-in-fact question (using the but-for or substantial factor tests) and a policy question (using the cut-off test). See Figure 13–1. Once we have answered the first question by concluding that the defendant was the cause in fact of the plaintiff's injury, we then ask the policy question of whether there is a need for a cut-off of the defendant's liability. The policy question is whether the defendant should be able to avoid liability for what he or she has caused in fact. The cut-off test is whether the injury suffered by the plaintiff was the foreseeable consequence of the original risk created by the defendant's unreasonable acts or omissions. If the answer is no, liability is cut off; the defendant will *not* be liable for what he or she has caused in fact. If the answer is yes, liability is not cut off; the defendant is liable for what he or she has caused in fact.

Although the phrase "proximate cause" refers to both the cause-in-fact issue and the policy issue, you will often see the phrase used in reference to the policy issue only. In this usage, someone might ask whether the defendant was the cause in fact of the injury and whether the defendant was the proximate cause of that injury.

> **EXAMPLE:**   Cliff speeds through a red light in his truck. He hits a car proceeding on a green light in the intersection. The plaintiff in the car suffers a broken arm from the collision, and the car is demolished.

> **CAUSE IN FACT:**   "But for" the way Cliff drove, the plaintiff would not have suffered the broken arm nor the property damage to the car; Cliff was certainly a substantial factor in producing the personal and property damage. Cliff is the cause in fact of both.

–3 Weight of the evidence on cause in fact: Eight possibilities.

HE BUT-FOR TEST:	USING THE SUBSTANTIAL FACTOR TEST:	CONSEQUENCES
1. The evidence is overwhelming that but for what the defendant did, the plaintiff's injury would not have occurred.	1. The evidence is overwhelming that the defendant was a substantial factor in producing the injury.	*If the case falls into any one of these three categories (1–3) for the but-for test or the substantial factor test, the plaintiff has carried the burden of proving by a preponderance of the evidence that the defendant was the cause in fact of the plaintiff's injury.*
2. The evidence shows it is highly likely that but for what the defendant did, the plaintiff's injury would not have occurred.	2. The evidence shows it is highly likely that the defendant was a substantial factor in producing the injury.	
3. The evidence shows it is more likely than not that but for what the defendant did, the plaintiff's injury would not have occurred.	3. The evidence shows it is more likely than not that the defendant was a substantial factor in producing the injury.	
4. The evidence is overwhelming that but for what the defendant did, the plaintiff's injury would still have occurred.	4. The evidence is overwhelming that the defendant was not a substantial factor in producing the injury.	*If the case falls into any one of these five categories (4–8) for the but-for test or the substantial factor test, the plaintiff has failed to carry the burden of proving by a preponderance of the evidence that the defendant was the cause in fact of the plaintiff's injury. Causation, therefore, cannot be established.*
5. The evidence shows it is highly likely that but for what the defendant did, the plaintiff's injury would still have occurred.	5. The evidence shows it is highly likely that the defendant was not a substantial factor in producing the injury.	
6. The evidence shows it is more likely than not that but for what the defendant did, the plaintiff's injury would still have occurred.	6. The evidence shows it is more likely than not that the defendant was not a substantial factor in producing the injury.	
7. The evidence shows a fifty/fifty possibility that but for what the defendant did, the plaintiff's injury would not have occurred.	7. The evidence shows a fifty/fifty possibility that the defendant was a substantial factor in producing the injury.	
8. The evidence shows there is a possibility that but for what the defendant did, the plaintiff's injury would not have occurred.	8. The evidence shows there is a possibility that the defendant was a substantial factor in producing the injury.	

PROXIMATE CAUSE: Cliff is also the proximate cause of the personal and property damage. The original risk created by speeding through a red light was the risk of hitting other cars and people. The plaintiff's broken arm and demolished car are foreseeable consequences of this original risk Cliff created. Hence, there is no need for a cut-off rule. Cliff is the proximate cause of what he caused in fact.

Let us look at another case:

EXAMPLE: Jim carelessly pushes Alice, who breaks a leg. Two weeks later, while walking on crutches, Alice falls and breaks her arm. Soon thereafter, she catches pneumonia because of her general rundown condition.

CAUSE IN FACT: "But for" Jim's push, Alice would not have suffered the leg injury, the arm injury, and the pneumonia. He is also a substantial factor in producing all three. He is the cause in fact of all three.

PROXIMATE CAUSE: When Jim pushed Alice, it was foreseeable that she could break a leg bone. This was within the original risk Jim created. It was also foreseeable that such an injury would require medical attention that would lead to the use of crutches. Everyone knows that walking on crutches is difficult. It is foreseeable that someone could fall on them and suffer further injury. Hence, the arm injury was also within the original risk created by Jim. Finally, it is foreseeable that an injured person would be in a rundown condition (initially created by the leg and arm injuries) and could contract an illness such as pneumonia. There is nothing unusual about this occurring. Jim, therefore, is the proximate cause of the leg injury, the arm injury, and the pneumonia. They are all foreseeable consequences of the original risk created by Jim's carelessness.

ASSIGNMENT

13.3

Peter is a passenger in a bus that is carelessly speeding. The bus crashes into another car. Peter is forced forward, injuring his arm. Moments after the crash, lightning strikes a tree, which falls on the part of the bus where Peter is sitting, injuring his leg. Is the bus company the proximate cause of the arm injury and the leg injury?

The conclusion that defendants are liable for the injuries they proximately cause is subject to the requirement that the plaintiff must take reasonable steps to **mitigate the consequences** of those injuries. (This duty to mitigate damages is also referred to as the doctrine of **avoidable consequences,** which is discussed more fully in Chapter 14.) Plaintiff, for example, cannot refuse all medical attention and then hold the defendant responsible for the **aggravation** of the injury caused by the refusal to see a doctor.

There are two major exceptions to the general cut-off test of proximate cause. They pertain to the unforeseeability of the extent of the injuries and of the manner of their occurrence.

Exceptions to Test

"Eggshell Skull" Rule—Extent of Injury   If it is foreseeable that defendant's unreasonable acts or omissions will result in any *impact on plaintiff's body,* and this impact does occur, the defendant will be liable for the foreseeable *and the unforeseeable* personal injuries that follow. The cut-off test of proximate cause will not prevent liability for unforeseeable personal injuries that follow from any foreseeable impact on the plaintiff's body. Assume that the defendant is carelessly running down the corridor and bumps into the plaintiff as the latter is turning the corner. Plaintiff is one month pregnant at the time. The accidental bump causes a miscarriage. Or, assume the defendant is driving 15 mph in heavy traffic. For a second, the defendant carelessly takes his eyes off the road and runs into the rear of the plaintiff's car. Only a slight dent is put on the plaintiff's car. The plaintiff, however, dies because the collision activates a rare disease. In both of these examples, the plaintiff had an **eggshell skull,** meaning a very high vulnerability to injury to any part of the body. The extent of the injury was not foreseeable by the defendant. The extent of the injury was not within the risk originally created by the defendant. In both cases, it was foreseeable that the defendant would cause an impact on someone's body, but the injury itself that resulted was clearly not foreseeable. In such situations, however, the defendant "takes the plaintiff as he finds him." There is no cut-off of liability. Note again, however, that this exception to the cut-off test applies only when it is foreseeable that there will be at least some body impact on the plaintiff.

The eggshell-skull rule is not limited to impact caused by negligence or unreasonableness. If the defendant makes impact on the plaintiff's body through an intentional tort such as battery, the defendant will be liable for all resulting injuries, foreseeable or not.

Phrased another way, the eggshell-skull exception means that the defendant will be deemed to be the proximate cause of all foreseeable and unforeseeable personal injuries that result from any foreseeable impact due to unreasonable or intentional conduct by the defendant.

Often, the plaintiff with the eggshell skull has a pre-existing condition, disease, or injury that has been aggravated by the defendant. The latter, of course, will not be responsible for the original existence of the pre-existing condition, disease, or injury, but will be responsible for its *aggravation*.

Suppose that the plaintiff goes insane or commits suicide because of despair over the initial injuries caused by the defendant. Assume that there was a foreseeable impact on the plaintiff's person. Courts differ as to whether the defendant will be held responsible. Some courts would say that insanity or suicide is so extreme that the cut-off principle of proximate cause will prevent liability for such a drastic consequence. Other courts would consider the suicide to be a superseding cause (to be considered later in this chapter), which would cut off liability. Many courts, on the other hand, will carry the eggshell-skull rule to its logical extreme and hold that the defendant is the proximate cause of the insanity or the death by suicide as long as there was a foreseeable impact on the body that the defendant carelessly or intentionally created.

Unforeseeability of Manner of Injury Frequently, the precise **manner** in which the damage or injury would occur is not foreseeable.

> **EXAMPLE:** Defendant is carelessly navigating a steamboat that rams into a bridge. The plaintiff was one of the workers repairing the bridge at the time. When the boat hit the bridge, the plaintiff fell onto a blowtorch he was using, resulting in blindness in both eyes.

In this case, it was foreseeable that some damage to the bridge and some kind of injury to someone on the bridge would occur from the careless navigation of a steamboat in the area of the bridge. Personal and property damage was foreseeable. But the *manner* in which the injury would result in this particular plaintiff—falling on the blowtorch—was not foreseeable to the defendant, who did not even know that the plaintiff was there working with a torch. Drowning or a severe concussion to anyone on the bridge may have been foreseeable to the defendant, but not the manner in which the injury in fact occurred in this case. The rule in such cases is as follows:

> The manner in which an injury occurs does not have to be foreseeable in order for the defendant to be the proximate cause of the injury, as long as the harm that resulted was within the risk originally created by the defendant's acts or omissions.

This then is the second major exception to the rule that you are not the proximate cause of an injury that is unforeseeable. You can be the proximate cause of a foreseeable injury that occurs in an unforeseeable manner.

The American Law Institute, in its *Restatement of Torts*, would agree that the particular manner of the occurrence of the harm need not be foreseeable in order for the defendant to be the proximate cause of the injury (or as the *Restatement* would phrase it, the "legal cause" of the injury). It is important to the *Restatement* (and to the courts that follow it) to assess whether the injury was a normal or ordinary consequence of the risk that the defendant created. Liability should be cut off, according to this view, only if we can say that the harm that resulted was in fact **highly extraordinary**.[3]

ASSIGNMENT
13.4

Tom, an adult, gives a loaded gun to Bob, a young boy. Tom asks Bob to deliver the gun to Jack. Bob takes his friend Bill with him to make the delivery. Upon arrival, Bob accidentally drops the gun on Bill's toe. The toe breaks. When the gun falls, it discharges immediately, killing Jack. Bob suffers a nervous breakdown over the incident. Is Tom the proximate cause of Bill's broken toe? Of Jack's death? Of Bob's nervous breakdown? See *Restatement (Second) of Torts* § 281, illustration 3 (1965).

---

[3]American Law Institute, *Restatement (Second) of Torts* § 435(2) (1965).

As we examine proximate cause, it is important that this element be kept in perspective with the other elements of negligence discussed thus far—duty (Chapter 11) and breach of duty (Chapter 12). A discussion of proximate cause assumes that the plaintiff has already been able to establish that a duty of reasonable care (the first element) exists between the plaintiff and defendant, and that the defendant has breached that duty (the second element) by unreasonable conduct. Note the role that foreseeability plays in each element:

Element I: Duty
Defendant owes plaintiff a duty of reasonable care if the defendant's act or omission has created a *foreseeable* risk of injury or damage to the plaintiff's person or property (the general rule; see Figure 11–1 in Chapter 11).

Element II: Breach of Duty
Defendant breaches a duty of reasonable care by failing to take precautions against injury to the plaintiff when the *foreseeability* of serious injury outweighs the burden or inconvenience of taking those precautions (see Figure 12–3 in Chapter 12).

Element III: Proximate Cause
Defendant is the proximate cause of every injury he or she in fact caused the plaintiff to suffer if those injuries were the *foreseeable* consequence of the original risk of injury created by the defendant's acts or omissions.

The foreseeability analysis that you must do to determine whether a duty exists (first element) is substantially the same foreseeability analysis that you must do to determine whether proximate cause exists (third element), or more accurately, whether the cut-off test of proximate cause will prevent the defendant from being liable for harm he or she has caused in fact. The very definition of the cut-off test requires you to refer back to the original risk created by the defendant. The relationship between the first element, duty, and the third element, proximate cause, is so close that you will sometimes see the proximate cause issue phrased in terms of duty: was the defendant under a duty to protect the plaintiff against the injury that resulted? Always keep in mind the two exceptions that operate to establish proximate cause for injuries that in extent or manner go beyond the original risk that was foreseeable. Aside from these two exceptions, you conduct the cut-off test of proximate cause by substantially repeating the same foreseeability analysis that you used to determine whether the first element of negligence (duty) applied.

Finally, we need to examine two special problem areas:

- the unforeseeable plaintiff
- intervening causes

Unforeseeable Plaintiff

We already looked at the problem of the **unforeseeable plaintiff** when we studied duty in Chapter 11. (See Figure 11–2.) What happens when injury to someone is foreseeable but not injury to the particular plaintiff who is injured? Is a duty (first element) owed to the unforeseeable plaintiff? As we saw in Figure 11–3, the Cardozo zone-of-danger test would say no, whereas the Andrews world-at-large test would say yes. If the Cardozo view is adopted in a state, the negligence case is over. The plaintiff loses for failure to establish one of the elements of negligence (duty). If the Andrews view is adopted in a state, the plaintiff will be successful in establishing the existence of a duty and must then move to the other elements of negligence, such as proximate cause. Because of the close relationship between duty and proximate cause, as we have seen, a plaintiff who successfully establishes duty is well on the way to establishing proximate cause as well. The cut-off principle of proximate cause will prevent liability only if the injury was beyond the scope of the foreseeable risk.

Intervening Causes

An **intervening cause** is a force that produces harm after the defendant's act or omission.

> **EXAMPLE:** Car #1 crashes into plaintiff's truck. While the plaintiff's truck is disabled in the middle of the road, car #2 crashes into the truck, but does not stop. Plaintiff sues car #1.

Car #2, the hit-and-run driver, is an intervening cause. The harm it caused occurred after the defendant's act or omission that led to the initial crash. Intervening causes operate subsequent to the involvement of the defendant. We need to examine the effect of an intervening cause on the defendant's liability. This is important because often the only party available to sue is the defendant; the person or entity that is the intervening cause may have disappeared, may have no assets (i.e., be **judgment proof**), or simply cannot be sued. The question, therefore, is whether the defendant is liable for the harm he or she originally caused *as well as* for the harm caused by what intervened. Phrased another way: is the defendant the proximate cause both of the harm he or she caused and of the harm produced by the intervening cause? First, we need to distinguish four different kinds of intervening causes:

- An **intervening force of nature** is a subsequent natural occurrence that is independent of human interference; it is an act of God. For example: The ABC Company carelessly builds a dam. Slight cracks become visible. A month after the dam is built, a severe tornado hits the area and the dam collapses. The tornado is an intervening force of nature.
- An **intervening innocent human force** is a subsequent occurrence caused by a human being who was not careless or wrongful. For example: Cynthia carelessly runs into the plaintiff crossing the street. While the plaintiff is on the ground, Tom's car hits the plaintiff. Tom was driving carefully when he hit the plaintiff. Tom is an intervening innocent human force.
- An **intervening negligent human force** is a subsequent occurrence negligently caused by a human being. For example: Alex carelessly runs into the plaintiff. Plaintiff is rushed to the hospital but is given negligent medical treatment by a nurse, causing further injury. The nurse is an intervening negligent human force.
- An **intervening intentional or criminal human force** is a subsequent occurrence caused intentionally or criminally by a human being. For example: George carelessly runs into the plaintiff. While at the hospital, the plaintiff sees his archenemy, who tries to poison him. The archenemy is an intervening intentional or criminal human force.

If any of these intervening forces can be classified as a **superseding cause,** the cut-off test of proximate cause will prevent the defendant from being responsible for the harm caused by the intervening force. If the intervening force is not a superseding cause, then the defendant will be found to be the proximate cause of the harm caused by the intervening force. Our question, therefore, becomes: when is an intervening force a superseding cause?

An intervening force becomes a superseding cause when the harm caused by the intervening force is beyond the foreseeable risk originally created by the defendant's unreasonable acts or omissions, and/or when the harm caused by the intervening force is considered highly extraordinary.

Hence, foreseeability and the original risk created by the defendant again become critical factors. Alternatively, the "highly extraordinary" test of the *Restatement* that we saw earlier can be used as a guide.

Intervening intentional or criminal human forces are often considered superseding causes, because they are either outside the scope of the original risk or are highly extraordinary. Examine again the example just given involving the archenemy's attempt to poison the plaintiff in the hospital. George initially hit the plaintiff in an automobile collision and is the proximate cause of the plaintiff's injuries sustained in the collision, but he is not the proximate cause of the poisoning. The latter was highly extraordinary and far beyond the original risk that George created by his careless driving. The injuries are the natural and foreseeable consequence of bad driving. The intentional and criminal act of poisoning is not reasonably connected with George's bad driving.

Intervening intentional or criminal human forces are *not* always considered superseding causes. What the defendant does or fails to do may increase the risk of such an intervention, making the latter neither unforeseeable nor extraordinary. Suppose the defendant gives loaded guns to a group of juvenile delinquents, who intentionally shoot the plaintiff. Or suppose a motel fails to provide any security in a section of the motel where the burglary or robbery of patrons is highly likely, and such a burglary or robbery in fact occurs. In these cases, the intentional or criminal intervening force was part of the foreseeable risk created by the defendant's acts or omissions. Such intervening forces are not superseding; defendant is the proximate cause of the harm produced by them.

Intervening innocent or negligent human forces are treated the same way. If their intervention was part of the original risk, then they were foreseeable and do not become superseding causes. In those cases, for example, where the plaintiff is further injured in a hospital (whether innocently or negligently) after being brought there for treatment for the injury originally caused by the defendant, the hospital injuries are usually considered to be part of the original risk and not highly extraordinary. So, too, if the plaintiff receives a second injury by a third party (whether innocently or negligently) at the scene of the accident. In all these cases, the defendant has rendered the plaintiff highly vulnerable to further injury. It is not uncommon for individuals to receive injuries in hospitals or on the road after the first injury, although it may be highly unusual for such second injuries to be produced intentionally or criminally.

What about intervening forces of nature? Here it is important to ask whether the injury or damage is of the same kind as would have occurred if the intervening force of nature had not intervened at all. If the same kind of injury or damage results, the intervening force of nature is not a superseding cause. Suppose, for example, that the defendant carelessly leaves explosives in an area where people would be hurt by an explosion. Because of the manner of storage, assume that the explosives could detonate on their own. Hence, unreasonable storage creates a risk of serious personal and property damage to people in the area. One day, lightning strikes the explosives, leading to serious personal and property damage. The lightning may have been unforeseeable, but the damage or injury caused by the intervention of the lightning was the same kind of damage or injury that the defendant's method of storage risked. Defendant is the proximate cause of what the lightning produced. The resulting damage or injury is not highly extraordinary, even though it may have been unforeseeable that it would occur in this way.

A different result is reached in many, but not all, courts when the intervening force of nature causes a totally different kind of injury than that originally foreseeable by the defendant's act or omission. Suppose, for example, that a truck company carelessly delays the delivery of the plaintiff's food goods, and the goods are destroyed by a storm. The destruction was not within the original risk created by the defendant (spoilage due to the delay), and some courts would therefore say that the intervening force of nature was a superseding cause.

OVERVIEW OF STEPS NEEDED TO ANALYZE PROXIMATE CAUSE

- Cause in Fact
  Apply the two tests for cause in fact. First ask if the plaintiff's injury would have occurred but for the acts or omissions of the defendant. Then apply the

substantial factor test, especially when more than one cause may have produced the plaintiff's injury. Was the defendant's act or omission *a* substantial factor in producing the plaintiff's injury? Plaintiff can establish cause in fact by *either* test.

- Burden of Proof

  Determine if there is enough evidence so that the fact finder (e.g., a jury) could at least say that it is more likely than not that the defendant's act or omission was a substantial factor in producing the plaintiff's injury. Or determine if there is enough evidence so that the fact finder could say it is more likely than not that but for the defendant's act or omission, the injury would not have occurred.

- Original Risk

  Turn the clock back to the time of the defendant's original act or omission. Identify the foreseeable risk as of that time. What kind of injury or damage was foreseeable or should have been foreseeable to the defendant?

- Eggshell Skull

  Determine whether the plaintiff has an "eggshell skull," or special vulnerability to injury. Was there a foreseeable impact on his or her body? If so, the resulting injuries are proximately caused by the defendant, even if the extent of the injuries was unforeseeable.

- Unforeseeable Manner

  Determine whether injury or damage was foreseeable because it was within the original risk created by the defendant and whether the only thing that was unforeseeable was the manner in which that injury or damage occurred. If so, the defendant is the proximate cause of the injury or damage, even though the manner of occurrence was unforeseeable.

- Intervening Human Force

  Determine whether any intervening human force was a causal factor in producing the injury or damage. If so, determine whether this human force was innocent, negligent, intentional, or criminal. Was the intervening human force within the scope of the original risk produced by the defendant? Was it foreseeable to the defendant? Did the human force proceed naturally out of what the defendant did or failed to do? Affirmative answers to these questions will make the defendant the proximate cause of what the intervening human force produced.

- Intervening Force of Nature

  Determine whether an intervening force of nature was a causal factor in producing the injury or damage. If so, ask whether the injury or damage that resulted was the same kind that would have occurred if the force of nature had not intervened. If so, the defendant is still the proximate cause of the injury or damage.

- Highly Extraordinary

  Can it be said that the injury or damage was highly extraordinary in view of what the defendant did or failed to do? If not, then the likelihood is that a court will find that the defendant was the proximate cause of the injury or damage.

- Causation v. Policy

  Make sure that your analysis has not confused the causation question with the policy question of proximate cause. The causation question involves a straightforward but-for or substantial factor assessment. The policy question involves the cut-off test that will prevent defendants from being responsible for injury or damage they have in fact caused. Do not worry about the policy question if cause in fact cannot be established.

ASSIGNMENT

13.5

Examine both issues of proximate cause (cause in fact and the cut-off principle) in the following situations:

a. Tom carelessly drives his motorcycle into Dan's horse. The horse goes wild and jumps over a five-foot fence (which it has never done before) and runs into traffic. Henry tries to turn his car away from the horse and accidentally hits Pete, who is a pedestrian on the sidewalk at the time of the collision. Pete sues Tom for negligence.

b. Same facts as in (a), except that Henry just misses Pete, rather than hitting him with his car. Pete and Henry begin an argument over Henry's driving. Henry hits Pete in the jaw. Pete sues Tom for negligence.

c. Mary gives a loaded gun to a ten-year-old girl who is Mary's neighbor. The girl takes the gun home. The girl's father discovers the gun but fails to take it away from his daughter. The girl shoots Linda with the gun. Linda sues Mary for negligence.

d. Harry carelessly hits Helen, a pedestrian, with his car in a busy intersection downtown. While Helen is lying on the ground, a person in another car accidentally hits Helen, causing further injuries. This other person is a hit-and-run driver who does not stop after hitting Helen. Helen sues Harry for negligence.

e. Pat carelessly leaves her keys in her car. A thief gets in the car and starts to speed away. Moments later, the thief hits Kevin with the car one block away from where Pat parked the car. Kevin sues Pat for negligence.

f. Same facts as in (e), except that the thief hits Kevin one month after he has stolen the car, in another section of the city.

SUMMARY

Proximate cause raises a causation issue (who caused what?) and a policy issue (is there a point at which the law should cut off liability for the harm we have caused?). There are two cause-in-fact tests. First, is it more likely than not that but for the defendant's unreasonable acts or omissions, the injury would not have been suffered by the plaintiff? (This test is used when there is only one alleged cause.) Second, is it more likely than not that the defendant's unreasonable acts or omissions were a substantial factor in producing the injury suffered by the plaintiff? (This test is used when there is more than one alleged cause.) The policy test used to determine whether to cut off liability is as follows: Was the injury suffered by the plaintiff the foreseeable consequence of the original risk created by the defendant's unreasonable acts or omissions?

In assessing cause in fact, our common sense relies on time (how soon after the defendant's act or omission did the injury occur?), space (how close was the defendant's act or omission to the area where the injury occurred?), and historical data (in the past, have acts or omissions similar to the defendant's led to this kind of injury?). The standard of proof used by the fact finder to decide the cause-in-fact issue is preponderance of the evidence.

If it is foreseeable that the defendant's unreasonable (or intentional) acts or omissions will result in any impact on the plaintiff's body, the plaintiff will be responsible for the foreseeable and the unforeseeable personal injuries that follow. The manner in which an injury occurs does not have to be foreseeable in order for the defendant to be the proximate cause of the injury as long as the harm that resulted was within the original risk created by the defendant's acts or omissions. Whether an intervening force is a superseding cause depends on whether the intervention was beyond the original risk or was highly extraordinary. Intervening intentional or criminal human forces are often considered superseding, unlike intervening innocent or negligent human forces. An intervening force of nature is not a superseding cause if it creates the same kind of injury or damage that the defendant's carelessness would have caused if nature had not intervened.

KEY TERMS

proximate cause   159

legal cause   159

cause in fact   160

but-for test   160

substantial factor test   160

sine qua non test   160

standard of proof   164

weight of the evidence   164

preponderance of the
    evidence   164

mitigate the consequences   167

avoidable consequences   167

aggravation   167

eggshell skull   167

manner   168

highly extraordinary   168

unforeseeable plaintiff   169

intervening cause   170

judgment proof   170

intervening force of nature   170

intervening innocent human
    force   170

intervening negligent human
    force   170

intervening intentional or
    criminal human force   170

superseding cause   170

Negligence: Element IV: Damages

Chapter Outline

KINDS OF DAMAGES

The plaintiff in a negligence action must suffer actual harm or loss to person or property. It is not enough that the defendant has engaged in unreasonable or even reckless conduct. Without actual harm or loss, the negligence action fails. Although the focus of this chapter is on damages in a negligence action, most of the principles discussed here also apply to intentional and strict liability torts.

Damages are monetary payments awarded for a legally recognized wrong. (The word *damage* also refers to any harm or loss.) Damages are a *legal* remedy, unlike an injunction, for example, which is an *equitable* remedy.[1] There are three main categories of damages: compensatory, nominal, and punitive.

Compensatory Damages

Compensatory damages are monetary payments awarded to make the plaintiff whole, to compensate him or her for the actual loss suffered. An important purpose of tort law is to return the plaintiff to the position he or she was in before the loss. The payment of money, of course, cannot always accomplish this. The payment of

---

[1]Equity was once a court system that was separate from the common law court system. The equity courts administered equitable remedies that were based on a somewhat flexible sense of fairness as opposed to the more rigid legal remedies available in the common law courts. Today the two court systems have merged in most states so that equitable remedies and legal remedies are usually available in the same court.

compensatory damages is designed to come as close as possible to returning the plaintiff to the status quo before the accident.

Compensatory damages cover two kinds of losses: economic and non-economic. Economic losses are **out-of-pocket** items—those things the plaintiff has already had to pay for or will probably have to pay for in the future. Economic losses can be objectively verified by examining the dollar amounts you would have to pay to replace whatever was lost.

EXAMPLES:

- present and future medical expenses
- burial costs
- loss of the use of property
- costs of repair
- costs of obtaining substitute domestic services
- present and future loss of earnings, loss of business or employment opportunities

Non-economic losses, on the other hand, are those losses for which no objective dollar amount can be identified. They are subjective to the plaintiff.

EXAMPLES:

- pain
- mental anguish
- inconvenience
- loss of companionship
- humiliation
- injury to reputation

Collectively, these non-economic damages are sometimes referred to as **pain and suffering** damages.

Another important classification of compensatory damages is the distinction between general and special damages. **General damages** are those compensatory damages that usually result from the kind of harm caused by the defendant's conduct. General damages naturally follow from the harm caused by such conduct. Pain and suffering, for example, naturally follow from a severe head injury. In most states, the complaint of the plaintiff does not have to allege general damages with specificity. The law will presume that general damages result from the wrong complained of. **Special damages,** on the other hand, are compensatory damages that are peculiar to the plaintiff. They would include medical expenses, loss of earnings, insanity, etc. The law does not presume that they exist. They must be specifically pleaded in the complaint. Special damages are also called **consequential damages.**

EXAMPLE: Sam is seeing a psychiatrist to help him overcome the anxiety he feels over the negligent conduct of the defendant who almost killed Sam with scalding water in a freak accident. The cost of the psychiatrist is part of Sam's special damages. His pain and suffering due to the anxiety are part of his general damages.

Nominal Damages

Nominal damages are a small monetary payment (often $1) awarded when the defendant has committed a tort that has resulted in little or no harm so that no compensatory damages are due. Nominal damages are not awarded in negligence cases since one of the elements of negligence is actual damages. Nominal damages are awarded in intentional tort and strict liability tort cases when there has been a technical commission of the tort but no actual harm. Attorneys usually do not take cases that do not present the possibility of substantial damages since fees are often a percentage of the damages award. When nominal damages are likely, the plaintiff's incentive to bring the case is to vindicate a right, to make a public record of the defendant's misdeed, or to warn the defendant that future misconduct of the same kind will lead to further lawsuits. If the attorney is not taking such a case **pro bono** (for free), he or she is probably being paid an hourly or set fee rather than a percentage.

Punitive Damages

Punitive damages are noncompensatory damages that seek to punish the defendant and to deter similar conduct by others. Punitive damages are awarded when the defendant has acted maliciously, outrageously, recklessly, or in conscious disregard for the safety of others. Mere negligence or unreasonable conduct is not enough. Nor is intentional conduct enough unless the court can conclude that the defendant acted in a morally reprehensible way. Punitive damages are also called **exemplary damages.**

PRESENT VALUE

By the time a trial ends, the court will want to reach one number to cover all past *and future* damages in what is called a **lump sum judgment.** The alternative would be for the court to retain jurisdiction of the case to keep it open for the life of the plaintiff in order to take account of actual medical costs, loss of income, inflation, and other uncertainties of the economy. This would create chaos in the court system since no tort case would ever end. Hence, the court will want to have a lump sum judgment. Normally, this judgment is paid at one time, although some states allow the amount to be paid in periodic payments over a set time. This may be required in certain kinds of tort cases such as medical malpractice.

Parties have more flexibility when negotiating a settlement. A **structured settlement,** for example, would consist of periodic payments for a designated period of time such as the life of the victim. The periodic payments are often paid through an annuity that the defendant funds. The settlement might call for a reduced lump sum payment with the balance covered by future periodic payments through an annuity.

Whenever you are entitled to a payment now to cover something that will happen in the future, the payment must be reduced to **present value.** Suppose, for example, that on January 1, you win a bet that will entitle you to $1,000 by the end of the year, but you are to be paid on January 1. On January 1, you are *not* given $1,000. If you were given this amount on this date, you could immediately invest it so that you would end up with more than $1,000 at the end of the year. Assume that you could invest $1,000 at 6 percent. At this rate, you would have $1,060 at the end of the year (6 percent of $1,000 is $60). To give you $1,000 at the beginning of the year, therefore, would amount to a $60 overpayment or **windfall,** which is an extra amount to which you are not entitled under the original understanding of the parties.

To avoid this windfall, you are given the present value of $1,000 (also called its **present cash value**). Present value is the amount of money an individual would have to be given now to produce or generate, through prudent investment, a certain amount of money in a designated period of time. (An example of a prudent investment might be a risk-free certificate of deposit or U.S. treasury bill.) If you were given $943.39 at the beginning of the year and invested it at 6 percent, you would have $1,000 by the end of the year ($999.99). The present value of $1,000, therefore, is $943.39. This is the amount you would be given on January 1. The calculation is called *reducing $1,000 to present value,* or phrased another way, *discounting $1,000 to present value.* The amount given now depends on what rate of interest we assume would be earned. Our example used a 6 percent rate. If the rate were 8.5 percent, the present value of $1,000 would be $921.57. If you were given this amount and invested it at 8.5 percent, by the end of the year you would have $1,000 ($999.90). A computer can easily calculate present value once we know the period of time to cover and the rate of return to use. We also need to know whether to use simple interest—as in the preceding examples—or compound interest so that interest is earned on interest as the year unfolds. If compound interest is used, you earn more and therefore need less at the outset to reach a given outcome. The percentage by which you reduce the amount you want to reach is called the **discount rate.**

The same process applies in tort litigation in the award of future economic damages such as expected medical expenses and lost wages.

> **EXAMPLE:** Early in 2000, Ted negligently injures Mary. During 2000, Mary pays $15,000 in medical bills. For each year from 2001 to the end of 2004, she is expected to spend $12,500 a year in further medical expenses. Assume that the negligence trial against Ted takes place at the end of 2000, at which time her total past and future economic damages for medical expenses are $65,000.

$$
\begin{array}{rl}
2000: & \$15,000 \quad \text{(past medical expenses)} \\
2001–2004: & \underline{50,000} \quad \text{(future medical expenses; } \$12,500 \times 4) \\
& \$65,000 \quad \text{(calculated as of the end of 2000)}
\end{array}
$$

She has already incurred a $15,000 loss for 2000. There is no problem in giving her this amount. We do not need to reduce this amount to present value since it is not a future loss. But what about the $50,000 loss she is expected to incur in the future? If we give her $50,000 at the end of 2000, she could immediately invest this money and thereby have considerably more than $50,000 by the end of 2004.

To prevent this overcompensation or windfall, the future economic loss must be reduced to present value or present cash value. We discount the $50,000. What sum of money must be awarded today so that she will end up with $50,000 by the end of 2004? If we gave her $40,322.49 now and she invested it at 6 percent (simple interest), she would have $50,000 in four years ($49,999.88). In this example, therefore, the present value of $50,000 is $40,322.49, assuming a discount rate of 6 percent. The present value number would be lower if we used compound interest. Again, computer programs are available to make these calculations quickly. (For an example, see Figure 14–2 later in the chapter.)

Figure 14–1 contains an example of a jury instruction on damages. Notice that the trial judge tells the jury that it must use present value for all future economic losses. Anything lost up to the date of the trial, however, is not reduced to present value. Also note that the instructions do not tell the jury to reduce non-economic losses such as pain and suffering to present value.

PAIN AND SUFFERING

Pain is often experienced when a tort is committed, at the time of medical treatment, and while recovering. During these periods, mental suffering or distress can also occur. For example:

- fright
- humiliation
- fear and anxiety
- loss of companionship
- unhappiness
- depression or other forms of mental illness

The amount recovered for pain and suffering will depend on the amount of time it was experienced and the intensity of the experience. Also considered are the age and condition of life of the plaintiff. It is, of course, very difficult to assign a dollar amount that will compensate the plaintiff for pain and suffering. The main guide available is the amount a reasonable person would estimate as fair. (See paragraph 5 in Figure 14–1.) A minority of states permit counsel to make a **per diem argument** to the jury whereby a certain amount is requested for every day the pain and suffering

If you find that the plaintiff is entitled to a verdict against the defendant, you must then award the plaintiff damages in an amount that will provide reasonable and fair compensation for each of the following elements of loss proved by the evidence to have resulted from the negligence of the defendant:

(1) The reasonable value of medical, hospital, and nursing care, services, and supplies reasonably required and actually given in the treatment of the plaintiff to the present time, and the present cash value of the reasonable value of similar items reasonably certain to be required and given in the future.

(2) The reasonable value of working time lost to date. In determining this amount, you should consider evidence of plaintiff's earnings and earning capacity, how he or she ordinarily occupied him- or herself, and find what was reasonably certain to have been earned in the time lost if there had been no injury. One's ability to work may have a monetary value even though that person is not employed by another. In determining this amount, you should also consider evidence of the reasonable value of services performed by another in doing things for the plaintiff which, except for the injury, plaintiff would ordinarily have performed for him- or herself.

(3) The present cash value of earning capacity reasonably certain to be lost in the future as a result of the injury in question.

(4) In computing the damages arising from the future because of expenses and loss of earnings, you must not simply multiply the damages by the length of time you have found they will continue or by the number of years you have found that the plaintiff is likely to live. Instead, you must determine their present cash value. "Present cash value" means the sum of money needed now, which, when added to what that sum may reasonably be expected to earn in the future through prudent investment, will equal the amount of the expenses and earnings at the time in the future when the expenses must be paid and the earnings would have been received.

(5) Reasonable compensation for any pain, discomfort, fears, anxiety and other mental and emotional distress suffered by the plaintiff and of which the injury was a cause and for similar suffering reasonably certain to be experienced in the future from the same cause. No definite standard or method of calculation is prescribed by law by which to fix reasonable compensation for pain and suffering. Nor is the opinion of any witness required as to the amount of such reasonable compensation. Furthermore, the argument of counsel as to the amount of damages is not evidence of reasonable compensation. In making an award for pain and suffering, you shall exercise your authority with calm and reasonable judgment and the damages you fix shall be just and reasonable in the light of the evidence.

FIGURE 14–1 Jury instructions on damages.

Adapted from David W. Robertson et al. *Torts* 349–350 (2d ed. 1998) and 2 *California Jury Instructions-Civil* §§ 14.00–14.13 (7th ed. 1986) (Book of Approved Jury Instructions (BAJI) of the Committee on Standard Jury Instructions, Civil, of the Superior Court of Los Angeles County, California); and Robert E. Keeton et al. *Tort and Accident Law* 449–450 (3d ed. 1998) and *Illinois Pattern Jury Instructions, Civil* §§ 30.01–30.07, 34.01, 34.02 (2d ed. 1971).

has been endured and is expected to continue. (The per diem argument is also called the **unit-of-time argument**.) Other states, however, do not allow such arguments on the ground that they are too arbitrary.

Damages for pain and suffering are controversial. The largest portion of an award of damages is usually the amount given for pain and suffering. Juries have been known to give amounts for pain and suffering that are fifty times the compensatory damages. It is sometimes said that pain and suffering "pays the attorney fees." Most attorneys in personal injury cases are paid a percentage of what the plaintiff receives. When the attorney walks away with a large fee, it is usually due to the pain and suffering portion of the final judgment or of the settlement if the case does not go to trial. Some states have passed reform proposals designed to set limits on damages for pain and suffering in certain categories of cases. For example, a state might pass a statute that limits (i.e., **caps**) damages for pain and suffering in medical malpractice cases at $250,000. As you might expect, trial attorneys are often vigorous opponents of such statutes.

Hedonic damages are compensatory damages that cover the victim's loss of pleasure or enjoyment for life's activities such as raising children, experiencing the morning sun, reading a good book, singing in a choir, and attending college. Some courts, however, say that an award of hedonic damages is improper because they are already provided for in the award of pain and suffering. If, however, the victim dies immediately, there may have been no pain and suffering. The concept of hedonic damages is relatively new; it is unclear how many states will allow juries to consider it.

Due to medical negligence during an operation, a patient becomes permanently comatose, although she did respond to certain stimuli such as light. What damages are possible?

Before a case goes to trial, a plaintiff will usually try to settle with the insurance company of the defendant, if any. How does a claims adjuster calculate damages? Although insurance companies do not all operate in the same way, there is a rough formula that many companies use as a starting point:

A claims adjuster begins with the medical expenses. Then the intangibles—pain and other non-economic losses—are multiplied by 1.5 to 2 times if the injuries are relatively minor, and up to 5 times if the injuries are particularly painful, serious, or long-lasting. Finally, lost income is added to that amount. Several factors raise the damages formula toward the 5-times end:

- more painful, serious, or long-lasting injuries
- more invasive or long-lasting injuries
- clearer medical evidence of extent of injuries
- more obvious evidence of the other person's fault[2]

SOFTWARE

Often a law office will use computer programs to help it calculate the damages that it will request. For example, Advocate Software, Inc. has software used in personal injury cases. It can be used to:

- convert future losses to present value
- calculate life expectancy
- calculate work life expectancy
- estimate average earnings for specific categories of work
- calculate household service values
- estimate fringe benefits a worker would have received
- prepare reports to be sent to insurers for settlement negotiations

See Figure 14–2, which provides damages projections for Robert Exemplar. When planning a case, the law office needs to calculate damages based on certain assumptions such as the discount rate and the rate of inflation. Software allows the office to change assumptions quickly and easily in order to assess alternatives.

PROPERTY DAMAGE

The defendant can inflict loss to property through the commission of a number of torts, such as negligence, trespass to chattels, and conversion. The measure of damages depends on the extent of the loss caused by the tort.

Property destroyed: The measure of damages is the fair market value of the property at the time of the destruction.

---

[2]Joseph Matthews, *Taking the Mystery Out of Personal Injury Claims,* Nolo News 9 (Fall 1994).

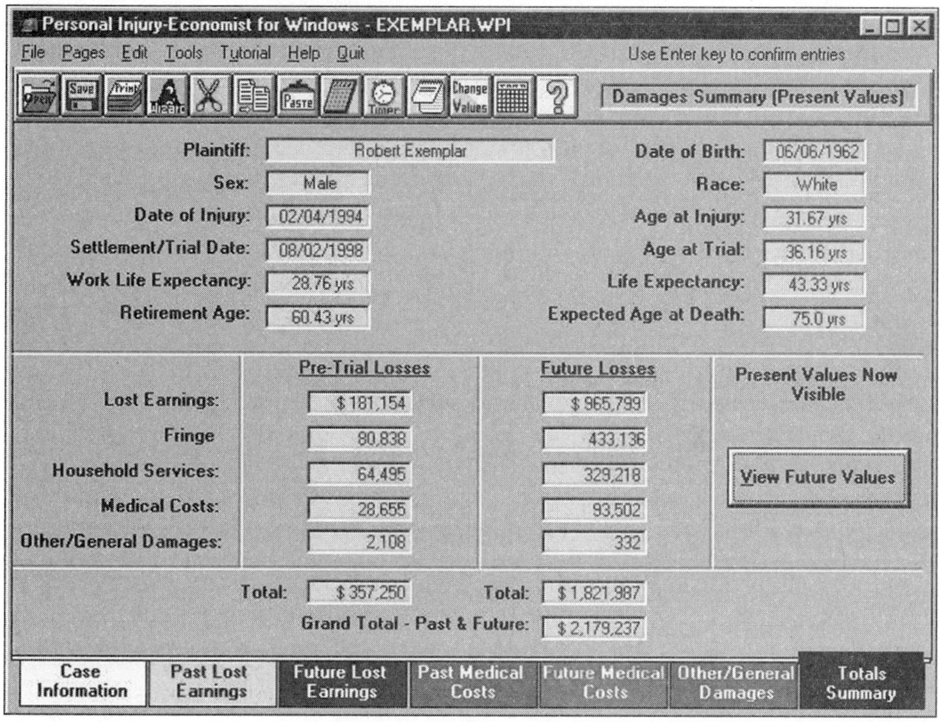

FIGURE 14–2
Software to help calculate damages.

Source: Advocate Software, Inc., Personal Injury-Economist.

Property damaged but not destroyed: The measure of damages is the difference between the fair market value of the property before the damage was done and its fair market value after the damage was done.

Deprivation of the use of the property: The measure of damages is the fair market value of the use of the property during the time the plaintiff was wrongfully deprived of its use.

Fair market value is what the property could probably have been sold for in the ordinary course of a voluntary sale by a willing seller to a willing buyer.[3] The fair market value of the use of the property might be the cost that an unpressured lessee would have to pay to rent the property from a willing lessor.

There are times when the fair market value of property is not a proper measure of damages. For example, a family portrait may have no exchange value or a dog may be trained to answer only one master. In such cases, other measures of damage might be used, e.g., replacement value, original cost, value of the time spent producing it.[4]

In addition, the plaintiff can recover for any mental distress that accompanied the destruction, damage, or deprivation of the property.

DOCTRINE OF AVOIDABLE CONSEQUENCES

Once plaintiffs have been injured, they must take reasonable steps to **mitigate the consequences** of their original injury. A defendant will not be liable for any further injury that the plaintiff could have reasonably avoided. This doctrine of **avoidable consequences** is different from contributory negligence. The latter is unreasonable conduct by the plaintiff that bars all recovery. It occurs before or simultaneously with the wrong committed by the defendant. The doctrine of avoidable consequences refers to unreasonable conduct by the plaintiff *after* the defendant has

---

[3]McCormick, *Handbook on the Law of Damages* 165 (1975).
[4]*Restatement (Second) of Torts* § 911, comment e (1979).

wronged the plaintiff. All recovery is not barred. The amount of the recovery is reduced to cover those damages the plaintiff brought on him- or herself by failing to use reasonable care.

The most obvious example is the plaintiff who fails to obtain medical help after being injured by the defendant. The plaintiff has thereby aggravated his or her own injury. The defendant will be liable for the initial injury, but not for the **aggravation** of that injury if the failure to seek medical assistance was unreasonable under the circumstances (e.g., such assistance was available, the plaintiff knew about it, and it had a good chance of helping the plaintiff).

The same principles apply to property loss. Suppose that the defendant negligently sets fire to a small portion of the plaintiff's barn. The plaintiff cannot sit by and watch the entire farm burn up if some reasonable steps by the plaintiff could have mitigated the loss (e.g., throwing an available bucket of water on the fire or calling the fire department).

ASSIGNMENT

14.2

Mary negligently hits a pedestrian. The pedestrian is rushed to the hospital and told that a blood transfusion is necessary. The pedestrian refuses on religious grounds. The pedestrian dies. For what damages will Mary be responsible in the negligence action brought by the pedestrian's estate?

COLLATERAL SOURCE RULE

When a person is injured or dies, he or she often receives funds or services from a variety of sources other than the defendant:

- the plaintiff's own medical or life insurance
- company insurance
- veteran's benefits
- Social Security
- wage continuation plans
- free medical care provided by a relative

These are all **collateral sources**—sources to which the defendant did not contribute. When the time comes to calculate the total amount in damages owed by the defendant to the plaintiff, should this amount be reduced by what the plaintiff has received through collateral sources? All states do not answer this question in the same way. Here are some of the approaches taken by different states:

- The damages are not reduced by collateral sources in any case even though the plaintiff, in effect, recovers twice for part or all of his or her injury. Furthermore, the defendant is not allowed to tell the jury about the collateral sources. The defendant is not given the benefit of the plaintiff's good luck or resourcefulness in obtaining benefits from collateral sources.
- The damages are not reduced by collateral sources in any case, but the defendant is allowed to tell the jury about the collateral sources in the hope that it might reduce the verdict because of them. (A reduction that is allowed but not required is called a **permissive offset**.)
- The damages are reduced by collateral sources, but only in certain kinds of cases such as medical malpractice. (A required reduction is called a **mandatory offset**.)
- The damages are reduced by collateral sources in all cases.
- The damages are reduced by some collateral sources. For example, the state may allow reduction of social security benefits, but not for life insurance proceeds or other death benefits.

JOINT TORTFEASORS

Joint tortfeasors fall into two categories:

* persons acting in concert to produce a wrong
* persons not acting in concert whose wrongs produce a single indivisible result[5]

The significance of being a joint tortfeasor is that each joint tortfeasor is **jointly and severally liable** for the entire harm suffered by the plaintiff. This means that the plaintiff can sue any individual joint tortfeasor for the entire harm or can join them all to recover for the entire harm. It does not mean that the plaintiff receives a multiple recovery. The plaintiff can receive only one satisfaction. Yet the plaintiff chooses whether to go after all of them or one of them. If the plaintiff sues one, but is unable to collect the full judgment, the plaintiff can sue the remaining tortfeasors until the full amount of the damages is recovered. Suppose only one joint tortfeasor pays the entire judgment. Can this person then collect anything from the other joint tortfeasors as their "share"? We will consider this separate topic later when we discuss *contribution*. It is of no concern to the plaintiff that the joint tortfeasors did not pay the judgment equally. They are left to fight this out among themselves. The plaintiff's only interest is in recovering full damages.

Persons Acting in Concert

Persons who act in **concert** to produce the negligent or intentional wrong are joint tortfeasors, and hence are jointly and severally liable for the harm they caused while on their **joint venture.**

> **EXAMPLES:**
>
> * Mary and Jane buy a truck to make deliveries together. One day, they are late in making a delivery. Mary, the driver, starts speeding. Jane urges her to go even faster. The truck negligently hits the plaintiff. Both Mary and Jane are joint tortfeasors.
> * Al and Donald agree to steal the plaintiff's goods. Al takes the goods while Donald acts as lookout. Both are joint tortfeasors.

There must be an express agreement or a tacit understanding that each will participate in the activity that produces the wrong. No such agreement or understanding would exist, for example, with a hitchhiker in the truck of Mary and Jane at the time of the accident in the first case. The hitchhiker would not be a joint tortfeasor along with Mary and Jane. To be a joint tortfeasor, the person must cooperate in the wrong, encourage it, or otherwise be an active participant. Someone who approves or **ratifies** the wrong after it is done for his or her benefit can also be a joint tortfeasor.

Persons Not Acting in Concert

Assume that two individuals, acting independently of each other, cause an accident.

> **EXAMPLE:**   Two cars carelessly collide on the highway. They both run into and kill a pedestrian.

The two drivers acted concurrently, but they were not acting in concert. There was no joint venture between them since they were operating independently. Yet, each was a substantial factor in producing a harm (the death of the pedestrian) that is **indivisible.** A result that cannot be practically divided is considered indivisible. In our example, we cannot separate the harm by determining which driver caused which

---

[5]Some authorities feel that it is a mistake to include such persons in the category of joint tortfeasors. Joint tortfeasors, according to this view, should be limited to defendants who act in concert and should not extend to independent defendants who concurrently produce the wrong.

part of the death. When two persons cause an indivisible harm, they are jointly and severally liable for the harm even though they were not acting in concert. They are treated the same as if they acted in concert.

If the harm is divisible, there is no joint tortfeasorship and no joint and several liability. Suppose that two companies independently pollute a stream with different chemicals, which can be separately identified. In such a case, each company will be liable only for that portion of the damage it caused. Suppose, however, that it is difficult to apportion the damages, because the companies used the same chemicals or because the different chemicals cannot be separately identified. The plaintiff and the defendants are in difficult positions. The plaintiff must do more than show that "somebody caused me harm." How is the plaintiff to meet his or her burden of proving what the individual defendants caused? From the defendants' perspective, it is unfair to saddle any one of them with the harm caused by the other defendants. A few courts shift the burden to the defendants and require them to establish who caused what. Most courts do not go this far; yet, they will assist the plaintiff in such cases by accepting a rough approximation of the portion of the harm caused by each defendant.

ASSIGNMENT

14.3

Ten families live in an apartment complex. They are very unhappy with the maintenance service provided by the landlord. Nine of the families begin throwing their garbage in a pile in one of the alleys next to the main building. The garbage draws many rats, which infest the apartment of the tenth family. This family sues the other nine families for negligence when it is forced to move out because of the rats. Are the nine families jointly and severally liable?

RELEASE

Satisfaction is the receipt of full payment or compensation by the plaintiff. If the satisfaction has been received from one joint tortfeasor, the others can no longer be sued by the plaintiff. A **release**, on the other hand, is the giving up of a claim. This may be done for "free" (**gratuitously**) or for money or something else of value (**consideration**).

> **EXAMPLE:** While Tim and Fred are fishing in a lake, they negligently destroy Diane's boat, which was moored at the dock. Because they were engaged in a joint enterprise, they are jointly and severally liable to her for the damage. Diane agrees, however, to give up (i.e., release) all her claims against Tim and Fred if they stop fishing in the lake where the accident occurred. They agree. If they abide by their agreement, Diane cannot later change her mind and sue them for the damage to her boat.

What happens if the plaintiff releases only one of the joint tortfeasors? Are the other joint tortfeasors likewise released? Yes. In most states, the release of one joint tortfeasor automatically releases the others. Statutes in some states change this result by providing that the release of one does not automatically discharge the others. The plaintiff under these statutes can still go after the other joint tortfeasors.

In states where the release of one discharges all the joint tortfeasors, there is a device designed to get around this result. The device works as follows: In the negotiation with one joint tortfeasor, the plaintiff does not provide a release. Rather, he or she makes a promise or **covenant not to sue** that joint tortfeasor. The covenant, unlike the release, does not act as a bar to go after the other joint tortfeasors.

CONTRIBUTION

Suppose that the plaintiff obtains satisfaction of the entire amount of damages from one of the joint tortfeasors. Can that tortfeasor now force the other joint tortfeasors to contribute their share of the amount paid? Can he or she obtain **contribution?** (Contribution is the right of one tortfeasor who has paid a judgment to be proportionately reimbursed by other tortfeasors who have not paid their share of the damages caused by all the tortfeasors.) States answer this question differently:

- Some states deny contribution among joint tortfeasors.
- Some states allow contribution only among joint tortfeasors against whom the plaintiff has secured a judgment. Those not sued would not have to contribute.
- Some states allow contribution only among joint tortfeasors who were negligent. Intentional joint tortfeasors cannot obtain contribution.

When contribution is allowed, the allocation is usually pro rata, or proportionate to the number of joint tortfeasors: two would be responsible for 50 percent each, three for 33⅓ each, etc. A few states, however, make the allocation according to the relative fault of the joint tortfeasors. Again, contribution is not a concern of the plaintiff who has received satisfaction. Contribution is a battle among the tortfeasors.

INDEMNITY

Indemnity is a device whereby one party who has paid the plaintiff can force another party to reimburse him or her for the full amount paid. Unlike contribution, which usually calls for a proportionate sharing of the loss, indemnity shifts the entire loss from the defendant who has paid onto someone else. Indemnity can arise by contract, where one person agrees to indemnify the other for any loss that results if the latter is sued. Indemnity can also arise by operation of law independent of any agreement between the parties.

> **EXAMPLES:**
>
> - An employer, who is vicariously liable for the tort committed by his or her employee, can seek indemnity from the employee. (Vicarious liability exists when a person becomes responsible for the tort or other wrong committed by another.) Seeking indemnity, of course, would be impractical if the employee has **shallow pockets** (inadequate resources from which a judgment can be collected).
> - The supermarket, which is strictly liable for a product it sold, can obtain indemnity from the negligent manufacturer who made the product.
> - One who has been passively negligent may be able to obtain indemnity from the person who was actively negligent or who acted intentionally.

The person seeking indemnity is liable for the tort. This person, however, is allowed to make someone else reimburse him or her for the judgment he or she has paid when it appears equitable to do so. The relationship between the party who has paid and the party against whom indemnity is sought must be such that in fairness we can say that the latter should pay.

SUMMARY

Damages are monetary payments awarded for a legally recognized wrong. Compensatory damages are monetary payments awarded to make the plaintiff whole for the actual loss suffered. These damages cover two kinds of losses: economic (out-of-pocket) losses and non-economic for which no objective dollar amount can be identified, e.g., pain and suffering. General damages are those compensatory damages that generally result from the kind of harm caused by the defendant's conduct. Special damages are compensatory damages that are peculiar to the plaintiff. Nominal damages are a small monetary payment awarded when the defendant has committed a tort that has resulted in little or no harm so that no compensatory damages are due. Punitive damages are noncompensatory damages that seek to punish the defendant and to deter similar conduct by others.

Future economic losses such as lost wages and medical expenses must be reduced to present value, which is the amount of money an individual would have to be given now to produce or generate, through prudent investment, a certain amount of money in a designated period of time.

Damages for pain and suffering are sometimes capped in certain kinds of cases. Hedonic damages are compensatory damages that cover the victim's loss of pleasure or enjoyment in life. Insurance claims adjusters sometimes use a rough formula in calculating the damages they may be willing to settle for. Software programs exist to help a law office calculate the variables involved in damage assessment. The measure of damages to property is often the fair market value of the property before and after the wrong. Under the doctrine of avoidable consequences, a defendant will not be liable for the additional or aggravated damages that the victim's reasonable steps could have avoided. Under the collateral source rule, the amount in damages owed by the defendant is not reduced by the injury-related funds received by the plaintiff from sources independent of the trial.

Joint tortfeasors are jointly and severally liable for the harm they wrongfully cause. They may have acted in concert or independently to produce an indivisible result. If the plaintiff receives full payment (satisfaction) from one joint tortfeasor, the other joint tortfeasors cannot be sued by the plaintiff. The relinquishment (release) of a claim against one joint tortfeasor usually acts to discharge the others. States differ on whether and when joint tortfeasors can seek contribution and thereby allocate the damages among themselves. Indemnity is the device whereby one party who has paid the plaintiff can force another party to reimburse him or her for the full amount paid.

KEY TERMS

CHAPTER

15

Negligence: Defenses

Chapter Outline

- Introduction
- Contributory Negligence
- Last Clear Chance
- Comparative Negligence
- Assumption of the Risk

INTRODUCTION

A **defense** is the response of a party to a claim of another party, setting forth the reason(s) the claim should be denied. In this chapter we consider the defenses of contributory negligence, last clear chance, assumption of risk, and the newest arrival, comparative negligence. Elsewhere in the book we examine other defenses to negligence such as the privileges and immunities covered in Chapter 23.

As we will see, the defenses of contributory negligence and assumption of risk are very harsh on the plaintiff. They nullify the effect of the defendant's negligence. To avoid the seeming unfairness of this result, doctrines such as last clear chance and, in particular, comparative negligence have been created. In many states, comparative negligence has merged into and led to the partial or total abolishment of contributory negligence and assumption of risk. We still need to cover contributory negligence and assumption of risk, however, since every state has not adopted comparative negligence, and even in states that have, contributory negligence and assumption of risk may still apply if the provisions of comparative negligence have not been met.

Here is an overview of comparative negligence and its impact on the other defenses:

Comparative negligence: The damages between the plaintiff and the defendant are allocated according to their relative fault. There is a formula that must be met before comparative negligence can apply. When the formula has been met, the damages are allocated.

Contributory negligence: *Before comparative negligence was adopted:* If the plaintiff's unreasonable conduct contributed to his or her own injury, the defendant paid no damages. Contributory negligence was a complete defense in spite of the defendant's negligence. *If comparative negligence applies:* Contributory negligence is not a complete bar to the plaintiff's recovery. The damages are allocated between the plaintiff and the defendant according to their relative fault.

Last clear chance: *Before comparative negligence was adopted:* The last-clear-chance doctrine offset the impact of contributory negligence. Contributory negligence was not a bar to the plaintiff's recovery if the defendant had the last clear chance to avoid the plaintiff's injury but failed to use this chance. *If comparative negligence applies:* There is no longer a need for the last-clear-chance doctrine since contributory negligence is no longer a complete bar to the plaintiff's recovery.

Assumption of the risk: *Before comparative negligence was adopted:* Assumption of risk was a complete defense. The plaintiff loses if he or she knowingly and voluntarily accepted the risk of being injured by the negligence of the defendant. This could occur in two ways: an express assumption of risk (the plaintiff knowingly and voluntarily accepts a risk by express agreement) and an implied assumption of risk (the plaintiff knowingly and voluntarily accepts a risk by reason of his or her knowledge and conduct). In either case, the defendant is not liable for the injury he or she negligently caused the plaintiff to suffer. *If comparative negligence applies:* The parties can still agree to an express assumption of risk. In a case of implied assumption of risk, the court will distinguish between primary assumption of risk and secondary assumption of risk. In primary assumption of risk, the plaintiff knowingly and voluntarily accepts a particular risk that the defendant did not have a duty to protect the plaintiff against. Hence the plaintiff recovers nothing. In secondary assumption of risk, the plaintiff knowingly and voluntarily accepts a particular risk that the defendant had a duty to protect the plaintiff against. The damages are allocated between the plaintiff and the defendant according to their relative fault.

We turn now to a closer examination of these principles.

CONTRIBUTORY NEGLIGENCE

Contributory negligence exists when the plaintiff's unreasonable conduct contributed to his or her own injury. Once established, the effect of this defense was drastic. It required the plaintiff to bear the full loss of his or her injury. The negligent defendant walked away without paying anything because the plaintiff was also negligent.

There were, however, limitations on the defense. The contributory negligence of the plaintiff prevented liability only when the defendant committed **ordinary negligence,** which is unreasonable conduct that is not reckless or gross. If the misdeed of the defendant went beyond ordinary negligence, the plaintiff's contributory negligence was not a defense. Conduct is **reckless** when a person acts with the knowledge that harm will probably result. **Gross negligence** is the failure to use even a small amount of care to avoid foreseeable harm. Contributory negligence was a defense to the defendant's ordinary negligence, but not to the defendant's recklessness or gross negligence. Also, contributory negligence was never a defense to any of the intentional torts the defendant might commit.

In most states, contributory negligence must be pleaded and proven by a preponderance of the evidence by the defendant. It is an affirmative defense. In a few states, however, the *plaintiff* had the burden of pleading and proving that the injury was not caused by his or her own negligence.

There are two major elements of contributory negligence:

- plaintiff's negligence (unreasonableness)
- cause in fact

Plaintiff's Negligence (Unreasonableness)

EXAMPLE: Ben is driving 40 mph in a 40 mph zone in rainy weather at night. Fred runs through a red light and hits Ben's car. Ben sues Fred for negligence. In Fred's answer, he raises the defense of contributory negligence.

In Chapter 12, we considered the standard that would apply to a defendant such as Fred who is sued for negligence: a defendant will be liable for acting unreasonably under the circumstances. This same test applies to determine whether a *plaintiff* has been contributorily negligent.

Plaintiffs must not take **unreasonable risks** of injuring themselves. There is a formula or equation that is used to determine whether someone has acted unreasonably. See Figure 15–1. This is the same equation used to determine whether the defendant was negligent or unreasonable. See Figure 12–3 in Chapter 12. The only difference between Figure 12–3 and Figure 15–1 is that in 15–1 our focus is on what a reasonable plaintiff would have done to prevent the injury to him- or herself, whereas in 12–3 the focus is on what a reasonable defendant would have done to prevent the injury to the plaintiff.

When you are charged with contributory negligence, the allegation is that you acted unreasonably for your own safety. To determine whether this was so, we apply the equation by asking a series of questions. How foreseeable was it to you that your conduct would contribute to an accident? How foreseeable should it have been to you? What kind of injury was foreseeable to you? What kind of injury should have been foreseeable to you? What were you trying to do before the accident? How important or socially beneficial was it? What kind of burden or inconvenience would you have had to endure in order to take added precautions to avoid injuring yourself? These are the questions that a reasonable person would ask.

If the danger of an accident causing serious injury to yourself outweighs whatever burden or inconvenience you would have had to go through to avoid this injury, then you were unreasonable and hence negligent in failing to take those preventive steps. The equation also considers the importance or social utility of what you were trying to do at the time. A reasonable person is more likely to take risks of injuring him- or herself when engaged in socially useful tasks than when engaged in minor or frivolous activities.

In the example involving Ben and Fred, was Ben contributorily negligent? He was driving 40 mph in a 40 mph zone in rainy weather at night. All of the circumstances of the accident would have to be considered in applying the equation. To determine the foreseeability of an accident, for example, we must know the condition of the road, the amount of traffic, visibility, etc. We have to *particularize* the event. It may be that Ben's speed was not unreasonable under the circumstances. What was Ben trying to do at the time? Simply get home as fast as possible to watch a football game, or get to a hospital as soon as possible to take a passenger to the emergency room? The more important or socially useful the goal of Ben at the time, the more reasonable it would be for him to take risks of his own safety. What was the burden or inconvenience on Ben of driving slower and hence taking less risk of injuring himself? All he had to do was not

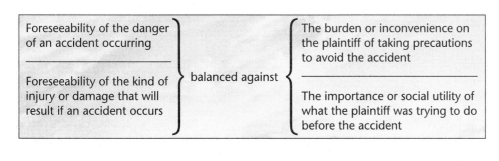

Foreseeability of the danger of an accident occurring	balanced against	The burden or inconvenience on the plaintiff of taking precautions to avoid the accident
Foreseeability of the kind of injury or damage that will result if an accident occurs		The importance or social utility of what the plaintiff was trying to do before the accident

FIGURE 15–1   Breach-of-duty equation.

press down so hard on the accelerator. A minimal burden. What was the inconvenience of doing this? Arriving a few seconds or minutes later? Whether this is much of an inconvenience may depend on where he was going and whether the extra time was needed for an important or socially useful purpose.

You will recall that special allowances are made for a defendant who has a physical defect or who is a child (see Chapter 12). The same allowances are made for a plaintiff who is alleged to be contributorily negligent. The test of reasonableness is what a reasonable person with the plaintiff's physical defects would have done under the circumstances, or what a reasonable person as young as the plaintiff would have done under the circumstances. Mental deficiencies of the party, however, are not taken into consideration. The standard of reasonableness is a mentally healthy person. Finally, if the plaintiff had any special knowledge or skills that would have helped to avoid the accident, the test of reasonableness is what a reasonable person with that knowledge or skill would have done under the circumstances.

In assessing the contributory negligence of a plaintiff, it is important to identify the particular risks that he or she undertook in order to determine whether these risks were in fact the risks that contributed to his or her injury. The general rule is that plaintiffs are contributorily negligent only if the risks they unreasonably created to their own safety are the *same* risks that eventually led to the injury.

> **EXAMPLE:** Tomas goes on Jim's land knowing that there are many dangerous animals on the land. While walking, Tomas falls into a concealed hole and breaks his leg. Tomas sues Jim for negligence. Jim raises the defense of contributory negligence.

Tomas was not contributorily negligent. Tomas may have created an unreasonable risk of injury to himself when he went on the land knowing dangerous animals were present, but this is not the particular risk that produced the broken leg—Tomas was not attacked by an animal. Nor is it significant that Tomas may have been a trespasser on Jim's land. Torts can be committed against trespassers (see Chapter 19).

Suppose that the plaintiff's negligence consists of a violation of a statute, ordinance, or regulation. A court will treat a violation by the plaintiff the same way that it will treat a violation by the defendant. The same analytical process is used whether we are assessing the negligence of the defendant (see Figure 12–5 in Chapter 12) or the contributory negligence of the plaintiff.

ASSIGNMENT 15.1

In the following situation, will the defendant be successful in raising the defense of contributory negligence?

A trucking company uses a public alley to load and unload its trucks. The manager warns a pedestrian to keep out because of the danger. The pedestrian ignores the warning and walks through. Two of the trucks collide. The collision causes a tremor in the alley. The tremor causes a large shovel to fall off a truck and hit the pedestrian. This truck was parked and was not part of the collision. The pedestrian sues the trucking company for negligence. The company asserts contributory negligence.

Cause in Fact

Once it is determined that the plaintiff was negligent (unreasonable), the next question is whether the plaintiff was a **cause in fact** of his or her own injury, along with the defendant. The question is whether both the plaintiff and the defendant caused the plaintiff's injury. The substantial-factor test is used to answer this question. The plaintiff caused his or her own injury if he or she was a substantial factor in producing the injury. The same test is used to determine whether the defendant caused the injury (see Chapter 13).

If the plaintiff acted unreasonably regarding his or her own safety, and this unreasonableness was a substantial factor in producing that injury, contributory negligence is established. It does not matter that the plaintiff was only slightly unreasonable when compared to the unreasonableness of the defendant, unless, as indicated, the defendant's unreasonableness could be categorized as reckless or gross.

In Chapter 14, on damages, we considered the doctrine of **avoidable consequences.** Assume that the defendant is liable in a case where there is no contributory negligence. Once the accident occurs, the plaintiff must take reasonable steps to mitigate or avoid aggravated or increased damages (e.g., by seeking proper medical attention). If the plaintiff does not take these steps, the defendant will not be liable for the aggravated or increased damages that could have been avoided. This is more of a damages issue than a contributory negligence issue.

Finally, the adoption of comparative negligence completely alters the impact of the plaintiff's contributory negligence. Under comparative negligence, damages are allocated between the plaintiff and the defendant according to their relative fault. Contributory negligence is no longer a complete defense if the state's comparative negligence law—to be examined shortly—applies.

LAST CLEAR CHANCE

Last clear chance is a pro-plaintiff doctrine that counteracts the drastic consequences of contributory negligence. A plaintiff found to be contributorily negligent can still recover if he or she can show that the defendant had the last clear chance to avoid the injury and failed to do so. Unfortunately, the doctrine is surrounded by a good deal of confusion, so that it is sometimes unclear whether a court will apply it.

It is important to distinguish the different predicaments in which plaintiffs can find themselves:

Plaintiff in helpless peril: A plaintiff is in **helpless peril** when his contributory negligence has placed him in a predicament that he *cannot* get himself out of. Even if the plaintiff now used reasonable care, he could not get out of the danger (e.g., plaintiff's foot is carelessly caught in a machine or in a railroad track).

Plaintiff in inattentive peril: A plaintiff is in **inattentive peril** when her contributory negligence has placed her in a predicament that she *could* get herself out of by the use of reasonable care, but the plaintiff remains negligently unaware of her peril up to the time of the accident (e.g., in a noisy section of town, plaintiff carelessly fails to hear or see a bus coming right at her on the street).

Plaintiff in Helpless Peril

If the defendant discovered the plaintiff in helpless peril and had an opportunity to avoid the accident but did not take it, then the plaintiff's contributory negligence will not bar recovery. The reason is that the defendant had and failed to take the last clear chance to avoid the injury.

Suppose, however, that the defendant did *not* discover the helpless plaintiff. Theoretically, the defendant did not have the last clear chance to avoid the accident. How can the defendant avoid what he or she does not know? Many states say that it is impossible, and hence deny the plaintiff the use of the last-clear-chance doctrine. This results in the plaintiff's loss of the case because of contributory negligence. Other states, however, take a different position, but only if the defendant *could have discovered* the helpless peril if the defendant had used reasonable care in his or her observation of the situation. For example, as the defendant railroad engineer approached the scene of the accident, the engineer failed to see the helpless plaintiff because the engineer negligently failed to maintain proper attention to the track directly in front. A few states treat "should-have-discovered" in the same way as "did-discover" and permit the plaintiff to recover in spite of the latter's contributory negligence if the defendant would have had a reasonable opportunity to prevent the accident at the last moment. The defendant must have been negligent in failing to discover the plaintiff and must have had a reasonable opportunity to prevent the accident if the plaintiff had been discovered.

Plaintiff in Inattentive Peril

If the defendant discovered the plaintiff in inattentive peril and had a reasonable opportunity to avoid the accident but did not take it, then the plaintiff's contributory negligence will not bar his or her recovery. The reason is that the defendant had and failed to take the last clear chance to avoid the injury. In other words, discovery of plaintiff in inattentive peril is treated in the same way as discovery of the plaintiff in helpless peril. The defendant does not have to have definite knowledge that the plaintiff was unaware of his or her peril, but the situation must be such that the defendant did see the plaintiff and should have known that the plaintiff was unaware or inattentive.

The most troublesome case is when the defendant failed to discover the plaintiff in inattentive peril because of the defendant's negligence at the time of the accident. Very few courts would permit the plaintiff to recover here. The negligence of both plaintiff and defendant resulted in their being ignorant of each other. Neither had the last clear chance. In most courts, therefore, the plaintiff's contributory negligence would bar his or her recovery.

ASSIGNMENT

15.2

Peter is negligently driving his car, which collides with Bill's car at an intersection. Peter is not injured, but his car is thrown onto the other side of the road, upon which Dan's car is approaching from the opposite direction. Dan is driving carelessly. Dan sees Peter's car, but instead of stopping, unreasonably thinks he can cut around Peter's car. The space is too narrow and Dan collides with Peter's car, causing Peter to break his leg. Peter sues Dan for negligence. Dan raises the defense of contributory negligence. Assess Dan's chances of succeeding with this defense.

A state that has adopted comparative negligence does not need the defense of last clear chance. When comparative negligence applies, contributory negligence is not a complete bar to recovery. Hence, there is no longer a need for a defense that offsets the all-or-nothing impact of contributory negligence.

COMPARATIVE NEGLIGENCE

Most states have adopted comparative negligence. The court first determines the total damages suffered by the plaintiff. Then it apportions these damages between the negligent plaintiff and the negligent defendant according to their relative fault. There are two main kinds of comparative negligence systems:

Pure Comparative Negligence

When the plaintiff sues the defendant for negligence and the defendant claims that the plaintiff's negligence contributed to the injury, a court will decide the percentage by which each side was negligent. Plaintiff's recovery is limited to that percentage of the award that was due to the defendant's negligence. If, for example, plaintiff suffered $100,000 in damages, and the court concludes that the defendant was 5 percent at fault and the plaintiff was 95 percent at fault in causing the injury, the plaintiff recovers $5,000 from the defendant—5 percent of $100,000. Plaintiff always recovers something if the injury was caused by the negligence of both parties, even if the plaintiff's fault was greater than the defendant's.

Restricted Comparative Negligence

Other states use different versions of comparative negligence that are not as comprehensive as the pure form. For example, some states will compare the negligence of the defendant and plaintiff in causing the plaintiff's injury and allow the plaintiff to recover only if the plaintiff's negligence was "slight" in comparison with the "gross" negligence of the defendant. Other states will compare the negligence of the defendant and that of the plaintiff in causing the plaintiff's injury and allow the plaintiff to recover only if the plaintiff's negligence is less than that of the defendant. In the latter states, if they are equally negligent, the plaintiff recovers nothing; if the plaintiff is 51 percent negligent and the defendant is 49 percent negligent, the plaintiff recovers nothing.

ASSUMPTION OF THE RISK

Assumption of the risk is the knowing and voluntary acceptance of the risk of being injured by someone's negligence. The plaintiff's conduct may amount to both contributory negligence and assumption of the risk. In a state that still has both defenses, the defendant can choose *either* to avoid liability. A basic difference between the two defenses, however, is that contributory negligence is determined by the **objective standard** of the reasonable person, whereas assumption of the risk is determined by a **subjective standard**—whether this particular plaintiff knowingly and voluntarily assumed the risk of the defendant's conduct.

> **Contributory negligence (objective test):** The plaintiff *should have known* that he or she was creating an unreasonable risk of injuring him- or herself and *should have taken* greater precautions against this risk.

> **Assumption of the risk (subjective test):** The plaintiff *actually knew* of the risk to his or her safety, but voluntarily chose to confront it.

There are two main elements of the defense of assumption of risk:

- Plaintiff understood the risks posed by the defendant's conduct to the plaintiff's safety.
- Plaintiff voluntarily chose to confront those risks.

Understanding the Risk

It is very easy to confuse assumption of the risk with contributory negligence. Suppose, for example, that Sam is injured in an electrical plant by coming into contact with large live wires that the plant negligently left on the floor. Sam never saw the wires in spite of their size. In Sam's negligence suit against the plant, can the plant use the assumption-of-the-risk defense? No. How could Sam have understood a risk in something that he did not see? If the plant says that Sam *should have seen* the wires because they were so large, the plant is confusing assumption of the risk with contributory negligence. If Sam did not see the wires but should have seen them if he had been acting reasonably as he walked, he was contributorily negligent, but it was impossible for him to have assumed the risk. Assumption of risk is subjective: the risk must be known and understood by a particular plaintiff before we can say that he or she assumed that risk. If all the defendant can say is that the plaintiff was stupid in failing to understand the risk, the defendant has conceded that assumption of the risk cannot apply.

To be sure, there will be some extreme cases in which no one will believe the plaintiff's claim that he or she did not understand the danger. A plaintiff, for example, who walks into a fire negligently set by the defendant would probably not be believed if the plaintiff says he or she did not know that the fire could cause serious injury.

ASSIGNMENT

15.3

Diane is a high school freshman. She has a part-time job at a convenience store in a run-down section of the city. There have been several robberies at the store, several of which Diane witnessed. The store manager carelessly fails to hire a guard or to install a security system. One day, a robber confronts Diane and demands all the cash in the register. Diane complies. She is traumatized by the incident and sues the store for negligently failing to have a guard or other security system. Can the store claim the defense of assumption of risk?

Voluntarily Confronting the Risk

We need to examine two categories of assumption of risk:

- the plaintiff's **express assumption of risk** in which the plaintiff knowingly and voluntarily accepts a risk by express agreement; the express assumption must not violate public policy
- the plaintiff's **implied assumption of risk** in which the plaintiff knowingly and voluntarily accepts a risk by reason of his or her knowledge and conduct; the implied assumption must not violate public policy

Express Assumption   People often enter into agreements limiting their liability to each other. For example, when someone stores a car or a coat in a warehouse or other business set up for this purpose, the parties may agree that the business will not be liable for certain kinds of damage to the car or coat. The owner of the car or coat in these situations is expressly assuming the risk of the damage.

But it must be clear that the parties agreed to such **limitation of liability.** The plaintiff must know about the limitation. A company may try to tell the customer that it will not be liable for negligence by putting a notice to this effect on a sign buried on a wall in the rear of a room, or in very small print on the back of a receipt check. Such communication will usually be insufficient. Customers do not agree to assume a risk of which they are unaware.

There are a number of situations in which the law will not permit or will restrict assumption-of-the-risk agreements even if the terms are made quite clear to both parties. This occurs mainly when there is a significantly unbalanced bargaining position between the parties. In such situations, the likelihood is that the weaker of the parties did not voluntarily agree to assume the risk. Considerable **coercion** or pressure took place. As a matter of **public policy,** the law will invalidate such "agreements."

> **EXAMPLES:**
>
> - An employer cannot ask an employee to assume all risks of injury on the job. The employer must provide a reasonably safe workplace.
> - Someone engaged in a public service (e.g., common carrier, innkeeper, public utility) cannot ask a customer to assume all risks of injury or damage while using the public service—but it can seek to limit its liability if the terms of the limitation are clearly communicated to the customer so that the latter knows what he or she is getting into.

Merchants often try to place a **release** clause in an agreement that they ask the consumer to sign. A release is the giving up or relinquishing of a claim. An agreement containing a release of liability for negligence or other wrongdoing is called an **exculpatory agreement.** Courts are often suspicious of such agreements, particularly when they are **adhesion contracts.** An adhesion contract is a standardized contract for goods or services offered on a take-it-or-leave-it basis without any realistic opportunity for bargaining between the buyer and seller.

Implied Assumption   The plaintiff can voluntarily assume the risk in ways other than by express agreement. An implied assumption of the risk arises because of the knowledge and conduct of the parties rather than because of an express agreement. If, for example, the plaintiff walks very close to the spot where fireworks are exploding and fully understands the dangers involved, the plaintiff has assumed the risk of injury due to the negligent setting off of the fireworks. This is an implied assumption of the risk. As with express assumption of the risk, however, there are some situations in which the law as a matter of public policy will not permit a plaintiff to impliedly assume the risk. Such a situation occurs, for example, when an employee works in an unsafe environment. The law may not permit express *or* implied assumption of the risk in such situations. With this qualification in mind, the rule on implied assumption of the risk, according to the *Restatement*, is as follows:

> A plaintiff who fully understands a risk of harm to himself or his things caused by the defendant's conduct or by the condition of the defendant's land, and who nevertheless voluntarily chooses to enter or remain, or to permit his things to enter or remain in the area of that risk, under circumstances that manifest his willingness to accept it, is not entitled to recover for harm within that risk.[1]

In effect, once you understand the risks and voluntarily proceed to confront them, you have decided to take your chances on injury or damage caused by the negligence of the defendant. Suppose that you buy a lawn mower, but before using it, you discover that it is defective. The blade has been negligently fastened to the body of the machine. You see the defect and understand the consequences of the blade's flying off while in use. If you decide to use it anyway, and are injured when the blade does come off, your negligence suit against the manufacturer will be defeated because of assumption of the risk. You have impliedly assumed the risk.

ASSIGNMENT

15.4

Examine the following situations to determine whether the plaintiff has voluntarily assumed the risk.

a. Plaintiff runs out into the street in the path of cars that are exceeding the speed limit. One of the cars hits the plaintiff. Plaintiff sues the driver.

b. Plaintiff agrees to take a joy ride with the defendant, who will drive on the beach in very shallow water. Neither party knows that the brakes are defective. The brakes fail and the car goes out to deep water, almost drowning the plaintiff. Plaintiff sues the defendant.

There is a form of pressure that a defendant can place on the plaintiff that can negate what would otherwise be an assumption of the risk. The pressure comes in the form of negligently leaving the plaintiff no reasonable alternative in protecting the plaintiff's rights.

> **EXAMPLE:** Defendant negligently sets fire to the plaintiff's car. The plaintiff tries to put out the fire and is burned. Plaintiff sues defendant for damage to the car and for personal injuries due to the burn. As to the personal injuries, the defendant raises the defense of assumption of the risk.

If the plaintiff acted reasonably in trying to put out the fire, he or she has not assumed the risk of being burned *even though the plaintiff fully understood the risks of being burned*. The risks were not voluntarily assumed. Defendant's negligent conduct put the plaintiff in the predicament of either watching the fire destroy the car or trying to stop the fire. The essential question is whether the plaintiff was reasonable in the course taken. This will depend on all the circumstances. How big was the fire at the

---

[1] *Restatement (Second) of Torts* § 496C (1965).

time the plaintiff tried to put it out? How old was the car? What was its value? How close was a fire station, and how difficult or easy was it to contact the station? What was in the car? Nothing? Valuable papers? An infant? Would the plaintiff have been stranded in an inhospitable area if he or she were not able to use the car? Taking all of these factors into consideration, if the attempt to put out the fire was reasonable, there was no voluntary assumption of the risk. If, on the other hand, the attempt was foolhardy because of the extraordinary danger of being seriously burned to protect a car of relatively little value, a court will conclude that there was an assumption of the risk. The plaintiff's protection of his or her rights or property must not be out of all proportion to the danger that the plaintiff walks or leaps into.

ASSIGNMENT 15.5

In the following cases, determine whether the defendant can successfully raise the assumption-of-risk defense.

a. Tony is building a new road in front of Alan's house. A ditch is dug in front of the house. Tony puts a thin piece of plywood across the ditch so that workers and Alan can cross over the ditch. A large "danger" sign is placed by Tony close to the plywood crossing. Alan sees the sign. While Alan is crossing over the plywood, it caves in, causing severe injuries. Alan sues Tony for negligence.

b. Bob's leg is injured in a hit-and-run accident. Along comes Tom in another car. Tom's car has defective brakes, and Bob knows this. Bob has no other way to get to a hospital for needed medical attention. Bob goes with Tom to the hospital. Along the way, the defective brakes cause another accident, in which Bob breaks his arm. Bob sues Tom for negligent injury to his arm.

We turn now to the effect of comparative negligence on assumption of risk.

First of all, express assumption of risk remains a defense, except in those cases where the court might rule that the agreement to limit liability is against public policy. All other assumption-of-risk cases fall into the category of implied assumption of risk. Does this category survive as a defense in states that have adopted comparative negligence? To answer this question, courts distinguish between two kinds of assumption of risk: primary and secondary.

Primary assumption of risk: The plaintiff knowingly and voluntarily accepts a particular risk that the defendant did not have a duty to protect the plaintiff against. The plaintiff recovers nothing in such cases.

> **EXAMPLE:** Paul buys an expensive season ticket to a professional basketball game. He sits in the front row, a few feet from the playing court. During play, a ball bounces off a player and hits Paul in the face, breaking his glasses. He sues the stadium for negligently failing to build a net in front of spectators to protect them from stray basketballs.

Paul loses. The stadium did not have a duty to protect spectators from being hit by a ricocheted basketball during an aggressive, but normally played, basketball game. The risk of serious injury from stray balls is relatively small. The burden on the stadium of preventing such accidents outweighs the risk of the injury. It would be impossible to keep the basketball in bounds at all times without fundamentally altering the competitive nature of the game. Stray balls are inevitable. Nets all around the court would impede vision. Spectators have the option of sitting further back from the playing court. In short, the stadium simply was not negligent. Another way of phrasing this conclusion is to say that a front-row spectator assumes the risk of being hit by stray basketballs during play even if the ball was carelessly thrown by a player before it ricocheted off the court. Yet, it would be more accurate to say that there was no negligence on the part of the defendant. Unfortunately, however, assumption-of-risk language is still used in these cases, but when the defendant had no duty to protect the plaintiff against a particular risk, many courts use the phrase *primary assumption of risk*.

If the state has comparative negligence, does the court compare the conduct of the parties and apportion liability? No. There is nothing to compare. The defendant simply was not negligent. Plaintiff recovers nothing in cases of primary assumption of risk because the defendant was not negligent—there is no reason to invoke the comparative fault principles of comparative negligence. This is so whether the plaintiff was reasonable or unreasonable in his or her own conduct.

Secondary assumption of risk: The plaintiff knowingly and voluntarily accepts a particular risk that the defendant had a duty to protect the plaintiff against.

> **EXAMPLE:** At a county fair, Mary agrees to ride in a horse-drawn carriage driven by a driver who is visibly drunk. Mary sees the driver's condition as he staggers onto the carriage, but decides to take the ride with him anyway. The driver carelessly drives too close to the edge of the road. The carriage tips over, injuring Mary.

This is a case of secondary assumption of risk. The driver had a duty to drive the carriage carefully and to protect passengers from injuries caused by unreasonable driving. Driving while intoxicated was certainly unreasonable. Mary, however, knew the driver was impaired and that this could affect the safety of the ride. She foolishly decided to ride with him. Arguably, she knowingly and voluntarily accepted the risk of injury from the ride. In cases of secondary assumption of risk, comparative negligence applies. Recovery is not barred because of assumption of risk. The court will compare the negligence of both parties and apportion the damages according to the comparative negligence rules in the state.

SUMMARY

Under the defense of contributory negligence, the plaintiff's unreasonableness in taking risks for his or her own safety is a complete bar to recovery of damages if it was a substantial factor in causing the injury. If, however, the defendant was reckless or grossly negligent, the contributory negligence of the plaintiff did not bar recovery. Plaintiff's contributory negligence is determined by the same formula used to determine the defendant's negligence: the foreseeability of the accident and of the kind of injury or damage that could result is weighed against the importance or social utility of what plaintiff was doing at the time and the burden or inconvenience of taking precautions to avoid the accident. Under comparative negligence, damages are allocated according to the relative fault of the parties. Contributory negligence is no longer a complete defense.

Contributory negligence does not bar recovery of damages if the defendant had the last clear chance to avoid the injury but failed to take it. If the defendant discovers (or could discover) the plaintiff in helpless peril and fails to take reasonable steps to avoid the accident, the plaintiff's contributory negligence is not a bar. The same is true if the defendant discovers the plaintiff in inattentive peril. A state that has adopted comparative negligence does not need the defense of last clear chance. Since contributory negligence is no longer a complete bar, there is no longer a need for a defense that offsets the all-or-nothing impact of contributory negligence.

Comparative negligence apportions the damages between the plaintiff and the defendant based on the extent to which each acted unreasonably. In a state that has adopted pure comparative negligence, the plaintiff's recovery is limited to the percentage of the harm that was due to the defendant's negligence. In a state that has adopted restricted comparative negligence, there may be no recovery unless the plaintiff's negligence meets a designated standard, such as being "slight" as opposed to the "gross" negligence of the defendant.

The plaintiff recovers nothing if he or she knowingly and voluntarily accepted (i.e., assumed) the risk of being injured by the negligence of the defendant. There must be actual knowledge of the risk. Generally, parties are free to enter agreements that limit their liability with each other. In an express assumption of risk, the plaintiff knowingly and voluntarily accepts a risk by express agreement. In an implied assumption of risk, the plaintiff knowingly and voluntarily accepts a risk by reason of his or her knowledge and conduct. Both kinds of assumption must not violate public policy. Under comparative negligence the parties can still agree to an express assumption of risk. For implied assumption of risk, a further distinction is made. In primary assumption of risk, the plaintiff knowingly and voluntarily accepts a particular risk that the defendant did not have a duty to protect the plaintiff against. Plaintiff recovers nothing. In secondary assumption of risk, the plaintiff knowingly and voluntarily accepts a particular risk that the defendant had a duty to protect the plaintiff against. Damages are allocated between the plaintiff and the defendant according to their relative fault.

KEY TERMS

defense   187

comparative negligence   187

contributory negligence   187

last clear chance   188

assumption of the risk   188

ordinary negligence   188

reckless   188

gross negligence   188

unreasonable risks   189

cause in fact   190

avoidable consequences   191

helpless peril   191

inattentive peril   191

objective standard   193

subjective standard   193

express assumption of risk   194

implied assumption of risk   194

limitation of liability   194

coercion   194

public policy   194

release   194

exculpatory agreement   194

adhesion contracts   194

primary assumption of risk   196

secondary assumption of
    risk   196

Products Liability

Chapter Outline

- Products Liability in the Media
- Categories of Defects
- Negligence
- Misrepresentation
- Warranty and Strict Liability
- Express Warranty
- Sale versus Service
- Implied Warranties
- Strict Liability in Tort
- Tobacco
- Reform

PRODUCTS LIABILITY IN THE MEDIA

Each year 29,000 deaths are associated with consumer products (not including automobiles and trucks). In addition, an estimated 33 million people are injured. The cost of injuries treated in hospital emergency rooms alone is about $10 billion a year. Yet the law of **products liability** is often misunderstood, particularly by the public. In part this is due to the media's fascination with the apparently frivolous case. For example:

- A man convinces a court that he became impotent after being shocked by a Pepsi Cola vending machine.
- A jury awards $2.7 million (later reduced to $640,000) to a woman against McDonald's because its coffee was so hot that she burned herself when she spilled some of it on her lap.

Reading about such cases in the media had many shaking their heads in disbelief. Warning labels were also ripe for comment. A sign on a baby stroller read, "Remove Child Before Folding." A Batman toy set warned that "Cape Does Not Enable User to Fly." The president of a stepladder company recently told a press conference of a case in which a man placed his ladder on frozen horse manure so that he could do some shingle work on his barn. As the manure melted, the ladder slipped. He fell and was injured. He then sued the ladder manufacturer and was awarded $330,000 on the theory that the manufacturer failed to provide adequate warning of the viscosity of manure! What does the need for such a warning say about the mentality of the American consumer? One commentator wonders whether we will one day see ladder warnings like the following:

- Avoid contact with electrical current. Never attempt to plug in a ladder.
- This warning sticker gets slippery when wet. That's why we put it on the side. If you're standing on this sticker, you've got the ladder pointed the wrong way.
- Never drink and climb. Always have a designated climber on hand.[1]

What's going on? Is the field of products liability law coming apart in a sea of ridicule? Not quite, but attorneys and the legal system have been taking a pounding. Talk-show hosts, late-night comics, and cartoonists are ever-available to give us the details of the latest seemingly absurd products liability case. In this environment of attack, humor, and exaggeration, it would be an understatement to say that many are confused about the law of products liability. Our goal in this chapter is to place this area of the law in perspective. An understanding of the basics will help separate the reality from the ridicule.

CATEGORIES OF DEFECTS

The term *products liability* does not refer to a particular tort. Rather, it is a shorthand term that covers a variety of causes of action that can be raised when a **defective** product causes injury or other harm. The causes of action are:

- negligence
- misrepresentation
- breach of express warranty
- breach of implied warranty of merchantability
- breach of implied warranty of fitness for a particular purpose
- strict liability in tort

In this chapter we begin our study of these causes of action.

The primary focus of a products liability case is on a product that is defective. Something is wrong with the product that makes it dangerous. As a result, someone is injured, property is damaged, or both. As we shall see, however, every product that causes injury or damage is not necessarily defective. A bottle of milk that falls and breaks a toe has caused an injury, but it is highly unlikely that the bottle fell because it was defective. The three broad categories of defectiveness are outlined in Figure 16–1.

Before we begin our study of negligence and the other causes of action based on these categories of defects, it is important to note that the status of the plaintiff or of the defendant can sometimes have a dramatic effect on the outcome of a case. The status possibilities of the plaintiff injured by the product are buyer, user (who is not the buyer), lessee (renter), bailee, and bystander (who is neither the buyer nor a user). The status possibilities of the defendant are manufacturer of the entire product, manufacturer of a part, supplier, wholesaler, retail seller, lessor, and bailor. For some causes of action, as we will see, if the status of the party changes, the applicable law might change as well.

NEGLIGENCE

The elements of negligence are duty, breach of duty, proximate cause, and damages. We examined these elements in Chapters 10 to 14 and the defenses to negligence in Chapter 15.

---

[1]Andrew J. McClurg, *Rungful Suits*, 83 ABA Journal 98 (June, 1997).

1. Manufacturing Defect

The product does not conform to its design. Something went wrong in the manufacturing process making the product dangerous. The defective product is different from the others. *Examples:* The screws on the wheels of the car were not tightened, a foreign substance was left in the soda bottle, a worker failed to follow instructions on the amount of a chemical to pour into the mold.

2. Design Defect

The product conforms to the design, but the design is defective. Something went wrong at the planning stage making the product dangerous. The defective product is exactly like all the others, but something is wrong with all of them because of the very design of the product. *Examples:* The kind of metal called for by the design is not strong enough to do the work of the product, a safety shield should have been built into the product, the driver's vision through the rear view mirror was blocked because of the amount and position of the paneling in the back of the car.

3. Warning Defect

There are no effective instructions or warnings to go with the product. This defect makes the product dangerous. The design of the product is otherwise reasonable and there are no manufacturing flaws in it, but the consumer should have been given more information about what the product can and cannot do. *Examples:* Consumers with a certain allergy should have been told not to use the drug, or should have been told to use it only under a doctor's supervision; consumers should have been told to keep the polish out of the reach of children.

FIGURE 19–1 Categories of defects in products.

Duty is relatively easy to establish since anyone who places a product on the market or sells it has engaged in affirmative conduct. As we saw in Figure 11–1 in chapter 11, when one's conduct creates a foreseeable risk of injury, a duty of reasonable care arises to take steps to avoid that injury. At one time, only parties in **privity** with each other could bring the negligence action. Privity means the relationship that exists between parties who have entered a contract with each other. Without privity there was no duty. If, for example, you go to Sears to buy a General Electric toaster that explodes, you could sue Sears in negligence, but not General Electric. Your contract was with Sears; you had no privity with General Electric. This rule has been changed. Today a duty of reasonable care is owed to all **foreseeable users** of a product (not just to those in privity) whenever it can be anticipated that harm will result if the product is defective.

The second element of negligence—**breach of duty**—is established by the operation of the breach-of-duty equation outlined in Figure 12–3 in Chapter 12. The defendant is unreasonable when the foreseeability of serious injury from the product outweighs the burden or inconvenience of steps that would avoid the injury and the defendant fails to undergo that burden or inconvenience. The more socially useful the product (particularly drugs), the more reasonable it would be for the defendant to create products that pose risks of injury. The defendant's duty is not to produce a safe product; the obligation is to provide a **reasonably safe** product. Manufacturers are not insurers. If manufacturers did everything reasonable to avoid the injury caused by their product, they would not be liable for negligence.

Establishing breach of duty is often a formidable task for plaintiffs. Furthermore, the contributory negligence of the plaintiff (his or her own carelessness in using the product) might be a complete defense that defeats the action. If the state has adopted comparative negligence, the court can apportion damages between the plaintiff and defendant. (See Chapter 15 on negligence defenses.) One of the reasons the law created a new tort called *strict liability in tort* was the difficulty faced by plaintiffs in winning a products liability case on a negligence cause of action. We will examine this new tort in detail after we review misrepresentation and the warranty causes of action.

MISREPRESENTATION

The tort of **misrepresentation** (also called deceit or fraud) is another cause of action that should be considered. Suppose a merchant knowingly makes a false statement of fact to a consumer about a product with the intent to deceive the consumer.

> **EXAMPLE:** Fred is a sales clerk in a department store where Mary is a prospective customer. She asks Fred if a particular mattress is flammable. Fred tells her it is not flammable. He knows this is not so, but feels that Mary would not make the purchase if she knew the truth. She buys the mattress. When she discovers the mattress is flammable, she sues the department store for misrepresentation.

If Mary is injured because of the false statement (e.g., being burned by the mattress), she can recover for her injury as well as for her loss in failing to get what she paid for. The critical element in the tort of misrepresentation is the intent to deceive—called **scienter.** This element exists when the defendant makes the statement knowing it is false, without a belief in its truth, or in reckless disregard of its truth or falsity, with the desire that the statement be believed and relied upon. This and other elements of misrepresentation will be examined in Chapter 22.

WARRANTY AND STRICT LIABILITY

A **warranty** action is a form of **strict liability,** meaning that a breach of the warranty will lead to liability whether the defendant acted intentionally, negligently, or innocently. The historical development of warranty shows that it has both contract and tort dimensions. The contract dimension is that the warranty grows out of a contract relationship. The major tort dimension is that there are consequences of violating or breaching the warranty that are imposed by law irrespective of what the parties to the contract agreed to do.

Three warranties need to be considered:

- express warranty
- implied warranty of merchantability
- implied warranty of fitness for a particular purpose

Since all three are strict liability causes of action, a plaintiff does not have to show that the defendant was negligent (or acted intentionally) in order to recover. Do not confuse the terms *strict liability* and *strict liability in tort*. "Strict liability" is a general term that means liability without fault—the imposition of liability without having to show negligence or intent. When we say that a cause of action imposes "strict liability," we are simply saying that there is no need to prove negligence or intent. The phrase "strict liability in tort," on the other hand, has a narrower meaning. It is an actual tort cause of action. Of course, the general meaning of liability without fault also applies to this tort. But since "strict liability in tort" is an actual cause of action, it has elements, as we shall see later in this chapter. Think of "strict liability" as a phrase applying to different causes of action, one of which being "strict liability in tort."

EXPRESS WARRANTY

The elements of an action for a breach of **express warranty** are as follows:

i. a statement of fact that is false
ii. made with the intent or expectation that the statement will reach the plaintiff
iii. reliance on the statement by the plaintiff
iv. damage
v. causation

Many states have passed § 2-313 of the **Uniform Commercial Code** (UCC),[2] a statute on express warranties.[3]

False Statement of Fact

The first element of a breach-of-express-warranty cause of action is that there must be a statement of **fact** that is false. A fact is a concrete statement that can be objectively established as true (e.g., "it's raining today"). An **opinion,** on the other hand, is a communication containing a relatively vague or indefinite value judgment that is not objectively verifiable (e.g., "the weather is refreshing"). The statement must be reasonably understood to be a fact.

Seller's talk or **puffing** is an expected exaggeration of quality, and as such, does not communicate facts. For example:

"The car is a great buy."

"The tool is excellent."

"It is the best buy around."

It does state a fact, however, to say that the glass in the car is "shatter-proof," and the statement would be false if a rock broke the glass. Sometimes it is difficult to classify a statement as fact or as seller's talk. Suppose that a merchant says that a chain saw is "durable." Has a fact been stated? The answer depends on how a reasonable listener would interpret the statement. It would be unreasonable to interpret the statement to mean that it will last forever. Arguably, however, the statement communicates that the saw is safe for ordinary uses.

The creation of the express warranty does not require the use of the words "warranty" or "guarantee." Any words describing a product can be sufficient so long as the words communicate statements of fact. The warranty can also be created by showing the plaintiff a model or sample. The defendant is stating that the product conforms to the model or sample.

The plaintiff does not have to prove that the defendant knew that the statement was false; it simply must be false. (If the defendant knew it was false and had the intent to deceive, a tort suit for misrepresentation would also be available.) Nor does the plaintiff have to show that the defendant acted negligently or intentionally in communicating the false statement.

ASSIGNMENT

16.1

Which of the following statements, if any, communicate statements of fact?

a. "The ladder will last a lifetime."

b. "The vaporizer is practically foolproof."

c. "These cigarettes are soothing."

d. "The detergent dissolves instantly."

e. "You can trust General Electric."

f. "If our tires save your life once, they are a bargain."

---

[2]The UCC is a set of statutes covering commercial transactions in areas where uniformity across state lines is desirable. (Section 2-313 is one of the statutes in the UCC.) The UCC was created by the National Conference of Commissioners on Uniform State Laws and the American Law Institute. The Conference then submitted it to each state's legislature, which was free to accept, modify, or reject its provisions. Although most legislatures adopted all of the UCC without significant modification, a researcher in any particular state must check the UCC in that state to determine its exact wording.

[3]See also § 402B of the *Restatement (Second) of Torts* on liability for misrepresentations of a material fact concerning the character or quality of a chattel that causes physical harm.

Intent or Expectation the Statement Will Reach the Plaintiff

The false statement of fact must be made to the plaintiff. If it is made to the public, the defendant must reasonably expect that the statement will reach someone like the plaintiff. Hence, statements made in general advertising would be covered. If the manufacturer makes statements in a manual that it distributes to retailers, the question will be whether the manufacturer could reasonably expect the retailer to tell consumers what is in the manual or to show the manual to them.

Reliance on Statement

Reliance means placing faith or confidence in someone or something. The statement of fact about the product must be **material** or important to the transaction. This is so when the plaintiff either buys the product or uses it because of what the defendant said about it. Of course, plaintiffs cannot rely on a statement unless they know about it. Hence, it must be shown that the plaintiff saw or heard the statement.

Damage and Causation

The reliance on the false statement of fact must cause the plaintiff's damage or injury. The plaintiff must show that "but for" the statement, the damage or injury would not have occurred, or that the statement was a substantial factor in producing the damage or injury.

SALE VERSUS SERVICE

The final three causes of action we will examine in this chapter are:

- breach of implied warranty of merchantability
- breach of implied warranty of fitness for a particular purpose
- strict liability in tort

A common component of all three is that they apply to **sales,** not to **services.** The distinction can be critical. If you are injured because of what the defendant *sold* you, the causes of action you can bring include negligence and the three strict-liability causes of action: breach of implied warranty of merchantability, breach of implied warranty of fitness for a particular purpose, and strict liability in tort. If, however, you are injured while the defendant is rendering a *service*, your cause of action is limited to negligence.[4] Phrased another way, if the defendant is engaged in a service, you must show that the defendant acted unreasonably; but if a sale is involved, you can use the strict-liability causes of actions without having to establish the defendant's unreasonableness, i.e., negligence. It is therefore to the plaintiff's advantage to be able to show that the defendant sold something.

A sale is the passing of title to tangible goods or products from a seller to a buyer for a price.[5] Courts, however, do not always use this definition. For example, when you rent or lease property, title does not pass, but the courts treat such transactions

---

[4]You can also sue for the tort of misrepresentation if you can establish intent (scienter). See Chapter 22. Of course, if the service provider has made express statements of fact about the service, a breach-of-express-warranty suit is a possibility as well. Express warranties can be made and breached in sales and in the rendering of services.

[5]Our focus here is on the sale of **personal property** rather than of **real property** or real estate. (Personal property, also called **chattels,** is movable property not attached to the land. Real property is land and anything permanently attached to the land.) There are some courts, however, that have allowed strict-liability causes of action in real estate transactions, particularly when the houses sold were mass-produced.

as "sales" for purpose of using the strict-liability causes of action. Also, every sale does not qualify. The sale must be by a merchant—someone in the business of selling. Hence, the strict-liability causes of action would not apply to the sale of a car between neighbors who are not car merchants.

ASSIGNMENT

16.2

Is there a sale in the following situations?

a. Fred is at a supermarket. He takes a bottle of catsup from the shelf, puts it in his cart, and heads for the checkout counter. While he is picking up the bottle from the cart to place it on the counter, it explodes, injuring Fred.

b. Mary is test driving a car that she is considering purchasing. She is alone in the car five blocks from the dealer. On her way back to the dealer, she decides against purchasing the car. Just as she drives in to the dealer's lot, the brakes malfunction, causing an accident, in which she is injured.

A service is an activity that is performed or a benefit that is provided as part of one's line of work, e.g., a doctor operating on a patient, an attorney conducting a trial, or a professor teaching a class. In general, if title does not pass, then what you have paid for is a service. The easiest services to recognize are the professional services of doctors, attorneys, and teachers. Such professionals are not strictly liable for the harm they cause. Suits against them must establish their negligence.[6]

A service does not become a sale simply because there is a sale dimension to what occurs. Suppose, for example, that a dentist uses a hypodermic needle in a patient's mouth. The needle is a product or "good" for which the patient is charged. Yet this does not change the character of the event from a service to a sale. There is no implied warranty that the needle is safe. There is no implied warranty that anything the dentist does is safe or effective. If the needle breaks in the patient's mouth, a suit against the dentist must show negligence.

What about a blood transfusion at a hospital? Assume that a hemophiliac contracts AIDS by receiving infected blood during a transfusion. Is the blood a "good" (a product) that has been purchased? Most courts say no. The blood transfusion is a service. (In some states this result is mandated by statute.) Negligence, therefore, must be shown, e.g., carelessness in the screening and testing procedures for those who donate blood.

Services are not limited to the professions. Hotels provide services, as do plumbers and carpenters. The gray area is again the situation where it appears that both a sale and a service exist. A beauty parlor, for example, provides a service. Yet, it uses and charges for products in rendering this service, e.g., a permanent-wave solution. Again, the general rule is that a service does not become a sale simply because a product is used or because there is a product component to what is predominantly a service. There are courts, however, that *are* willing to chip away at this rule when nonprofessional services are involved. In the beauty parlor case, for example, there is a well-known New Jersey opinion that held there was a sale of the permanent-wave solution by a beauty parlor. When the solution caused injury, strict liability was imposed without the need to prove negligence.[7] The same result would be reached if a plaintiff at a restaurant were injured by food or drink. They are sales.

Defendants understandably want to classify what they do as services in order to avoid any form of strict liability. If they are correct that they are engaged in a service, the plaintiff must prove that the injury was negligently produced.

---

[6]Unless, of course, they have guaranteed their service (in which case they may be liable for a breach of express warranty) or lied about some critical aspect of their service (in which case they may be liable for the tort of misrepresentation). See also footnote 4.

[7]*Newmark v. Gimbel's Inc.* 102 N.J. Super. 279, 246 A.2d 11, *aff'd,* 54 N.J. 585, 258 A.2d 697 (1969).

Bob is an independent paralegal in your state. He is authorized to represent clients in cases before the Social Security Administration for which he can legally charge a fee. For $25 extra, he sells clients a packet of forms that they can use to fill out themselves. Mary is one of his clients. She pays him his fee plus $25 for the forms. When opening the packet of forms at home, she cuts herself on a small razor that Bob had carelessly left in the packet. Mary wants to sue Bob. Does she have to prove negligence?

IMPLIED WARRANTIES

There are two implied warranties:

- implied warranty of merchantability
- implied warranty of fitness for a particular purpose

They are imposed by the law and not through agreement of the parties. You will find these warranties in state statutory codes. State legislatures created the warranties by modeling them on § 2-314 (merchantability) and § 2-315 (fitness) of the Uniform Commercial Code (UCC) (see footnote 2). Like the breach of an express warranty, the breach of these two implied warranties imposes strict liability, in that the plaintiff does not have to establish that the defendant intended to breach them nor that the defendant was negligent in breaching them.

Our discussion of the implied warranties will cover the following topics:

- elements of breach
- problems of privity
- defenses

Implied Warranty of Merchantability

The elements of a breach of an **implied warranty of merchantability** are:

- i. sale of goods
- ii. by a merchant of goods of that kind
- iii. the goods are not merchantable
- iv. damage
- v. causation

Sale of Goods   Sales are covered, but not services. See the earlier discussion in this chapter on the problems of distinguishing a sale (which does carry an implied warranty of merchantability) and a service (which does not).

Merchant of Goods of that Kind   This warranty does not apply to the occasional seller of goods, such as a cab driver who sells a watch to a fellow cab driver or to a customer in the cab. The defendant must be a merchant in the business of selling goods of the kind in question. There is an implied warranty of merchantability in a car sold by a car dealer, but not in a rifle sold by the car dealer.

Goods Are Not Merchantable   Goods are **merchantable** when they are fit for the ordinary purposes for which the goods are used. (As we shall see in the next section, this is a broader test than that used for *strict liability in tort*, which requires that the product be unreasonably dangerous.) The following are examples of products that are not merchantable:

- vinegar bottles that contain particles of glass
- shoes with heels that break off with normal use soon after purchase
- aspirin that causes infertility

If, however, regular shoes fall apart when the plaintiff is mountain climbing, there is no implied warranty of merchantability, because the shoes were not being used for their ordinary purpose. If the plaintiff who bought the shoes can establish the elements of an implied warranty of fitness *for a particular purpose,* strict liability will be imposed on that theory. Otherwise, the defendant is not liable without a showing of negligence.

There is no requirement that plaintiffs prove they actually relied on the merchantability of the goods before purchase. This reliance is assumed. Suppose, however, that there are obvious defects in the product, which a reasonable inspection of the goods would reveal to the typical consumer. There is no implied warranty with respect to such defects so long as the consumer had full opportunity to inspect.

Damage and Causation   The damage or injury to the person or property of the plaintiff must be caused by the fact that the goods were not fit for their ordinary purpose. The traditional but-for or substantial factor test will be applied to establish causation.

ASSIGNMENT

16.4

There is a small fire in Mary's apartment. When she tries to smother it with a blanket, she is burned by the flames that come from the blanket, which caught fire the moment she placed it on the small fire. In a suit against the manufacturer of the blanket, can she claim breach of implied warranty of merchantability?

Implied Warranty of Fitness for a Particular Purpose

Next we examine the **implied warranty of fitness for a particular purpose.** The elements of a breach of this warranty are:

   i. sale of goods
   ii. seller has reason to know the buyer's particular purpose in buying the goods
   iii. seller has reason to know that the buyer is relying on the seller's skill or judgment in buying the goods
   iv. the goods are not fit for the particular purpose
   v. damage
   vi. causation

Particular purposes must be distinguished from the ordinary purposes of a product. Ordinary purposes are the customary uses of the product. The following are examples of particular purposes:

- shoes to be used to climb mountains
- sunglasses to be used by a professional baseball player
- a dog chain to hold a 300-pound dog

The seller must know or have reason to know about the particular purpose, and know that the buyer is relying on the seller's skill and judgment. The buyer must in fact rely on this skill and judgment. A buyer who makes a careful inspection of the product may have difficulty proving reliance. A good deal will depend on the extent of the inspection and on the expertise of the buyer in the use of the product. If the buyer relies on his or her own skill and judgment rather than on that of the seller, the buyer cannot use this cause of action. Of course, if the product is also not fit for its *ordinary* purpose, the plaintiff can sue under the merchantability warranty. Otherwise, there is no recovery unless the plaintiff establishes negligence.

Privity

Earlier when we discussed negligence in a products liability case, we saw that privity is no longer needed to bring a negligence action. Privity is the relationship that exists between parties who have entered a contract with each other.

> **EXAMPLE:** Helen buys a General Electric blender from Macy's. One day in Helen's kitchen, the blender explodes, injuring Helen, her young daughter, and a visiting neighbor. When the accident occurred, they were all gathered around the blender ready to taste a new drink the blender was mixing.

Helen is in privity with Macy's, but not with General Electric. Her daughter and neighbor are in privity with no one. Under the modern rule, however, they can all sue General Electric for negligence. The absence of privity will not be a bar since they are all foreseeable users of the blender, which is dangerous if defectively made.

Suppose, however, that Helen, her daughter, and her neighbor want to sue General Electric for breach of any of the warranties. Will the lack of privity be a bar? States do not answer this question in the same way:

Who Can Sue for Breach of Warranty

- A few states cling to the old rule that there must be privity, which can exist only between an immediate buyer and the immediate seller.
- Some states permit the immediate buyer and members of the buyer's family or household to bring the warranty action.
- Some states permit the immediate buyer and any person who may reasonably be expected to be affected by the goods to bring the warranty action, e.g., a bystander who is hit by a car.

Who Can Be Sued for Breach of Warranty

- A few states cling to the old rule that there must be privity, which can exist only between an immediate buyer and the immediate seller.
- Some states permit designated nonprivity plaintiffs (see "Who Can Sue") to bring direct warranty actions against the manufacturer when the product is designed to come into contact with the body, e.g., food, home permanent solution.
- Some states permit designated nonprivity plaintiffs (see "Who Can Sue") to bring direct warranty actions against the manufacturer for any product.

Defenses to Warranty Actions

The following defenses will be briefly discussed:

- disclaimer
- notice
- contributory negligence
- assumption of the risk

Disclaimer of Warranty   Under certain conditions, parties to a sales contract can agree that some or all warranties do not exist, i.e., the warranties are disclaimed. The **disclaimer** must be conspicuous and unambiguous so that it is clearly communicated to the buyer. A disclaimer buried in small print on the back of a standardized contract form will probably be held to be ineffective against the ordinary consumer. A court may rule that the disclaimer is invalid because it is **unconscionable.** Something is unconscionable when it is substantially unfair due to a highly unequal bargaining position of the parties. If the defendant is the seller or manufacturer of mass-produced goods, courts are likely to find that nonconspicuous disclaimers are unconscionable against the average consumer. Statutes may impose special requirements for disclaimers to be effective. For example, a disclaimer of the warranty of merchantability must mention the word "merchantability" in the language of the disclaimer. Finally, if a nonpurchaser is allowed to bring a warranty action (see the discussion on privity), disclaimers are generally ineffective against them.

Notice   It is a defense to a warranty action that the injured plaintiff failed to give **notice** to the defendant of the breach of the warranty within a reasonable time after the breach was discovered or should have been discovered. Since many plaintiffs wait a good deal of time before taking action, they fall into the trap of this defense. Some courts, however, disregard the notice requirement when the breach of warranty causes personal injury or when the plaintiff is a nonpurchaser. Even if a court will not go this far, the tendency is to be lenient to plaintiffs in deciding whether they waited an unreasonable time to notify the defendant.

Contributory Negligence   Generally, contributory negligence is not a defense to a breach-of-warranty action.

Assumption of Risk   Assumption of the risk *is* a defense to a breach-of-warranty action. The defendant must show that the plaintiff had actual knowledge and an appreciation of the danger and yet still voluntarily proceeded to use the product.

STRICT LIABILITY IN TORT

One of the most dramatic developments in the law of torts since the 1960s has been the creation of a new tort called **strict liability in tort.** As we will see, it provides considerable advantages to an injured consumer over the other products liability causes of action. We begin our study of this important tort by an overview that places it in context.

 Strict Liability in Tort Checklist:

Definitions, Relationships, Paralegal Roles, and Research References

Category
Strict liability in tort is a strict liability tort. There is no need to show intent or negligence. In many states, however, negligence concepts are relevant to design defects.

Interest Protected by This Tort
The right to be free from injuries due to products that are defective and unreasonably dangerous.

Elements of This Tort
  i. seller
 ii. a defective product that is unreasonably dangerous to person or property
iii. user or consumer
 iv. physical harm (damages)
  v. causation

Definitions of Major Words/Phrases in These Elements
Seller: A person engaged in the business of selling products for use or consumption.
Defective product: At the time the product leaves the seller's hands, it has a manufacturing, design, or warning defect.
Unreasonably dangerous: The product is dangerous to an extent beyond that which would be contemplated by the ordinary consumer who purchases it, with the ordinary knowledge common to the community as to its characteristics. (Note: Some courts use other tests.)
User or consumer: Anyone who uses or consumes the product (some courts have extended the definition to cover bystanders).
Physical harm: Damage to person or property.
Causation: "But for" the defect, the physical harm would not have occurred, or the defect was a substantial factor in producing the physical harm.

Major Defenses and Counterargument Possibilities That Need to Be Explored
  1. The defendant is not a seller.
  2. The injury came from a service, not a product.
  3. The product is not defective.
  4. The product is not unreasonably dangerous.
  5. The plaintiff is not a user or consumer.

Strict Liability in Tort Checklist Continued

6. There was no physical harm to person or property of the plaintiff.
7. The defendant did not cause the physical harm.
8. There was unforeseeable, extreme misuse of the product by the plaintiff.
9. The plaintiff assumed the risk of the danger in the product.
10. The plaintiff failed to take reasonable steps to mitigate the harm caused when the defendant committed strict liability in tort; therefore, damages should not cover the aggravation of the harm caused by the plaintiff (on the doctrine of avoidable consequences, see Chapter 14).

Damages

In most states, damages for strict liability in tort cover physical harm to persons or property, but not economic loss alone. Once physical harm to persons or property is established, compensatory damages can include medical bills, pain and suffering, etc. Punitive damages are also possible. (On the categories of damages, see Chapter 14.)

Relationship to Criminal Law

A state might impose criminal penalties on a company for selling designated products, e.g., drugs, explosives. The company would also be subject to civil liability—strict liability in tort—if the product is defective (unreasonably dangerous) and causes injury.

Relationship to Other Causes of Action

Breach of express warranty: Available if the product does not conform to a representation made by the seller of the product.
Breach of implied warranty of merchantability: Available if the product is not fit for its ordinary purpose.
Breach of implied warranty of fitness for a particular purpose: Available if the product is not suitable for a particular purpose when the buyer relied on the seller's skill or judgment on the product's suitability for that purpose.
Misrepresentation: Defendant must have knowingly made false statements of fact about the product that led to the injury and must have had the intent to deceive (scienter).
Negligence: Plaintiff must prove that the injury from the product was caused by the absence of reasonable care on the part of the seller.

Federal Law

a. Under the Federal Tort Claims Act, the United States Government will *not* be liable for a tort based on strict liability committed by one of its federal employees within the scope of employment. Sovereign immunity is not waived as to such torts. (See Figure 23–7 in Chapter 23.)
b. The United States Consumer Product Safety Commission (CPSC) has authority to protect the public against unreasonable risks of injury associated with designated consumer products. Penalties can be imposed for violation of CPSC mandates.
c. Other federal agencies also have jurisdiction over specific consumer products, e.g., the Food and Drug Administration, the National Highway Transportation and Safety Administration. Such agencies write administrative regulations that impose safety and other standards governing these products. These standards must be examined to assess their relevance to litigation on strict liability in tort.

Employer-Employee (Agency) Law

An employer who is a seller is strictly liable in tort for harm caused by a product sold by one of its employees within the scope of employment if the product is defective and unreasonably dangerous (respondeat superior). On the factors that determine the scope of employment, see Figure 12–7 in Chapter 12.

Paralegal Roles in Strict Liability in Tort Litigation

Fact finding (help the office collect facts relevant to prove the elements of strict liability in tort, the elements of available defenses, and extent of injuries or other damages):
• client interviewing
• field investigation
• online research (e.g., identity of board of directors of a manufacturer)

Strict Liability in Tort Checklist Continued

File management (help the office control the volume of paperwork in a strict liability in tort litigation):
- open client file
- enter case data in computer database
- maintain file documents

Litigation assistance (help the trial attorney prepare for a trial and appeal, if needed, of a strict liability in tort case):
- draft discovery requests
- draft answers to discovery requests
- draft pleadings
- digest and index discovery documents
- help prepare, order, and manage trial exhibits (visuals or demonstratives)
- prepare trial notebook
- draft notice of appeal
- order trial transcript
- cite check briefs
- perform legal research

Collection/enforcement (help the trial attorney for the judgment creditor to collect the damages award or to enforce other court orders at the conclusion of the strict liability in tort case):
- draft postjudgment discovery requests
- field investigation to monitor compliance with judgment
- online research (e.g., location of defendant's business assets)

Research References for Strict Liability in Tort

Digests

In the digests of West, look for case summaries of court opinions on this tort under key topics such as:

Products liability	Damages
Drugs and narcotics	Torts
Sales	Negligence

Corpus Juris Secundum and American Jurisprudence 2d

In these legal encyclopedias, look for discussions under topic headings such as:

Products liability	Damages
Drugs and narcotics	Torts
Food	Negligence
Sales	Death

Legal Periodical Literature

There are two index systems to use to locate articles on this tort:

INDEX TO LEGAL PERIODICALS AND BOOKS (ILP)	CURRENT LAW INDEX (CLI)
Check subject headings such as:	Check subject headings such as:
Products Liability	Products Liability
Warranty	Insurance,
Strict Liability	Products Liability
Insurance,	Product Recall
Products Liability	Manufacturers
Product Recall	Torts
Manufacturers	Damages
Torts	Negligence
Damages	Warranty
Negligence	

Strict Liability in Tort Checklist Continued

Example of a legal periodical article you can locate on this tort by using *ILP* or *CLI*:

Strict Liability in Tort: Reliance on Circumstantial Evidence to Prove a Defect by Donald J. O'Meara, 27 Federation of Insurance Counsel Quarterly 129 (1977).

A.L.R., A.L.R.2d, A.L.R.3d, A.L.R.4th, A.L.R.5th, A.L.R. Fed.
Use the *ALR Index* to locate annotations on this tort. In this index, check subject headings such as:

Products liability	Absolute liability
Warranty	Negligence
Warnings	Torts
Drugs and narcotics	Repairs and maintenance

Example of an annotation you can locate through this index on strict liability in tort:

Products Liability: Modern Cases Determining Whether Product is Defectively Designed by Kristine Cordier Karnezis, 96 A.L.R.3d 22.

Words and Phrases
In this multivolume legal dictionary, look up *strict liability, warranty, defect, dangerous,* and every other word or phrase connected with strict liability in tort discussed in this section of the chapter. The dictionary will give you definitions of these words or phrases from court opinions.

CALR: Computer-Assisted Legal Research

Example of a query you could ask on WESTLAW to try to find cases, statutes, or other legal materials on strict liability in tort: **"strict liability in tort"/p damages**

Example of a query you could ask on LEXIS to try to find cases, statutes, or other legal materials on strict liability in tort: **strict liability in tort/p damages**

Example of search terms you could use on an Internet legal search engine such as LawCrawler (http://lawcrawler.findlaw.com) to find cases, statutes, or other legal materials on this tort: **"strict liability in tort"**

Example of search terms you could use on an Internet general search engine such as Alta Vista (http://www.altavista.com) to find cases, statutes, or other legal materials on this tort: **"strict liability in tort"**

More Internet sites to check to find materials on strict liability in tort and other torts:
Jurist: (http://jurist.law.pitt.edu/sg_torts.htm)
LawGuru: (http://www.lawguru.com/search/lawsearch.html)
See also Tort Law Online at the end of Chapter 1.

In several significant ways, strict liability in tort is different from the products liability causes of action we have been considering thus far in this chapter: negligence, misrepresentation, implied warranty of merchantability, and implied warranty of fitness for a particular purpose. In an action for strict liability in tort:

- The plaintiff does not have to prove that the defendant was negligent (although negligence concepts may be relevant when the plaintiff alleges that the injury was caused by a design defect).
- The plaintiff does not have to prove that the defendant knew of the defect or intended to deceive the plaintiff.
- The plaintiff does not have to establish privity with the defendant.
- The defendant cannot disclaim the obligation of safety no matter how conspicuous the disclaimer.
- Before being able to sue, the plaintiff has no duty to notify the defendant of the injury caused by the product.

There are five elements to the strict liability in tort cause of action:

1. seller
2. a defective product that is unreasonably dangerous to person or property

3. user or consumer
4. physical harm (damages)
5. causation

These elements are based on the highly influential § 402A of the American Law Institute's *Restatement (Second) of Torts*. Most courts have adopted these five elements of § 402A. As we shall see, however, there are a number of courts that have modified some of the elements. Also, the American Law Institute has itself made significant changes in its more recent *Restatement (Third) of Torts*, particularly as to design defects. Yet, the principles that dominate this area of the law in most states continue to be those embodied in § 402A of *Restatement (Second) of Torts*.

Seller

The defendant must be a **seller.** Seller has a broad definition: any person engaged in the business of selling products for use or consumption. Not covered is the occasional seller of a product who is not engaged in selling as part of his or her business. If, for example, one student sells another student a defective car, there is no strict liability in tort, because the student is not in the business of selling products. If the student is liable at all, negligence will have to be shown. Isolated sales that are not part of the usual course of business of the seller are not covered.

The following would be sellers under the first element:

- manufacturer of entire product
- assembler
- wholesaler
- operator of a restaurant
- supplier of a part
- distributor
- retailer

Some states do not impose strict liability in tort on the manufacturer of a defective **component part** of a product. Its liability would have to be based on negligence. Other courts, however, treat the manufacturer of a component part like everyone else in the **chain of distribution** and impose strict liability in tort.

Assume that at a small neighborhood hardware store you buy a defective hammer that is manufactured by a company located a thousand miles away. Both the store (a retailer) and the manufacturer are subject to strict liability in tort. They are both in the chain of distribution to the plaintiff. The store manager cannot say, "I didn't make the hammer; go sue the manufacturer." The store is a seller engaged in the business of selling, and hence is subject to strict liability in tort. To recover, the plaintiff does not have to prove that the store manager was negligent.

Someone who *rents* products as a business is also considered a seller. A company that rents cars, planes, or other equipment, for example, can be strictly liable in tort. Section 402A does not cover sales of real property. As we saw with implied warranty of merchantability, however, some states are willing to extend strict liability to sellers of houses, particularly mass-produced structures. (See footnote 5.)

Strict liability in tort applies to the *sale of products,* not to *services.* See the earlier discussion of this distinction in this chapter, particularly with reference to the problem of transactions that have both sale and service components.

Defective Product That Is Unreasonably Dangerous

There are two requirements for this element under § 402A of *Restatement (Second) of Torts*: the product must be both defective *and* **unreasonably dangerous.** Earlier in Figure 16–1, we examined the three major categories of defects:

manufacturing defects: Something never intended went wrong when the product was being put together. The product does not conform to its design.

design defects: The product conforms to what the planners intended, but something is wrong with their design.

warning defects: The instructions or warnings for the product are either missing or are inadequate.

The plaintiff does not have to prove that the defendant was negligent in creating any of these defects. A defendant who has "sold" a defective product can be strictly liable in tort even if the defendant used all reasonable care. The problem, however, is that it is sometimes difficult to avoid discussing negligence concepts, particularly when the product is alleged to have design defects. Part of the confusion is the use of the phrase "unreasonably dangerous" in § 402A of *Restatement (Second) of Torts*. This phrase certainly suggests the reasonableness analysis that dominates any discussion of negligence. In theory, however, we need to separate negligence from strict liability in tort. They are different causes of action.

When is a product unreasonably dangerous? Section 402A uses the "ordinary consumer" test:

> A product is unreasonably dangerous when it is dangerous to an extent beyond that which would be contemplated by the ordinary consumer who purchases it, with the ordinary knowledge common to the community as to its characteristics.

Note that the test is not whether the injured plaintiff thought the product was unreasonably dangerous. All injured plaintiffs undoubtedly would. The test is **objective:** what would an ordinary consumer think or expect?

In many cases there is little difficulty establishing unreasonable danger by using the test of the ordinary consumer. Such consumers, for example, would not expect a bottle of catsup to have arsenic in it and would expect a bus to be designed with handrails within easy reach during a sudden stop. They are also aware of the danger that is inherent in some products, e.g., knives, matches, bug sprays. If these products are not defectively made or designed, they are not unreasonably dangerous. Aware of the obvious danger, the ordinary consumer takes obvious precautions, e.g., lifts a knife by its handle rather than by its blade.

Other products, however, are not so easy to assess. Assume, for example, that the plaintiff eats a bowl of fish chowder at a New England restaurant and suffers severe injuries when a fish bone gets caught in the throat. Is the product unreasonably dangerous? Probably not. An ordinary consumer would expect to find some bones in this kind of soup. There is danger from bones in the soup, but not an unreasonable danger. Note that we do not ask whether the restaurant used reasonable care to remove bones from the fish chowder. The use of reasonable care is a negligence standard. The test here is the expectation of the ordinary consumer.

There are some courts that argue that a product is unreasonably dangerous if it contains a substance that is "foreign" to the product. Most courts, however, reject this view and say that even a substance that is "natural" to the product can be unreasonably dangerous.

A manufacturer or retailer is not required to sell a product that will never cause injury. Nor are they required to sell a product in the safest condition possible. A car built like a tank may be the safest vehicle on the road, but a car manufacturer is not strictly liable in tort for failing to build its cars to be as strong as tanks. Why? Because ordinary consumers do not expect cars to be built this way for their safety.

ASSIGNMENT

16.5

Are the following products unreasonably dangerous?

a. Linda goes into a bar and orders a martini. She breaks a tooth on an unpitted olive.

b. George chokes on a cherry pit in a pie he purchases from a school vending machine.

   c. Sara chokes on a whole peanut found in "extra creamy" peanut butter she purchases at the supermarket.

   d. Tom, age twelve, buys a bicycle from the Cycle and Sports Store. The bike does not have a headlight on it. While carefully driving the bike at night, Tom is hit by a car. Assume that the accident would not have occurred if the bike had a headlight on it.

Many products can become dangerous to a consumer who overuses or overconsumes them, but they are not necessarily unreasonably dangerous. Good, "wholesome" whiskey is not unreasonably dangerous because it can be deadly to alcoholics. Uncontaminated butter is not unreasonably dangerous because it can bring on heart attacks for people who need a low-cholesterol diet.

Nor is a product unreasonably dangerous because it fails to warn against every possible danger that could be caused by its use.

> The seller may reasonably assume that those with common allergies, as for example to eggs or strawberries, will be aware of them, and he is not required to warn against them. Where, however, the product contains an ingredient to which a substantial number of the population are allergic, and the ingredient is one whose danger is not generally known, or if known is one which the consumer would reasonably not expect to find in the product, the seller is required to give warning against it, if he has knowledge, or by the application of reasonable, developed human skills and foresight should have knowledge, of the presence of the ingredient and the danger. Likewise in the case of poisonous drugs, or those unduly dangerous for other reasons, warning as to use may be required. *Restatement (Second) of Torts* § 402A, comment j (1965).

Once a warning is clearly and conspicuously given, the seller can assume that it will be read and followed.

Unavoidably unsafe products are those that are incapable of being made safe due to the current state of technology and science. A certain drug, for example, may be extremely valuable, but have a high risk of dangerous side effects. If the drug is properly prepared and marketed, and an adequate warning is given of the risk, the drug is neither defective nor unreasonably dangerous. Properly prepared means that all feasible tests were conducted on the drug before it was placed on the market. Properly marketed might mean that it is sold only by prescription through a doctor.

Design defects pose the greatest headaches for the courts. The first problem is to make the distinction between the **intended use** and the **foreseeable use** of a product:

> **intended use:** What the manufacturer wanted the product used for; the purpose for which the product was built and placed on the market.

> **foreseeable use:** What the manufacturer anticipates or should be able to anticipate the product will be used for; a foreseeable use may not be the intended use.

A product must not be unreasonably dangerous both for its intended use *and* for its foreseeable use.

EXAMPLES:

- Chair
  Intended Use: To sit on
  Foreseeable Use: To stand on in order to store things in a closet
  Unforeseeable Use: To provide extra support for an elevated car while changing a tire

- Cleaning Fluid

Intended Use:	To clean floors
Foreseeable Use:	To be swallowed by children
Unforeseeable Use:	As a lighter fluid for a barbecue

If a plaintiff is injured when a chair on which he or she is standing collapses, the manufacturer cannot escape strict liability in tort by arguing that the plaintiff was not using the product for its intended purpose. It is foreseeable that at least a fair number of users will stand on chairs. Therefore, the product must not be unreasonably dangerous for this foreseeable purpose—the chair must be built strongly enough to accommodate this purpose, or adequate warnings against use for this purpose must be provided. An ordinary consumer would expect the product to be reasonably safe for all foreseeable purposes, including, of course, its intended purposes.

Nor will the defendant be able to raise the defense that the plaintiff misused the product. It is not a **misuse** of a product to use it for a purpose that the manufacturer should have anticipated. Or, viewed from another perspective, if it is a misuse, it is a foreseeable misuse that should have been guarded against in the design or through a warning. Similarly, it is foreseeable that small children will swallow cleaning liquid. Therefore, the manufacturer should provide safety precautions against such use, e.g., a warning on the bottle addressed to parents that the substance is toxic and should be kept out of the reach of children, or instructions on the bottle of what to do if someone swallows the contents.

Unforeseeable uses, however, are another matter. To make a manufacturer strictly liable in tort for injuries caused by products put to unforeseeable uses would be to make the manufacturer an insurer. Liability does not extend this far.

Of course, liability for unreasonably dangerous products put to foreseeable uses is not limited to the manufacturer that designed the defective product. The local department store is also strictly liable for such products. Anyone who is a "seller" in the chain of distribution has committed strict liability in tort.

ASSIGNMENT

16.6

a. For the following products, identify what you think are:
- the intended uses
- possible unintended uses that are foreseeable
- possible unintended uses that are unforeseeable
  a. a screwdriver
  b. shampoo for a dog
  c. a lawn mower
  d. bug spray

Assume that each time the product was used for one of the three categories of use, an injury occurred because the product was defective and dangerous for that use.

b. The Smith family live in a hot neighborhood. To keep out insects, they have placed standard removable screens on the windows of their second floor apartment. One day their eleven-month-old, twenty-eight-pound child accidentally falls on the screen, pushing it out. The baby falls to the ground outside, sustaining severe injuries. The Smith's sue the screen manufacturer for strict liability in tort. What arguments will the Smiths make and what will be the response of the manufacturer?

An important design defect issue concerns the **crashworthiness** of automobiles—the problem of the second injury or the second collision. An automobile accident often involves two events: the impact with the other car or object and the impact of the plaintiff *inside* the car with the steering wheel, window, dashboard, or car roof. The design of the car may have nothing to do with the initial accident, yet have a great deal to do with the extent of the injury suffered by the plaintiff. The question is: how crashworthy does the car have to be? Does the manufacturer have the responsibility of designing the car so that the plaintiff is not injured through internal impact with the car's steering wheel, dashboard, gas tank, or other component? It is highly foreseeable that a plaintiff will receive serious injury following an initial crash. This risk must be weighed against the cost of designing the car to minimize the risk. A court may conclude, for example, that a dashboard made out of a hard metal is unreasonably dangerous, or that the placement of the gas tank is unreasonably dangerous because alternative designs were feasible and would have lessened the danger of the second injury.

Many state and federal statutes and regulations exist on consumer products. Is a product that conforms to all of them automatically deemed to be reasonably safe even though it causes an injury? Yes, according to some courts, particularly if the statute explicitly exempts the defendant from liability when there is compliance. Many courts, however, say that a product that conforms to all of the statutes and regulations can still be unreasonably dangerous, because they may cover only what is minimally required for safety. Compliance is merely some evidence—or at most, raises a presumption—that the product is not defective or unreasonably dangerous.

Other Tests?

Thus far we have been focusing on the ordinary consumer test for unreasonable danger presented in § 402A of *Restatement (Second) of Torts*. Some states do not accept this test for determining all kinds of product defects. Everyone knows, for example, that products do not last forever. But how is an ordinary consumer supposed to identify the exact life of a particular product such as a tire, engine, or drug during which it should remain reasonably safe? Ordinary consumers (with the "ordinary knowledge common to the community") often do not know enough to be able to judge the amount of danger that should have been designed out of a particular product.

In part because of this difficulty, some states do not use the ordinary consumer test for all products, particularly when a design defect is alleged. Here is a sample of the language used in some states:

- The risks of the product's design outweigh its benefits.
- The risks of the product are so great that a reasonable seller, knowing the risks, would not place the product on the market.
- The product is defective and this defect caused injury in reasonably foreseeable use.

The focus of these tests is not the expectations of the ordinary consumer. Most of the tests require the kind of **risk-benefit analysis** that courts traditionally use when determining negligence:

The foreseeability of serious harm: The greater the foreseeability of serious harm, the more care, time, and expense are needed to design the product to avoid or minimize the harm.

The importance or social utility of the product: How valuable or significant is the product? The more importance or social utility it has, the more reasonable it is to take risks in putting the product on the market.

The burden or inconvenience on the manufacturer of redesigning the product to make it safer: What would have been the expense of adding an extra safety precaution? If it is slight, it probably should have been taken. If, however, the cost is so excessive as to make the product close to unmarketable, the precautions may not need to be taken. A warning might be sufficient. Note, however, that although warnings might be the cheapest and least burdensome precaution, they are not a substitute for reasonable design changes that would take the danger out of the product or significantly reduce it.

This kind of analysis is also referred to as **risk-utility analysis** or **risk-utility balancing**.

Risk-utility analysis has recently been adopted by the American Law Institute, the creator of the *Restatements*. As indicated earlier, the American Law Institute has made a significant change in strict liability in tort. It no longer recommends that courts use the unreasonable danger and ordinary consumer test of § 402A of the *Restatement (Second) of Torts* as the exclusive test for design defects. The new *Restatement (Third) of Torts* (1997) on products liability now recommends a different test for design defects:

> The product is defective in design when the foreseeable risks of harm posed by the product could have been reduced or avoided by the adoption of a reasonable alternative design . . . and the omission of the alternative design renders the product not reasonably safe. § 2.

Hence, the new test on design defects is the availability of a **reasonable alternative design**. It replaces the "ordinary consumer" expectations test from § 402A of *Restatement (Second) of Torts*. Of course, the availability of an alternative design was also relevant under § 402A of *Restatement (Second) of Torts*. Yet, this availability was often judged from the perspective of the ordinary consumer's expectations.

Under the new test, how do you determine whether a reasonable alternative design was possible? By going through a risk-benefit analysis or risk-utility balancing. The *Restatement's* new test does not mean that the expectations of the ordinary consumer are discarded. They are still considered. Under the new test, however, consumer expectations do not constitute an independent standard for judging the defectiveness of product designs.

This change has been controversial; it is unclear how many states will adopt the new test of *Restatement (Third) of Torts*. In a recent case, a court said that "the majority of jurisdictions *do not* impose upon plaintiffs an absolute requirement to prove a feasible alternative design."[8] Clearly, the law on this element of strict liability in tort is not settled. We can expect to see continued developments in the determination of what constitutes a product defect.

User or Consumer

The third element of a cause of action for strict liability in tort is that the plaintiff must be a user or consumer. The plaintiff does not have to be the purchaser of the product. A state that follows § 402A will require only that the plaintiff be a user or consumer.

> **EXAMPLE:** Tom is driving a car that is unreasonably dangerous because of defective brakes. Jim is his passenger. There is an accident caused by the brakes. Tom and Jim are injured as well as Mary, who was a pedestrian crossing the street when the car hit her.

Tom is a user or consumer whether or not he is the purchaser of the car. So is Jim. Passengers certainly use cars. Mary, however, is not a user or consumer. She is a **bystander**. Under § 402A, Mary cannot sue the car manufacturer for strict liability in tort unless the state expands the tort to cover anyone who is foreseeably injured by the unreasonably dangerous product. There are a number of states that have done so. This would cover Mary. It is highly foreseeable that cars with defective brakes will go out of control and injure pedestrians or other bystanders.

---

[8] *Potter v. Chicago Pneumatic Tool Co.*, 694 A.2d 1319, 1331 (Conn. 1997)(emphasis in original).

In the fact situation just mentioned involving Tom, Mary, and the defective brakes, could Mary sue Tom for strict liability in tort?

Physical Harm

The tort covers actual damage to property (e.g., demolished car) or to person (e.g., broken arm, death). If no such damage has occurred, and the plaintiff has suffered economic damage only, most courts do not allow recovery under strict liability in tort. If the plaintiff is the purchaser, he or she may be able to sue under some other cause of action. The plaintiff, for example, buys a boat that is defective and unreasonably dangerous because of the design of the motor. The boat cannot be used in the plaintiff's business. No one is injured and no damage occurs to the boat itself. Only an economic loss has been suffered. The plaintiff may be able to sue for breach of contract, for breach of warranty, or perhaps even for misrepresentation. Most courts, however, do not provide strict liability in tort as a remedy for purely economic loss.

Causation

The plaintiff must show that the product was defective at the time it left the hands of the defendant and that this defect caused the physical harm. Causation is established by the but-for test (but for the defect, the harm would not have resulted), or the substantial factor test when more than one cause is involved (the defect was a substantial factor in producing the harm).

> The seller is not liable when he delivers the product in a safe condition, and subsequent mishandling or other causes make it harmful by the time it is consumed. . . . If the injury results from abnormal handling, as where a bottled beverage is knocked against a radiator to remove a cap, or from abnormal preparation for use, as where too much salt is added to food, or from abnormal consumption, as where a child eats too much candy and is made ill, the seller is not liable.[9]

Causation can sometimes be difficult to prove when the defendant is a remote manufacturer and the product has passed through many hands before it injured the plaintiff. A court will not allow causation to be established by mere speculation. This does not mean that the plaintiff must eliminate every possible cause other than the defendant. Where there is some evidence of other causes, however, the plaintiff must either negate them or show that the defendant was at least a substantial factor along with the other causes in producing the injury.

Causation by Market Share

In Chapter 12, we saw that the courts created the doctrine of res ipsa loquitur to help plaintiffs who would otherwise have great difficulty establishing the second element of negligence: breach of duty (unreasonableness). The doctrine allowed the jury to draw the inference of unreasonableness even though there was no direct or specific evidence of it.

We now look at a similar problem pertaining to the element of causation.

---

[9] *Restatement (Second) of Torts* § 402A, comment g (1965).

> **EXAMPLE:** During pregnancy a woman takes DES (diethylstilbestrol), a synthetic form of estrogen, designed to prevent miscarriage. She gives birth to a daughter. When the child grows up, she develops cervical cancer, which was caused by the DES taken by her mother. Which manufacturer of DES can the daughter sue? At least 200 manufacturers used an identical formula to produce DES. But the daughter cannot determine which manufacturer made the DES pills that her mother took. The pharmacist used by her mother is no longer in business, and no records are available.

The drug was obviously defective, and unreasonably so. A duty of reasonable care existed, the duty was breached, and an injury resulted. But *who caused the injury?* We know *what* caused the cancer, but we do not know *who* caused it. Under traditional rules, it is fundamental that the plaintiff establish which manufacturer made the defective pills taken by her mother. But she has no way of doing so on these facts.

In most states, she loses her case. A minority of states, however, are more sympathetic. In *Sindell v. Abbott Laboratories,*[10] for example, a California court held that if the plaintiff:

* established that DES caused the cancer, and
* sued a substantial share of the DES manufacturers who were selling in the market in which her mother purchased the drug,

then each defendant/manufacturer would be liable for the proportion of the plaintiff's damages represented by its share of that market unless it could prove that it could not have made the DES pill that caused plaintiff's injuries.[11] If a particular defendant/manufacturer could not prove this, then it would be liable for that part of the judgment that was proportional to its market share. This approach has been called **market share liability.**

Using this method of handling causation has been highly controversial. Some fear that it might open a floodgate of liability.

Although *Sindell* was dramatic in its approach, there are limitations to its use. The product made by the manufacturers must be identical, or nearly so. If the products are simply similar and are not made in the same dangerous way, this approach cannot be used. *Sindell* arguably would not apply, for example, if different manufacturers used different proportions of ingredients to make what would otherwise be considered the same product. Also, a large number of manufacturers must be sued so that it can be said that they constitute a significant or substantial share of the market.

Defenses to Strict Liability in Tort

Misuse   Every misuse of the product is not a defense. As indicated earlier, the simple fact that a consumer does not use a product for its intended purpose does not necessarily mean that it has been misused. A product must be reasonably safe for the foreseeable uses of the product. Furthermore, a manufacturer must plan for a certain amount of foreseeable misuse. Misuse is a defense when it is unforeseeable and when it is extreme. Such misuse occurs, for example, when the plaintiff knowingly violates the plain, unambiguous instructions on using the product or ignores the clear warnings provided.

Contributory Negligence   In most states, contributory negligence is *not* a defense when the plaintiff's conduct consists of failing to discover the danger. Assume the defendant rents a defective car to Bob Smith. On the dashboard, there

---

[10]26 Cal. 3d 588, 607 P.2d 924, 163 Cal. Rptr. 132, 2 A.L.R.4th 1061 (1980).
[11]W. Page Keeton et al., *Prosser and Keeton on the Law of Torts* 271 (5th ed. 1984).

is a red light signaling trouble to the driver. Smith does not see the light and keeps driving. An accident occurs because of the defect in the car that makes it unreasonably dangerous. It is no defense that Smith failed to discover the danger—even if a reasonable person would have discovered it by checking the dashboard and seeing the red light. Smith's own negligence in failing to discover the danger to himself is not a defense.

Contributory negligence is a defense only when it constitutes the extreme, unforeseeable misuse described above, or an assumption of the risk described below.

Comparative Negligence   There are some states that apply their comparative negligence rules to strict-liability-in-tort cases, even though there is no need for the plaintiff in such cases to establish the negligence of the defendant. The damages suffered by the plaintiffs are proportionately reduced by whatever percentage of the harm the plaintiffs caused themselves through carelessness.

Assumption of the Risk   If the plaintiff has actual knowledge of the danger and voluntarily proceeds to use the product in spite of the danger, there has been an assumption of the risk, which *is* a defense to strict liability in tort. The plaintiff must have actually discovered the danger. For a discussion of assumption of the risk, see Chapter 15.

ASSIGNMENT 16.8

Tom buys a lawn mower from a department store. A string is tied around the top of the mower attached to a tag that says "WARNING: BEFORE USING, READ INSTRUCTION BOOK CAREFULLY." Tom sees this sign but fails to read the instruction book. In the book, the consumer is told never to use the mower on a steep hill. Tom is injured while mowing on a steep hill in his yard. The mower tipped over and fell on him. Is the department store strictly liable in tort?

TOBACCO

"Vicious!" said the plaintiff's attorney when he saw a roadside billboard display in the city where he was suing a tobacco company. The display, paid for by tobacco companies, contained a photo of an obviously wealthy and obnoxious attorney sitting by a pool with his golf clubs and Mercedes in the background. The caption on the billboard read in large letters:

"1-800-I-Sue-4-You."

In response, anti-smoking ads were available in abundance in the same city. One TV ad showed a tobacco executive at a "Demon Award" ceremony. As he accepted the award, he said, "This is for all you smokers out there." Among the executive's admirers in the audience were murderers, drug dealers, Adolf Hitler, and Joseph Stalin.[12] Such ads and counter-ads are a not-very-subtle attempt to influence juries, judges, legislators, and the general public. The tobacco wars were being waged on all fronts.

For years, smokers lost their cases in court because they were portrayed as foolish people who wanted someone else to pay for their lack of self-control. They knew smoking was hazardous to their health; since 1966 every pack of cigarettes bluntly told them so. In legal terms, they assumed the risk of health problems by continuing to smoke. Juries consistently came to this conclusion, in part, because the general

---

[12]*Blowing Smoke: Cigarette Maker Taunts Lawyers in Ad Campaign,* Wall Street Journal October 20, 1998, at B1.

public had little sympathy for the smoker. A political cartoon by Signe Wilkinson in the Philadelphia Daily News shows a distraught but sincere woman on the witness stand telling the judge and jury, "The cigarette that I was forced to smoke dropped ashes on the silicone breasts I was forced to implant and they melted over the hamburger I hadn't cooked so that's why I deserve $325 million." So prevalent was this anti-consumer attitude that a number of states even passed statutes that banned most smoker lawsuits on the ground that the dangers of tobacco use were well known. Prior to the 1990s, tobacco companies (e.g., American Tobacco Company, Brown & Williamson, Liggett & Myers, Lorillard, Philip Morris, R.J. Reynolds, and United States Tobacco Company) were not concerned by individual lawsuits brought by smokers since few of them succeeded, the awards were small, and every victorious plaintiff was overturned on appeal.

Such legal victories by the tobacco industry were remarkable in the face of a drumbeat of news that over 400,000 people per year died in the United States from smoking-related diseases such as cancer, heart disease, and emphysema. The Secretary of the United States Department of Health and Human Services estimated that smoking-related health costs exceeded $45 billion a year, particularly through Medicare and Medicaid. If you include fire damage, absenteeism, and lost productivity, the total economic cost of tobacco use was said to exceed $145 billion a year. Nevertheless, the tobacco industry kept winning in the courtroom.

Since the mid-1990s, however, the tide has turned. For years, tobacco companies denied that their product was addictive, unhealthy, or targeted at young people. Internal documents, however, have dramatically shown otherwise. For example, extensive media attention has been given to reports that the tobacco industry considered teenagers to be "replacement smokers" for the hundreds of thousands of smokers dying each year from lung cancer and other smoking-related diseases. A 1975 memo (marked "secret") of R.J. Reynolds made the following stunning statement about children as young as fourteen:

> To ensure increased and long-term growth for CAMEL FILTER, the brand must increase its share penetration among the 14–24 age group which have a new set of more liberal values and which represent tomorrow's cigarette business.

A paralegal played a prominent role in this drama. Merrell Williams was a paralegal who once worked at Wyatt, Tarrant & Combs, the largest law firm in Kentucky. The firm represented Brown & Williamson (B&W), maker of Kool and Viceroy. While Merrell Williams worked at the firm, he secretly photocopied and distributed confidential internal memos, letters, and other documents between the law firm and its client. The documents demonstrated that the corporation knew about the danger of smoking, but tried to cover it up. The news media made extensive use of this material. Here is how a Los Angeles Times article described this development:

> Big tobacco is known as a formidable legal adversary, skilled and even ruthless in the courtroom. Yet the industry is being slowly undone by its former secrets. . . . Disclosure of documents [containing these secrets], many dating back 40 years, has done enormous damage, outraging citizens and forcing once-helpful politicians to climb on the anti-tobacco bandwagon. . . . The ground shifted in 1994, when an obscure paralegal, who had secretly stolen thousands of pages of documents from a [law firm representing] B&W, leaked the purloined papers to Congress and the media. The documents were an instant sensation. In one 1963 memo, for example, the [tobacco] company's former general counsel declared, "We are, then, in the business of selling nicotine, an addictive drug.". . . Now the blood was in the water, and so were the sharks. For 1994 also marked the formation of a powerful alliance of products liability lawyers and state attorneys general, who began filing immense new claims against the industry.[13]

---

[13]Myron Levin, *Years of Immunity and Arrogance Up in Smoke,* Los Angeles Times, May 10, 1998, at D1, D17.

Wyatt, Tarrant & Combs obtained an injunction against Merrell Williams to prevent him from continuing to reveal what he learned while he was a paralegal at the firm. The law firm says "Williams broke his employment contract which requires confidentiality, and stole photocopies of documents from the law office." An ex-smoker himself, Williams has undergone quadruple bypass surgery and has sued Brown & Williamson for his own health problems.[14]

The onslaught of litigation against tobacco companies fell into several categories:

- states sued for the Medicaid costs they paid to treat smoking-related illnesses;
- private citizens who were smokers or ex-smokers brought class action suits in state and federal courts on behalf of large numbers of sick and deceased smokers;
- private citizens who were smokers or ex-smokers brought individual suits in state and federal courts for the illness or death brought on by smoking;
- private citizens who were not smokers or ex-smokers brought individual or class action suits in state and federal courts for the illness or death caused by second-hand smoking.

The largest number of these cases, many of which take years to litigate, were filed during the period when the media were revealing the contents of the internal tobacco documents.

Class actions in tobacco cases have not done well in federal courts. For example, a federal court refused to certify a nationwide class action on behalf of "all nicotine dependent persons in the United States." The class could have involved 50 million smokers. The court concluded that the criteria for a class action in federal court had not been met.

State courts, however, have not been as reluctant as federal courts to certify a nationwide class. In 1996, one of the smaller cigarette manufacturers, Liggett Group (maker of Chesterfield, L&M, and Eve), broke ranks and settled a class action that was filed in an Alabama state court on behalf of a nationwide class of smokers.[15] The Alabama court certified this action as a settlement class and preliminarily approved the proposed settlement. A nationwide campaign of notice then took place in newspapers across the country. Under the settlement, Liggett admitted that smoking causes various health problems and that nicotine is addictive. Liggett also agreed to pay 7.5 percent of its pre-tax income to a Settlement Fund for the next twenty-five years. To the dismay of the rest of the tobacco industry, Liggett also agreed to "cooperate fully" in "lawsuits against the other cigarette manufacturers."

In June of 1997, the front pages of every major newspaper in the country reported that cigarette makers and forty states had reached a settlement that would provide $368.5 billion over twenty-five years to cover Medicaid money that states have paid to treat sick smokers.[16] Although this settlement eventually collapsed, many were amazed at what the tobacco industry had agreed to do:

- give the United States Food and Drug Administration (FDA) expanded authority to regulate the level of nicotine in cigarettes;
- cease all outdoor tobacco advertising and eliminate cartoon characters and human figures, such as Joe Camel and the Marlboro Man, two tobacco icons, which the public health community had long assailed as advertising appealing to our nation's youth; and
- subject tobacco manufacturers to severe financial surcharges in the event underage tobacco use did not decline radically over the next decade.

---

[14]Mark Curriden, *DOJ (Department of Justice) Probes Law Firms: Paralegal Who Copied Documents Subpoenaed,* 80 American Bar Association Journal 14 (June 1994); *It Started with a Paralegal,* 13 Legal Assistant Today 18 (May/June 1996).

[15]You can examine the court documents in this state case on the Internet at <www.liggett.net>.

[16]The details of the settlement were posted on the Internet at <http://stic.neu.edu/settlement/6-20-settle.htm> and also at <www.tobaccoresolution.com>.

This settlement required legislation by Congress since it involved major policy changes such as the scope of the FDA's regulatory power. Public health groups, however, attacked the deal as too weak since companies could simply pass on their added costs to smokers. The American Lung Association called it a "bailout for the industry." In the end, Congress failed to act, and the settlement fell apart.

Several states pursued their own actions against the tobacco industry to recover their Medicaid costs. Individually, the states of Mississippi, Florida, Texas, and Minnesota reached settlements. The total involved in these four states was over $40 billion.

In the meantime, efforts to achieve a broader settlement continued. The breakthrough came in November of 1998 when the other forty-six states reached a settlement that called for the payment of $206 billion over 25 years for smoking-related health costs. Note that the claimants in these settlements were *not* smokers who arguably assumed the known risks of smoking. The claimants were the state governments who wanted to recoup the billions of dollars they spent for smoking-related diseases. The governments had not assumed any risks. States do not inhale!

The settlements did not increase the authority of the FDA to regulate nicotine in tobacco or other aspects of the manufacture and marketing of tobacco products. The courts have ruled that the FDA would have to obtain this authority through new legislation from Congress. Nor did the settlements put an end to individual lawsuits or class actions brought by smokers. They still had the right to prove their case in court. Individual smokers were not part of the settlements that the tobacco industry made with the fifty state governments.

In 1999, a San Francisco jury awarded a smoker $51.5 million from Philip Morris Company, fifty million of which was for punitive damages. The plaintiff was a 52-year-old woman who said she had inoperable lung cancer from 35 years of smoking. The size of the verdict frightened the tobacco companies. The punitive damages were more than three times the $15 million she asked for. She also was not expected to be a sympathetic plaintiff since she tried to stop smoking only once in 35 years. Yet, she walked away with a $51.5 million judgment. Although this amount was eventually cut in half on appeal, the size of the verdict has encouraged other individual smokers to bring their own cases. By the end of 1998, for example, Philip Morris said that it was defending over 500 smoking and health cases filed by individuals, an increase of just under 30 percent from the previous year. Class action filings had also jumped from 50 to 60 in the same period. This is the experience of only one manufacturer. In Florida, five of the largest tobacco manufacturers lost the first state class action case ever to be tried by a jury. It returned a staggering punitive damages award of $144 billion! Many feared that the judgments coming out of such suits may be so large that the tobacco companies will be forced into bankruptcy. And in 1999, the federal government sued the tobacco industry to recover the billions it spends treating smoking-related diseases of Medicare patients, military veterans, and federal employees. Clearly, the tobacco industry is not close to achieving resolution of the tort litigation crisis it faces.

Manufacturers of other allegedly dangerous products have not been encouraged by what has happened to tobacco companies. Who is next? they wonder. Manufacturers and distributors of intoxicating liquor? Those who make and sell guns? Attempts to subject these other industries to litigation have not yet been successful, but the attempts are continuing. A few years ago, no one would have predicted that tobacco companies would be facing multibillion-dollar liability payments through settlements and judgments. There are numerous tort attorneys in the United States looking around for other deep pockets.

REFORM

Federal involvement in this area of the law has been relatively minor, including the work of the Consumer Product Safety Commission, whose role has primarily been that of a monitor and information collector in spite of its authority to force companies to recall their products.

Most products liability law is created and applied at the state level, which is true for most of tort law. This, of course, means that each state is free to develop its own products liability law. Critics say that this system has produced chaos, and that we need a federal products liability law. Although Congress has considered a number of proposals to implement such a law, none has been enacted to date. Here are selected aspects of some of the proposed reforms:

- The creation of federal standards governing the litigation of disputes arising out of injuries caused by defective products. These standards would **preempt** (take the place of, be controlling over) state law.
- The creation of an expedited settlement system to be available at the outset of every case.
- The imposition of a cap on non-economic damages that can be awarded.
- The creation of standards for when punitive damages can be obtained from a defendant.
- A uniform statute of limitations for bringing a case.

SUMMARY

Products liability is not a cause of action. It is a general term that covers different causes of action based on products that cause harm. These causes of action are negligence, misrepresentation, breach of express warranty, breach of implied warranty of merchantability, breach of implied warranty of fitness for a particular purpose, and strict liability in tort. There are three categories of defects in products: manufacturing defects, design defects, and warning defects.

For purposes of a negligence suit, the defendant owes a duty of reasonable care to all foreseeable users of the product if it can be anticipated that substantial harm to person or property will result if the product is defective. Privity is not necessary. Breach of duty is established when the defendant fails to take reasonable steps to prevent injury caused by the product. Another traditional cause of action is misrepresentation, which can be used when the defendant makes a false statement about a product with the intent to mislead (scienter) that causes injury.

Breach of express warranty requires proof of a false statement of fact, the intent or expectation that the statement will reach the plaintiff, reliance on the statement by the plaintiff, and causation of damage or injury.

The following causes of action apply to sales rather than to services: breach of implied warranty of merchantability, breach of implied warranty of fitness for a particular purpose, and strict liability in tort. For a breach of implied warranty of merchantability, goods must be sold by a merchant of that kind. The goods are not merchantable and cause damage or injury. For a breach of implied warranty of fitness for a particular purpose, goods must be sold by a seller who has reason to know that the buyer has a particular purpose in buying the goods and is relying on the seller's skill or judgment. The goods cause damage or injury because they are not fit for that particular purpose.

To bring a warranty action, the general rule is that there must be privity, or a contractual relationship, between the defendant and the person injured. Some states have abolished the privity requirement in designated kinds of cases such as when the person injured is in the immediate family of the person who bought the product. Defenses to actions for breach of warranty include valid disclaimers, failure of the plaintiff to provide notice within a reasonable time after the breach was discovered or should have been discovered, and assumption of the risk. Contributory negligence is generally not a defense.

In an action for strict liability in tort, the defendant must be a seller, which includes most companies in the chain of distribution. Companies in the business of renting products are also included. The product must be defective and unreasonably dangerous for its intended use and its foreseeable use. States differ on the tests they use to determine when a defect is unreasonably dangerous. The, predominant test is the expectations of the ordinary consumer. Some states, however, use other tests, particularly for design defects. A recent proposal for such defects is the availability of a reasonable alternative design as determined by a risk-benefit analysis. The defect in the product must cause physical harm in the plaintiff, who is either a user or consumer of the product, or, in some states, anyone who is foreseeably injured, which could include a bystander. Misuse is a defense when it is unforeseeable and is extreme. Assumption of the risk is also a defense. Generally, contributory negligence is not. A state may compare the fault of the plaintiff and the defendant and apportion the damages according to its applicable formula.

For years, tobacco companies were very successful in court, particularly with the argument that smokers were assuming a known risk. The tide, however, has turned in large part because of leaked tobacco company documents that show that the companies knew about the danger of smoking and targeted young people. States sued for the Medicaid costs; private citizens brought class actions and individual lawsuits for the illnesses caused by direct and secondhand smoke. After Liggett Group broke ranks and settled, forty-six states agreed to a $206 billion settlement. (Four other states reached individual settlements.) The settlements did not put an end to individual lawsuits or class actions brought by smokers. They still had the right to prove their case in court.

KEY TERMS

products liability   199

defective   200

manufacturing defect   201

design defect   201

warning defect   201

duty   201

privity   201

foreseeable users   201

breach of duty   201

reasonably safe   201

misrepresentation   202

scienter   202

warranty   202

strict liability   202

express warranty   202

Uniform Commercial Code   203

fact   203

opinion   203

puffing   203

reliance   204

material   204

sales   204

services   204

personal property   204

real property   204

chattels   204

implied warranty of merchantability   206

merchantable   206

implied warranty of fitness for a particular purpose   207

disclaimer   208

unconscionable   208

notice   208

strict liability in tort   209

§ 402A   213

seller   213

component part   213

chain of distribution   213

unreasonably dangerous   213

objective   214

unavoidably unsafe products   215

intended use   215

foreseeable use   215

misuse   216

crashworthiness   216

risk-benefit analysis   217

risk-utility analysis   218

risk-utility balancing   218

reasonable alternative design   218

bystander   218

market share liability   220

preempt   225

Survival and Wrongful Death

Chapter Outline

- Introduction
- Survival of Torts Unrelated to Death
- Wrongful Death
- Avoiding Double Recovery

INTRODUCTION

Distinguish between the following situations:

Case I.   Dan steals Paul's watch. Paul then sues Dan for the tort of conversion. Within two weeks of filing the suit, Paul dies in a car accident and Dan dies in an earthquake.

Case II.   Barbara negligently drives her car into Sam's car. Sam dies from the injuries resulting from the crash.

In Case I, the plaintiff (Paul) died from a cause unrelated to Dan's tort of conversion; the tort did not cause Paul's death. The same is true of the defendant (Dan)—his death had nothing to do with the tort. Case II presents a very different situation. Barbara's negligence caused the death of Sam. It was a **wrongful death** because it was caused by a tort. (It, therefore, is also referred to as a **tortious** death.) We need to determine whether the tort action survives the death of either the victim or the **tortfeasor** in Cases I and II. (A tortfeasor is a wrongdoer who has committed a tort.) **Survival** is the continuation of a cause of action such as a tort after the death of either the victim or the alleged wrongdoer. As we will see, not all tort actions survive.

SURVIVAL OF TORTS UNRELATED TO DEATH

First, we examine the survival of a tort cause of action when a death has occurred that had nothing to do with the tort (Case I in the preceding example). The survival of the tort depends in part on the kind of injury or harm that the tort inflicts. Three main categories of torts exist: personal torts, personal property torts, and real property torts. **Personal torts** injure the person.

Tom invades Pete's privacy, defames Pete, or batters him. These are examples of torts against Pete's *person*.

Personal property torts damage movable property, which is any property not attached to the land.

Tom converts Pete's car or negligently damages Pete's livestock. These are examples of torts against Pete's *personal property*.

Real property torts damage land and anything attached to the land.

Tom trespasses on Pete's land or negligently damages Pete's house. These are examples of torts against Pete's *real property*.

In all of these examples, assume that Tom or Pete dies from a cause unrelated to the tort. What survives? Logically, you would think that the death of the victim or of the tortfeasor from an unrelated cause would not affect the litigation of the tort action. If the tortfeasor dies, the victim's **estate** should be able to bring the tort claim against the tortfeasor. (An estate consists of all the assets and debts left by a decedent. The estate can sue and be sued; it acts through a personal representative appointed by the decedent's will or by the court.) If, on the other hand, it is the tortfeasor who dies, the victim should be able to bring the tort action against the tortfeasor's estate. Logic, however, has not always ruled this area of the law.

Common Law and Statutory Law

First, we will examine survival of the three categories of torts (personal, personal property, and real property) at **common law.** (Common law is judge-made law in the absence of statutes or other higher law to the contrary.) Then, more important, we will examine what survives under statutory law that has changed the common law. Such statutes are often called *survival statutes*.

Personal Torts

Common law: At common law, torts against the person of the victim did not survive the death of either the victim or the tortfeasor. If the victim dies, the action could not be brought by the victim's estate. If the tortfeasor dies, the action could not be brought against the estate of the tortfeasor.

Statutory law: All states have passed survival statutes that have changed the common law, but not completely. In most states, the personal torts that are invasions of **tangible** interests survive, but the personal torts that are invasions of **intangible** interests do not. Something is tangible if we can make contact with it through our senses such as touch. For example, a human body is tangible. Since battery is a tort against the body, it is a tort that protects a tangible interest and, therefore, would survive. Something is intangible, however, if it cannot be perceived by the senses. For example, a person's reputation or privacy is intangible. Hence, personal torts that protect these interests such as defamation and invasion of privacy would not survive.

Personal Property Torts

Common law: At common law, torts against the personal property of the victim survived the death of the victim but did not survive the death of the tortfeasor.

Statutory law: Survival statutes have changed the common law. In all states, torts against personal property survive both the victim and the tortfeasor.

Real Property Torts

Common law: At common law, torts against the real property of the victim did not survive the death of the victim or the tortfeasor.

Statutory law: Survival statutes have changed the common law. In all states, torts against real property survive the death of either the victim or the tortfeasor.

Hence, if a tort action survives today, it is because the action is one of the few that survived at common law, or because a survival statute has established that it survives.

Characteristics of Actions That Survive

Let us focus on a tort action that survives the death of the victim, again keeping in mind that we are not yet talking about a death that is caused by the tort. Before the victim brings any action against the tortfeasor, the victim dies from a cause unrelated to the tort. The action is brought after this death. Note the following characteristics of this action:

- The action is brought by the estate of the victim through the personal representative of the estate.
- The action is not a new or independent action. It is the same action that the victim would have had if he or she had lived.
- The plaintiff in the action is not an heir or relative of the victim unless the heir or relative happens to be the personal representative of the victim's estate.
- Heirs or relatives do not directly receive any benefit from a damage award in the tort action that survives. If they benefit from the award, they do so through the estate as beneficiaries of a will or via **intestacy** (the distribution of a decedent's estate when no valid will exists).
- There is no recovery for the death of the victim, because we are examining a case in which the tort did not cause the death of the victim; the decedent was the victim of a tort that did not cause death.
- Any defenses the tortfeasor would have had against the victim, had the latter lived (e.g., contributory negligence, assumption of the risk, self-defense), are available to the tortfeasor in the action that survives.

WRONGFUL DEATH

Common Law

Now we move to the situation in Case II presented at the beginning of this chapter: what happens when the victim of a tort dies *because* of the tort? Here we are talking about a tortious or wrongful death. At common law, a tort action for this death could not be brought against the wrongdoer. If, however, the act that caused the death of the victim constituted a crime, the wrongdoer might be prosecuted in a criminal court, but no civil tort action could be brought. If the wrongdoer committed a non-deadly tort against the victim or a tort against the property of a victim who was still alive, there *could* be recovery against the wrongdoer, but not if the latter had killed the victim. It was cheaper, therefore, to kill the victim!

Needless to say, statutes were passed to change this absurdity. Every state now has a remedy for wrongful death. The remedy is not the same in each state. Although your primary concern will be the law of your state, you will need to be aware of the major remedies available in other states, because it is not uncommon for an office to work on a case involving the death of someone in another state.

Elsewhere in this book, we discuss the law of workers' compensation (Chapter 24). If an employee dies from an injury that arises out of and in the course of employment, compensation to heirs or relatives is received through the workers' compensation statute, whether or not the employer wrongfully caused the death. In most states, workers' compensation replaces any other civil remedy. Hence, the following discussion does not apply to death due to an employment accident or disease.

Recovery for Wrongful Death

States differ on how they allow recovery for wrongful death. Two common methods include:

- enlarging the survival statute to include death, and
- enacting a wrongful death statute (Lord Campbell's Act)

Enlarging the Survival Statute to Include Wrongful Death We saw earlier that survival statutes have been passed to permit most kinds of tort actions to survive the death of the victim of the tort. In some states, the death of the victim caused by the tort is handled as follows:

- The tort action of the victim survives his or her death and covers damages that accrued up to the moment of death.
- Damages resulting from the death can be recovered in the same survival action.

No new cause of action is created because of the death. The victim's cause of action is continued by the personal representative of his or her estate. In this action, any defense is available that could have been brought had the victim lived. The damages that are recoverable in this action usually include:

- pain and suffering of the victim from the time of the injury to the time of death
- medical, hospital, and funeral expenses
- lost net earnings and savings the victim would have accumulated if he or she had lived to his or her life expectancy

Enacting a Wrongful Death Statute (Lord Campbell's Act) Most states create a new cause of action for designated relatives of the deceased victim, e.g., spouse and children. A statute creating this wrongful death cause of action is usually modeled after **Lord Campbell's Act** in England and is sometimes referred to as a "pure" death action, as distinguished from the enlarged survival action, which continues the victim's claim. The new cause of action is brought by a representative for the benefit of the relatives or beneficiaries, or in some states, by the beneficiaries themselves. The damages that are recoverable in this action are usually limited to **pecuniary losses.** This covers the loss of the economic value of the support, services, and contributions that the beneficiaries would have received if the victim had lived to his or her life expectancy.

Damages are *not* recoverable in this action for:

- pain and suffering of the victim, medical bills, lost wages, or any other loss that the victim would have had against the tortfeasor (damages for such items are recoverable in a separate survival action, which is often brought along with the beneficiaries' action—see the following discussion on Avoiding Double Recovery)
- mental suffering and grief experienced by the survivor-beneficiaries because of the death of the victim, and loss of consortium rights (see Chapter 18), particularly the right to the companionship and society of the deceased (some states, however, have changed this rule and allow recovery for such **nonpecuniary losses**)

Under most wrongful death statutes, the defendant can raise any defense he or she would have had against the victim if death had not occurred. For example, the defendant may assert that the death was not wrongful. The defendant may have caused the death—but not tortiously. There must be an underlying intentional, negligence, or strict-liability tort before the beneficiaries can recover anything in the wrongful death action. Also, defenses of contributory negligence, assumption of the risk, or any of the privileges will usually defeat the wrongful death action. In most states, the statute of limitations runs from the time of death and not from the date of the injury.

AVOIDING DOUBLE RECOVERY

Some states have both a survival statute (covering the victim's pain and suffering, loss of earnings, medical expenses up to death, etc.) *and* a wrongful death statute (covering the beneficiaries' pecuniary loss of the support, services, and contributions that the victim would have provided them if he or she had not died). The survival action and the wrongful death action can usually be brought concurrently. When both actions are possible, there is a fear of double recovery, especially with respect to the lost earnings of the victim. The following describes the basic conflict and how it may be handled:

> An injured person's own cause of action in tort, which at common law would have ended abruptly at death, is now preserved and vested in his personal representative by means of a survival statute, one of which obtains in every jurisdiction. The existence of such a measure side by side with a wrongful death provision has proved to be a source of concern arising from fear that a duplication of damages could result. Indeed such a fear is not without foundation: Whenever an injured victim while still alive can demonstrate that the impairment of his bodily condition is sufficiently serious to shorten his life expectancy he will become entitled to damages sufficient to replace the lost earnings that otherwise would have been in prospect for him. It is not to be expected that this right would be expunged in the event that death does indeed foreshorten his life before the award has been made. In theory, this element of loss should persist and remain available to his personal representative under a survival statute. If, however, to this survived claim for lost future earnings there were superadded a separate award for his dependents' loss of support under a [wrongful] death statute, the prospect of a duplication of damages would face the defendant. This dilemma has been dealt with in a bewildering variety of ways. In a few states a binding election must be made between a survival claim and an action for wrongful death (e.g., Ky. and Wyo.). Occasionally the survival suit is arbitrarily restricted to those claims of the deceased that were unrelated to his death (e.g., W.Va.). In other states the lawmakers have deliberately omitted a separate death statute, and lost future earnings in full are provided under the survival measure (e.g., Conn.). There are numerous other varieties in approach. The one that is most satisfactory and which has been most widely adopted is that of affording recognition of both the survival claim and the wrongful death claims but with damages for loss of earnings under the survival suit limited exclusively to those earnings that were lost between the time of accident and the moment of death. All pecuniary loss accruing thereafter must be recovered solely under the [wrongful] death statute. It is noteworthy, however, that funeral expenses, which do not accrue, of course, during the lifetime of the deceased, are frequently made recoverable by express provision in the survival statute.[1]

SUMMARY

An action for a personal tort that does not cause death, such as defamation, does not survive the death of either the tortfeasor or the victim when the tort protects an intangible interest such as reputation or privacy. A personal tort that does not cause death, such as battery, and that protects tangible interests, does survive the death of either the tortfeasor or the victim. A personal property tort or a real property tort that does not cause death also survives the death of either. The tort action that survives is the same action that the victim would have brought if he or she had lived.

When the tort causes the death of the victim, a state might enlarge its survival statute to allow the personal representative of the deceased's estate to recover damages for wrongful death in the survival action. On the other hand, the state might create a separate cause of action for wrongful death for designated relatives of the deceased. Special provisions are often necessary to avoid double recovery for lost earnings (in the survival action) and loss of support (in the wrongful death action).

---

[1]W. Malone, *Injuries to Family, Social and Trade Relations* 44–45 (1979).

KEY TERMS

Torts Against and Within the Family

Chapter Outline

- Torts Derived from Other Torts
- Torts Not Derived from Other Torts
- Prenatal Injuries
- Wrongful Life, Birth, Pregnancy
- Wrongful Adoption
- Intrafamily Tort Immunity

TORTS DERIVED FROM OTHER TORTS

Loss of Consortium

Consortium is the companionship, love, affection, sexual relationship, and services (e.g., cooking, making repairs around the house) that one spouse provides another. There can be a recovery for a tortious injury to consortium. At one time, only the husband could recover for **loss of consortium.** In every state, this view has been changed by statute or has been ruled unconstitutional as a denial of the equal protection of the law. Either spouse can now recover for loss of consortium.

> **EXAMPLE:**
>
> - Rich and Ann are married.
> - Paul, a stranger, injures Ann by negligently hitting her with his car.
> - Ann sues Paul for negligence. She receives damages to cover her medical bills, lost wages, and pain and suffering.
> - Rich then brings a *separate* suit against Paul for loss of his wife's consortium. He receives damages to compensate him for whatever loss or impairment he can prove to the companionship he had with Ann before the accident—to the love, affection, sexual intercourse, and services that she gave him as his wife before the accident.

In Rich's action against Paul, Rich cannot recover for injuries sustained by Ann. Ann must recover for such injuries in her own action against Paul. Paul's liability to Rich is limited to the specific injuries sustained by Rich—the loss or impairment of his wife's consortium. If Ann loses her suit against Paul, e.g., because she was contributorily negligent, Rich will not be able to bring his consortium suit. To recover for loss of consortium, there must be an underlying successfully litigated tort.

Most states deny recovery for loss of consortium to individuals who are not married.

> **EXAMPLES:**
>
> - Jim and Rachel are engaged to be married. The defendant negligently incapacitates Rachel the day before the wedding. Rachel sues the defendant to recover for her injuries.
> - Mary and John have lived together for forty years. They have never married and do not live in a state that recognizes common law marriage. The defendant negligently incapacitates John, who sues the defendant to recover for his injuries.
> - George and Bob are homosexuals who have lived together as a couple for ten years. The defendant negligently incapacitates Bob, who sues the defendant to recover for his injuries.

Clearly, Jim, Mary, and George have experienced a loss of consortium. They arguably have suffered in the same manner as Rich, whose wife, Ann, was negligently hit by Paul. The difference, however, is that Jim, Mary, and George (unlike Rich) were not married at the time their consortium was damaged. Most states deny an unmarried person the right to sue for loss of consortium. This may seem unfair, particularly to a couple who is hours away from being married. The law, however, must draw a line somewhere. A court would have a difficult time distinguishing between Jim and Rachel (a day away from their wedding) and an engaged couple whose wedding is one or two years away. What about someone six months or six weeks away? The practical problem of drawing the line plus the bias of the law in favor of marriage has led courts to limit the action for loss of consortium to married individuals.

The word *consortium* sometimes also refers to the normal companionship and affection that exists between a parent and a child. The right of a child to the companionship and affection of a parent is referred to as **parental consortium.** The right of a parent to the companionship and affection of a child is referred to as **filial consortium.**

> **EXAMPLES:**
>
> - Bill is the father of Sam.
> - The defendant negligently incapacitates Bill, who sues the defendant to recover for Bill's injuries.
> - The defendant negligently incapacitates Sam, who sues the defendant to recover for Sam's injuries.

In the first case, Sam has also suffered a loss—a loss of parental consortium. Yet, most states do *not* allow suits for damage to this kind of consortium. Suppose, however, that the parent (Bill) dies from the defendant's negligence. There are some states whose wrongful death statute gives children the right to damages for the loss of companionship and affection they had with their parent (in addition to the financial losses caused by the death). But most states would *not* allow a suit for loss of parental consortium when the injured parent is still alive. (On wrongful death, see Chapter 17.)

In the second case, Bill has also suffered a loss—a loss of filial consortium. As we will see in a moment, parents can sue someone who interferes with their right to receive the services of their children such as doing household chores. States differ, however, on the parent's right to recover for interference with the companionship and affection the parent has with a child—filial consortium. Many states deny such recovery. There are, however, a fair number of states that take a different position and allow recovery for interference with filial consortium.

Loss of Services

A parent has the right to the services of his or her **unemancipated** child. This would include tasks such as cutting the grass and running errands for the household. (Unemancipated means legally dependent on one's parent or legal guardian. A child is **emancipated** if he or she becomes legally independent such as by marrying.)

> **EXAMPLE:** Mary is the twelve-year-old child of Victor and Helen. The defendant negligently injures Mary in a car accident. In a negligence action against the defendant, Mary can recover damages for her injuries.

Victor and Helen can also recover damages from the defendant for causing a **loss of services** by Mary to them. As a twelve-year-old who is dependent on her parents, Mary is unemancipated. She probably helps around the house. The parents can recover for any interference with these services that are wrongfully caused.

TORTS NOT DERIVED FROM OTHER TORTS

Other tort actions that can be brought by one family member because of what the defendant did with or to another family member include the following:

- alienation of affections
- criminal conversation
- enticement of spouse
- abduction or enticement of a child
- seduction

To establish one of these causes of action, there is no need to prove an underlying tort; they are torts in their own right. A number of states, however, have passed statutes (sometimes called **heart-balm statutes**) that have abolished some or all of these tort actions.

Alienation of Affections

Elements
i. The defendant intended to diminish the marital relationship (love, companionship, and comfort) between the plaintiff and the latter's spouse.
ii. Affirmative conduct by the defendant.
iii. Affections between the plaintiff and spouse were in fact alienated.
iv. The defendant caused the alienation (but for the defendant, the alienation would not have occurred, or the defendant was a substantial factor in producing the alienation).

Criminal Conversation

Element
The defendant had sexual relations with the plaintiff's spouse (adultery).

Enticement of Spouse

Elements
i. The defendant intended to diminish the marital relationship between the plaintiff and the latter's spouse.
ii. Affirmative conduct by the defendant either:
   a. to entice or encourage the spouse to leave the plaintiff's home, or
   b. to harbor the spouse and encourage the latter to stay away from the plaintiff's home.
iii. The plaintiff's spouse left home.
iv. The defendant caused the plaintiff to leave home or to stay away (but for what defendant did, the plaintiff would not have left home or stayed away; or, the defendant was a substantial factor in the spouse's leaving or staying away).

Abduction or Enticement of a Child

Elements

     i. The defendant intended to interfere with the parent's custody of the child.

    ii. Affirmative conduct by the defendant:

       a. to abduct or force the child from the parent's custody,

       b. to entice or encourage the child to leave the parent, or

       c. to harbor the child and encourage the latter to stay away from the parent's custody.

    iii. The child left the custody of the parent.

    iv. The defendant caused the child to leave or to stay away (but for what the defendant did, the child would not have left or stayed away; or, the defendant was a substantial factor in the child's leaving or staying away).

ASSIGNMENT

18.1

Olivia is the mother of Irene, who is married to George. Olivia begged Irene not to marry George—to no avail. After the marriage and the birth of a son, Olivia warns Irene that George has a violent disposition. Irene and George separate. Irene takes their son to live with Olivia. Has Olivia committed any torts?

Seduction

Element

The defendant had sex with the plaintiff's minor daughter by force or with the consent of the daughter.

PRENATAL INJURIES

It is possible to commit a tort against an unborn child.

> **EXAMPLE:** Mary is pregnant. While on the freeway one day, Tom negligently drives his car into Mary's car. The impact causes a head injury to the unborn child Mary is carrying.

Mary, of course, can sue for her own injuries and for damage to her car caused by the defendant's negligence. Also, if the child is later born alive, an action can be brought on its behalf to cover the head injury. Suppose, however, the prenatal injury results in the death of the child. In such cases, many states will allow a wrongful death action to be brought (see Chapter 17), but only if the child was **viable** at the time of death. (*Viable* means able to live indefinitely outside the womb by natural or artificial support systems.)

WRONGFUL LIFE, BIRTH, PREGNANCY

Doctors and pharmaceutical companies have been sued for negligence that results in the birth of an unwanted child. When the child is born deformed or otherwise impaired, two categories of suits have been attempted:

Wrongful life: An action by or on behalf of an unwanted child who is impaired; the child seeks its own damages in this action.

Wrongful birth: An action by the parents of an unwanted child who is impaired; the parents seek their own damages in this action.

Suppose, for example, a woman contracts German measles early in her pregnancy. Her doctor negligently advises her that the disease will not affect the health of the child. In fact, the child is born with severe defects caused by the disease. If the woman had known the risks, she would have had an abortion.

In such cases, a small number of states allow suits for wrongful life to cover the child's damages. The vast majority of states, however, do not. Courts are very reluctant to recognize a right not to be born. Several reasons account for this result. One is the enormous difficulty of calculating damages. According to a New Jersey court, it is literally impossible to measure the difference in value between life in an impaired condition and the "utter void of nonexistence." *Berman v. Allen*, 404 A. 2d 8, 12 (N.J. 1979). Some courts also feel that allowing the suit might encourage unwanted children to sue for being born to a poverty-stricken family or to parents with criminal records. Finally, anti-abortion activists have argued that no one should be allowed to sue for missing the opportunity to have been aborted.

Wrongful birth cases, on the other hand, have been more successful. Here the parents sue for their own damages to cover their emotional distress, the cost of prenatal care and delivery, and other expenses attributed to the child's impaired condition.

Finally, we examine negligence that leads to the birth of an unwanted *healthy* child:

> **Wrongful pregnancy:** An action by the parents of an unwanted child who is healthy; the parents seek their own damages in this action.

Cases of wrongful pregnancy (also called wrongful conception) are allowed in most states. The most common example is a suit against a doctor for negligently performing a vasectomy or against a pharmaceutical company for producing defective birth control pills. Damages are limited to the expenses of prenatal care and delivery; they rarely extend to the costs of raising a healthy child. Furthermore, the unwanted healthy child is usually not allowed to bring the same kind of action in his or her own right.

WRONGFUL ADOPTION

Suppose that an adoption agency misrepresents the physical or mental health of a child or misrepresents the medical history of the child's birth family.

> **EXAMPLE:** Alice and Stan Patterson want to adopt a child. They go to the Riverside Adoption Agency (RAA), which introduces them to Irene, an infant available for adoption. The Pattersons adopt Irene. Before the adoption, RAA told the Pattersons that Irene did not have any genetic disorders. This turned out to be false. Also, RAA knew that Irene had been sexually abused, but they did not inform the Pattersons of this. After Irene has been living with the Pattersons for a while, they discover that she has severe medical and psychological problems.

Can the Pattersons sue RAA for damages covering the increased cost of child rearing? The period for challenging the adoption itself may have passed. Furthermore, the adoptive parents may have bonded with the child and do not want to "send" the child back even if it were possible to annul or abrogate the adoption. In such cases, some states have allowed the adoptive parents to sue, particularly when they made clear to the agency that they did not want to adopt a problem child. Their argument is that they would not have adopted the child if they had been presented with all the facts. They cannot expect a guarantee that the child will be perfect. But they are entitled to available information that might indicate a significant likelihood of future medical or psychological problems. The failure to provide such information may constitute the tort of **wrongful adoption**. In an action for this tort, the adoptive parents seek damages from the adoption agency for wrongfully stating or failing to disclose available facts on the health or other condition of the child (the adoptee) that would have been relevant to their decision of whether to adopt.

INTRAFAMILY TORT IMMUNITY

Finally, we consider **intrafamily torts,** which are torts committed by one family member against another. Historically, an intrafamily **immunity** existed for most of these torts. (An immunity is a defense that prevents someone from being sued for what would otherwise be wrongful conduct.) Courts have always been reluctant to permit tort actions among any combination of wife, husband, and unemancipated child. (If a state refuses to allow one spouse to sue another for a specific category of tort, the immunity is referred to as **interspousal immunity.**) This reluctance to allow family members to sue each other is based on the theory that family harmony will be threatened if members know they can sue each other in tort. If the family carries liability insurance, there is also a fear that family members will fraudulently try to collect under the policy by fabricating tort actions against each other. A more technical and brutal reason was given at common law for why husbands and wives could not sue each other—the husband and wife were considered to be one person, and that one person was the husband! Hence, to allow a suit between spouses would theoretically amount to one person suing himself. With the passage of the Married Women's Property Acts and the enforcement of the laws against sex discrimination, a wife now retains her separate identity so that she can sue and be sued like anyone else.

Reform in the law, however, has not meant that **intrafamily tort immunity** no longer exists. A distinction must be made between a suit against the person (such as battery) and a suit against property (such as conversion). For torts against property, most states allow suits between spouses and between parent and child. Many states, however, retain the immunity in some form when the suit involves a tort against the person. The state of the law is outlined in Figure 18–1.

FIGURE 18–1
Intrafamily torts.

Spouse against Spouse

1. In most states, spouses can sue each other for intentional or negligent injury to their property, e.g., negligence, trespass, conversion.
2. In some states, spouses cannot sue each other for intentional or negligent injury to their person—a personal tort action, e.g., negligence, assault, battery.
3. Some states will permit personal tort actions if the man and woman are divorced or if the tort is covered by liability insurance.
4. Some states will permit intentional tort actions against the person to be brought by spouses against each other, but continue to forbid negligence actions for injury to the person.

Child against Parent(s)

1. In all states, a child can sue the parent for intentional or negligent injury caused by the parent to the child's property, e.g., negligence, trespass, conversion.
2. In many states, a child cannot sue a parent for intentional or negligent injury caused by the parent to the child's person, e.g., negligence, assault, battery, particularly in cases where the parent was disciplining the child. Parents have a privilege to discipline their children.
3. If the child is emancipated (e.g., married, member of the armed forces, self-supporting), the child in all states can sue the parent for intentional or negligent injury caused by the parent to the child's person, e.g., negligence, assault, battery.
4. Some states will permit any child (emancipated or not) to sue the parent for intentional torts causing injury to the person, but continue to forbid actions for negligence causing injury to the person.
5. A few states allow the child to sue the parent for all intentional torts causing injury to the person, except where a tort arises out of the parent's exercise of discipline over the child.

Other Related Persons

Brothers and sisters, aunts and uncles, grandparents and grandchildren, and other relatives can sue each other in tort. The restrictions imposed on spouse suits and child suits do not apply to tort actions involving other relatives.

ASSIGNMENT

18.2

Dave knows that he has contagious genital herpes, but does not tell Alice, who contracts the disease from Dave. Can Alice sue Dave for battery? For intentional infliction of emotional distress? For deceit or fraud? Does it make any difference whether the disease was communicated before or after Dave and Alice were married? Does it make any difference that they are now divorced?

SUMMARY

Loss of consortium is an independent action brought by a person whose spouse has been tortiously injured. The action covers the loss of love, affection, sexual relationship, and services that one spouse normally provides another. When a parent is injured, most states do not recognize an action for loss of parental consortium in which a child sues for the tortious interference with the normal companionship and affection children have with their parents. When a child is injured, states differ on whether parents can sue for tortious interference with filial consortium, the normal companionship and affection parents have with their children. An action for loss of services can be brought by a parent against a defendant who has tortiously injured a child to the extent that the child cannot render services that rightfully are due the parent.

Other torts against the family include alienation of affections (the defendant causes the deprivation of love, companionship, and comfort between the plaintiff and the plaintiff's spouse); criminal conversation (the defendant has sex with the plaintiff's spouse); enticement of spouse (the defendant causes the plaintiff's spouse to leave home or to stay away); abduction or enticement of a child (the defendant causes the plaintiff's child to leave home or to stay away); and seduction (the defendant has sex with the plaintiff's minor daughter, with or without the latter's consent). Many states have abolished these torts.

Unborn children can sue for prenatal injuries. If the child dies from the injuries, many states allow a wrongful death action if the child was viable at the time of death. Courts are reluctant to allow an unwanted impaired child to bring an action for wrongful life for his or her own damages in being negligently born. Wrongful birth actions in which parents seek damages for the negligent birth of an unwanted impaired child are usually permitted, as are wrongful pregnancy actions, in which parents seek damages for the negligent birth of an unwanted healthy child. The failure of an adoption agency to give prospective adoptive parents available information about the health or other condition of the prospective adoptee may constitute the tort of wrongful adoption.

Intrafamily torts that damage property are often treated differently from torts that injure the person. Generally, spouses can sue each other for negligent or intentional damage to property. The same is true for such damage caused by the parent to a child's property. There is no immunity for property torts. For torts against the person, in some states, one spouse cannot sue another, and an unemancipated child cannot sue a parent; immunity does apply to torts against the person in such states. There are some exceptions. For example, many states grant this immunity only for negligent injury to the person; thus, any family member can sue another for intentional injury to the person in such states. Other family members such as siblings and other relatives do not have intrafamily tort immunity.

KEY TERMS

consortium   233

loss of consortium   233

parental consortium   234

filial consortium   234

unemancipated   234

emancipated   235

loss of services   235

heart-balm statutes   235

alienation of affections   235

criminal conversation   235

enticement of spouse   235

abduction or enticement of a
   child   236

seduction   236

viable   236

wrongful life   236

wrongful birth   236

wrongful pregnancy   237

wrongful adoption   237

intrafamily torts   238

immunity   238

interspousal immunity   238

intrafamily tort immunity   238

Torts Connected with Land

Chapter Outline

- Introduction
- Trespass to Land
- Nuisance
- Traditional Negligence Liability

INTRODUCTION

An **interest** is a right, claim, or legal share of or in something. There are a variety of interests you can have in land based on your relationship to the land. You can be:

- an owner who is occupying the land
- a nonoccupying owner who is the landlord (i.e., lessor) of a tenant (i.e., lessee) who is occupying the land
- a nonoccupying owner of vacant land
- a tenant (lessee) of the land
- a subtenant (sublessee) who is renting the land from the tenant
- a trespasser who now claims to own the land as an adverse possessor

This chapter is primarily about the torts that can be committed by and against individuals with these relationships to—these interests in—land. The topics we will consider are:

- trespass to land
- nuisance due to trespass, negligence, or strict liability
- negligence

In Chapter 9, we examined a separate tort called strict liability of abnormally dangerous conditions or activities, which is often committed by occupiers of land.
We begin with an overview of **trespass to land.**

TRESPASS TO LAND

 ## Trespass to Land Checklist

Definitions, Relationships, Paralegal Roles, and Research References

Category
Trespass to land is an intentional tort.

Interest Protected by This Tort
The interest in the exclusive possession of land in its present physical condition.

Elements of This Tort
  i. An act
  ii. Intrusion on land
  iii. In possession of another
  iv. Intent to intrude
  v. Causation of the intrusion

Definitions of Major Words/Phrases in These Elements
Act: A voluntary movement of the body that leads to the intrusion.
Intrusion: a. Physically going on the land,
        b. Remaining on the land,
        c. Going to a prohibited portion of the land, or
        d. Failing to remove goods from the land.
Possession: a. Actual occupancy with intent to have exclusive control over the land, or
        b. The right to immediate occupancy when no one else is actually
          occupying it with intent to control it.
Intent to Intrude: The desire to intrude on the land or the knowledge with
substantial certainty that an intrusion will result from what you do or fail to do.
Causation: But for what the defendant did, the intrusion would not have occurred,
or the defendant was a substantial factor in producing the intrusion.

Major Defenses and Counterargument Possibilities That Need to Be Explored
  1. The defendant did not voluntarily go on the land, remain on the land, go to a pro-
     hibited portion of the land, or fail to remove goods from the land.
  2. The plaintiff did not have possession of the land.
  3. The plaintiff had no reasonably beneficial use of the land that the defendant entered
     (e.g., the air space over the land).
  4. There was no intent to intrude: the defendant did not desire to intrude or know with
     substantial certainty that an intrusion would result from what the defendant did.
  5. The defendant did not cause the intrusion (but for what the defendant did or failed
     to do, the intrusion would have occurred anyway; the defendant was not a substan-
     tial factor in bringing about the intrusion).
  6. The plaintiff consented to the defendant's intrusion (on the defense of consent, see
     Chapter 23).
  7. The intrusion occurred while the defendant was defending property (on necessity and
     other self-help privileges, see Chapter 23).
  8. The intrusion occurred while the defendant was abating a nuisance (see discussion of
     this self-help privilege later in this chapter).
  9. The plaintiff's suit against the government for trespass committed by a government
     employee may be barred by sovereign immunity (on sovereign immunity, see
     Chapter 23).
  10. The plaintiff's suit against the government employee for trespass may be barred by
     public official immunity (on official immunity, see Chapter 23).
  11. The plaintiff's suit against the charitable organization for trespass committed by some-
     one working for the organization may be barred by charitable immunity (on charita-
     ble immunity, see Chapter 23).

Damages
If actual harm or damage was done to the land, the plaintiff can recover compensatory
damages, e.g., cost or repair. If no harm or damage was done (a technical violation only),

Trespass to Land Checklist Continued

nominal damages can be recovered. If the defendant acted out of hatred and malice, punitive damages are possible. (On the categories of damages, see Chapter 14.)

Relationship to Criminal Law
It may be a crime in certain states to enter designated land, e.g., government property.

Relationship to Other Torts
Negligence: If the defendant does not intentionally enter the plaintiff's land, the defendant may have entered negligently, e.g., due to an unreasonable mistake. The tort of negligence is committed if actual damage results from the negligent entry.
Nuisance: The defendant may commit a private or public nuisance while entering the plaintiff's land.
Strict Liability for Abnormally Dangerous Activities: The defendant may enter the land while engaged in abnormally dangerous activities, which could be the basis of strict liability.

Federal Law
a. Under the Federal Tort Claims Act, the United States Government *will* be liable for trespass to land committed by one of its federal employees within the scope of employment (respondeat superior). (See Figure 23–7 in Chapter 23.)
b. There may be liability under the Civil Rights Act if the trespass to land was committed while the defendant was depriving the plaintiff of federal rights under color of law. (See Figure 23–8 in Chapter 23.)

Employer-Employee (Agency) Law
An employee who commits a trespass to land is personally liable for this tort. His or her employer will *also* be liable for trespass to land if the conduct of the employee was within the scope of employment (respondeat superior). The employee must be furthering a business objective of the employer at the time. Intentional torts such as trespass to land, however, are often outside the scope of employment. If so, only the employee is liable for the trespass to land. (On the factors that determine the scope of employment, see Figure 12–7 in Chapter 12.)

Research References for Trespass to Land

Digests
In the digests of West, look for case summaries on trespass to land under key topics such as:

Trespass   Adverse Possession

Corpus Juris Secundum and American Jurisprudence 2d
In these legal encyclopedias, see the discussions under topic headings such as:

Trespass   Adverse Possession
Forcible Entry and Detainer

Legal Periodical Literature
There are two index systems to use to locate legal periodical literature on trespass to land:

INDEX TO LEGAL PERIODICALS AND BOOKS (ILP)	CURRENT LAW INDEX (CLI)
Check subject headings such as:	Check subject headings such as:
Trespass	Trespass
Forcible Entry and Detainer	Torts
Torts	Riparian Rights
Adjoining Landowners	Real Property
	Damages

Example of a legal periodical article you will find using *ILP* or *CLI:*

Invasion of Radioactive Particulates as a Common Law Trespass 3 Urban Law Review 206 (1980).

Trespass to Land Checklist Continued

A.L.R., A.L.R.2d, A.L.R.3d, A.L.R.4th, A.L.R.5th, A.L.R. Fed.
Use the *Index to Annotations* to locate annotations on trespass to land. In this index, check subject headings such as:

Trespass	Adverse possession
Forcible Entry and Detainer	Torts

Example of an annotation on trespass to land you can locate through this index:

Liability for Personal Injury or Death Caused by Trespassing or Intruding Livestock by James L. Rigelhaupt, 49 A.L.R.4th 710 (1987).

Words and Phrases
In this multivolume legal dictionary, look up *trespass to land, intrusion, land, real property, ejectment, detainer,* and every other word or phrase connected with trespass to land discussed in this section of the chapter. The dictionary will give you definitions of these words or phrases from court opinions.

CALR: Computer-Assisted Legal Research
Example of a query you could ask on WESTLAW or on LEXIS to try to find cases, statutes, or other legal materials on trespass to land: **trespass /s damages**

Example of search terms you could use on an Internet legal search engine such as LawCrawler (http://lawcrawler.findlaw.com) to find cases, statutes, or other legal materials on trespass to land: **"trespass to land"**

Example of search terms you could use on an Internet general search engine such as Alta Vista (http://www.altavista.com) to find cases, statutes, or other legal materials on trespass to land: **"trespass to land"**

More Internet sites to check for materials on trespass to land and other torts:
Jurist: (http://jurist.law.pitt.edu/sg_torts.htm)
LawGuru: (http://www.lawguru.com/search/lawsearch.html)
See also Tort Law Online at the end of Chapter 1.

Plaintiffs in a Trespass Action

You do not have to own land to bring a suit against someone who is trespassing on the land. Plaintiffs in trespass cases can include tenants and anyone else who has a present or future right to possess the land (referred to as someone with a **possessory interest**). A major reason to bring a trespass action is to prevent someone from taking it away by **adverse possession.** This is a method of acquiring title to land without buying it or receiving it as a gift through a will or other traditional means. The law allows a trespasser to obtain title to land by occupying it in a hostile and visible manner for a designated number of continuous years. This method of acquiring title is designed to prevent speculators from buying land and leaving it vacant for long periods of time until its price increases. If these speculators want to avoid losing their land, they must bring trespass actions against anyone claiming it by adverse possession.

The elements of trespass to land are act, intrusion on land, in possession of another, intent to intrude, and causation of the intrusion. See the definition of these elements in the checklist at the beginning of this chapter. Before leaving the relatively uncomplicated tort of trespass to land, we need to explore briefly the nature of the required intent, the definition of land, and the issue of damages in a trespass case.

Intent

The intent required for this tort is the intent to enter upon the particular piece of land in question. The defendant does not have to show that the plaintiff intended to violate defendant's rights. Hence, it is no defense for the plaintiff to be able to show that he or she was reasonable in thinking there was a right to enter. For example, the defendant has committed trespass to land even though the defendant reasonably, but mistakenly, believed that he or she owned the land. "The defendant is liable for an intentional entry although he acted in good faith, under the mistaken belief, however reasonable, that he was committing no wrong."[1]

Although this element is called the "intent to intrude," intrude or intrusion simply means physically going on the land, remaining on the land, going to a prohibited portion of the land, or failing to remove goods from the land.

Land

Land does not consist solely of ground. It also includes that portion of the air space above the ground over which the plaintiff can claim a **reasonable beneficial use.** If a defendant throws a brick over the plaintiff's land, a trespass has occurred even if the brick never touches the plaintiff's home or ground. Assume that it finally lands beyond the plaintiff's property line. The plaintiff has the use of the air space immediately above the ground. Hence, there has been a trespass to land. The case is different, however, for the space one mile above the ground that is used by airplanes. The latter do not commit trespass.

Damages

Actual destruction or harm to the land does not have to be shown. The actual entry is damage enough. If nothing more has occurred, the plaintiff can at least recover **nominal damages** and prevent someone else from obtaining title by adverse possession.

ASSIGNMENT 19.1

Has a trespass to land been committed in the following cases?   *yes*

a. Jim sells automobiles on the Internet. He obtains Dan's e-mail address and sends Dan a message announcing an automobile sale. Dan sends an e-mail back telling Jim not to send him any unsolicited messages (spam). Jim responds by sending Dan another automobile sale message.

b. Same facts as in (a) except that the spam contains an ad for a pornographic site on the Internet and a new ad is sent every day.   *yes*

NUISANCE

There is no separate tort of **nuisance.** The word describes two different kinds of harm produced by specific tortious or other wrongful conduct. The kinds of harm are **private nuisance** (an unreasonable interference with the reasonable use and enjoyment of private land) and **public nuisance** (an unreasonable interference with a right that is common to the general public). While all private nuisances involve interference with land, some public nuisances do not.

Private Nuisance

The tort of trespass to land protects one's interest in the exclusive possession of land. Private nuisance, on the other hand, is an interference with one's interest in the reasonable use and enjoyment of land. While the same conduct of the defendant can be both a trespass to land and a private nuisance, the wrongs involved are distinct.

---

[1] W. Page Keeton et al., *Prosser and Keeton on the Law of Torts* 74 (5th ed. 1984).

Whoever has the right to the use and enjoyment of the land can sue for its interference. This can include a tenant. It can also include a nonoccupying owner or landlord if the harm to the land is likely to last beyond the tenancy.

Interference with the use and enjoyment of land occurs when the plaintiff's **peace of mind** is disturbed because of the defendant's conduct. The interference can be in the form of loud noises, flooding, constant telephone calls, odors, gasses or other pollution, keeping a house of prostitution next door, etc.

The interference must be **unreasonable.** The test is whether a person who is not unduly sensitive would be annoyed or disturbed by what the defendant has done. In making this determination, a court will consider seven main factors, no one of which is usually determinative.

1. *The gravity and character of the harm.* The interference must be substantial. This is likely to be the case if the interference has visibly altered the physical condition of the plaintiff's land (e.g., dumping chemicals on it). Being emotionally upset, however, because a neighbor's child occasionally cries in an adjoining yard would probably not be considered an unreasonable interference no matter how upset the plaintiff is by the noise.

2. *The social value of the use the plaintiff is making of the land.* **Social value** means quality as measured by the general public good. Using one's land for residential, business, or recreational purposes has considerable social value. This is not so, however, if the plaintiff's land is vacant or unoccupied.

3. *The character of the locality.* Here the question is how suitable to the environment is the defendant's conduct and the plaintiff's use of his or her land. Zoning is one measure of suitability. Even if no zoning ordinances exist, however, a court will want to know whether an area consists primarily or exclusively of residences, heavy industry, small business, agriculture, etc. If the plaintiff's use of his or her land is suitable to a locality, a court will be more likely to conclude that the defendant's interference with this use is unreasonable. In mixed residential and commercial areas, plaintiffs cannot be as sensitive to interferences as they can be in single-use or homogenous areas. The cases that are most difficult to resolve are those in which the plaintiff's use of his or her land and the defendant's conduct are both in conformity with the locality.

4. *The extent of the burden on the plaintiff of avoiding or minimizing the interference.* A court is unlikely to rule that an interference is unreasonable if minimal effort by the plaintiff will take care of the problem. A minimal burden might be to close the window to prevent occasional pollutants from flying in. A substantial burden might be to have to move away to escape the constant flow of pollution.

5. *The motive of the defendant.* If a defendant is acting out of spite to harm the plaintiff, a court is more inclined to rule that the interference is unreasonable than if the defendant is merely acting out of self-interest.

6. *The social value of the defendant's conduct.* Just as we examined the social value of the plaintiff's use of land, so we must ask about the extent of the social value of the defendant's conduct that has led to the interference. For example, the defendant's operation of a legitimate business certainly has social value. The court will take this into consideration in balancing the conflicting interests of the plaintiff and defendant.

7. *The extent of the burden on the defendant of avoiding or minimizing the interference.* If it would take very little effort for the defendant to solve the problem, the failure to exert this effort would encourage a court to rule that the interference is unreasonable. The case becomes more difficult if radical and expensive measures would have to be taken.

ASSIGNMENT

19.2

Examine the following situations. What questions would you want answered in order to determine whether there has been an unreasonable interference with the use and enjoyment of land for purposes of establishing a private nuisance?

a. The plaintiff lives next door to a small nursing home. The home has a large air conditioner motor in the backyard. The plaintiff is very upset about the noise given off by this motor.

b. The defendant is an excellent mechanic. She works on cars as a hobby after her regular job hours. She frequently works on her car and the cars of her friends until late at night. The plaintiff, a neighbor, is bothered by the bright lights the defendant uses while working on the cars and by the constant coming and going of her friends who visit to talk about cars.

c. The local church runs a bingo game every Thursday night. This is extremely upsetting to the plaintiff, who lives next door to the church.

d. A factory employing five hundred people has a chimney that sends black smoke into the air. Particles in the smoke sometimes fall on the plaintiff's house. The plaintiff is worried that the particles will damage her property.

e. Tom lives two floors above Mary's apartment in a four-story apartment building. Mary is a cigarette smoker and her boyfriend smokes a cigar. Whenever either of them smokes, the secondhand smoke travels up through the walls into Tom's apartment. It also goes into several of Tom's windows when they are open.

A private nuisance to the plaintiff's land can be created negligently (e.g., carelessly allowing waste to flow on private land), intentionally (e.g., purposefully dumping the waste on private land), or through an abnormally dangerous condition or activity (e.g., blasting in the area, which causes the waste to go on private land).

If the plaintiff wins, he or she can ask for **damages,** an award of money. The amount might be the difference between the value of the land before and after the interference, or it might be the **cost of restoration** of the land to the state or condition it was in before the interference. An equitable remedy such as an **injuction** is also a possibility. This would consist of a court order that the defendant prevent the interference from occurring or from continuing. Courts are reluctant to award injunctions when their effect would be drastic on a community such as the loss of many jobs due to the closing of a plant.

Self-help is another possible remedy in which victims of a tort take corrective steps on their own without resort to the courts. There is a common law privilege to **abate the nuisance.** This consists of reasonable steps to correct the private nuisance that is interfering with the use and enjoyment of land. The aggrieved person must act within a reasonable time after discovering the interference and, if practical, notify the wrongdoer that he or she will remove the interference if the wrongdoer does not do so. Suppose, for example, that Tom comes home one day from a vacation and is shocked to find that Mary has parked her car in his driveway, blocking the entrance to his garage. She has committed a private nuisance. When he unsuccessfuly tries to find Mary, he gets in her car, releases the emergency brake, and rolls the car out of his way. Tom has properly exercised his privilege to abate a nuisance.

Public Nuisance

A public nuisance is an unreasonable interference with a right common to the general public. Examples include keeping diseased animals that will be sold for food, operating a house of prostitution, operating an illegal gambling parlor, obstructing a public highway, polluting a public river, wiretapping conversations in a judge's chambers or in a jury room, maintaining unsafe apartment buildings, and using public profanity. Conduct that constitutes a public nuisance may also be a private nuisance (if it results in unreasonable interference with the use and enjoyment of private land) and a crime (if it violates the criminal code). A public nuisance must unreasonbly interfere with a public right involving more than a few members of the public. Reasonableness is determined by many of the same factors discussed earlier in assessing reasonableness in a private nuisance, e.g., the gravity of the interference and the burden of avoiding or minimizing the interference.

<table>
<tr><td>**ASSIGNMENT**
19.3</td><td>Do you think that manufacturers of a legal product can commit a public nuisance? Assume that five gun manufacturers make 95 percent of the guns used in the commission of crime in a large city. They place gun ads in media outlets that are distributed in high crime areas. They know that hundreds of guns are purchased at one time by individuals not connected with gun stores. The police believe that these individuals sell the guns to minors, gang members, ex-felons, and others who cannot obtain a gun permit. Have the manufacturers committed a public nuisance?</td></tr>
</table>

A public nuisance can be created negligently (e.g., carelessly allowing logs to fall off a truck and block a public highway), intentionally (e.g., pouring pollutants into a public lake knowing that they will make the lake unusable for fishing), through an abnormally dangerous condition of activity (e.g., blasting in the area, which causes substantial damage to surrounding buildings through vibrations), or by violating a statute, ordinance, or regulation (e.g., opening a house of prositution).

A public official such as the mayor can sue the wrongdoer in civil court or, if a crime is alleged, can urge the prosecution of the wrongdoer in criminal court. A private citizen can also sue if he or she has suffered in a way that is different in kind from every other member of the public affected by the public nuisance. If the private citizen has "only" suffered more of the same harm that everyone else has suffered, he or she would not have **standing** to sue. (Standing is the right to bring an action because of the sufficiency of one's personal interest in the outcome of the proposed litigation or because a special statute grants this right.) Suppose, for example, that the wrongdoer obstructs a public highway, necessitating a substantial detour. A private citizen does not have standing to sue for public nuisance if that citizen suffers the same inconvenience of the detour as everyone else—even if the citizen suffers it more in degree because of the frequency of his or her need to use that road. Suppose, however, that a citizen crashes into the obstruction. This individual has suffered personal or property damage that is different in kind from having to make a detour. Consequently, he or she *would* have standing to sue the wrongdoer for public nuisance.

TRADITIONAL NEGLIGENCE LIABILITY

In this section, we consider negligence liability to persons who are injured on someone's premises or in the immediate environment. In Chapters 11 through 14, we studied the elements of negligence:

- duty
- breach of duty
- proximate cause
- damages

The major headache in the area of **premises liability** is the first element: duty. In Chapter 11 the general rule on duty is stated as follows:

Whenever one's conduct creates a foreseeable risk of injury or damage to someone else's person or property, a duty of reasonable care arises to take precautions to prevent that injury or damage.

When discussing the negligence liability of occupiers of land, this general rule on duty is unfortunately riddled with exceptions depending on the status of the plaintiff:

- adult trespasser
- child trespasser
- licensee
- invitee

and the status of the defendant:

- owner-seller
- owner-buyer
- tenant

Every time the status of the plaintiff or defendant changes, we must ask whether the court will apply a different standard of duty (other than the general duty of reasonable care) for purposes of negligence liability.

A few courts have recently discarded all these special rules and exceptions, and have declared that the duty is reasonable care for all categories of plaintiffs and defendants. The status of the plaintiff or defendant is simply one of the factors to be taken into consideration in deciding whether there has been a breach of this duty. The status of the plaintiff as trespasser, licensee, or invitee, for example, would be relevant solely in determining the extent to which their presence on the land was foreseeable to the defendant. A separate duty would not exist for each category of plaintiff under this minority view. Because most courts, however, do not take this position, we must examine each status separately.

Throughout the discussion, we will be asking whether a duty of **reasonable care** is owed by the defendant, and if not, what *lesser standard of care* is owed. In some situations, it may be that *no duty* of care is owed, so that the defendant will not be liable for the injury suffered by the plaintiff.

The following themes will guide our discussion:

1. the duty of occupiers of land to persons outside the land
2. the duty of occupiers of land to trespassers, licensees, and invitees on the land
3. the special problems of the seller and buyer of land (vendor and vendee)
4. the special problems of the landlord and tenant (lessor and lessee)

By **occupier** we mean anyone in possession of the land claiming a right to possession, e.g., an owner personally using the premises, a tenant, or an adverse possessor.

1. Persons Outside the Land

A person traveling in front of the defendant's land or living close by can be injured in a number of ways. The injury can come from a natural condition on the defendant's land (e.g., a tree limb falls on the plaintiff who is walking on a sidewalk), or from a non-natural condition on the defendant's land (e.g., a building collapses on a car parked on a street in front of the defendant's land), or from some business or personal activity taking place on the defendant's land (e.g., a bucket falls from a plank used by painters, and the bucket hits a pedestrian). See Figure 19–1 for the defendant's duty with respect to each category.

The rules in Figure 19–1 apply if the injury results from anything that the defendant's employees do or fail to do within the scope of their employment. Suppose, however, the defendant hires an **independent contractor** over whom the defendant usually has little control concerning the manner in which the work is done. If injury occurs to plaintiffs not on the land due to the activity of independent contractors on

The Condition or Activity	The Duty Owed
1. *Natural conditions on the defendant's land* (e.g., natural lakes, trees, rocks)	**1.** Generally, the defendant owes *no* duty of care to prevent injury to persons outside the land who might be injured by natural conditions on the defendant's land. If, however, the defendant owns *trees* in an *urban* area, he or she does owe a *duty of reasonable care* to inspect the trees and make sure that they are safe to persons outside the land. In most states, there is *no* duty owed if the trees are in a *rural* area.
2. *Non-natural or artificial conditions on the defendant's land* (e.g., fence, swimming pool, building)	**2.** The defendant owes a *duty of reasonable care* to prevent injury to persons outside the land who might be injured by non-natural or artificial conditions on the defendant's land.
3. *Business or personal activity taking place on the defendant's land* (e.g., steam blasting the wall of a building)	**3.** The defendant owes a *duty of reasonable care* to prevent injury to persons outside the land who might be injured by business or personal activities being conducted by the defendant on the land.

the land, the independent contractor and not the defendant will be liable for the negligence. An exception exists when the defendant hires the independent contractor to do inherently dangerous work. The defendant will be liable for injuries resulting from such activities. When, however, the injury results from the manner or method of work of the independent contractor not involved in inherently dangerous work, the defendant-occupier of the land is not liable.

2. Trespassers, Licensees, and Invitees

Everyone who comes on the land will fall into one of the three categories of trespasser, licensee, or invitee. (See the definitions in Figure 19–2.) The highest standard of care is owed the invitee, who must be accorded full reasonable-care treatment by the land occupier. Although the trespasser is given the lowest standard of care of the three, there are important exceptions that have the effect of elevating the amount of care owed the trespasser.

Trespassers

Trespassers have neither consent nor privilege to be on the land or on designated portions of the land. The privileges would include necessity, recapture of chattels (for a discussion of these self-help privileges, see Chapter 23), and abatement of a nuisance.

Trespasser: A person who enters the land without the consent of the occupier and without any privilege to do so.

Licensee: A person who enters the land for his or her own purposes, but with the express or implied consent of the occupier. A licensee does not enter to pursue a purpose of the occupier.

Invitee: A person who enters the land upon the express or implied invitation of the occupier in order to use the land for the purposes for which it is held open to the public or to pursue the business of the occupier.

The general rule is that the occupier owes *no duty of care* to a trespasser unless the trespasser falls into one of the following categories:

- discovered trespasser anywhere on the land
- foreseeable constant trespassers on limited areas of the land
- child trespasser anywhere on the land

Discovered trespasser anywhere on the land   An occupier cannot commit any *intentional* harm on a known trespasser unless the occupier has a privilege (e.g., self-defense, defense of others) to use such force. A spring gun, for example, cannot be used to catch an unsuspecting trespasser. What about *negligence* liability? A known trespasser is owed a duty of reasonable care by the occupier. If, for example, a railroad engineer sees a trespasser ahead, reasonable care must be used to avoid hitting the trespasser. Actual knowledge of the trespasser is not necessary as long as the occupier has enough information to lead a reasonable person to know that a trespasser is present.

Reasonable care does not mean that the occupier must make the land safe for the trespasser. It simply means that once discovered, the occupier must use reasonable care to avoid injuring the trespasser. Ordinary care under the circumstances will be sufficient. A warning, for example, may be required to alert the trespasser to dangerous activities or conditions on the land, which the trespasser might not be expected to notice. No such warning would be needed, however, for natural conditions on the land such as a lake or clearly visible ice.

A few courts take a more simplistic view and argue that the only duty of the occupier to the known trespasser is to avoid injuring the trespasser by willful or wanton conduct.

Foreseeable constant trespassers on limited portions of the land   The occupier has a duty of reasonable care to discover and provide protection for trespassers who frequently enter limited areas of the land. For example, a railroad may know (or should know) that large numbers of people regularly walk across the track at a designated spot. The area must be limited and the trespassing in that area must be constant. As with the known trespasser, the occupier does not have a duty to inspect his or her land in order to make it injury-proof. The duty is to use reasonable care under the circumstances, which may include a warning, fencing, extra lighting—but only on the limited area where constant trespassers are foreseeable. The more dangerous the condition or activity in that area, the greater the precaution the occupier must take to prevent the injury. No such precautions are usually needed for natural conditions on the limited area of the land that the trespassers can be expected to protect themselves against. If the trespasser is injured in spite of the reasonable steps taken by the occupier, the latter will not be liable for negligence.

Child trespassers anywhere on the land   Children are given special protection in the law of premises liability. A **child** is usually defined as someone who is too young to appreciate the dangers that could be involved in a given situation. There is no age limit that sets the boundary line for the level of immaturity that is required, but in the vast majority of cases that have provided this special protection, the plaintiff has been under fifteen.

The special protection is embodied in the **attractive nuisance doctrine**, which says a duty of reasonable care is owed to prevent injury:

1. to a trespassing child unable to appreciate the danger
2. from an artificial condition or activity on land
3. to which the child can be expected to be drawn or attracted

The word "nuisance" is used in its generic sense of something that is mischievous; it has no reference to the rules on private and public nuisance discussed earlier.

A more modern statement of the "attractive nuisance" rule or doctrine has been provided by the *Restatement of Torts*[2], which provides that an occupier of land is liable for physical harm caused by artificial conditions on the land if:

1. the artificial condition is on a place on the land that the occupier knows or has reason to know that children will trespass upon, and
2. the occupier knows or has reason to know that the artificial condition will involve an unreasonable risk of serious injury to the trespassing children, and
3. the trespassing children are too young to discover the artificial condition or to appreciate the danger within it, and
4. the utility to the occupier of maintaining the condition and the burden or inconvenience of eliminating the danger are slight when compared to the risk to the trespassing children, and
5. the occupier fails to take those reasonable steps that would protect the child.

This list is a specific application of the traditional breach-of-duty equation we examined in Chapter 12, which balances the factors that help the court determine what is and is not unreasonable conduct. (See Figure 12–3 in Chapter 12.)

The foreseeability of serious injury to the child is measured or weighed against what the defendant was trying to accomplish by the artificial condition, and the burden or inconvenience on the defendant to protect the child against this condition.

Artificial conditions include tracks, vehicles, rope, fences, barns, and factories. Under the *Restatement*'s formula, the attractiveness of the condition is important mainly on the issue of the foreseeability of the child's presence.

The duty of reasonable care is usually not applied when the child is injured by natural conditions on the land (e.g., lakes, rivers, and natural rock formations) unless the defendant has significantly altered these conditions through strip-mining or other processes.

ASSIGNMENT

19.4

What questions would you investigate to decide whether the defendant in the following cases owed and breached a duty of reasonable care to the plaintiff?

a. A ten-year-old boy is trespassing on the defendant's land. He leans against a fence on the land and badly injures his back against a protruding nail.

b. A nine-year-old girl is trespassing on the defendant's land. She watches workers climb a pole on the land. After the workers leave, the girl puts on a pair of spiked or cleated shoes that she owns and tries to climb the pole. She falls and severely injures herself.

Licensees

Licensees are on the land with the express or implied permission of the occupier. The licensees, however, are present for their own purposes.

EXAMPLES:

- someone taking a shortcut through the land
- someone soliciting money for charity
- a trespasser who has been allowed to remain, e.g., a loiterer
- a person who comes to borrow a tool
- a social guest, even if invited

The last example has caused some difficulty. Because **social guests** are invited, one would normally tend to classify them as invitees. Only a few courts, however, take

---

[2]*Restatement (Second) of Torts* § 339 (1965).

this position. In most states, a social guest is a mere licensee, no matter how much urging the occupier may have used to get the guest to come and even though the guest may perform some incidental chores or tasks for the occupier while there. A **business guest,** however, who comes for the purpose of doing business with the occupier, *is* an invitee.

What standard of care is owed by the occupier to the licensee?

1. First, the occupier owes the licensee at least the same duty of care that he or she owes the trespasser, as discussed previously.
2. The occupier must warn the licensee of dangerous natural *or* artificial conditions (a) if the owner knows about these conditions or has reason to know about them—actual knowledge, and (b) if they are **latent** so that the occupier should expect that the licensee would not discover them. (Note: the occupier does not have a duty to inspect his or her premises to discover such danger. This duty to inspect *will* exist for the protection of an invitee.)
3. Third, if the condition is extremely dangerous, the occupier's duty may be to take active, reasonable precautions to protect the licensee rather than to simply warn him or her of the condition.
4. Fourth, for any activities being conducted on the land, the occupier owes the licensee a duty of reasonable care to avoid injuring the licensee, which may call for a warning or for more active safety precautions.

Suppose that there is a fence on the land in a state of disrepair. The occupier does not know or have reason to know about this artificial condition but should know about it if he or she were acting reasonably. The licensee is injured when the fence falls on him or her. On these facts, the occupier would not be liable to the licensee for negligence. The occupier has no duty to inspect for dangerous *conditions*. If the occupier has actual knowledge of the dangerous condition (artificial or natural), then he or she must either warn the licensee of it or make it safe, depending on the nature of the danger. *Activities,* such as operating machinery on the land, however, call for reasonable care.

If the occupier knows that third persons are on the land who are likely to injure the licensee, the occupier has a duty to at least warn the licensee of the presence of such third persons, e.g., known criminals or individuals who have told the occupier that they want to harm the licensee.

An analogous situation involves automobiles. If the social guest is a licensee in an automobile, the same rules apply: the driver has a duty to use reasonable care in driving the car (an activity), but has no duty to inspect the car to make sure that it is safe. When the driver knows of defective conditions in the car, he or she must warn the guest of them. As indicated in Chapter 12, however, there are automobile guest statutes in some states that change this common law, often making the driver liable only for wanton or reckless conduct in driving the car. A **passenger,** however, is often treated differently than a mere social guest. In many states, a duty of reasonable care is owed passengers. To be a passenger, the plaintiff's presence must confer some benefit on the driver other than the benefit of his or her company or the mere sharing of expenses, although the latter can be a factor to show that the plaintiff is a passenger if other benefit to the driver is also shown. If the plaintiff is paying for the ride, or if the driver is trying to solicit business from the plaintiff, the latter is a passenger to whom a duty of reasonable care is owed.

ASSIGNMENT 19.5

A door-to-door salesperson slips and falls on a child's skate upon approaching the front door of a residence. What standard of care would the occupier owe this person?

Invitees

The highest degree of care by the occupier of land is owed an invitee. An invitee is someone present on the land with the express or implied invitation of the occupier to use the land for a purpose for which it is open to the public or to use the land to pursue the business of the occupier.

> **EXAMPLES:**
>
> - a customer in a department store
> - someone browsing in a department store, even if nothing is purchased
> - a user of a laundromat to wash clothes (a person who is present in the laundromat to wait for a bus or to get out of the rain, however, is probably a licensee only)
> - someone attending a free public lecture on religion
> - a user of a library (a person who is there to meet a friend, however, is probably only a licensee)
> - a patron at a restaurant, theater, amusement park, or similar establishment
> - someone who goes to a garage to find out if it sells a certain part for a car

There must be an element of invitation that is much stronger than mere permission or consent that the person be on the land. The invitation is an implied or direct statement of a desire by the occupier that the person be present. A greater standard of care is owed to an invitee than to a trespasser or a licensee because the invitation justifies the invitee's belief that the premises are safe.

Public employees injured on the premises often pose a problem. They include police officers, fire fighters, sanitation workers, postal workers, and meter readers. What is their status? If they are not present in their official capacity within working hours, their status is determined like that of any other citizen. Indeed, they could have the status of trespasser. When present in an *official* role, are they invitees or licensees?

In most states, police officers and fire fighters are licensees only, to whom a duty of reasonable care is owed for activities conducted on the premises, but no duty concerning dangerous conditions unknown to the occupier. The theory behind this position is that these public employees are likely to go to parts of the premises that the occupier has no reason to expect, especially in emergency situations. As to such areas, the occupier has made no implied or direct representation that they are safe. Other public official entrants, however, are given the status of invitees on the somewhat strained theory they are present for a business purpose of the occupier.

A few states disregard this distinction and classify all public entrants as invitees.

ASSIGNMENT

19.6

Are the following individuals invitees, licensees, or trespassers?

a. Tom enters a restaurant solely to use its bathroom. He slips on the bathroom floor.

b. Mary wants to visit a friend who is staying at a hotel. She goes to the room of the friend. While there, she is assaulted by another guest.

c. Fred goes to a railroad station to meet a passenger. While there, he falls over a hose on the ramp.

d. Linda goes to a soccer game to pass out religious literature. She falls down a flight of steps.

e. Jim is in a restaurant eating. He notices that there are cries of distress coming from the kitchen. He passes through the kitchen door on which a sign is posted reading, "Authorized Personnel Only." He discovers that nothing is wrong, but slips on the kitchen floor.

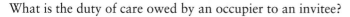

What is the duty of care owed by an occupier to an invitee?

1. First, the occupier owes the invitee at least the same standard of care owed the trespasser, as discussed previously.
2. Second, the occupier owes the invitee at least the same standard of care owed the licensee, as discussed previously.
3. Third, the occupier owes the invitee a duty of reasonable care to inspect *and discover* dangerous artificial conditions on the land, dangerous natural conditions on the land, and dangerous activities on the land.
4. Fourth, depending on the extent of the danger in the condition or activity, the occupier must either warn the invitee or make the condition or activity safe.

Again, no more than reasonable care is required to discover the danger and protect the invitee from it. The occupier is not the insurer of the invitee.

3. The Special Problems of the Seller and Buyer of Land (Vendor and Vendee)

When land is sold, the general rule is that the seller (**vendor**) has no further tort liability for injuries that occur on the land, either to the buyer (**vendee**) or to a third person. The buyer, under the theory of **caveat emptor** (buyer beware), takes the land as he or she finds it. The buyer is expected to make an inspection of the premises before purchasing. The seller will not be liable if the buyer is injured by a condition on the land, even if the condition was present when the land was sold. Third parties injured by such conditions must look to the new owner for liability.

A number of exceptions exist to this rule. If there is a hidden or latent condition on the land that is dangerous and if the seller knows about the condition (or has reason to know about it), the seller has a duty either to warn the buyer of the condition or to repair it before turning the land over to the buyer. Examples of latent conditions include deep holes in the yard covered by thin plywood, and ceilings infested with termites not visible on the surface. A seller does not have a duty to inspect the premises to discover defects that are latent. There is a duty to warn or repair only when the seller knows about such defects or has reason to believe they exist. If this duty is breached, injuries sustained by the buyer can lead to negligence liability against the seller. The buyer may also be able to assert the tort of fraud or misrepresentation.

Another exception concerns conditions on the land that are dangerous to persons *outside the land* at the time of the sale. These conditions sometimes amount to a public or private nuisance, although the seller's liability for injury caused to a plaintiff outside the land is not dependent on the existence of a nuisance. The seller's liability exists only for a reasonable time to enable the buyer to discover such conditions and therefore assume responsibility for them.

4. The Special Problems of the Landlord and Tenant (Lessor and Lessee)

Normally, a landlord (**lessor**) is not entitled to possession of the land, but has a **reversionary interest** in the land, which comes into effect after the tenancy is over. (A reversionary interest is a right to the future enjoyment of land that is presently occupied by another). The general rule is that the tenant (**lessee**) assumes all liability for injuries caused by conditions or activities on the land. There are a number of exceptions to this general rule.

Statutes may exist in a state requiring the landlord to maintain the premises, particularly apartment houses, in a safe condition. The violation of such statutes may impose negligence (and in severe cases, criminal) liability on the landlord.

The landlord will be liable to the tenant and to third parties for injuries caused by latent dangerous conditions on the land at the time of the lease which the landlord has actual knowledge of or has reason to believe exist. In most states, the landlord has no duty to inspect and discover such conditions, but must know of them or have reason to believe that they are present. The conditions must be latent or concealed—not obvious to the tenant.

Often the landlord does not lease the entire building or land to the tenant(s). The landlord may retain control over certain **common areas,** such as hallways, stairways, elevators, boiler rooms. The landlord has a duty of reasonable care to inspect these common areas and make sure that they are safe for those who are entitled to use them, e.g., the tenants and people using the land as invitees.

Another exception occurs when the landlord leases the premises for a purpose that involves the admission of the public, e.g., theater, pier, hotel, and department store. In such cases, the landlord has a duty to inspect the premises and to repair any dangerous conditions that exist at the time of the lease, *before* the tenant takes over. Reasonable care must be used to make sure that the land is not turned over in a dangerous condition. If a member of the public is injured by such a condition that was unreasonably not discovered and repaired by the landlord before the tenant took over, the landlord will be liable, even if the lease agreement provides that the tenant shall assume all responsibility for repairs. The landlord cannot shift the responsibility to the tenant in this way. The duty is non-delegable.

Suppose that the dangerous condition arises *after* the land is leased. The general rule is that injured third parties must look to the tenant for liability rather than to the landlord. If, however, the landlord is obligated to make repairs by the terms of the lease, failure to do so will lead to negligence liability in most states. In such cases, the tenant can argue that the tenant did not make the repairs because of reasonable reliance on the landlord's contract obligation to do so. There are some states, however, that do not impose tort liability on the landlord for a failure to make agreed-upon repairs. In such states, only the tenant is liable in tort to injured third parties. The tenant's recourse in such states is a breach-of-contract action against the landlord. If the landlord does undertake the repairs but performs them negligently, the landlord will be liable in tort.

SUMMARY

Trespass to land is an intentional intrusion on land in possession of another. The intent to enter does not require proof of an intent to enter wrongfully. Land includes the ground and the air space above the ground over which the plaintiff has reasonable beneficial use. Actual harm to the land does not have to be shown.

A private nuisance is an unreasonable interference with the reasonable use and enjoyment of private land. This occurs when one's peace of mind is disturbed while on the land. In determining whether the interference is unreasonable, the court will consider a number of factors: the gravity and character of the harm, the social value of the use the plaintiff is making of the land, the character of the locality, the extent of the burden on the plaintiff of avoiding or minimizing the interference, the motive of the defendant, the social value of the defendant's conduct, and the extent of the burden on the defendant of avoiding or minimizing the interference. A private nuisance can be created negligently, intentionally, or through an abnormally dangerous condition or activity. Any person who has the right to the use and enjoyment of the land can bring the action. The remedies might include money (damages,) injunction, and self-help via the privilege to abate the nuisance.

A public nuisance is an unreasonable interference with a right common to the general public. It can be created negligently; intentionally; through an abnormally dangerous condition or activity; or by violating a statute, ordinance, or regulation. A public official can sue the wrongdoer. A private citizen can also sue if he or she has suffered in a way that is different in kind from every other member of the public affected by the public nuisance.

Traditional negligence liability may depend on the status of the parties. To persons outside the land, occupiers owe a duty of reasonable care as to non-natural or artificial conditions on the land and as to business or personal activity taking place on the land. No duty of care is owed to trespassers unless they are discovered on the land, are constant trespassers on limited areas of the land, or are trespassing children (under the attractive nuisance doctrine). Licensees must be warned of dangerous natural or artificial conditions on the land if the occupier knows or has reason to know about the conditions and if they are latent so that the licensee is not expected to discover them. More than a warning is needed if the condition is extremely dangerous. Licensees must be accorded reasonable care as to activities on the land. For invitees, the occupier must take reasonable steps to inspect and discover dangerous artificial or natural conditions and dangerous activities on the land. The occupier must then use reasonable care to protect the invitee from such conditions and activities. The seller of land can be liable for known latent defects that injure the buyer or a third person on the land. A landlord can be liable to tenants and others injured by latent dangerous conditions on the land that the landlord knows about or should know about. The landlord must use reasonable care to make common areas safe.

KEY TERMS

interest   241

trespass to land   241

possessory interest   244

adverse possession   244

reasonable beneficial use   245

nominal damages   245

nuisance   245

private nuisance   245

public nuisance   245

peace of mind   245

unreasonable   245

social value   246

damages   247

cost of restoration   247

injunction   247

self-help   247

abate the nuisance   247

standing   248

premises liability   248

reasonable care   249

occupier   249

independent contractor   249

trespasser   250

licensee   250

invitee   250

child   251

attractive nuisance doctrine   251

social guests   252

business guest   253

latent   253

passenger   255

vendor   255

vendee   255

caveat emptor   255

lessor   255

reversionary interest   255

lessee   255

common areas   255

Defamation

Chapter Outline

INTRODUCTION

In Shakespeare's *Othello,* Iago says to Othello:

> Good name in man and woman, dear my lord,
> Is the immediate jewel of their souls.
> Who steals my purse steals trash;
> 'Tis something, nothing;
> 'Twas mine, 'tis his, and has been slave to thousands;
> But he that filches from me my good name
> Robs me of that which not enriches him,
> And makes me poor indeed. Act III, scene 3.

Defamation covers injuries to a person's good name and reputation. There are two defamation torts: libel and slander. **Libel** consists of defamation that is written (e.g., in a book) or embodied in a physical form (e.g., a photograph, a film, an effigy). **Slander** consists of defamation that is spoken (e.g., a conversation) or gestured as a substitute for speech (e.g., a nod of the head, a wave of the hand). Defamation on a television program would be considered libel since it has relative permanence in the physical form of film or video.[1] The elements of libel and slander are the same with the major exception of the element of damages.

---

[1]At one time, defamation on radio or television was referred to as **defamacast.**

The United States Supreme Court significantly changed the common law of defamation when the alleged defamer is a newspaper, a television program, or other member of the media. To preserve the freedom-of-the-press protection under the First Amendment of the *United States Constitution*, the Court made it considerably harder to win a defamation suit against the media than against any other category of defendant. Some believe that the Court will eventually impose the same or similar rules in all defamation suits. To date, however, the Court has not constitutionalized all of defamation law. Hence, we need to examine both the common law of defamation (covering primarily non-media defendants) and the constitutional law of defamation (covering primarily media defendants). Constitutional law will be covered throughout the chapter, but primarily when we study the falsity of a defamatory statement. This is where the most significant changes have been made.

 Defamation Checklist

Definitions, Relationships, Paralegal Roles, and Research References

Category
At common law, defamation was a strict-liability tort except for the element of publication. For media defendants, this has been changed by constitutional law. For such defendants, defamation is now a tort that requires a showing of fault.

Interest Protected
The right to one's good name and reputation.

Elements
Defamation consists of two torts: libel and slander. The elements of these torts are the same. When we study the first and fourth elements, however, we will find that there can be important differences depending on the identity of the parties and the kind of defamation alleged.

   i. A defamatory statement by the defendant
   ii. Of and concerning the plaintiff
   iii. Publication
   iv. Damages
   v. Causation

Definitions of Major Words/Phrases in These Elements
Defamatory Statement: A statement of fact that would tend to harm the reputation of the plaintiff in the eyes of at least a substantial and respectable minority of people by lowering the plaintiff in the estimation of those people or by deterring them from associating with the plaintiff.
Of and Concerning the Plaintiff: A statement reasonably understood to refer to the plaintiff.
Publication: A communication of the statement to someone other than the plaintiff.
Damages (in non-media cases): Slander:
   a. Special damages are not required if the slander is *slander per se.*
   b. Special damages must be proven if the slander is *slander per quod.*
     Libel:
   a. In some states, libel never requires special damages.
   b. In other states, only libel on its face does not require special damages. In such states, libel per quod requires special damages.
Causation: But for the defendant's statement, the plaintiff would not have suffered harm to reputation; or, the defendant's statement was a substantial factor in bringing about the harm to the plaintiff's reputation.

Major Defenses and Counterargument Possibilities That Need to Be Explored
(Constitutional law has changed a good deal of the common law of defamation as it applies to the media. In the following list, if the item has been applied only to media defendants, it will so indicate.)

   1. The statement did not tend to harm the reputation of the plaintiff in the eyes of at least a respectable and substantial minority of the community.

Defamation Checklist Continued

2. Only the plaintiff thought that the statement harmed his or her reputation, or that it had a tendency to do so.

3. The defendant's statement cannot reasonably be understood in a defamatory sense.

4. The defendant's statement was not in fact understood in a defamatory sense.

5. The defendant merely stated an opinion, which did not expressly or impliedly communicate any statements of fact.

6. The defendant's statement could not reasonably be understood to refer to the plaintiff.

7. The group the defendant defamed was too large for the plaintiff (who was part of the group) to be able to reasonably say that the statement was of and concerning the plaintiff.

8. The defendant neither intended to refer to the plaintiff nor was negligent in referring to the plaintiff (for media defendants only).

9. The defendant's statement was not communicated to someone other than the plaintiff.

10. The defendant neither intended to communicate the statement to someone other than the plaintiff nor was negligent in this regard.

11. The defendant's oral defamatory statement is not slander per se and the plaintiff has failed to prove special damages.

12. The defendant's statement is libel per quod and the plaintiff has failed to prove special damages.

13. The harm suffered by the plaintiff was not caused by the defendant's defamatory statement.

14. The defendant's defamatory statement was true.

15. The defamatory statement pertained to a matter of public concern about a public official or a public figure and the plaintiff has not shown actual malice by clear and convincing evidence (for media defendants only).

16. The defamatory statement pertained to a matter of private concern about a public official or a public figure and the plaintiff has not shown the defendant's fault as to truth or falsity by clear and convincing evidence (for media defendants only).

17. The defamatory statement pertained to a matter of public or private concern about a private person and the plaintiff has not shown the defendant's fault as to truth or falsity by clear and convincing evidence (for media defendants only).

18. The defendant had an absolute privilege to utter the defamatory statement.

19. The defendant had a qualified or conditional privilege to utter the defamatory statement and the privilege was not lost by abusing it.

20. The defendant consented to the publication of the defamatory statement (on the defense of consent, see Chapter 23).

21. The plaintiff's defamation suit is a "slapp" suit that should be dismissed.

22. The plaintiff's suit against the government for defamation committed by a government employee may be barred by sovereign immunity (on sovereign immunity, see Chapter 23).

23. The plaintiff's suit against the government employee for defamation may be barred by public official immunity (on official immunity, see Chapter 23).

24. The plaintiff's suit against the charitable organization for a defamation committed by someone working for the organization may be barred by charitable immunity (on charitable immunity, see Chapter 23).

25. The plaintiff's suit against a family member for defamation may be barred by intrafamily immunity (on intrafamily immunity, see Chapter 18).

Damages
At common law, defamation plaintiffs can receive presumed damages; special damages do not have to be proven. (Special damages are actual monetary or pecuniary losses.) In many states, special damages must be proven if the defamation is slander per quod. In some states, libel never requires special damages. In others, this is so only for libel on its face. For media defendants, in almost all cases there can be no presumed damages.

Defamation Checklist Continued

Relationship to Criminal Law
Certain forms of defamation are crimes in some states if the defamatory statement is intentionally published. Truth is usually not a defense to the crime of criminal defamation.

Relationship to Other Torts
Abuse of Process: While abusing legal process, the defendant may also defame the plaintiff.

Alienation of Affections: While alienating the affections of a spouse, the defendant may also defame the plaintiff.

Assault: While assaulting the plaintiff, the defendant may also defame the plaintiff.

Battery: While battering the plaintiff, the defendant may also defame the plaintiff.

Disparagement: Defamation protects the personal reputation of the plaintiff. Disparagement is an attack against the goods or property of the plaintiff beyond ordinary commercial competition. While committing disparagement, the defendant may also defame the plaintiff if the attack against the plaintiff's goods or property is also an express or implied personal attack on the reputation of the plaintiff.

False Imprisonment: While falsely imprisoning the plaintiff, the defendant may also defame the plaintiff.

Intentional Infliction of Emotional Distress: The defendant's defamatory statement may not be actionable because it is true or because it is not communicated to a third person. Yet, the statement might be so outrageous as to constitute the tort of intentional infliction of emotional distress.

Invasion of Privacy: The facts that give rise to false light invasion of privacy often also give rise to an action for defamation.

Malicious Prosecution: While committing malicious prosecution, the defendant may also defame the plaintiff.

Federal Law
a. Under the Federal Tort Claims Act, the United States Government will *not* be liable for libel or slander committed by one of its federal employees within the scope of employment (respondeat superior). (See Figure 23–7 in Chapter 23.)
b. There may be liability under the Civil Rights Act if the libel or slander was committed while the defendant was depriving the plaintiff of federal rights under color of law. (See Figure 23–8 in Chapter 23.)

Employer-Employee (Agency) Law
An employee who commits libel or slander is personally liable for this tort. His or her employer will *also* be liable for libel or slander if the conduct of the employee was within the scope of employment (respondeat superior). The employee must be furthering a business objective of the employer while defaming the plaintiff. (On the factors that determine scope of employment, see Figure 12–7 in Chapter 12.)

Paralegal Roles in Defamation Litigation
Fact finding (help the office collect facts relevant to prove the elements of libel or slander, the elements of available defenses, and extent of injuries or other damages):
- client interviewing
- field investigation
- online research (e.g., locating news stories about the defendant)

File management (help the office control the volume of paperwork in a libel or slander litigation):
- open client file
- enter case data in computer database
- maintain file documents

Litigation assistance (help the trial attorney prepare for a libel or slander trial and appeal, if needed):
- draft discovery requests
- draft answers to discovery requests
- draft pleadings
- digest and index discovery documents

Defamation Checklist Continued

- help prepare, order, and manage trial exhibits (visuals or demonstratives)
- prepare trial notebook
- draft notice of appeal
- order trial transcript
- cite check briefs
- perform legal research

Collection/enforcement (help the trial attorney for the judgment creditor to collect the damages award or to enforce other court orders at the conclusion of the libel or slander case):

- draft postjudgment discovery requests
- field investigation to monitor compliance with judgment
- online research (e.g., location of defendant's business assets)

Research References for Defamation

Digests
In the digests of West, look for case summaries on defamation under key topics such as:

Libel and Slander	Damages
Constitutional Law (90)	Torts

Corpus Juris Secundum
In this legal encyclopedia, see the discussions under topic headings such as:

Libel and Slander	Damages
Constitutional Law (585)	Torts

American Jurisprudence 2d
In this legal encyclopedia, see the discussions under topic headings such as:

Libel and Slander	Constitutional Law
Damages	Torts

Legal Periodical Literature
There are two index systems to use to try to locate articles on defamation:

INDEX TO LEGAL PERIODICALS AND BOOKS (ILP)	CURRENT LAW INDEX (CLI)
Check subject headings such as:	Check subject headings such as:
Libel and Slander	Libel and Slander
Constitutional Law	Liberty of the Press
Freedom of the Press	Constitutional Law
Torts	Torts
Damages	Damages

Examples of legal periodical articles on defamation you will find by using *ILP* or *CLI:*

Pornography as Defamation and Discrimination by Catherine MacKinnon, 71 Boston University Law Review 793 (1991)

Old Doctrines on a New Frontier: Defamation and Jurisdiction in Cyberspace by R. Timothy Muth, Wisconsin Lawyer 10 (Sept. 1995) [WESTLAW at 68-SEP WILAW 10]

A.L.R., A.L.R.2d, A.L.R.3d, A.L.R.4th, A.L.R.5th, A.L.R. Fed.
Use the *ALR Index* to find annotations on defamation. In this index, check subject headings such as:

Libel and Slander	Radio and Television
Freedom of Speech and Press	Damages
	Torts
Privileges and Immunities	New York Times Rule
Newspapers	

Defamation Checklist Continued

Example of an annotation on defamation you will find by using this index:

Who Is "Public Figure" for Purposes of Defamation Action by Tracy A. Bateman, 19 A.L.R.5th 1 (1995).

Words and Phrases

In this multivolume legal dictionary, look up *slander per se, libel per quod, defamatory statement, publication, special damages,* and every other word or phrase connected with defamation discussed in this chapter. The dictionary will give you definitions of these words or phrases from court opinions.

CALR: Computer-Assisted Legal Research

Example of a query you could ask on WESTLAW to try to find cases, statutes, or other legal materials on defamation: **"defamatory statement" /p slander**

Example of a query you could ask on LEXIS to try to find cases, statutes, or other legal materials on defamation: **defamatory statement /p slander**

Example of search terms you could use on an Internet legal search engine such as LawCrawler (http://lawcrawler.findlaw.edu) to find cases, statutes, or other legal materials on defamation: **defamation AND tort**

Example of search terms you could use on an Internet general search engine such as Alta Vista (http://www.altavista.com) to find cases, statutes, or other legal materials on defamation: **+defamation tort**

More Internet sites to check for materials on defamation and other torts:
Jurist: (http://jurist.law.pitt.edu/sg_torts.htm)
LawGuru: (http://www.lawguru.com/search/lawsearch.html)
See also Tort Law Online at the end of Chapter 1.

DEFAMATORY STATEMENT

Introduction

A **defamatory statement** is a statement of fact that would tend to harm the reputation of the plaintiff in the eyes of at least a substantial and respectable minority of people by lowering the plaintiff in the estimation of those people or by deterring them from associating with the plaintiff. More specifically, it is a statement of fact that tends to disgrace a person by holding him or her up to hatred or ridicule, or by causing others to avoid him or her. The people who express this hatred or ridicule must not be extreme or antisocial in their reaction. For example, although it is possible to find people who hate members of a particular race, it is not defamatory for someone to say that you like or support the rights of members of that race, even if a large number of bigots hold you in contempt for this position.

Facts and Opinions

Defamatory opinions are rarely actionable. An **opinion** is defined as a relatively vague or indefinite value judgment that is not objectively verifiable. ("The speaker was boring.") Opinions are often the basis of endless debate. A **fact,** on the other hand, is a concrete statement that can be objectively established as true or false. ("The speaker lied about his credentials.") There is a difference between saying, "Helen's behavior is disgraceful" and saying, "Helen stole $100." Only the latter is a statement of fact. In general, you cannot sue someone for expressing a defamatory opinion unless the opinion implies the existence of undisclosed defamatory facts as the basis for the opinion. The statement, "The food at the City Deli is uneatable" is an opinion, but it is arguably based on the unstated defamatory fact that the speaker has eaten spoiled food at this restaurant. According to the United States Supreme Court:

> [E]xpressions of "opinion" may often imply an assertion of objective fact. If a speaker says, "In my opinion John Jones is a liar," he implies a knowledge of facts which lead to the conclusion that Jones told an untruth. Even if the speaker states the facts upon which he bases his opinion, if those facts are either incorrect or incomplete, or if his assessment of them is erroneous, the statement may still imply a false assertion of fact. Simply couching such statements in terms of opinion does not dispel these implications. . . .[2]

The statement, "In my opinion John Jones is a liar," communicates a fact because you can objectively verify whether someone has told the truth. On the other hand, the following statement does not communicate undisclosed facts: "In my opinion Mayor Jones shows his abysmal ignorance by accepting the teachings of Marx and Lenin." It would be impossible to prove that someone is ignorant because of a belief in a particular political or social philosophy.

There is no doubt that opinions can be derogatory and harmful. Yet, it is very difficult to win suits that grow out of defamatory opinions. There are two main reasons for this. First, everyone has a privilege to express opinions on matters of public interest, even if the opinions are defamatory. ("The contest is rigged.") This privilege is known as **fair comment.** It prevents liability for defamation so long as the comment, no matter how unreasonable, was the actual opinion of the critic and was not made solely for the purpose of causing harm to the person about whom the comment was made. Second, when the media is the defendant, the First Amendment of the *United States Constitution* gives wide latitude in the expression of ideas and opinions. In a famous line in *Gertz v. Welch*, the United States Supreme Court said,

> Under the First Amendment, there is no such thing as a false idea. However pernicious an opinion may seem, we depend for its correction not on the conscience of judges and juries but on the competition of other ideas.[3]

This does not mean that the media has a constitutional right to express any opinion. As we have seen, opinions based on undisclosed defamatory facts can lead to liability for defamation. Yet, winning a defamation suit based on such an opinion is extremely difficult for reasons we will examine shortly.

ASSIGNMENT

20.1

Are any of the following statements defamatory? Assume that each of the statements is made in front of third persons.

a. Vince calls Nick a "closet Republican." Nick is a registered Democrat.

b. Tom calls Juanita a "Socialist."

c. Ed calls Bill a "tree-hugger."

d. Rich is a member of a union who returns to work during a strike. Hank, another union member, calls Rich a traitor.

e. Mary is the ex-wife of John, now married to Linda. Mary says she had a dream last night and knows it is going to come true. In the dream, Linda wanted to "murder me."

f. Don Adams is the sports announcer for the city's major league baseball team. Sam says, "Adams is the only sportscaster in town who is enrolled in a course for remedial speaking."

---

[2]*Milkovich v. Lorain Journal Co.*, 497 U.S. 1, 19, 110 S. Ct. 2695, 2706, 111 L. Ed. 2d 1 (1990).
[3]418 U.S. 323, 339, 94 S. Ct. 2997, 3007, 41 L. Ed. 2d 789, 805 (1974).

EXTRINSIC FACTS

Some statements are not defamatory on their face because you cannot understand the defamatory meaning simply by examining the words or images used. For example, to say that "Mary gave birth to a child today" is not defamatory **on its face** because you need to know the **extrinsic fact** that Mary has been married only a month. When extrinsic facts are needed, they are alleged in the part of the complaint called the **inducement**. The explanation of the defamatory meaning of words alleged by inducement is called the **innuendo**.

FALSITY OF THE STATEMENT

At common law, the plaintiff did not have to prove the statement was false. It was assumed to be false. Truth was an **affirmative defense,** which meant that the defendant had to allege and prove it. (An affirmative defense to a claim or charge is a response that is based on new factual allegations by the defendant not contained in the complaint of the plaintiff.) Also, there was no need at common law to show **fault** in the defendant. The mere fact that the statement was defamatory was enough to establish liability. A plaintiff did not have to show that the defendant knew the statement was false, or was reckless or negligent as to the truth or falsity of the statement. The United States Supreme Court, however, has dramatically changed the common law when the defendant is part of the media. When the media publishes a defamatory statement, the common law on falsity does *not* apply. The statement is not assumed to be false; the defendant does not have the burden of proving that the statement is true as an affirmative defense. The plaintiff has the burden of proving the falsity of the statement and must do so by showing fault. There are three possible standards of fault: the media knew the statement was false, was reckless as to its truth or falsity, or was negligent as to its truth or falsity. There can be no strict liability against the media in defamation cases.

> **EXAMPLE:** A local newspaper publishes a story that Jim Franklin recently sold a stolen Picasso painting. Unfortunately, this statement turns out to be false. Examine the following four possibilities.
>
> A. The editor knew that the painting was not stolen.
> B. The editor did not know the story was false. An anonymous source told the editor that the painting was stolen. This is the basis of the story. The editor was told that three other sources would cast serious doubt on whether the painting was stolen. The editor, however, decides not to check these sources or any other evidence.
> C. The editor did not know the story was false. An anonymous source told the editor that the painting was stolen. This is the basis of the story. The editor does no more checking to find out if there are any other sources that will confirm or deny the claim that the painting was stolen.
> D. The editor did not know the story was false. An anonymous source told the editor that the painting was stolen. Three other sources, however, cast serious doubt on whether the painting was stolen. The editor carefully checks all of these sources as well as others.

In Case A, the editor knew the story was false. In Case B, the editor printed the story in reckless disregard for the truth or falsity of the story. Not checking three known sources seems to be extraordinarily poor judgment. Recklessness means an egregious or blatant disregard of what should appear to be an obvious step to take to determine the accuracy of a story. To rely on one anonymous source and to disregard known contrary sources is reckless. In Case C, the editor is negligent. There was no

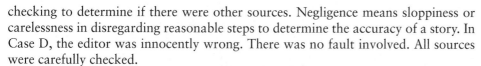

checking to determine if there were other sources. Negligence means sloppiness or carelessness in disregarding reasonable steps to determine the accuracy of a story. In Case D, the editor was innocently wrong. There was no fault involved. All sources were carefully checked.

We said that a plaintiff suing a media defendant for a defamatory statement must prove fault. We now address the question of which standard of fault must be established. This depends on the answer to two questions:

- What is the status of the plaintiff?
- Is the defamatory statement about a matter of public concern or about a private matter?

Status. There are three categories of plaintiffs in media cases: public officials, public figures, and private persons. A **public official** is a government employee who has significant authority, e.g., mayor, police officer. A **public figure** is a nongovernment employee who has assumed special prominence in the affairs of society. There are two categories of public figures. An all-purpose public figure is a person of general power, influence, or notoriety (e.g., a prominent actor). A limited-purpose public figure is a person who has voluntarily become involved in a controversy of interest to the general public (e.g., a death-penalty activist). A **private person** is everyone else. Private persons are those who are neither public officials nor public figures. An example might be your retired Uncle Ed or the local supermarket clerk.

Public concern/private matter. Defamatory statements about a plaintiff fall into two main categories: those that involve public issues or matters of public concern and those that involve private matters.

EXAMPLES:

- The Detroit Daily News prints a story that says Sam Smith tried to pour poison into the drinking reservoir of the city.
- A TV show called *Revelations* says that Sam Smith once took a male impotency pill.

Assume that both statements are false and defamatory. For the moment, we will not concern ourselves with whether Smith is a public official, public figure, or private person. Let us simply classify the category of defamatory statement in each example. The statement about the poison clearly involves a matter of public concern. The public has an interest in the safety of its drinking water. The statement about impotency medication, however, appears to be little more than barnyard gossip. The kind of medication someone may have taken for a sexual problem is a private matter, not a public one.

Once we identify the category of the plaintiff and the category of the defamatory statement about the plaintiff, we now turn to the law that applies to the media defendant. There are three main kinds of cases:

1. *The plaintiff is a public official or a public figure who is suing the media for a defamatory statement about the plaintiff that pertains to a matter of public concern.* The plaintiff must prove by clear and convincing evidence that:

- the media knew the statement was false *or*
- the media was reckless in determining the truth or falsity of the statement

Either standard of fault is sufficient. Knowledge of falsity or recklessness is referred to as **actual malice** or **constitutional malice**.[4] Negligence is not enough. There is no liability if the media negligently publishes a defamatory falsehood of this kind about a public official or public figure. Nor is there any liability if it was innocently published.

---

[4]It is also called **New York Times malice** because the standard was first announced in the case of *New York Times v. Sullivan*, 376 U.S. 254, 84 S. Ct. 710, 11 L. Ed. 2d 686 (1964).

2. *The plaintiff is a public official or a public figure who is suing the media for a defamatory statement about the plaintiff that pertains to a private matter.* The plaintiff must prove by clear and convincing evidence that:

- the media knew the statement was false *or*
- the media was reckless in determining the truth or falsity of the statement *or*
- the media was negligent in determining the truth or falsity of the statement

A state is free to select one of these three standards. Fault must be established. There is no liability if the media innocently publishes a defamatory falsehood of this kind about a public official or public figure.

3. *The plaintiff is a private person who is suing the media for a defamatory statement about the plaintiff that pertains to a public or a private matter.* The plaintiff must prove by clear and convincing evidence that:

- the media knew the statement was false *or*
- the media was reckless in determining the truth or falsity of the statement, *or*
- the media was negligent in determining the truth or falsity of the statement

The state is free to select one of these three standards. Fault must be established. There is no liability if the media innocently publishes a defamatory falsehood about a private person. Most states have chosen the negligence standard, making it somewhat easier for private persons in these states to win defamation cases than public officials or public figures alleging defamation on matters of public concern.

Suppose that the defendant in a defamation case is not part of the media, e.g., your neighbor calls you a thief, a bank teller accuses you of forging a check. The common law of defamation applies. The defamatory statement is assumed to be false and there is no need for the plaintiff to prove that the defendant knew the statement was false, or was reckless as to its truth or falsity, or was negligent as to its truth or falsity.

As indicated earlier, however, some believe that the United States Supreme Court will eventually change defamation law for non-media defendants in the same way it has revolutionized the law governing media defendants. The law of defamation is still evolving. Our society places a high value on robust debate in the free exchange of ideas. Making defamation suits harder to win arguably supports this value. Yet, there is still a need for individuals to be able to protect their name and reputation. As the Court tries to balance these interests, it is unclear whether the trend toward narrowing the torts of libel and slander will continue.

ASSIGNMENT 20.2

In the following cases, what is the standard of fault that the plaintiff must prove in order to win the defamation case against the defendant?

a. A national television news report says that the president of the United States is a "philanderer."

b. Dr. Adams is a twenty-five-year-old biologist who teaches at the local community college. He applies for and is given a $1,500 government grant to study whether fleas can understand Italian. A columnist in a local newspaper awards him the "Golden Fleece Award of the Month" for the absurd use of public funds.

c. The front page of a newspaper contains a story that the mayor illegally grants city contracts to his "cronies and friends." The mayor sues for defamation. You are a paralegal who works for the law firm that represents the mayor. What facts would you try to investigate in order to determine whether the newspaper published the story with constitutional malice?

d. Explain why the following statement is true: The media has a constitutional right to negligently publish defamatory statements about public officials or public figures on matters of public concern.

OF AND CONCERNING THE PLAINTIFF

The defamatory statement must be **of and concerning the plaintiff.** This requires proof by the plaintiff that a recipient of the statement reasonably understood that it referred to the plaintiff. Occasionally, extrinsic facts are needed to make this determination. Suppose the defendant says that "the head guard at Fulton Prison has stolen state funds." On the face of this statement, we cannot identify who was defamed. We need to know who was the head guard at the time the statement was made. The plaintiff can introduce the extrinsic fact that he or she was the head guard at the time, and that, therefore, the statement was reasonably understood to refer to the plaintiff. The part of the complaint in which the plaintiff alleges that the defamatory statement was of and concerning the plaintiff is called the **colloquium.**

Suppose that the defendant defames a group, e.g., "all Italians are thieves" or "Boston doctors are quacks." The groups defamed here are too large; no individual Italian or Boston doctor can say that the statement can be reasonably understood to refer to him or her as an individual. The larger the group, the less reasonable such an understanding would be.

ASSIGNMENT

20.3

Can defamation actions be brought because of the following statements? If so, by whom?
a. "The jury that acquitted John Gotti was bribed."
b. "Cab drivers always cheat."
c. "The Titon University football players take steroids."
d. "The money was stolen by Tom or Fred."

PUBLICATION

There must be a **publication** of the defamatory statement by the defendant. Publication means that the statement is communicated to someone other than the plaintiff. Publication has always been a fault element. The defendant must intentionally or negligently allow someone else to read or hear the statement.

> ▪ **EXAMPLE:** Ted telephones Paulette in order to accuse her of being a thief.

There is no publication if Paulette is the only person who heard the statement.

> ▪ **EXAMPLES:** Ted telephones Paulette in order to accuse her of being a thief. He knows that she has her speakerphone on.
>
> Ted sends Paulette a postcard in which he accuses her of being a thief.

In both of these cases, Paulette can try to prove that Ted knew or should have known that someone other than Paulette would hear or see the statement, e.g., evidence that Ted knew that Paulette had roommates who would probably listen to all phone messages, or that others picked up her mail for her and could easily read a postcard. If such evidence does not exist, the publication of the defamatory statement was unintentional or innocent and therefore not actionable.

> **EXAMPLE:** Alice sends Dan a letter in which she says he is a child molester. On the cover of the envelope, Alice prints the words, "PERSONAL AND CONFIDENTIAL." Unknown to Alice, however, Dan has asked his mother to open and sort all his mail. Or, Dan's neighbor steals the letter and reads it.

In both instances, Alice was not at fault in communicating the statement to a third person. She did not intend someone else to read it and there is no indication that she was careless or negligent in allowing this to occur. She sealed the letter in an envelope, using language alerting everyone that the letter was for Dan's eyes only. Hence, the element of publication has not been established.

ASSIGNMENT

20.4

Nina writes a note on a piece of paper in which she says that George's divinity degree is a fake. She intends to hand the note to George in person. She places the note in her purse and boards a bus. Carelessly, however, she leaves her purse on the bus. A bus driver finds the purse and reads everything in it, including the note to George. Has Nina published the note?

REPUBLICATION

Someone who repeats another's defamatory statement has *republished* it and can sometimes be subject to the same tort liability as the person who originated the statement.

> **EXAMPLE:** Ted works for the Ajax Company in the town of Salem. At a staff meeting, he hears Thomas Sanford, another employee, say that "Senator Bill Crowley is a crook." The next morning, Ted says to a friend, "Thomas Sanford said that Senator Bill Crowley is a crook."

If Sanford made this statement, he published a defamatory statement at the meeting. But Ted *also* published (or republished) the defamatory statement the next morning when he repeated the statement to a friend. Ted's **republication** is treated as a publication. Crowley can sue Sanford and Ted for defamation.

The media can also be a republisher.

> **EXAMPLE:** The Salem News prints a news article on a staff meeting held at the Ajax Company in Salem. The article reports that Thomas Sanford told the assembled employees that "Senator Bill Crowley is a crook."

The newspaper has republished the defamatory statement. Winning a defamation case against the media, however, can be difficult. As we have seen, a public figure like Senator Crowley must establish that a defamatory falsehood on a matter of public concern was published with actual malice. Also, many states give the media a **fair report privilege.** This privilege allows the media to publish fair and accurate stories on government reports and proceedings, even if the stories contain defamatory statements made in the government reports or proceedings. This privilege would not apply to the Salem News case in our example since the news story was not about a government report or proceeding. Yet, Senator Crowley would still have a difficult time suing Salem News because he would have to prove actual malice.

Other individuals and businesses are also engaged in republication. Examples include bookstores, news carriers, libraries, message deliverers, and printers. Are they liable for the defamatory statements contained in the products that they deliver or transmit? Since it would be too burdensome for them to check the content of everything they distribute, they are *not* liable for defamation unless they have reason to know that the book, article, message, or other communication contains defamatory material. The same is true of telephone and telegraph companies.

CYBERSPACE DEFAMATION

The coming of the Internet has raised the issue of defamation in cyberspace through the Internet. **Cyberspace** "refers to the interaction of people and businesses over computer networks, electronic bulletin boards, and commercial online services. The largest and most visible manifestation of cyberspace is the Internet."[5] Over 100 million regular users of the Internet exist. One of the main Internet service providers is America Online (AOL), which allows its subscribers to send and receive information through AOL's computer network. This is done in a variety of ways, including:

- electronic mail or e-mail, which consists of private electronic communications addressed to specific recipients
- message boards, which are topical forums where subscribers post messages that may be read by all other subscribers
- chat rooms, which are forums in which two or more subscribers may conduct real-time, computer-to-computer conversations, with the statements of each speaker briefly appearing on the computer screens of other participating subscribers[6]

The quantity of material exchanged through these methods is staggering. AOL alone processes over 30 million e-mail messages a day and oversees over 19,000 chat rooms.

What happens when one subscriber defames another through one of these vehicles?

> **EXAMPLE:** Mary and George are AOL subscribers. On a message board, Mary sends a message to George that says, "Jim Thompson beats his wife." Thousands of other subscribers read this.

Mary has published a defamatory statement to George. Clearly, Thompson can sue her for defamation. What about AOL? Hasn't it *also* published the defamatory statement?

Congress has definitively answered *no* to this question. In 1996, it passed a law that prohibited tort actions that seek to treat an entity such as AOL as the "publisher or speaker" of messages transmitted over its service by third parties:

> "No provider . . . of an interactive computer service shall be treated as the publisher or speaker of any information provided by another information content provider. . . . No cause of action may be brought and no liability may be imposed under any State or local law that is inconsistent with this section." 47 U.S.C. § 230(c)(1) & (d)(3).

In our example, AOL is a "provider" of an "interactive computer service." Mary is an "information content provider", she provided the "information" that "Thompson beats his wife." Under the protection granted by Congress, the victim of defamation delivered in this manner cannot sue the interactive computer service. The victim must go after the originator of the defamatory speech. Online providers such as AOL will not be treated as newspapers, magazines, and television and radio stations that have more control over the content of their products. In effect, Congress granted tort **immunity** to Internet intermediaries that are providers of interactive computer services. This was done to encourage further robust development of the Internet:

> The purpose of this statutory immunity is not difficult to discern. Congress recognized the threat that tort-based lawsuits pose to freedom of speech in the

---

[5]R. Timothy Muth, *Old Doctrines on a New Frontier: Defamation and Jurisdiction in Cyberspace,* Wisconsin Lawyer 10, 11 (Sept. 1995).
[6]*Doe v. America Online, Inc.,* 25 Media L. Rep. 2112, 1997 WL 374223 (Fla. Cir. Ct. 1997).

new and burgeoning Internet medium. The imposition of tort liability on service providers for the communications of others represented, for Congress, simply another form of intrusive government regulation of speech. [The immunity] was enacted, in part, to maintain the robust nature of Internet communication and, accordingly, to keep government interference in the medium to a minimum.[7]

The immunity is also a recognition of the near impossibility of requiring providers of online services to edit the vast quantity of information passed between the millions of connected computers all over the world.

DAMAGES

At common law, once the plaintiff proved that the defendant published a defamatory statement, the jury was allowed to presume that the plaintiff suffered humiliation or harm to reputation. There was no need for the plaintiff to offer specific evidence of these consequences. Such damages were called **presumed damages.** If, in addition, the plaintiff suffered actual dollar losses such as medical expenses or lost income, they could be recovered as **special damages.** These are actual economic or pecuniary losses. Today, there can be no presumed damages against media defendants charged with making defamatory statements on matters of public concern *unless* the plaintiff can prove actual malice—the defendant knew the statement was false or was reckless as to its truth or falsity.[8]

The following discussion of damages in libel and slander is limited to suits against non-media defendants.

Libel

In most categories of libel, presumed damages can be awarded and there is no need to prove that special damages were suffered. In some states, however, if the plaintiff is alleging **libel per quod,** special damages must be shown. Libel per quod is a written statement that requires the reader to know extrinsic facts (see earlier section on extrinsic facts) to understand its defamatory meaning. Special damages in libel cases are not required in any state if the statement is defamatory on its face.

Slander

Slander per se does not require proof of special damages, but slander per quod does.

Slander per se is an oral statement that is defamatory in one of the following four ways:

- It accuses the plaintiff of a crime (e.g., "Ed stole a car").
- It accuses the plaintiff of having a loathsome communicable disease (e.g., "Ed has venereal disease").
- It accuses the plaintiff of sexual misconduct (e.g., "Ed is an adulterer").
- It adversely affects the plaintiff's trade, profession, or office (e.g., "Ed forged his license to sell liquor").

A slanderous statement that does *not* fall into one of these four categories (e.g., "Ed is illegitimate") is called **slander per quod.** In a few states, this phrase has the additional meaning of an oral statement that requires extrinsic facts to understand its defamatory meaning.

---

[7]*Zeran v. America Online, Inc.,* 129 F.3d 327, 330 (4th Cir. 1997).
[8]A private person, however, can obtain presumed damages if the defamatory statement did not involve an issue of public concern. *Dun & Bradstreet,* 472 U.S. 749, 105 S. Ct. 2939, 86 L. Ed. 2d 593 (1985).

PRIVILEGE

There are a number of situations in which a defendant has, in effect, a **privilege** to defame. A privilege is the right to act contrary to another individual's right without being subject to tort or other liability. The existence of a privilege is a defense to the tort action. Two kinds of privileges exist: absolute and qualified.

Absolute Privilege

An **absolute privilege** is a privilege that cannot be lost because of the bad motives of the party asserting the privilege. The holder of such a privilege is not subject to defamation liability even though he or she knows the statement is false and has personal ill will toward or intends to harm the subject of the defamation. In short, the privilege is absolute.

> **EXAMPLE:** Judge Smith says to attorney Jones during a trial, "your incompetence knows no equal among the practicing bar in the state."

Judge Smith has an absolute privilege to utter this defamatory statement even if the judge knows it is false and utters it solely out of hatred of Jones.

There are several categories of individuals who can assert this absolute privilege:

1. Judges, attorneys, parties, witnesses, and jurors while performing their functions during judicial proceedings.
2. Members of Congress, the state legislature, and city councils or other local legislative bodies while the members are performing their functions during legislative proceedings. Witnesses testifying before these bodies also have an absolute privilege to defame.
3. High executive or administrative officers of the government while performing their official duties.

Qualified Privilege

A **qualified privilege** (also called a *conditional privilege*) is a privilege that can be lost if it is not exercised in a reasonable manner for a proper purpose.[9] Some states are more specific on how this privilege can be lost in defamation cases. For example, some states say it is lost if the defamer did not believe the statement was true or did not have reasonable grounds to believe the statement was true. Other states say that the privilege is lost only if the defamer was reckless in determining its truth or falsity.

Who can assert qualified privileges? As we saw earlier, everyone has a right to make a *fair comment* on a matter of public interest. This is a qualified privilege that can be lost if it is abused. We also saw that many states have a *fair report* privilege that allows the media to publish stories on government reports and proceedings, even if the stories contain defamatory statements made in the government reports or proceedings. This privilege can be lost if the media's story is not fair and accurate.

The most common qualified privilege is the privilege to protect your own legitimate interests.

> **EXAMPLE:** Tony calls Diane a "liar" after Diane says Tony stole her money.

Tony has defamed Diane. If she sues him for defamation, his defense is the qualified privilege of protecting his interest in his own integrity. The privilege would be lost, however, if Tony goes beyond the scope of protecting his interest such as by calling Diane a prostitute or by responding solely out of revenge to hurt Diane.

---

[9]W. Page Keeton et al., *Prosser and Keeton on the Law of Torts* 832 (5th ed. 1984).

Under limited circumstances, a person also has a qualified privilege to defame in order to protect *others*. The defamer must be under a legal or moral obligation to protect the other and must act reasonably in believing the protection is necessary.

> **EXAMPLE:** Lena tells her daughter that it would be disastrous for her to marry "a bum and a gigolo like Paul."

Finally, people who share a *common interest* have a qualified privilege to communicate about matters that will protect or advance that interest.

> **EXAMPLE:** One employee of a company says to another, "don't buy anything from the Eagle Supplier Corp. since all of its goods are stolen."

ASSIGNMENT
20.5

In the following cases, what defenses, if any, can the defendant raise in the defamation action?

a. Alex calls ABC Insurance Company and says that Jackson, his neighbor, has filed fraudulent automobile-accident claims against the company. The neighbor sues Alex for defamation.

b. Same facts as in (a). ABC Insurance Company tells a different insurance company that Jackson has been charged with filing fraudulent claims. Jackson sues ABC Insurance Company for defamation.

SLAPP SUITS

It is relatively easy to sue someone. All you need is an allegation and court filing fees. Many defendants, however, are quite upset when they find out they are being sued, particularly after a process server formally hands them the official documents that signal the beginning of litigation. In this environment of tension, some individuals use defamation suits to intimidate those who have complained about something.

> **EXAMPLE:** Mary Adams tries to organize fellow trailer-home owners against the fees imposed by the park where the trailers are located. She writes a newsletter in which she says that the park owner, Ron Ullson, should be reported to the government for imposing "greedy" fees. Ullson then sues Adams for defamation.

Arguably, the defamation suit is meritless and Ron Ullson is simply trying to use the suit to intimidate Mary Adams—to scare her off. Even if he loses the defamation suit, he may cause her so much agony that she will drop her efforts to organize the trailer-home owners. Emotional and financial costs of defending the defamation action can be overwhelming.

If this is Ullson's motive, his suit is known as an intimidation suit. It is also called a **SLAPP suit,** which stands for "strategic lawsuit against public participation." They are meritless suits brought primarily for the purpose of chilling the defendant's exercise of the right to free speech and to petition the government for a redress of grievances. The cause of action in these suits is usually defamation, but other causes of action are also common such as the tort of interference with economic advantage, which we will consider in Chapter 22.

What can a defendant do in such cases, particularly the defendant who does not have the economic resources of the party who "slapped" the defendant with the intimidation suit? As we discussed in Chapter 6, the defendant can sue the plaintiff for the tort of malicious prosecution, but this can be a cumbersome and expensive remedy.[10] A more direct method of relief is to use the anti-SLAPP statute that about eight states have passed to help curb the use of intimidation suits to muzzle citizens. In California, for example, victims of SLAPP suits can assert a special motion to strike the defamation or other suit. The motion will be granted unless there is a probability that the plaintiff will prevail on the claim. This can end a meritless suit well before the full ordeal of a trial is played out. Furthermore, the defendant may be able to recover his or her attorney fees and costs in defending the SLAPP suit.

"VEGGIE LIBEL"

Occasionally, people will make unflattering comments about certain consumer products, e.g., "there are dangerous pesticides in Idaho potatoes." Can you defame a potato? Several states have enacted statutes that allow suits for maligning or disparaging certain products. The media has labeled such suits "veggie libel cases." We will consider them later in Chapter 22.

SUMMARY

There are two defamation torts: libel (written or embodied in a physical form) and slander (spoken or gestured). A statement of fact is defamatory if it would tend to harm the reputation of the plaintiff in the eyes of at least a substantial and respectable minority of people by lowering the plaintiff in the estimation of those people or by deterring them to associate with the plaintiff. In general, defamatory opinions are not actionable unless they imply the existence of defamatory facts, i.e., facts that can be objectively established as true or false. The privilege of fair comment and the media's First Amendment rights make defamation suits based on derogatory opinions difficult to win.

When extrinsic facts had to be alleged for the explanation of the defamatory statement (the innuendo), the facts were pleaded in the inducement. At common law, the falsity of the statement was assumed; truth was an affirmative defense. Constitutional law has changed this for media defendants. Fault must be proven. If the defamatory statement pertained to a matter of public concern about a public official or a public figure, the plaintiff must show by clear and convincing evidence that the defendant knew the statement was false or was reckless as to its truth or falsity (actual malice). If the defamatory statement pertained to a matter of private concern about a public official or a public figure, the plaintiff must show by clear and convincing evidence that the defendant knew the statement was false or was reckless or negligent as to its truth or falsity. If the defamatory statement pertained to a matter of public or private concern about a private person, the plaintiff must show by clear and convincing evidence that the defendant knew the statement was false or was reckless or negligent as to its truth or falsity.

The defamatory statement must be of and concerning the plaintiff. Extrinsic facts may need to be pleaded in the colloquium of the complaint to establish that the defamatory statement was of and concerning the plaintiff. Publication of the statement occurs when it is intentionally or negligently communicated to someone other than the plaintiff. The repetition or republication of a defamatory statement by someone else is treated as a publication of the statement. The media, however, has the protection of the new constitutional law of defamation and, in

---

[10]A party can also file an ethics charge against the attorney who helped the plaintiff bring the SLAPP suit. It is unethical for an attorney to assert a frivolous claim for a client. The ethics charge, however, is resolved later; it does not stop the SLAPP suit.

some states, a fair report privilege. Entities that merely deliver or transmit the defamatory statement such as bookstores and telephone companies, however, are not liable for defamation unless they have reason to know that they are transmitting defamatory material. Providers of interactive computer services on the Internet have an immunity from tort liability based on defamatory statements made by others on the online service of the providers.

In non-media cases, most libel on its face does not require special damages. Libel per quod does in some states, slander per se does not, and slander per quod does.

Judges, attorneys, parties, witnesses, and jurors have an absolute privilege to make defamatory statements while performing their duties in judicial proceedings. The same is true of legislators, legislative witnesses, and high executive officers. An absolute privilege cannot be lost by bad motives. Under certain circumstances, defendants have a qualified privilege to defame in order to protect their own legitimate interests, the interests of others, or common interests. Everyone has the qualified privilege of fair comment on a matter of public interest or concern, and in some states, the media has the qualified fair report privilege. A qualified privilege can be lost if it is not exercised in a reasonable manner for a proper purpose.

Plaintiffs sometimes "slapp" defendants with meritless defamation suits solely to intimidate them. Several states give SLAPP victims the right to assert special motions designed to end such suits quickly.

KEY TERMS

Invasion of Privacy

Chapter Outline

- Four Torts
- Intrusion
- Appropriation
- Public Disclosure of Private Fact
- False Light
- Media Defendants

FOUR TORTS

Invasion of privacy consists of four torts: intrusion, appropriation, public disclosure of private fact, and false light. Each has its own elements. In general, the torts are designed to protect an individual's interest in being left alone that is violated because of an unreasonable form of attention or publicity.

 Invasion-of-Privacy Checklist

Definitions, Relationships, Paralegal Roles, and Research References

Interests Protected by These Torts
Intrusion: The right to be free from unreasonable intrusions into a person's private affairs or concerns. This tort is also called *intrusion on seclusion*.
Appropriation: The right to prevent the unauthorized use of a person's name, likeness, or personality for someone else's benefit.
Public Disclosure of Private Facts: The right to be free from unreasonable disclosures of private facts about a person's life that are not matters of legitimate public concern.
False Light: The right to be free from false statements that unreasonably place a person in a false light in the public eye.

Elements of These Torts
1. Intrusion:
    i. an act of intrusion into someone's private affairs or concerns
    ii. highly offensive to a reasonable person
2. Appropriation:
    i. the use of the plaintiff's name, likeness, or personality
    ii. for the benefit of the defendant
3. Public disclosure of private fact:
    i. publicity
    ii. concerning the private life of the plaintiff
    iii. highly offensive to a reasonable person

Invasion-of-Privacy Checklist Continued

    4. False light:
        i. publicity
        ii. placing the plaintiff in a false light
        iii. highly offensive to a reasonable person

Definitions of Major Words/Phrases in These Elements

Intrusion: Prying, peering, or probing.

Private: Pertaining to facts about an individual's personal life that have no reasonable or logical connection to what the person does in public and that the person does not consent to reveal.

Reasonable Person: An ordinary person who is not unduly sensitive.

Benefit: Deriving some advantage.

Publicity: Communication to the public at large or to a large group of people.

Major Defense and Counterargument Possibilities That Need to Be Explored

1. There was no prying, peering, or probing (for Intrusion).
2. What the defendant did related to the public activities of the defendant (for Intrusion, Public Disclosure of Private Fact, and False Light).
3. The defendant did not use plaintiff's name, likeness, or personality (for Appropriation).
4. The defendant did not derive benefit from the use of the plaintiff's name, likeness, or personality—or derived only incidental benefit from such use (for Appropriation).
5. The statement about the plaintiff was not communicated to the public at large nor to a large group of people (for Public Disclosure of Private Fact and False Light).
6. No inaccurate impression or statement was made about the plaintiff (for False Light).
7. The plaintiff consented to what the defendant did (for all four torts)(on the defense of consent, see Chapter 23).
8. The defendant's conduct occurred while the defendant was arresting the plaintiff, protecting the defendant's own property, or giving testimony in a public proceeding (for Intrusion, Public Disclosure of Private Fact, and False Light)(on the privilege of arrest, see Chapter 5; on defense of property and other self-help privileges, see Chapter 23).
9. The plaintiff's suit against the government employee for invasion of privacy may be barred by public official immunity (for all four torts)(on official immunity, see Chapter 23).
10. The plaintiff's suit against the charitable organization for invasion of privacy committed by someone working for the organization may be barred by charitable immunity (for all four torts)(on charitable immunity, see Chapter 23).
11. The plaintiff's suit against a family member for invasion of privacy may be barred by intrafamily immunity (for all four torts)(on intrafamily immunity, see Chapter 23).
12. The plaintiff failed to take reasonable steps to mitigate the harm caused by the defendant's invasion of privacy; therefore, damages should not cover the aggravation of the harm caused by the plaintiff (for all four torts) (on the doctrine of avoidable consequences, see Chapter 14).

Damages

The plaintiff can recover compensatory damages for humiliation or embarrassment caused by the defendant. If the plaintiff suffered mental or physical illness due to the tort committed by the defendant, recovery can also include damages for the illness. If the defendant's conduct constituted more than one of the four torts, there can be only one recovery. If the defendant acted with a malicious motive to harm or injure the plaintiff, punitive damages are possible. (On the categories of damages, see Chapter 14.)

Relationship to Criminal Law

If the defendant committed Intrusion by wiretapping or other electronic devices, the conduct may also violate the criminal law.

Relationship to Other Torts

Defamation: Libel or slander may be committed along with False Light if the statement is also derogatory (harms the plaintiff's reputation).

Intentional Infliction of Emotional Distress: This tort is committed along with any of the four invasion-of-privacy torts if the defendant committed an outrageous act with the intent to cause severe emotional distress.

Invasion-of-Privacy Checklist Continued

Malicious Prosecution: One example of Intrusion is to pry into the plaintiff's private affairs through procedural devices such as subpoenas. In such cases, malicious prosecution may also be committed.

Misrepresentation: Misrepresentation may be committed along with False Light when the following elements can be established: a false statement of fact, intent to deceive, intent that the plaintiff rely on the statement, justifiable reliance, and actual damages.

Prima Facie Torts: If the plaintiff cannot establish the elements of any of the four invasion-of-privacy torts, the plaintiff should check prima facie tort in those states that recognize it.

Federal Law

a. Under the Federal Tort Claims Act, the United States Government can be liable for invasion of privacy committed by one of its federal employees within the scope of employment (respondeat superior) (see Figure 23–7 in Chapter 23).

b. There may be liability under the Civil Rights Act if the invasion of privacy was committed while the defendant was depriving the plaintiff of federal rights under color of law (see Figure 23–8 in Chapter 23).

Employer-Employee (Agency) Law

An employee who commits an invasion of privacy is personally liable for this tort. His or her employer will *also* be liable for invasion of privacy if the conduct of the employee was within the scope of employment (respondeat superior). The employee must be furthering a business objective of the employer at the time. (On the factors that determine scope of employment, see Figure 12–7 in Chapter 12.)

Paralegal Roles in Invasion-of-Privacy Litigation

Fact finding (help the office collect facts relevant to prove the elements of the four invasion-of-privacy torts, the elements of available defenses, and extent of injuries or other damages):

• client interviewing
• field investigation
• online research (e.g., obtaining public records)

File management (help the office control the volume of paperwork in an invasion-of-privacy litigation):

• open client file
• enter case data in computer database
• maintain file documents

Litigation assistance (help the trial attorney prepare for an invasion-of-privacy trial and appeal, if needed):

• draft discovery requests
• draft answers to discovery requests
• draft pleadings
• digest and index discovery documents
• prepare trial notebook
• draft notice of appeal
• order trial transcript
• cite check briefs
• perform legal research

Collection/enforcement (help the trial attorney for the judgment creditor to collect the damages award or to enforce an injunction or other court order at the conclusion of the invasion-of-privacy case):

• draft postjudgment discovery requests
• field investigation to monitor compliance with judgment
• online research (e.g., location of defendant's business assets)

Invasion-of-Privacy Checklist Continued

Research References for Invasion-of-Privacy Torts

Digests
In the digests of West, look for case summaries on these torts under key topics such as:

Torts   Constitutional Law (274)
Damages

Corpus Juris Secundum
In this legal encyclopedia, see the discussions under topic headings such as:

Constitutional Law (582)   Torts
Right of Privacy   Damages

American Jurisprudence 2d
In this legal encyclopedia, see the discussions under topic headings such as:

Privacy   Damages
Constitutional Law (503)   Fright, Shock, and
Torts   Mental Disturbance

Legal Periodical Literature
There are two index systems to use to locate articles and other legal periodical literature on these torts:

INDEX TO LEGAL PERIODICALS (ILP)	CURRENT LAW INDEX (CLI)
Check subject headings such as:	Check subject headings such as:
Right of Privacy	Right of Privacy, Liberty of the Press
Eavesdropping	Torts
Torts	Damages
Freedom of the Press	
Damages	

Example of a legal periodical article you can find by using *ILP* or *CLI*:

Invasion of Privacy: New Guidelines for the Public Disclosure Tort by Greg Trout, 6 Capitol University Law Review 95 (1976).

A.L.R., A.L.R.2d, A.L.R.3d, A.L.R.4th, A.L.R.5th, A.L.R. Fed.
Use the *ALR Index* to locate annotations on these torts. In this index, check subject headings such as:

Privacy   Newspapers
Harassment   Torts
Eavesdropping   Damages

Example of an annotation you can locate through this index on these torts:

Publication of Address as well as Name of Person as Invasion of Privacy by Phillip E. Hassman, 84 A.L.R.3d 1159 (1978).

Words and Phrases
In this multivolume legal dictionary, look up *invasion of privacy, intrusion, appropriation, false light,* and every other word or phrase connected with the four invasion-of-privacy torts discussed in this chapter. The dictionary will give you definitions of these words or phrases from court opinions.

CALR: Computer-Assisted Legal Research
Example of a query you could ask on WESTLAW to try to find cases, statutes, or other legal materials on these four torts: **"invasion of privacy"/p damages**

Example of a query you could ask on LEXIS to try to find cases, statutes, or other legal materials on these four torts: **invasion of privacy/p damages**

Invasion-of-Privacy Checklist Continued

Example of search terms you could use on an Internet legal search engine such as LawCrawler (http://lawcrawler.findlaw.com) to find cases, statutes, or other legal materials on these four torts: **"invasion of privacy" AND tort**

Example of search terms you could use on an Internet general search engine such as Alta Vista (http://www.altavista.com) to find cases, statutes, or other legal materials on these four torts: **+invasion of privacy" +tort**

More Internet sites to check for materials on invasion of privacy and other torts:
Jurist: (http://jurist.law.pitt.edu/sg_torts.htm)
LawGuru: (http://www.lawguru.com/search/lawsearch.html)
See also Tort Law Online at the end of Chapter 1.

INTRUSION

The elements of the tort of **intrusion** (also called *intrusion on seclusion*) are:

1. an act of intrusion into someone's private affairs or concerns
2. highly offensive to a reasonable person

Intrusion consists of prying, peering, or probing of some kind, e.g., wiretapping, opening mail, filing subpoenas that require disclosure of records, making persistent phone calls. Such methods of intrusion must be directed at something that is considered one's **private affairs.** It is usually not an intrusion to follow the plaintiff in a department store or to photograph him or her in a park. In these settings, the plaintiff is engaging in public activity. There are a number of factors a court will consider in determining whether something is private, none of which is usually conclusive alone. These factors are outlined in Figure 21–1.

Not every intrusion into private matters is tortious. The intrusion must be highly offensive to a **reasonable person.** The test is objective—what the reasonable person considers **highly offensive.** The plaintiff may be greatly offended by a call from a bill collector at the plaintiff's workplace. But a reasonable person would probably not be highly offended by such a call. The case may be different, however, if calls are made every fifteen minutes starting at midnight while the plaintiff is trying to sleep at home.

A. "Yes" answers to the following questions will help persuade a court that the activity was *not* private:

*   Was the plaintiff in a public place at the time?
*   Was the activity of the plaintiff observable by normal methods of observation?
*   Was the activity of the plaintiff already a matter of public record before the defendant became involved?
*   Was the plaintiff drawing attention to him- or herself?

B. "Yes" answers to the following questions will help persuade a court that the activity *was* private:

*   Was the plaintiff caught off guard through no fault of his or her own?
*   Did the defendant take advantage of a vulnerable position that the plaintiff was in?
*   Was the activity of the plaintiff something that society would consider none of anyone else's business?

FIGURE 21–1
Factors a court will consider when deciding whether plaintiff was engaged in a private activity.

ASSIGNMENT

21.1

Has the tort of intrusion been committed in any of the following situations?

a. Tim photographs Karla at an amusement park in the fun house at the moment an air vent on the floor blows up her dress.

b. At a bus terminal, a wall television camera is clearly visible in the men's room.

c. General Motors hires a prostitute to solicit Ralph Nader to engage in sexual activities. Ralph refuses.

APPROPRIATION

The elements of the tort of **appropriation** are:

1. the use of the plaintiff's name, likeness, or personality
2. for the benefit of the defendant

The first element is present if the plaintiff is specifically identifiable through the use of his or her name, likeness, or personality. To make a statue or mannequin of the plaintiff is not sufficient unless the plaintiff is clearly recognizable.

The defendant must derive benefit from the use. In some states, the benefit must be commercial or pecuniary, e.g., impersonating the plaintiff to obtain credit, or using the plaintiff's name or picture in a business ad to give the appearance of an endorsement. But in most states the benefit does not have to be financial. The second element would be met, for example, if the defendant pretended to be a famous photographer as part of his effort to seduce women.

ASSIGNMENT

21.2

The plaintiff is a "human cannonball" who shoots himself out of a cannon at county fairs. Do either of the following situations constitute appropriation?

a. The defendant tapes a video of the stunt and shows it at home to friends and relatives.

b. The defendant is a television station. One of its employees videotapes the stunt and shows it both on the evening news and on its "Incredible People" variety show. (See the last section of this chapter on Media Defendants.)

PUBLIC DISCLOSURE OF PRIVATE FACT

The elements of the tort of **public disclosure of private fact** are:

1. publicity
2. concerning the private life of the plaintiff
3. highly offensive to a reasonable person

For purposes of this tort, "publicity" has a different meaning from "publication" in the law of defamation. **Publication** is the communication of the defamatory statement to at least one person other than the plaintiff. **Publicity**, however, means communication to the public at large. More than a few people must hear or read the statement.

Review the factors mentioned in the section on intrusion that are used to determine whether something is private (see Figure 21–1). Most of these factors are also relevant to determine whether there has been a public disclosure of a private fact.

There is no disclosure of a private fact when publicity is given to something that is already a matter of public record (e.g., a document filed in court, the names of contributors to a political candidate). Some subject matter, however, is clearly private, either by law or by custom. Data provided on income tax returns and census forms, for example, are protected from disclosure by law. Also legally protected are confidential communications between attorney and client, doctor and patient, and minister and penitent. One's sexual inclinations are also private, because in our society such matters are considered no one's business. Of course, if a plaintiff flaunts such information, he or she may be considered to have consented to the disclosure.

If there has been a disclosure of a private fact, it is no defense that the fact is true. Falsity is not one of the elements of this tort.

It is not enough that the plaintiff considers the publicity discomforting or embarrassing. It must be highly offensive to a reasonable person. A reasonable person, for example, would not be highly offended by a story about an individual's having his deceased dog cremated, but would probably be offended by a story about the individual's three unsuccessful operations to cure his impotency. Here are some other disclosures that might be highly offensive to a reasonable person:

- a sign placed in the defendant's window that the plaintiff does not pay his or her debts
- an interoffice memo sent to thirty employees that a fellow employee is a homosexual
- a video shown in a tavern of a woman nursing her baby on her backyard porch

---

ASSIGNMENT

21.3

Tom is an ex-convict who served time for murder twenty-five years ago. He is now a reformed citizen living an outstanding life in a new community. Bill finds out about Tom's past and lets everyone know at a town meeting. Does Tom have a cause of action against Bill?

FALSE LIGHT

The elements of the tort of **false light** are:

1. publicity
2. placing the plaintiff in a false light
3. highly offensive to a reasonable person

The first element of false light is publicity. It has the same meaning as publicity in the tort of public disclosure of private fact: communication to the public at large—not just to a few people.

False light is similar to defamation in that the statement about the plaintiff must be false. Unlike defamation, however, false light can be established without the statement harming the plaintiff's reputation, although most usually do. When is a person placed in a false light? Broadly speaking, whenever an impression or conclusion is given about a person that is not accurate.

EXAMPLES:

- falsely stating in a report that a doctor has given AIDS to one of his patients during an operation
- falsely claiming that the plaintiff has written a pornographic novel
- signing the name of a pro-choice plaintiff on a pro-life petition without permission.

These cases of false light would be considered highly offensive by a reasonable person. Not all false light, however, falls into this category. Misspelling the plaintiff's name on a notice places him or her in a false light, but this would hardly be deemed highly offensive, even if the plaintiff was very embarrassed by the incident. A reasonable person would not take such offense.

ASSIGNMENT

21.4

a. At a banquet honoring the retirement of Linda, her boss rises to make a speech. The boss gives some details of Linda's life, including the fact that she was married on June 26, 1968 and gave birth to her first child on July 1, 1968. In fact, the child was born on June 30, 1969. Linda sues her boss for false light. What result?

b. George Jones is a practicing attorney. He decides to hire two attorneys as associates (not partners). The name of the firm is "Jones & Associates." Jones decides to take out a Yellow Pages listing under this name. When the Yellow Pages come out, his firm is listed as "Jones & Ass." Have any torts been committed?

MEDIA DEFENDANTS

Special protections exist for the press, television, radio, or other members of the media who are defendants in invasion-of-privacy tort suits. The media has a constitutional right under the First Amendment to publicize **newsworthy** people and events. This covers a broad range of matters of **legitimate public interest.** Media defendants are often charged with false light invasion of privacy, particularly by a **public official** or a **public figure.** (A public figure is someone who has assumed special prominence in the affairs of society because of power, influence, or voluntary involvement in a controversy of interest to the general public.) In such a case, there must be proof that the media defendant either knew that the publication placed the plaintiff in a false light or acted in reckless disregard of whether it did so. (This is known as **constitutional malice** or **actual malice.**) These rules also apply to defamation cases against the media. See Chapter 20 where the rules are more fully discussed.

SUMMARY

There are four invasion-of-privacy torts that protect an individual's interest in being left alone: intrusion, appropriation, public disclosure of private fact, and false light.

Intrusion is prying, peering, or probing into the plaintiff's private affairs or concerns when it is considered highly offensive to a reasonable person. Appropriation is the use of the plaintiff's name, likeness, or personality for the benefit of the defendant. In most states, this benefit does not have to be pecuniary. Public disclosure of private fact is a communication of a statement to the public at large (publicity) concerning the private life of the plaintiff when such publicity is considered highly offensive to a reasonable person. False light is publicity that inaccurately portrays the plaintiff when such publicity is considered highly offensive to a reasonable person.

Media defendants in an action for appropriation or for public disclosure of private fact often have the defense that the information was a matter of legitimate public interest, which the media has a constitutional right to make public. In an action for false light against a media defendant, the plaintiff who is a public official or a public figure must prove that the defendant knew the statement placed the plaintiff in a false light or acted in reckless disregard of whether it did so.

KEY TERMS

Misrepresentation, Tortious Interference, and Other Torts

Chapter Outline

- Misrepresentation
- Interference with Contract Relations
- Interference with Prospective Advantage
- Tortious Interference with Employment (Wrongful Discharge)
- Disparagement
- Injurious Falsehood
- Prima Facie Tort
- Bad Faith Liability
- Dram Shop Liability

MISREPRESENTATION

The tort of **misrepresentation** (sometimes called **deceit** or **fraud**) primarily covers **pecuniary loss** caused by false statements. A pecuniary loss is a loss of money.

> **EXAMPLE:** When George sells Brenda a used computer for $500, he tells her that it has a modem. He knows that this is not true.

George lied about the features of the computer. Contrary to his statement, it does not have a modem. He probably has committed the tort of misrepresentation, although we must examine all of the elements of this tort to be sure. Brenda has suffered a pecuniary loss. She received a computer that is worth less than the one George described.

There has been no property damage or bodily injury as a result of what George did. If such damage or injury does result from a false statement (e.g., Sam becomes ill after drinking what Mary told him was a healthy fruit drink when she knew there was poison in it), many courts will allow recovery for the property damage or bodily injury in the misrepresentation suit. It would be more common, however, for this kind of recovery to be sought under other torts such as battery, conversion, or negligence.

Misrepresentation Checklist

Definitions, Relationships, Paralegal Roles, and Research References

Category
Misrepresentation is an intentional tort. (In many states, however, negligence is also a basis for liability—negligent misrepresentation.)

Interest Protected by This Tort
The right to be free from pecuniary loss resulting from false statements.

Elements of This Tort
  i. Statement of fact
  ii. Statement is false
  iii. Scienter (intent to mislead)
  iv. Justifiable reliance
  v. Actual damages

Definitions of Major Words/Phrases in These Elements
Fact: An express or implied communication containing concrete information that can be objectively established as true or false. (An opinion is an express or implied communication containing a relatively vague or indefinite value judgment that rarely, if ever, is objectively verifiable.)

Intent to Mislead (Scienter): Making a statement knowing it is false, or without a belief in its truth, or in reckless disregard of its truth or falsity—with the desire that the statement be believed and relied upon.

Justifiable Reliance: Being reasonable in taking action (or in refraining from taking action) because of something such as what someone has said or done.

Major Defense and Counterargument Possibilities That Need to Be Explored
  1. The defendant made no statement of past or present fact.
  2. The defendant concealed no past or present fact.
  3. The defendant had no duty to disclose the fact; there was no fiduciary or other relationship of trust and confidence between the parties.
  4. The statement was not false, incomplete, ambiguous, or misleading.
  5. The defendant did not have a state of mind that differed from what he or she expressed.
  6. The defendant did not know or believe the statement was false or inaccurate.
  7. The defendant did not act in reckless disregard of the truth or falsity of his or her statement.
  8. The defendant did not intend the plaintiff to rely on the defendant's statement, and had no reason to expect that the plaintiff would rely on it.
  9. The plaintiff did not in fact rely on the defendant's statement.
  10. The defendant's statement was not a substantial factor in the plaintiff's action or inaction.
  11. The plaintiff's reliance was not justifiable.
  12. The defendant did not take advantage of idiosyncrasies of the plaintiff.
  13. A cursory investigation by the plaintiff would have revealed the truth or falsity of the defendant's statement.
  14. The plaintiff suffered no actual damages.
  15. The plaintiff's suit against the government for misrepresentation committed by a government employee may be barred by sovereign immunity (on sovereign immunity, see Chapter 23).
  16. The plaintiff's suit against the government employee for misrepresentation may be barred by public official immunity (on official immunity, see Chapter 23).
  17. The plaintiff's suit against the charitable organization for misrepresentation committed by someone working for the organization may be barred by charitable immunity (on charitable immunity, see Chapter 23).
  18. The plaintiff failed to take reasonable steps to mitigate the harm caused when the defendant committed misrepresentation; therefore, damages should not cover the aggravation of the harm caused by the plaintiff (on the doctrine of avoidable consequences, see Chapter 14).

Misrepresentation Checklist Continued

Damages
Actual damages must be proved. Some courts use the out-of-pocket measure of damages, whereas other courts allow a benefit-of-the-bargain measure of damages. Traditionally, misrepresentation covered only pecuniary or economic damages. Many courts now also allow recovery for injury to person or property caused by the false statement. Punitive damages are also possible. (On the categories of damages, see Chapter 14.)

Relationship to Criminal Law
In all states, embezzlement is a crime. In many states there is a crime called false pretenses. False statements of fact are often made by the defendant in the commission of both crimes.

Other Torts and Related Actions
Battery: One way to commit battery is to induce the plaintiff to give consent to a touching by falsely stating facts (e.g., defendant falsely claims to be a doctor and examines the plaintiff).
Breach of Express Warranty: Under the Uniform Commercial Code (UCC), a cause of action for breach of an express warranty is possible if the defendant makes a false statement of fact with the intent that the plaintiff rely on the statement, which in fact occurs, to the detriment of the plaintiff.
Conversion: One way to commit this tort is to take possession of the plaintiff's property by falsely stating the authority to do so.
Defamation: Defendant can defame the character of the plaintiff by making false statements about the plaintiff.
False Imprisonment: One way to commit this tort is to confine the plaintiff by falsely stating the authority to do so.
Intentional Infliction of Emotional Distress: One way to commit this tort is to tell a particularly vicious lie to an unsuspecting plaintiff.
Negligence: The tort of negligence can be committed when the defendant causes injury to plaintiff's person or property by carelessly stating facts (e.g., carelessly telling the plaintiff that the milk is safe to drink when in fact it is not).
Trespass to Land: One way to commit this tort is to get someone to go onto the plaintiff's land by making false statements about who owns the land.

Federal Law
a. Under the Federal Tort Claims Act, the United States Government will *not* be liable for misrepresentation committed by one of its federal employees within the scope of employment. (See Figure 23–7 in Chapter 23.)
b. There may be liability under the Civil Rights Act if the misrepresentation was committed while the defendant was depriving the plaintiff of federal rights under color of law. (See Figure 23–8 in Chapter 23.)

Employer-Employee (Agency) Law
An employee who commits a misrepresentation is personally liable for this tort. His or her employer will *also* be liable for misrepresentation if the conduct of the employee was within the scope of employment (respondeat superior). The employee must be furthering a business objective of the employer at the time. Many times, intentional torts such as misrepresentation, however, are outside the scope of employment. If so, only the employee is liable for the misrepresentation. (On the factors that determine scope of employment, see Figure 12–7 in Chapter 12.)

Research References for Misrepresentation
Digests
In the digests of West, look for case summaries on this tort under the following key topics:

Fraud	Torts
Vendor and Purchaser	Damages
Negligence	

Misrepresentation Checklist Continued

Corpus Juris Secundum
In this legal encyclopedia, see the discussion under topic headings such as:

Fraud	Torts
Vendor and Purchaser	Damages
Negligence	

American Jurisprudence 2d
In this legal encyclopedia, see the discussion under topic headings such as:

Fraud and Deceit	Sales
Fraudulent Conveyances	Damages
Vendor and Purchaser	Torts
Negligence	

Legal Periodical Literature
There are two index systems to use to locate legal periodical articles on this tort:

INDEX TO LEGAL PERIODICALS AND BOOKS (ILP)	CURRENT LAW INDEX (CLI)
Check subject headings such as:	Check subject headings such as:
Fraud	Fraud
Negligence	Negligence
Torts	Torts
Debtor and Creditor	Damages

Example of a legal periodical article you can find by using *ILP* or *CLI*:

Misrepresentation of Sterility or of Use of Birth Control by J. Mann, 26 Journal of Family Law 623 (1987–88).

A.L.R., A.L.R.2d, A.L.R.3d, A.L.R.4th, A.L.R.5th, A.L.R. Fed.
Use the *ALR Index* to locate annotations on this tort. In this index, check subject headings such as:

Fraud and Deceit	Negligence
Fraudulent Conveyance	Torts
Vendor and Purchaser	Damages
Debtors and Creditors	

Example of an annotation you can find through this index:

Consumer Class Action Based on Fraud or Misrepresentations by Mary J. Cavins, 53 A.L.R.3d 534.

Words and Phrases
In this multivolume legal dictionary, look up *misrepresentation, deceit, fraud, scienter, fact, opinion, justifiable reliance,* and every other word or phrase connected with misrepresentation discussed in this chapter. The dictionary will give you definitions of these words or phrases from court opinions.

CALR: Computer-Assisted Legal Research
> Example of a query you could ask on WESTLAW or on LEXIS to try to find cases, statutes, or other legal materials on misrepresentation: **misrepresentation /p damages**

> Example of search terms you could use on an Internet legal search engine such as LawCrawler (http://lawcrawler.findlaw.com) to find cases, statutes, or other legal materials on misrepresentation: **misrepresentation AND tort**

> Example of search terms you could use on an Internet general search engine such as Alta Vista (http://www.altavista.com) to find cases, statutes, or other legal materials on misrepresentation: **+misrepresentation +tort**

Misrepresentation Checklist Continued
More Internet sites to check for materials on misrepresentation and other torts:
Jurist: (http://jurist.law.pitt.edu/sg_torts.htm)
LawGuru: (http://www.lawguru.com/search/lawsearch.html)
See also Tort Law Online at the end of Chapter 1.

Statement of Fact That Is False

The first element of misrepresentation is that the defendant has made a statement of **fact.** The second element is that the fact is false. (Sometimes the first element is expressed as a statement of material fact. In this chapter, however, we will cover materiality under a different element of the tort—the element of justifiable reliance.) A fact is an express or implied communication containing concrete information that can be objectively established as true or false. When I tell you that a particular pen has red ink in it, I have communicated a fact. There is an objective way to find out if my statement is true: we simply write with the pen to check the color of its ink. An **opinion,** on the other hand, is an express or implied communication containing a relatively vague or indefinite value judgment that is not objectively verifiable. When I tell you that a particular product is "wonderful," I have communicated an opinion. Whether something is "wonderful" could be the subject of endless debate. There is no way to prove—objectively—that the statement is true or false.

Controversy often arises in sales transactions where **puffing** is common. Puffing is an expected exaggeration of quality. An example would be a seller telling a buyer that the XYZ brand of shampoo is "fabulous." Such comments are mere puffing, not statements of fact. Furthermore, there cannot be justifiable reliance (an element we will consider later) on puffing.

Some opinions contain implied statements of fact.

> **EXAMPLE:** Vince is trying to sell Linda an automobile. He tells her that the car is in "excellent condition." Once Linda buys the car, she discovers that it has no engine.

Vince's comment about the car is an opinion, but it implied the fact that the car had at least the basic equipment in it—such as an engine!

If you state an opinion that you do not believe, you have lied about your state of mind. When you communicate your state of mind, you are communicating a fact. While an opinion itself is not a fact, a communication about your state of mind is a fact.

> **EXAMPLE:** A stock broker says, "I believe this stock is a dream come true." The broker, however, knows that the stock is worthless and highly unlikely to appreciate in value or to earn income.

The statement that the stock is a "dream come true" is an opinion. It is a vague value judgment that cannot be objectively proven or disproved. But whether the broker believes the statement at the time he or she made it is a fact that can be proven or disproved. He either thinks highly of the stock or he doesn't. A false representation of a state of mind is a false representation of a fact.

Words are not always necessary to communicate a fact. Someone who turns back the odometer without saying a word, for example, is making a factual statement about the number of miles a vehicle has traveled to date. Occasionally, the active concealment of a fact can lead to liability for misrepresentation. For example, the defendant paints over cracks in an engine in order to conceal its defects from a potential buyer.

Silence can also communicate facts, e.g., not telling someone that a house has termites could constitute a communication that the house is termite-free. Communicating facts through silence, however, is not sufficient to impose liability for misrepresentation unless there is an obligation to disclose the facts. Two strangers usually do not have this obligation to each other. Suppose, however, that two people have a **fiduciary relationship,** sometimes called a **confidential relationship.** A fiduciary relationship exists when one of the parties owes the other loyalty, candor, and fair treatment. Examples would be business partners, doctor and patient, bank and depositor, and husband and wife. When this relationship exists, silence can be the basis for the tort of misrepresentation when the fact should have been communicated because of the fiduciary relationship.

Scienter

Scienter is the intent to mislead. This means that the defendant knows the statement is false, or does not believe in its truth, or acts in **reckless disregard** for its truth or falsity. Scienter also includes an intent that the audience of the statement believe it and act in reliance on its truth. The audience consists of those individuals the defendant intends to reach with the statement. Some states go further and extend liability to those individuals the defendant has reason to expect will learn about and act on the statement, even though the defendant never actually intended to reach them.

Negligent Misrepresentation

Suppose the defendant's misrepresentation does not encompass scienter because there was no knowledge of the statement's falsity, no lack of belief in its truth, or no reckless disregard for truth or falsity. The defendant may simply have been careless in making the false statement, such as by not taking reasonable steps to check the accuracy of the statement before making it. If this leads to physical harm (e.g., plaintiff is injured because the car brakes failed after defendant carelessly told the plaintiff that the brakes were safe), a traditional negligence suit can be brought. If, however, only pecuniary harm results (e.g., the plaintiff loses $10,000 because of a careless statement by the defendant on the value of a painting), many states will allow the plaintiff to sue for **negligent misrepresentation** as long as he or she was one of the individuals the defendant intended to reach by the careless statement. In many states, individuals within a relatively small group can also sue if the defendant knows that at least someone in a group will learn about the statement and rely on it, even if the defendant does not know which specific individual will do so.

Justifiable Reliance

To recover, the plaintiff must rely on the statement of the defendant, and it must be a **justifiable reliance.** If the plaintiff is foolish in believing and acting on the defendant's statement, recovery for misrepresentation may be denied unless the defendant knew about and took advantage of the plaintiff's intellectual vulnerabilities. The fact on which the plaintiff relies must be **material,** meaning that it was important to the transaction. In selling the plaintiff a car, for example, it is not material that the defendant falsely tells the plaintiff that the defendant likes bananas, if all the statements about the car itself are accurate. If, however, the defendant knows that the plaintiff attaches significance to a peculiar fact and intentionally misleads him or her as to that fact, recovery may be allowed.

ASSIGNMENT	
22.1	Diane has just been hired as a telemarketer for a museum. She calls Harry, a stranger, to solicit a contribution. She tells Harry that the museum has important works of art in it and therefore deserves the support of the community. In fact, none of the works of art is valued over $500. During the conversation, Diane learns that Harry is a Catholic. She tells Harry that she too is a Catholic. In fact,

she has always been a practicing Lutheran. She is married to a Catholic and attends Catholic church services once or twice a year. Harry tells his wife about the museum. His wife decides to donate $10,000. When she finds out that the museum has a very weak collection and that Diane is not a Catholic, she sues Diane for misrepresentation. What result?

INTERFERENCE WITH CONTRACT RELATIONS

Suppose that Fred has a contract to build a bridge for Sam. If Fred fails to build the bridge, Sam can sue Fred in a contract action—for breach of contract. Now suppose that a third party, Dan, persuades Fred not to build Sam's bridge so that Fred can build one for Dan. At this point two legal actions are possible:

- a *contract* action (Sam v. Fred) for breaching the contract to build a bridge for Sam
- a *tort* action (Sam v. Dan) for inducing a breach of the contract Sam had with Fred

The tort is called **interference with contract relations.** Its elements are as follows:

  i. an existing contract
 ii. interference with the contract by defendant
iii. intent
 iv. damages
  v. causation

Existing Contract

There must be a contract with which the defendant interferes. The enforcement of the contract must not violate public policy. A contract to marry, for example, cannot be the subject of a breach of contract action. It is against **public policy** to enforce such contracts by requiring someone to go through with a marriage he or she no longer wants. Therefore, it would not be a tort to induce someone to breach a contract to marry. So too, it is not a tort to induce the breach of an illegal gambling contract or a prostitution contract.

Suppose that the contract is **voidable,** i.e., unenforceable at the option of one of the parties. A voidable contract remains in effect if the option to terminate is not exercised. A contract might be voidable because it is not in writing or because one of the parties is a minor. Is it a tort to interfere with such a contract? Yes, as long as the contract is in existence and is not contrary to public policy as just discussed. The contract does not have to be enforceable to be the foundation of this tort. There is always the possibility that the party to the contract will *not* exercise his or her option to get out of it; hence, it is a wrong (a tort) for a third party (the defendant) to induce its breach.

Many contracts, particularly employment contracts, are **terminable at will,** meaning that either party can get out at any time for any reason. Some courts conclude that it is not a tort to induce the termination of a contract at will since the parties to the contract are always free to terminate it without committing a breach of contract to each other. Most courts, however, disagree. It is a tort in most states to interfere with a contract at will. The injured party to the contract had a valuable expectation that the other party would not terminate—until the defendant came along. It is a tort to upset the contract relationship that existed.

Interference

The interference with the contract can take a number of forms:

- inducing one party to the contract to breach it
- making it impossible for one party to perform the contract
- making it substantially more difficult for one party to perform the contract

Intent

The plaintiff must show that the defendant intended to interfere with the contract relation by inducing the breach, or by rendering performance impossible or more burdensome. The defendant must desire this interference or know with substantial certainty that the interference will result from what the defendant does or fails to do. Negligence is not enough. Suppose that the XYZ Company has a contract to supply lake water to a city, and the defendant (a third party) negligently pollutes this water before delivery. The defendant has surely interfered with XYZ's contract with the city, but no intentional tort has been committed by the defendant because there was no intent to interfere with the contract. The XYZ Company or the city may be able to sue the defendant for negligence in polluting the water, but there can be no suit for interference with contract. The defendant must know about the contract and intend to interfere with it.

Damages

The damages for this tort cover the loss of the contract or the diminished value of its performance. Most courts require a showing of actual damages, even though they may be nominal. In addition, damages for mental suffering are usually allowed, and if malice is shown, punitive damages can be awarded. As indicated in the bridge example at the beginning of this section involving Fred, Sam, and Dan, the plaintiff may have a breach of contract action against the other party to the contract *and* a tort action against the third party for inducing the breach or for diminishing the value of performance. To avoid double recovery, however, the amount recovered in the tort action is reduced by whatever the plaintiff recovers in the contract action. When the defendant has threatened an interference with the contract, or when the interference is continuing, many courts will grant an **injunction** against the defendant because of the inadequacy of damages as a remedy.

Causation

The plaintiff must show that either:

- but for the action or inaction of the defendant, the plaintiff would not have suffered the damages that are provable, or
- the defendant was a substantial factor in producing these damages

Privilege to Interfere

One of the major defenses to this tort is the privilege to interfere in order to protect one's own interest. Assume, for example, that Len has a contract to furnish goods to Ted. Len will obtain these goods from Mary with whom Len has a separate contract. If Mary feels that Len is violating his contract with her, she can take steps to protect her own interest. This might include stopping delivery of the goods to Len. This, of course, would have the effect of interfering with Ted's contract with Len. Mary has not committed a tort, however, as long as she is acting reasonably to protect her own interest.

There may also be a privilege to interfere in order to protect the interest of someone else if there is a legal or moral duty to protect this other person (e.g., a doctor caring for a patient, an attorney advising a client). The interference could take the form of a recommendation that the person remove him- or herself from certain contract obligations that are reasonably thought to be detrimental to the welfare of that person. For example, the doctor might tell the patient that continuing to work at a particular plant could lead to a further deterioration of the patient's health.

This privilege is lost if the interference was **malicious.** In this context, malice means not acting reasonably—acting for a purpose other than to protect a legitimate interest, e.g., interfering with someone's contract in order to seek revenge.

ASSIGNMENT
22.2

Helen works for Linda. One day, Helen borrows $500 from Linda to repair a fence at Helen's home. Linda has difficulty collecting this money from Helen. Linda tells her father, Ed, about the loan. He advises Linda to fire Helen if she does not repay the loan. Linda tells Helen that she will lose her job if she does not repay the loan within a week. Helen is fired when she does not make the payment within the time designated. Does Helen have a cause of action against Ed?

INTERFERENCE WITH PROSPECTIVE ADVANTAGE

Next, we consider the tort called **interference with prospective advantage,** which has the following elements:

  i. reasonable expectation of an economic advantage
 ii. interference with this expectation
iii. intent
 iv. damages
  v. causation

In this tort, there is no existing contract with which the defendant has interfered. All that is needed is a reasonable expectation of some economic advantage. The defendant usually has committed other torts that have led to this interference, e.g., misrepresentation, defamation, assault, and battery.

In the business world, most of the cases that have arisen under the tort of interference with prospective advantage have involved what is loosely called **unfair competition.**

> **EXAMPLES:**
>
> • The plaintiff is trying to lure ducks at a public pond, which he or she will then kill and try to sell. The defendant intentionally fires a gun into the air in order to scare the ducks out of the plaintiff's range. The defendant is a competitor of the plaintiff in the sale of ducks.
> • The defendant threatens a third party not to go to work for the plaintiff (no employment contract yet exists). The goal of the defendant is to get the third party to go to work for the defendant.
> • The defendant pours some foul-smelling chemicals on his or her own property, which is next door to the plaintiff's, in order to scare the latter's potential customers away. The defendant wants the plaintiff to leave the area so that the defendant can rent the premises now occupied by the plaintiff.

The defendant has a privilege to protect his or her own business interests by engaging in fair competitive practices. Deceptive advertising and monopolistic steps, of course, constitute unfair (and illegal) competition. When these devices are not used, the defendant is free to use tactics such as high pressure advertising, price cutting, and rebates in order to lure prospective customers away from other merchants.

Courts are often reluctant to allow the tort of interference with prospective advantage when business or commercial interests are not involved, e.g., a defendant pressures a person to remove the plaintiff as the beneficiary of a will. There are a few courts, however, that will allow recovery in such situations, when there is a reasonable degree of certainty that the plaintiff would have received the expected benefit if there had been no interference by the defendant. In most cases of interference with prospective advantage, causation is a problem. It can be very difficult to prove that the benefit would have been obtained but for what the defendant did, or that the defendant was a substantial factor in the loss of the benefit. This is because the plaintiff had no contract right to the benefit at the time of the interference. Yet, if causation can be shown with reasonable certainty, recovery is allowed.

TORTIOUS INTERFERENCE WITH EMPLOYMENT (WRONGFUL DISCHARGE)

Most people are employed "at will," which, as indicated earlier, simply means that either the employee or the employer can terminate the relationship at any time and for any reason. There is no obligation to explain why or to state a cause. If, on the other hand, an express contract of employment exists for a designated period of time (e.g., a one-year union contract), the termination of the relationship within this period must comply with the terms of the contract. This usually means that terminations are allowed only for **cause**; employees with contract protection cannot be fired at will. In this context, cause means a justifiable reason such as incompetence.

The traditional rule on **employment at will** has been undergoing some modification. There are now some circumstances in which the law *will* protect the employee at will. Suppose, for example, that the employer fires the employee because the latter reported fire hazards in the employer's building to the city, or because the employee filed a workers' compensation claim. This **retaliatory discharge** violates public policy, because it obviously discourages employees from engaging in important activity such as fire prevention and in exercising rights such as those provided by the workers' compensation system.

What is the remedy for such retaliation? It is difficult to categorize the remedy within the traditional causes of action. A breach of contract action is somewhat strained, because there is no express contract that was violated. Some courts say that in the employment relationship there is an implied condition that forbids the employer from terminating the relationship for a reason that violates public policy. Most courts take a different approach by concluding that a tort has been committed—the **tortious interference with employment** (also called **wrongful discharge**). This tort differs from the tort of interference with contract relations (discussed earlier), in which a *third party* has wrongfully caused the interference.

DISPARAGEMENT

The tort of **disparagement** covers attacks made against the business or property of the plaintiff. The elements of this tort are as follows:

   i. false statement of fact
  ii. disparaging the plaintiff's business or property
 iii. publication
 iv. intent
  v. special damages
 vi. causation

The attack might cast doubt on the plaintiff's title to property (called **slander of title**) or attribute a quality to goods that make them undesirable for sale or other commercial use (called **trade libel**). The effect of the disparaging statement is to cause others not to deal with the plaintiff or to cause some other similar disadvantage.

> **EXAMPLES:**
>
> - Sam falsely states that he holds a mortgage on the plaintiff's farm, which the latter has on the market for sale.
> - Tom falsely says that he owns the land that Jim is trying to sell.
> - Sarah falsely states that the tires being sold by XYZ as radials are not radials.

Some statements constitute the tort of disparagement and the tort of defamation. Disparagement discredits the quality of or title to *goods or property.* Defamation consists of a derogatory statement about the *person* of the plaintiff (see Chapter 20). Compare the following statements:

"Prostitutes regularly use the XYZ Hotel for their clients."
"Fred, the manager of the XYZ Hotel, takes a cut of the fee charged by prostitutes in exchange for the use of the hotel for their clients."

The first statement disparages the hotel—the business. The second statement disparages the hotel *and* personally defames the manager.

The plaintiff must plead and prove **special damages,** which are specific economic or pecuniary losses. It is usually not enough for the plaintiff to prove that there was a general loss of business following the disparaging statements of the defendant. The plaintiff must show specifically identified contracts or customers that were lost. Or, the plaintiff must show he or she had to sell goods at a lower price to specific customers as a result of the disparagement.

Defendants have a privilege to protect their own interest. For example, a defendant can state that he or she owns property the plaintiff is trying to sell. This disparages the property of the plaintiff, but it is privileged as long as the defendant is acting in the honest belief that he or she is protecting his or her own interest. Malice, however, defeats the privilege.

There is also a general privilege to compete in the business world by exaggerating the qualities of your own products compared to the products of others. There is a privilege, for example, to say that "no car is more economical" than the car being offered for sale. As indicated earlier, such statements are viewed either as nonfactual statements (hence not qualifying as the first element of disparagement) or as **fair competition.**

Special Statutes: "Veggie Libel"

Some statements about consumer products can have a major impact on their sale. Suppose, for example, that a guest, a reporter, or a host on a national talk show or newsmagazine says, "The pesticides used on all broccoli cause cancer in children." This could devastate the broccoli market.

Several states have passed special statutes that give producers of perishable food products a cause of action when they lose business because of false statements that disparage the safety of their products. The media has called such actions "**veggie libel.**"

> **EXAMPLES:**
>
> - Ranchers sued television talk-show host, Oprah Winfrey, and a guest who said American beef was largely infected with bovine spongiform encephalopathy, or "mad cow disease." (WINFREY: "You said this disease could make AIDS look like the common cold?" GUEST:

> "Absolutely." WINFREY: "Now doesn't that concern you-all a little bit right here, hearing that? It has just stopped me cold from eating another burger. I'm stopped.")
>
> • Washington State apple growers sued the CBS television show *60 Minutes* for alleging in a segment called, "*A* Is for Apple" that Alar, a chemical growth regulator, dramatically increased cancer risks.
> • Emu ranchers sued Honda Motor Company for a Honda advertisement that said the emu was the "pork of the future."

Almost all cases of this kind are lost by the plaintiffs who bring them. It is often very difficult to prove that the statements are false. This is particularly true in those states where the plaintiff must prove that the defendant knew the statement was false. Also some courts are not receptive to an allegation of group disparagement that is not directed at a particular grower or food producer. Furthermore, there is reason to believe that the United States Supreme Court will eventually impose severe constitutional limitations on disparagement suits of this kind against the media as it has in the area of defamation. The inclination of the Court is to interpret the First Amendment as encouraging robust speech. "Veggie libel" laws arguably do the opposite.

ASSIGNMENT

22.3

Did President George Bush commit a tort when he told the media, "I hate broccoli and we don't serve it here at the White House"?

INJURIOUS FALSEHOOD

The phrase **injurious falsehood** is sometimes used interchangeably with the word "disparagement," but injurious falsehood is a broader concept. Disparagement is an example of an injurious falsehood. An injurious falsehood can consist of a statement of fact that injures someone economically in a way other than disparaging goods or a business.

> **EXAMPLES:**
>
> • a false statement to the immigration officials that results in the deportation of the plaintiff
> • a false statement by an employer of the income paid to an employee, resulting in tax evasion charges against the employee

The same elements for disparagement are required for injurious falsehood, except for the second element: disparaging the plaintiff's business or property. Instead of showing that the statement disparages the business or products of the plaintiff, the broader tort of injurious falsehood requires only that the statement be harmful to the interests of the plaintiff. The other elements are the same: false statement of fact, publication, intent, special damages, and causation.

ASSIGNMENT

22.4

Tom dies intestate, i.e., without a valid will. There are only two survivors: Mary, a daughter, and George, a nephew. Under the intestate law of the state, all property goes to legitimate children. If no legitimate children survive, the property goes to other relatives. George claims that Mary is illegitimate. Mary hires an attorney who helps establish that she is legitimate. What tort or torts, if any, has George committed?

PRIMA FACIE TORT

Negligence is a catchall tort that encompasses a very wide variety of wrongful conduct that is considered unreasonable. There is no comparable catchall tort for conduct that is intentional. We cannot say that all intentional conduct causing harm is tortious. If the defendant's actions or inactions do not fall within the elements of negligence, the plaintiff must look to the approximately thirty other torts, e.g., battery, deceit, malicious prosecution, and others listed in Figure 1–3 of Chapter 1. If these torts do not fit, then the plaintiff must suffer the loss, unless, of course, workers' compensation and no-fault insurance (see Appendix A) provide some form of relief.

Some consider it unfortunate that the law does not provide a clear tort remedy for a defendant's intentional conduct that harms someone even though the facts do not fit within the traditional torts. In a sense, the torts of injurious falsehood and interference with prospective advantage try to fill some of the holes left by the traditional torts. Yet, as we have seen, even these torts have limitations on what intentional conduct they will or will not cover.

In a few states (including New York), small efforts toward the creation of a generic intentional tort have been made in the form of the **prima facie tort.** Although this tort is not limited to the business world, most of the cases applying it have involved commercial matters. The elements of the prima facie tort are:

   i.   infliction of harm
   ii. intent to do harm (malice)
   iii. special damages
   iv. causation

It is sometimes said that the tort does not exist unless the defendant acted "maliciously and without justification." It is not always clear whether malice means a desire to harm someone or simply an intentional act or omission.

In theory, the prima facie tort is available when the facts of the case do not fit the pigeonholes of any of the traditional torts. It does not follow, however, that the prima facie tort will apply every time the other torts do not. The requirement of special damages, for example, tends to limit the applicability of the prima facie tort, due to the difficulty of proving specific economic or pecuniary loss (i.e., special damages).

The vast majority of states do *not* recognize the prima facie tort. Too many problems exist in defining it and in defining the defenses to it. Rather than create a new tort, most states would prefer to try to stretch the boundaries of the existing torts so that plaintiffs will not be without a remedy when defendants have intentionally caused injury.

BAD FAITH LIABILITY

A relatively recent basis of liability against insurance companies is called **bad faith liability.** It consists of an unreasonable denial or delay in paying an insurance claim within policy limits.

> **EXAMPLE:** Jackson has a $100,000 liability policy with an insurance company. He has an accident and is sued for $250,000 by Pamela. The latter offers to settle for $80,000. Jackson's attorney notifies the insurance company of the offer, but the company takes an unreasonable amount of time to respond. Pamela proceeds with litigation and obtains a $200,000 judgment against Jackson. The insurance company pays $100,000 of this judgment, the maximum under the policy.

Jackson can now sue the company for the tort of bad faith in handling the insurance claim. His argument is that the company's unreasonable delay in processing his claim led to a judgment far in excess of policy limits.

DRAM SHOP LIABILITY

A number of states have what is called a Civil Liability Act or Dram Shop Act that imposes liability on those who give liquor to someone who is visibly intoxicated when the intoxication causes an injury to a third person. The basis of **dram shop liability** can differ from state to state. Negligence may have to be shown: the person giving the liquor created an unreasonable risk that the person receiving the liquor might injure others. Some states impose strict liability, especially if the person receiving the liquor is a minor. In such states there is no need for the injured third party to show that the person giving the liquor was negligent.

Many states impose dram shop liability only when the liquor is *sold* and only when the buyer is already visibly intoxicated. In a few states, however, liability is not dependent on a sale. A social host can also be held to dram shop liability when a *gift* of intoxicating liquor causes an injury.

> **EXAMPLE:** Bob holds a high school graduation party in his home for his daughter and her friends. He serves liquor at the party. One of the guests is Kelly, who is intoxicated. While driving home from the party, Kelly hits a pedestrian. Kelly became intoxicated at the party and the intoxication was a substantial factor in causing the pedestrian's injury. The latter can now seek dram shop liability against Bob.

ASSIGNMENT

22.5

The XYZ Supermarket has a liquor section. Davidson, an adult, buys a six-pack of beer at XYZ. At the time of the purchase, his speech was slightly slurred from drinking earlier in the day. He goes to his car in the parking lot of XYZ and drinks all the beer he just bought. Would dram shop liability apply in the following cases?

a. After Davidson drives out of the XYZ Supermarket parking lot, he goes to a nearby parking lot. He has a fist fight with another driver in an argument over a parking space. Davidson knocks the other driver unconscious. This driver now wants to sue the XYZ Supermarket for selling Davidson the beer.

b. After Davidson drives out of the XYZ Supermarket parking lot, he hits a tree and is killed. His family now wants to sue the XYZ Supermarket for selling Davidson the beer.

SUMMARY

Misrepresentation covers pecuniary loss caused by false statements of fact, by the active concealment of a fact, by the nondisclosure of a fact that someone had a duty to disclose, and by the statement of opinion containing false implied facts. There must be scienter, the intent to mislead, which is established by showing that the defendant made a statement knowing it is false, without a belief in its truth, or in reckless disregard of its truth or falsity, with the desire that the statement be believed and relied upon. An action for negligent misrepresentation can be brought in many states for the careless communication of a false statement of fact brought by someone whom the statement was intended to reach. There must be justifiable reliance, which means that the plaintiff was reasonable in taking action because of the plaintiff's statement. The exception is when the defendant knows the plaintiff is particularly vulnerable to whatever the defendant says.

It is a tort to interfere with contract relations by intentionally inducing another to breach a contract or to make it impossible or more difficult to perform. There must be an existing contract with which the defendant intends to interfere. The plaintiff's damages include compensation to cover the loss of the contract or the diminished value of its performance. One of the defenses to this tort is the privilege to protect one's own interest or the interest of another. If the plaintiff does not have a contract, but the defendant interferes with the plaintiff's reasonable expectation of an economic advantage, the defendant may have committed the tort of interference with prospective advantage. Most cases raising this tort in the business world involve unfair competition. Some states will allow an employee at will to sue an employer for tortious interference with an employment relationship through a retaliatory discharge. When the employment is at will, this tort is an exception to the traditional rule that at-will employees can be fired at any time for any reason.

To commit the tort of disparagement, the defendant must publish a false statement of fact that casts doubt on the plaintiff's title to property (slander of title) or attributes a quality to the plaintiff's goods that makes them undesirable for commercial use (trade libel). A defendant has the privilege to protect his or her own interest and to engage in fair competition in the business world. Some states have passed "veggie libel" statutes that give producers of perishable food products a cause of action when they lose business because of false statements that disparage the safety of their products. These cases are difficult to prove and are subject to constitutional challenge.

In a few states, if the defendant causes special damages by intentionally inflicting harm, the plaintiff may be able to bring an action for prima facie tort when the conduct does not fit within any of the traditional torts.

Insurance companies that unreasonably delay acting on insurance claims within policy limits may be subject to bad faith liability when the litigated claim results in a judgment against the plaintiff that is over the limits of the policy. Businesses that sell liquor to intoxicated persons who then injure others can be subject to dram shop liability. Some states also impose this liability on hosts who serve liquor to intoxicated guests at social gatherings.

KEY TERMS

misrepresentation   287

deceit   287

fraud   287

pecuniary loss   287

fact   291

opinion   291

puffing   291

fiduciary relationship   292

confidential relationship   292

scienter   292

reckless disregard   292

negligent misrepresentation   292

justifiable reliance   292

material   292

interference with contract
    relations   293

public policy   293

voidable   293

terminable at will   293

injunction   294

malicious   295

interference with prospective
    advantage   295

unfair competition   295

cause   296

employment at will   296

retaliatory discharge   296

tortious interference with
    employment   296

wrongful discharge   296

disparagement   296

slander of title   297

trade libel   297

special damages   297

fair competition   297

veggie libel   297

injurious falsehood   298

prima facie tort   299

bad faith liability   299

dram shop liability   300

Additional Tort Defenses

Chapter Outline

- Introduction
- Consent in Tort Law
- Self-Help Privileges
- Sovereign Immunity
- Official Immunity: The Personal Liability of Government Employees
- Charitable Immunity
- Intrafamily Tort Immunity

INTRODUCTION

A **defense** is the response of a party to a claim of another party, setting forth the reason(s) the claim should not be granted. Sometimes the defense is a simple denial ("I didn't do it"). More often the response is more specific (e.g., "the law allowed me to do what I did because. . . ."). Throughout this text, we have studied defenses to specific torts, e.g., Chapter 15 (defenses to negligence) and Chapter 20 (defenses to defamation). In this chapter, almost all the defenses we will study apply to more than one tort.

Many defenses are privileges or immunities. A **privilege** is a justification for what would otherwise be wrongful or tortious conduct. A privilege is the right of an individual to act contrary to the right of another individual without being subject to tort or other liability. Self-defense is an example. Using physical force against another usually constitutes a battery. If, however, you used this force to protect yourself against attack, you may have a defense when you are sued for battery—the privilege of self-defense. Technically, a tort cannot exist if the defendant had a privilege to do what the plaintiff is now complaining about. An **immunity,** on the other hand, is a special protection given to someone who *has* committed a tort. Sovereign immunity is an example. Suppose, for example, that a government employee defames you. The defense of sovereign immunity may prevent you from suing the government for this tort, and the defense of official immunity may prevent you from suing the employee for this tort. The practical effect of privileges and immunities is the same: they both are defenses that prevent liability for damage or injury. Because of this similarity of effect, you will sometimes see the words "privilege" and "immunity" used interchangeably.

Privileges that are defenses to tort actions are different from evidentiary privileges that operate to prevent a jury from considering otherwise admissible evidence. Examples of evidentiary privileges are attorney-client privilege, doctor-patient

303

privilege, and privilege against self-incrimination. In this chapter, we are concerned with the privileges that prevent tort liability.

CONSENT IN TORT LAW

A central principle of the law is **volenti non fit injuria**: no wrong is done to one who consents. If the plaintiff consented to the defendant's conduct, the defendant should not be liable for the resulting harm. When the defendant is charged with negligence or strict liability in tort, the consent defense is the closely related concept of assumption of risk, which we examined in Chapters 15 and 16. Here, our focus is consent as a defense to intentional torts such as assault, battery, and trespass.

The basic elements of **consent** are presented in Figure 23–1.

FIGURE 23–1
Elements of consent.

> **1.** Plaintiff (P) must have the capacity to consent to the conduct of Defendant (D).
> **2.** There is an express or implied manifestation from P of a willingness to let the conduct of D occur.
> **3.** P's willingness is voluntary.
> **4.** D reasonably believes that P is willing to let D's conduct occur.
> **5.** P has knowledge of the nature and consequences of D's conduct.
> **6.** D's conduct is substantially the same as the conduct P agreed to.

Capacity to Consent

The person giving consent must have the capacity to consent. A young girl, for example, may agree to sexual intercourse with an older male, but the latter can still be guilty of statutory rape. If the girl later sues the male for battery in a civil case, the male cannot raise the defense of consent, just as he could not raise it in the criminal case. The young girl does not have the capacity to consent if she is below the age designated by law. So too, there are statutes intended to protect children from working in dangerous conditions. If a child is injured in working conditions that violate the statute, the employer will not be able to say that the child consented to work there and took the risk of being injured—even if the child understood those risks and willingly proceeded. The statutes will probably be interpreted as taking away the child's capacity to consent.

A person can also lack the capacity to consent by being too young or ill to understand the conduct involved. Unless an authorized parent or guardian gives consent for this person, the consent is invalid.

Suppose that the conduct to which consent is given is criminal conduct. Paul and Dan agree to a duel or boxing match that is illegal. Both are prosecuted under criminal law. Paul then sues Dan for damages in a civil battery case. Dan's defense is that Paul consented to being hit. Courts differ on how they handle this problem. Some hold that the consent will be a good defense, barring the civil action. Other courts, however, do not recognize the consent as valid on the theory that no one has the power or capacity to consent to a crime. Since the consent is invalid, the civil battery action can be brought. As a consequence, a plaintiff can receive damages growing out of a criminal act in which the plaintiff willingly participated. Of course, if both Paul and Dan were injured in their illegal fight with each other, each of them could sue the other for civil battery in a state where the consent will not be recognized.

Manifestation of Willingness

A person can demonstrate or manifest willingness in a variety of ways. There can be an express manifestation such as telling someone he or she can enter the land or use a car. Written or verbal manifestation is not always needed. The wave of a hand can indicate consent to come on one's land. Consent by silence is also common if the person would normally be expected to speak if he or she objected to conduct about to occur. If a trespasser enters your yard and you fail to object or fail to take steps to remove the individual, your silence or nonaction is strong evidence that you do not object. This is an **implied consent.** If you voluntarily agree to play football, you are implying consent to the kind of rugged contact that is usually associated with this sport. If you walk downtown into a crowded store, you are implying consent to the kind of everyday contact that is normal in crowds.

ASSIGNMENT

23.1

a. Henry and Fred are having an argument. Henry is about to hit Fred with a baseball bat. In response, Fred punches Henry with his fist and breaks Henry's jaw. While Henry is unconscious on the ground, Fred stabs him in the leg. Henry later sues Fred for injury to his leg in a civil battery case. Fred raises the defense of consent. What result and why?

b. At a college dance, Jessica asks Dan, a stranger, to dance. After the dance, Jessica kisses Dan on the cheek and walks away. Dan sues Jessica for battery. Does she have a defense?

Voluntariness

If the plaintiff has been coerced into agreeing to the defendant's conduct, the consent is invalid. **Coercion** is the use of such strength or pressure to secure compliance that the compliance is not the product of a free will. Coercion renders consent involuntary, invalidating the defense. Suppose that a foreign passenger about to enter port does not want to be vaccinated, but nevertheless rolls up her sleeve to the doctor injecting the needle. Her conduct led the doctor to believe that she consented. She may have been under pressure to be vaccinated in order to avoid the hassle of being detained at port, yet the consent was still the product of a free will. The consent was voluntary.

Extreme or drastic pressure, however, can be enough to invalidate consent, e.g., a threat of force against the plaintiff or a member of the plaintiff's family, or a threat against the valuable property of the plaintiff. The plaintiff's agreement as a result of such pressure would probably not be voluntary.

Reasonable Belief

The defendant must be reasonable in believing that the plaintiff has consented to the conduct in question. Problems often arise when the defendant claims to have relied on the plaintiff's implied consent. Suppose that the defendant has always played practical jokes on the plaintiff, to the latter's great amusement, e.g., squirting the plaintiff with a water pistol or pretending to steal the plaintiff's hat. It would be reasonable for the defendant to believe that the plaintiff would continue to agree to such jokes as long as they were of the same kind as practiced in the past. If the plaintiff has decided that enough is enough and does not want to be subjected to such jokes anymore, he or she must communicate this to the defendant. Otherwise, the defendant is justified in believing that plaintiff continues to consent. The test of consent is not what the plaintiff subjectively thinks, but what someone reasonably interprets the plaintiff to be communicating based upon the latter's words, actions, silence, and any relevant cultural customs in the area on how people normally interpret each other's behavior.

ASSIGNMENT

23.2

a. Tom calls Linda on the phone and tells her that he has her very valuable painting, which he will destroy if she does not come to his apartment and engage in sexual intercourse. Linda is frantic about the painting. She goes to his apartment and has sex with him. He then gives her the painting. Later, she brings a civil battery action against him. Does he have a defense? Would it make any difference if his threat was to harm Linda's neighbor?

b. Mary is riding in her car when she spots Alex injured on the side of the road. Mary pulls over to try to help. She sees that his arm is broken and puts it in a sling. Later, Alex sues Mary for battery. Does she have a defense? Does it make any difference that Mary is a doctor? Why or why not?

Knowledge

The plaintiff must know what conduct is being consented to and its probable consequences in order for the consent to be an effective bar to a later tort action against the defendant. If a doctor obtains the consent of a patient to undergo an operation, but fails to tell the patient of the very serious probable side effects of the operation, the patient has not consented to the operation. The defendant has not provided the patient with the basic knowledge to enable the patient to give an **informed consent.** As we saw in Chapter 12, if an emergency exists, the doctor can proceed with treatment to save the patient's life or to avoid serious further injuries if it is not possible or practical to obtain the patient's consent and the doctor does not have an express prior direction to the contrary from the patient.

Consent obtained by trickery or misrepresentation is not effective. The classic case is the plaintiff who buys candy that turns out to be poisoned. The implied representation of the seller is that the candy is wholesome. The plaintiff consented to eat candy, not poison. So too if the defendant entices the plaintiff to play a game of ice hockey in order to get the plaintiff into a position where the defendant can intentionally cut the plaintiff with skates, the defendant cannot later claim that the plaintiff consented to such contact. The plaintiff's consent was obtained by misrepresentation.

When the plaintiff has made a mistake about what he or she is consenting to, it is important to know whether the defendant caused the plaintiff's mistake and whether the defendant knew about it. If the mistake was not caused by and was not known to the defendant, the consent is still valid as long as the defendant was reasonable in believing that the plaintiff consented. If, for example, the plaintiff agrees to let the defendant ride a truck over one parcel of land, but makes a mistake and lets the defendant ride over a different parcel of land, the consent is valid and defeats a trespass action as long as the defendant neither knew about nor procured the error that the plaintiff made. The consent is invalid if the defendant either knew about or caused the plaintiff to make the mistake, as through misrepresentation.

Substantially the Same Conduct

If the defendant's conduct deviates in a minor way from the conduct the plaintiff consented to, the consent is still effective. The deviation must be substantial for the consent to be invalid. If, for example, the plaintiff agrees to let the defendant throw a bucket of water on him or her, the consent is still effective if the same approximate amount of water is poured on the plaintiff by using a garden hose. The defendant's conduct is substantially different, however, if the bucket of water contains rocks, unknown to the plaintiff.

Sexual fidelity can sometimes raise consent issues.

> **EXAMPLE:** In the case of *Neal v. Neal,* Thomas and Mary Neal are married. They engage in sexual relations during a time that Thomas is having an affair. When Mary finds out about the affair, she brings a battery action against Thomas for those times they had sexual relations while the affair was going on. Tom's defense is that Mary consented to these relations.

If Mary had known of Thomas's sexual involvement with another woman, she says she would not have consented to continue having sex with him since sexual relations under those circumstances "would have been offensive to her." Therefore, she contends that his failure to disclose the fact of the affair rendered her consent ineffective and subjects him to liability for battery. In *Neal v. Neal*, the trial court ruled in favor of Thomas on the ground that Mary's consent was valid since sexual relations with her husband "was not actually offensive at the time it occurred." The appellate court reversed because the ruling of the trial court "ignores the possibility that Mary Neal may have engaged in a sexual act based upon a substantial mistake concerning the nature of the contact or the harm to be expected from it, and that she did not become aware of the offensiveness until well after the act had occurred. . . . To accept that the consent, or lack thereof, must be measured by only those facts which are known to the parties at the time of the alleged battery would effectively destroy any exception for consent induced by fraud or deceit. Obviously if the fraud or deceit were known at the time of the occurrence, the 'consented to' act would never occur." *Neal v. Neal*, 125 Idaho 617, 622, 873 P.2d 871, 876 (1994).

ASSIGNMENT

23.3

In the case of Thomas and Mary Neal, assume that several weeks after Mary found out about Thomas's affair, she resumed sexual relations with her husband. Later, however, she still sues him for battery to cover the time they had sexual relations when she was unaware of the affair. Does Thomas now have a better argument that her consent was valid during this time?

The defendant must substantially comply with any restrictions or conditions imposed on the consent by the plaintiff that are communicated to the defendant. If, for example, the plaintiff tells the defendant that he or she can cut one truckload of timber from the plaintiff's land on January 3 or 4, the defendant will be liable for trespass to land if he or she cuts three truckloads on those dates, or if any timber is cut on January 10.

ASSIGNMENT

23.4

Ted and Maureen agree to have sexual intercourse. Maureen gets venereal disease from Ted and sues him for battery. How, if at all, would the following factors affect Ted's defense of consent?

a. Ted was a prostitute and Maureen knew it.

b. Ted led Maureen to believe that he was a virgin.

c. Ted and Maureen confided to each other that both had had many lovers before.

d. Ted lied to Maureen about wanting to marry her.

e. Maureen lied to Ted about wanting to marry him.

f. This was the first time Ted and Maureen met.

g. Ted and Maureen are married to each other.

SELF-HELP PRIVILEGES

When serious conflict arises, our society encourages people to use the legal system—the courts—to resolve the conflict. In effect, we say, "don't take the law into your own hands; tell it to a judge!" There are situations, however, where it simply is not practical to ask the courts to intervene. A person may need to act immediately to protect an interest or a right. Such immediate, protective action is called **self-help.** Self-help is justified when there is a privilege to act without first obtaining the permission or involvement of the legal system.

We shall consider nine self-help privileges:

1. self-defense
2. defense of others
3. necessity
4. abating a nuisance
5. defense of property
6. recapture of chattels
7. retaking possession of land forcibly
8. discipline
9. arrest

The question often arises whether a defendant loses the protection of a privilege because the defendant has made a *mistake.* As we shall see, some reasonable mistakes do not destroy the privilege, whereas other mistakes—even if reasonably made—do destroy it.

Self-Defense

The privilege of **self-defense** is the use of reasonable force to prevent an immediate harmful or offensive contact against you by someone who is making an apparent threat of this contact. In short, it is the right to protect yourself from immediate physical harm. The threat must be immediate (today, you cannot hit someone who has threatened to hurt you tomorrow) and the force used to prevent the threat must be reasonable (you cannot shoot someone who has threatened to blow smoke in your face).

What happens if you make a mistake in trying to protect yourself?

> **EXAMPLE:** Nathan sees Diana running toward him with a raised baseball bat. Thinking that she is going to hit him, Nathan throws a brick at Diana, breaking her leg. In fact, unknown to Nathan, Diana was simply expressing jubilation after just coming from a baseball game that her team won.

Nathan acted in self-defense, but he made a mistake. There was no actual threat to him from Diana. In most states, the defense is not lost if this mistake was reasonable as to the amount of force needed for self-protection or, indeed, as to whether any protection was needed. Figure 23–2 presents an overview of the elements of the privilege of self-defense, examples of the kinds of torts to which this privilege can be used as a defense, examples of paralegal interviewing and investigation tasks to uncover facts that are relevant to proving that the privilege applies (including the reasonableness of mistakes), and a list of facts that could make it impossible to use the privilege.

ASSIGNMENT

23.5

In the following situations, assess whether the defendant can successfully raise the privilege of self-defense.

a. Richard raises his cane over his head and shouts at Gary, saying, "If my daughter wasn't here with me, I'd smash you in the head." Gary is afraid. He grabs Richard's cane and knocks him down. Richard then sues Gary for battery.

b. Jane asks Clayton to leave Jane's store because she does not like the color of Clayton's clothes. Clayton refuses to leave. Jane comes at Clayton with a broom. Jane is over twenty-five feet away and is on crutches. As Jane approaches, Clayton shoots her. Jane sues Clayton for battery.

c. Lou is in Robin's home. Lou starts yelling obscenities at Robin in front of Robin's family. Lou spits in Robin's face and throws Robin's coat out the window. Just as Lou is about to spit in Robin's face again, Robin stabs Lou. Lou sues Robin for battery.

FIGURE 23–2 An overview of the privilege of self-defense.

Elements of the Privilege of Self-Defense	The Torts Involved (Examples)	Paralegal Tasks: What to Find Out Through Interviewing and Investigation	Facts That Destroy the Privilege
a. Reasonable belief by D that P will immediately inflict harmful or offensive contact on D. **b.** Reasonable force used by D to prevent P from carrying out the apparent threat of an immediate harmful or offensive contact on D. (See the notes on mistakes, deadly force, and attacks in a residence.)	• *Battery* P is about to hit D. To prevent this, D knocks P down. P sues D for battery. D can raise the defense of self-defense. • *Assault* P is about to hit D. To prevent this, D threatens to hit P. P sues D for assault. D can raise the defense of self-defense. • *False Imprisonment* P is about to hit D. To prevent this, D locks P in a room. P sues D for false imprisonment. D can raise the defense of self-defense.	• Has P threatened D in the past? • Has P hit D in the past? • Does P have a reputation for aggressiveness? • What age and strength differences appear to exist between P and D? • How close was P to D at the time of the threat? • What did P threaten D with? • Did the threat occur in D's residence? • Did P say anything to indicate how serious the threat was? • How much time did D have before P would carry out P's threat? • Was P's threat to inflict future or present harm on D? • Did D know or believe that P was only bluffing? • Did D have time to warn P that D would inflict force on P? • In the past, has D ever consented to the kind of contact that P threatened?	• D's response to the threat of P was disproportionate to the danger posed by P. (D cannot kill P to prevent a shove by P when the shove does not threaten D's life or limb with serious bodily harm.) • P's threat was to inflict future harm on D. • P was merely insulting D and not threatening D with bodily harm or offensive contact. • D was acting solely to protect D's honor and not to prevent a harmful or offensive contact by P. • D was acting out of revenge and not to prevent immediate harm to D. • D was not threatened at D's residence and could have retreated without responding with deadly force or force calculated to impose serious bodily harm on P. • D knew or believed that P was only bluffing.

Notes:

- If D makes a mistake on whether P is about to inflict an immediate harmful or offensive contact on D, or if D makes a mistake on the amount of force needed to prevent the immediate threat, the privilege of self-defense is still valid if the mistake was reasonable under the circumstances.
- Reasonable force can include deadly force or force calculated to cause serious bodily harm *only if* D reasonably believes D is threatened with death or serious bodily harm from P.
- If D is in his or her residence, D does not have to retreat before inflicting deadly force or force calculated to cause serious bodily harm if such force is otherwise reasonable.
- States differ on whether such retreat is needed if D is *not* in his or her residence.

Defense of Others

We are also allowed to defend others. The privilege of the **defense of others** is the use of reasonable force to prevent an immediate harmful or offensive contact against a third person by someone who is making an apparent threat of this contact. This privilege is similar to self-defense in that the threat must be immediate and the use of force must be proportionate to the threat. A major distinction between the two privileges concerns the effect of a mistake. As we just saw, the privilege of self-defense is not lost if you make a reasonable mistake in what you thought was needed to protect yourself. Suppose, however, you make a mistake when trying to protect a third person.

> **EXAMPLE:** Dan sees that Paul is about to knock Bill down. To prevent this, Dan runs over and pushes Paul away. Paul sues Dan for battery. Dan raises the defense of the defense of others—Dan was trying to prevent Paul from harming Bill. Unknown to Dan, however, Bill had just pulled a knife on Paul. Paul was acting in self-defense when he was about to knock Bill down. Hence, Paul had a privilege to harm Bill.

In this case, the third person—Bill—was the aggressor against Paul. Dan didn't know this. He made a mistake. Does this mistake mean that Dan loses the defense of defense of others? Yes, in most states. Even a reasonable mistake will not save Dan. When you intervene to protect a third person, you take the risk that this third person has no right to be protected. In a minority of states, however, a reasonable mistake *will* preserve the defense. In our example, if Dan was reasonable in thinking that Bill needed protection, Dan can use the defense of defense of others to defeat Paul's battery action against him. But this is so only in a minority of states.

Figure 23–3 presents an overview of the elements of this privilege, examples of the kinds of torts to which this privilege can be used as a defense, examples of paralegal interviewing and investigation tasks to uncover facts that are relevant to proving that the privilege applies, and a list of facts that could make it impossible to use the privilege.

Necessity

Necessity is the privilege to make a reasonable use of the property of others to prevent immediate harm or damage to persons or property. The property can be **chattels** (personal property) or land.

> **EXAMPLES:** Without permission, you use a stranger's car to drive a member of your family to the emergency room of a hospital.
>
> Without permission, you burn the crops of a neighbor in order to stop the spread of a fire that is headed toward the town on the other side of the neighbor's field containing the crops.

When you use someone's property in this way, do you have to compensate them for any damage that you do? The answer depends on the kind of necessity that existed. You must provide compensation if a **private necessity** existed. This is the privilege to make a reasonable use of someone's property to prevent immediate private harm or damage. The use of the car in the first example demonstrates a private necessity. You were trying to protect a member of your family. A **public necessity,** on the other hand, is the privilege to make a reasonable use of someone's property to prevent immediate public harm or damage. This was the case in the second example. There was a danger of the town going up in flames—clearly a public danger. There is no requirement to provide compensation to someone whose property is used to prevent public harm or danger. In many states, however, special statutes exist that provide compensation in these cases, particularly when the damage is done by public employees such as the police or fire department.

Figure 23–4 presents an overview of the elements of the privilege of necessity, examples of the kinds of torts to which the privilege can be used as a defense, examples of paralegal interviewing and investigation tasks to uncover facts that are relevant to proving that the privilege applies, and a list of facts that could make it impossible to use the privilege.

ASSIGNMENT

23.6

Tom has a contagious disease. He has no money to buy medicine and no hospitals are in the area. Tom breaks into a doctor's office at night and steals what he thinks is medicine that will help. In fact, he takes the wrong medicine. The doc-

FIGURE 23–3 An overview of the privilege of defense of others.

Elements of the Privilege of Defense of Others	The Torts Involved (Examples)	Paralegal Tasks: What to Find Out Through Interviewing and Investigation	Facts That Destroy the Privilege
a. Belief by D that P will immediately inflict harmful or offensive contact on a third person. b. Reasonable force used by D with the intent to prevent P from carrying out the apparent threat of an immediate harmful or offensive contact on the third person. c. P did not have a privilege to threaten the third person. (See the notes on the minority rule on the third element, the use of deadly force, and the identity of the third person.)	• *Battery* P is about to hit a third person. D sees this and hits P to prevent P's attack on the third person. P sues D for battery. D can raise the defense of the defense of others. • *Assault* P is about to hit a third person. D sees this and threatens to hit P if P does not stop. P sues D for assault. D can raise the defense of defense of others. • *False Imprisonment* P is about to hit a third person. D sees this and locks P in a "bear hug" until the third person can escape. P sues D for false imprisonment (and for battery). D can raise the defense of the defense of others.	• Has P threatened the third person in the past? • Has P hit the third person in the past? • Does P have a reputation for aggressiveness? • What age and strength differences appear to exist between P and the third person? Between P and D? • How close was P to the third person at the time of P's threat? • What gestures or words were used by P to the third person that D could observe or hear? • How much time appeared to exist before P would carry out P's threat against the third person? • Was P's threat against the third person immediate or for the future? • Did P appear to be bluffing? • Did D have time to warn P that D would use force against P if the latter did not stop trying to harm the third person? • Did the third person appear to be consenting to contact from P, e.g., in a football game?	• D's response was disproportionate to the harm P was threatening the third person with. • P's threat was to impose future harm on the third person. • P was merely insulting the third person and not threatening the latter with immediate harm. • D knew P was bluffing. • D was acting out of revenge and not to prevent immediate harm to the third person. • In most states, D loses the privilege if D made a mistake and the third person turns out to have been the aggressor against P. This is so even if the mistake was reasonable. In a minority of states, however, the privilege is *not* lost if D's mistake was reasonable.

Notes:

• A minority of states do not include the third element listed in the first column (c) as long as D was reasonable in what turns out to be a mistake as to the third party's right to be protected.

• As to the amount of force that is reasonable, D stands in the shoes of the third person. D can use the amount of force that the third person could have reasonably used to protect him- or herself. This could include deadly force *only if* the third person was in danger of death or serious bodily harm from P.

• The third person does not have to be a member of D's family. In most states, the third person whom D tried to protect can be a stranger.

tor sues Tom for conversion. Does Tom have a defense? If Tom has a defense, does he still have to pay the doctor for losses sustained due to the break-in?

Abating a Nuisance

There are times when a defendant has a privilege to enter someone's land in order to **abate a nuisance.** This is the privilege to take reasonable steps to correct a nuisance that is interfering with the use and enjoyment of your land. The privilege is a defense to the tort of trespass to land. For a discussion of this privilege, see Chapter 19.

FIGURE 23–4 An overview of the privilege of necessity.

Elements of the Privilege of Necessity	The Torts Involved (Examples)	Paralegal Tasks: What to Find Out Through Interviewing and Investigation	Facts That Destroy the Privilege
a. Reasonable belief by D that persons or property will be immediately harmed or damaged. **b.** Reasonable use by D of P's chattels (personal property) or land to prevent the immediate harm or damage.	• *Conversion* D destroys P's liquor to prevent it from getting into the hands of an invading army. P sues D for conversion. D can raise the defense of public necessity and avoid paying P for the loss D caused. • *Conversion* D is injured in a car accident and uses P's scarf as a tourniquet. The scarf is ruined. P sues D for conversion. D can raise the defense of private necessity, but must compensate P for any damage done to P's scarf. • *Trespass to Land* D runs onto P's land to escape a bear. P sues D for trespass to land. D can raise the defense of private necessity but must compensate P for any damage D does to P's land, e.g., to a fence.	• What alternatives, if any, were available to D and how realistic were they? • How much time did D have to act? • How much damage did D do? • What were the indications that the public was in danger (for public necessity)? • Did D seek advice on what to do—if any time was available?	• D's belief in the existence of the danger was unreasonable. • D's use of P's chattels or land was disproportionate to the danger. (For example, D cannot blow up P's house to prevent the spread of a fire when the fire is minor and water is easily available to put it out.)

Defense of Property

The privilege of the **defense of property** is the right to use reasonable force to prevent an immediate interference with your property or to end an interference that has begun. The property can be land or chattels (personal property). You cannot use deadly force, however, to protect your property.

There are two major kinds of mistakes possible in trying to use this privilege:

- mistake on the amount of force needed to protect your possession, and
- mistake on whether you had the right to possess the property you protected.

A reasonable mistake on the amount of force needed will not defeat the privilege. Any mistake, however, on your right to possession *will* defeat the privilege, regardless of how reasonable your mistake might have been.

> **EXAMPLE:** Dan buys a painting from Kevin, a reputable art dealer, not knowing that Kevin stole the painting from Peter. When Peter sees the painting on Dan's wall, Peter starts to take the painting off the wall. To prevent this, Dan pushes Peter away. Peter sues Dan for battery.

In the battery action, Dan cannot use the defense of defense of property. He made a reasonable mistake in believing that he had a right to possess the painting since he bought it from a reputable dealer without knowing the dealer was a thief. Mistakes on the right to possession, however, destroy the privilege to defend property—even reasonable mistakes. The only exception would be if the person with the superior right to possession caused the other person to make the mistake.

Figure 23–5 presents an overview of the elements of this privilege, examples of the kinds of torts to which this privilege can be used as a defense, examples of paralegal interviewing and investigation tasks to uncover facts that are relevant to proving that the privilege applies, and a list of facts that could make it impossible to use the privilege.

Recapture of Chattels

The defense-of-property privilege is used when you have possession of property with which someone is interfering. Suppose, however, you no longer have possession. Someone has wrongfully dispossessed you of a chattel and you want to recapture it. The

FIGURE 23–5   Overview of the privilege of defense of property.

Elements of the Privilege of Defense of Property	The Torts Involved (Examples)	Paralegal Tasks: What to Find Out Through Interviewing and Investigation	Facts That Destroy the Privilege
a. D has possession of land or chattels (personal property). **b.** D's right to possession is superior to P's claim of possession, if any. **c.** D has a reasonable belief that immediate force is needed to prevent P's present threat to or continued interference with D's possession. **d.** D requests that P cease the threatened or continued interference with D's possession, unless the request would be unsafe or impractical for D. **e.** D uses reasonable force against P to prevent the threatened or continued interference by P of D's possession.	• *Battery* P enters D's land and refuses to leave when D asks him to do so. D takes P by the collar and pushes him out. P sues D for battery. D can raise the defense of defense of property. • *Assault* P reaches for D's purse on the table. D raises her fist at P and shouts at him to keep away from her purse. P sues D for assault. D can raise the defense of defense of property.	• Did D have possession of the land or chattel? • What indications were there that P was going to interfere immediately or was going to continue the interference? • What did P say or do? • What alternatives to force, if any, were available to D? • What age and strength differences existed between P and D? • What harm was P subjected to by D's use of force to prevent P's threatened or continued interference? • Did D ask P to stop the interference? Would such a request have been realistic? • Did P's interference with D's land or chattel in any way threaten D's personal safety or that of others?	• P had a privilege to be on the land or to possess the chattel. • P's right to possession was superior to D's. • P's threat to interfere was in the future—it was not an immediate threat. • D's use of force was disproportionate to the threat posed by P to D's possession. • D was motivated solely by hatred and revenge. D was not trying to prevent interference by P. • D knew that P was bluffing when P threatened interference. • D did not ask P to cease the threatened or actual interference by P. The request would have been reasonable or practical. • D used deadly force or force calculated to cause serious bodily harm even though neither D nor anyone else was threatened with death or serious bodily harm by P.

Notes:

• In most states, D cannot use deadly force or force calculated to cause serious bodily harm (e.g., shoot P), even if D adequately warns P that such force will be used. D has a privilege to use great force *only if* P's interference with property also threatens life or limb of others.

• D is still protected by the privilege if D makes a reasonable mistake on the amount of force needed, but not if D makes even a reasonable mistake on D's right to possession of the land or the chattel, unless P caused D to make the mistake.

• In this privilege, we are not talking about D's privilege to *recapture* possession from P. Recapture will be considered later in Figure 23–6.

privilege you need to try to use in this situation is called **recapture of chattels.** It is the right to use reasonable force to obtain the return of personal property (chattels) shortly after someone obtains them wrongfully. Before force is used, a request for the return of the chattel must be made unless such a request would be impractical or unsafe. Like the defense of property, you cannot use deadly force to recapture the chattels. Also, the privilege of recapture does not apply unless the chattel was taken from you wrongfully.

> **EXAMPLE:** David lets his friend, Paul, use David's bike for a brief ride in the playground. When Paul is on the bike for a few moments, he decides not to return it and tells David this. David immediately pushes Paul off the bike and retrieves it. Paul sues David for battery.

Paul wins. David cannot use the defense of recapture of chattels because Paul initially obtained possession of the bike rightfully—David agreed to let him use it. The privilege does not apply unless it is being used to obtain it back from someone who obtained it wrongfully. Paul rightfully obtained possession, but he has wrongfully kept it. To get the bike back in such a case, David must resort to the courts. The case would be different if Paul took the bike without permission. Then David would have the privilege to recapture.

You must be sure that you have the right to possess the chattel you want to recapture. If you make a mistake—even a reasonable one—the privilege is destroyed and you can be liable for any torts resulting from your use of force. To demonstrate this, let us change the facts of our bike example:

> **EXAMPLE:** David sees Paul, a total stranger, take a bike out of the playground. David immediately pushes Paul off the bike and retrieves it. In fact, Paul was riding his own bike, which looked exactly the same as David's bike. Paul sues David for battery.

Paul wins. David made a mistake about his right to possess the bike. Even though the mistake may have been reasonable since the bikes looked alike, the mistake is fatal. If you use force to recapture a chattel, you must have the right to possess that chattel. The only exception would be if the person with the superior right to possession caused the other person to make the mistake.

Figure 23–6 presents an overview of the elements of this privilege, examples of the kinds of torts to which this privilege can be used as a defense, examples of paralegal interviewing and investigation tasks to uncover facts that are relevant to proving that the privilege applies, and a list of facts that could make it impossible to use the privilege.

| **ASSIGNMENT** **23.7** | In the following situations, determine whether the defendant can claim the defense of recapture of chattels. |

a. Tom is playing football. He asks Fred to hold his watch. While Tom is on the field, Fred suddenly must leave. Fred asks Joe to hold the watch for Tom. Fred does not know that Joe is Tom's archenemy. When Tom finds out that Joe has the watch, he asks for it back. Joe refuses. Tom hits Joe over the head with a football helmet and takes the watch back. Joe sues Tom for battery.

b. Sam steals John's ring and sells it for $1 in a dark alley to Fred, who knows neither John nor Sam. Two weeks after John finds out that Fred has the ring, John breaks into Fred's house and takes the ring from Fred's jewelry box. Fred sues John for trespass to land.

Retaking Possession of Land Forcibly

Only under limited circumstances is a defendant entitled to retake possession of *land* from a plaintiff with the use of force, e.g., the plaintiff him- or herself has directly and wrongfully dispossessed the defendant. State statutes exist in most states

FIGURE 23–6 Overview of the privilege of recapture of chattels (personal property).

Elements of the Privilege of Recapture of Chattels	The Torts Involved (Examples)	Paralegal Tasks: What to Find Out Through Interviewing and Investigation	Facts That Destroy the Privilege
a. P acquired possession of the chattel wrongfully, e.g., by fraud or force. **b.** D has the right to immediate possession. **c.** D requests that P return the chattel. This request is made before D uses force to recapture it unless the request would be unrealistic or unsafe for D. **d.** D's use of force to recapture the chattel occurs promptly after P took possession of the chattel (sometimes referred to as **fresh pursuit**), or promptly after D discovered that P took possession. **e.** D uses reasonable force (not force calculated to cause death or serious bodily injury) with the intent to recapture the chattel from P.	• *Battery* P has just stolen D's television, and refuses to return it. D pushes P aside in order to take the television back. P sues D for battery. D can raise the defense of recapture of chattels. • *Assault* Same facts as above, except that instead of pushing P, D raises his fist and threatens to hit P if P does not return the television. P sues D for assault. D can raise the defense of recapture of chattels. • *Trespass to Land* Same facts as above on the television. P has the television in his garage. When D finds out, D immediately goes into the garage to recapture the television. P sues D for trespass to land. D can raise the defense of recapture of chattels.	• How did P get possession of the chattel? • Did P claim P had a right to possession? If so, on what basis? • What is D's basis for the claim that D had a right to possess the chattel? • Did either P or D claim that they owned the chattel, that they had properly rented it, or that they were properly holding it for someone else? • Did P originally get possession with the consent of D? • Did D request P to return the chattel? Was such a request realistic and safe? • When did D discover that P had possession, and how long after discovery did D try to recapture it? • Could D have discovered that P had possession sooner? Why or why not? • Could D have acted sooner to recapture the chattel? Why or why not? • How much force was necessary to take the chattel back from P? Could less force have been used? Why or why not? • What did P and D say to each other just prior to D's use of force?	• P did not have actual possession nor did P control possession. • P in fact got possession rightfully (even though P's *continued* possession may now be wrongful, in which case D does not have the privilege of recapture—D must use the courts to get the chattel back). • D has no right to possession. • D failed to request a return when such a request was practical and safe. • D took too long to discover that P had possession. • D took too long to recapture after D knew or should have known that P had possession. • D used a disproportionate amount of force to recapture the chattel. • D was acting solely from the motive of hatred and revenge and did not limit the force to what was necessary to recapture the chattel.

Notes:

• D's mistake about P's right to possession destroys the privilege even if the mistake was reasonable (unless P caused D to make the mistake).

• The **shopkeeper privilege** allows a merchant to detain a person for a reasonably short time for the purpose of investigating whether there has been a theft. The merchant must reasonably believe the person detained is a thief. (See Chapter 5 on false imprisonment.)

• For each example in the second column, D must establish compliance with the five elements of the privilege listed in the first column, e.g., the demand for a return is made when realistic and safe.

governing the repossession of land through the use of court proceedings, particularly when a landlord is trying to remove (evict) a tenant.

Discipline

Parents have the privilege of disciplining their children. This can include physically hitting and confining the children, as long as such force is reasonable. (Teachers and others who stand in the place of parents—*in loco parentis*—also have this privilege unless it has been restricted by special statute.) Suits within the family are discussed elsewhere. See Figure 18–1 in Chapter 18.

Arrest

When a public officer or a private citizen tries to arrest someone, the latter might respond with a suit for battery, assault, or false imprisonment. The privilege of **arrest** can be raised as a defense to such suits. The elements of this privilege and its special circumstances are considered in Chapter 5 on false imprisonment and false arrest. The arrest of an individual can also raise issues of defamation, invasion of privacy, malicious prosecution, and abuse of process. Finally, the arrested person might claim a violation of his or her civil rights.

SOVEREIGN IMMUNITY

When is a government liable for the torts committed on its behalf? The old answer was: never. The King cannot be sued because the King can do no wrong. This was the essence of the doctrine of **sovereign immunity.** Over the years, however, the government (i.e., the sovereign) has agreed to be sued for torts in limited situations. In this section, we will discuss the boundaries of what is now a limited sovereign immunity. Government, of course, acts only through its agents or employees. Hence, when the government is liable, it will be on a theory of **respondeat superior:** let the master answer for the acts of its servant. The servant is the government employee. We also need to explore when this employee is *personally* liable for the torts he or she commits while carrying out governmental functions. In summary, the issues are:

1. When has the *federal* government agreed to be liable for the torts of its employees?
2. When has the *state* government agreed to be liable for the torts of its employees?
3. When have *local* governments agreed (on their own or on order from the state government) to be liable for the torts of their employees?
4. When is a federal, state, or local government employee independently and personally liable for the torts he or she commits on the job? As we will see later, when government employees are not personally liable for such torts, it is because they enjoy what is called **official immunity,** which is separate from sovereign immunity.

If you are the victim of a tort committed by a government employee (e.g., slander, conversion), you will have no one to sue if both sovereign immunity and official immunity apply.

Before we examine these immunities, two closely related issues need to be mentioned. First, legislatures sometimes pass special legislation that allows a private individual to sue the government when the individual's suit would otherwise be barred by sovereign immunity. This waiver from immunity is more narrow than the general waiver for designated classes of torts or other claims that are our concern here. Second, if the government forces you to give up your land for a public purpose (e.g., to build a road through it), you must receive **just compensation.** This is because the constitution forbids government **taking of property** from a private individual without just compensation. To the extent that the government is forced by the constitution to provide compensation for a "taking," the government is waiving its sovereign immunity.

Federal Government

The basic law containing the federal government's consent to be sued is the **Federal Tort Claims Act** (FTCA).[1] By no means does the FTCA abolish sovereign immunity for the federal government. The general rule established by the FTCA is as follows: The United States (this phrase refers to the federal government) will be liable for its torts in the same manner as a private individual would be liable according to the local law in the place where the tort occurs, *unless* the United States is specifically exempted for that tort in the FTCA.

Assume that a federal employee in Delaware commits a tort such as negligence against you. According to the general rule, if the negligence law of the state of Delaware would make a private person liable for negligence for doing what the federal employee did, then the federal government will be liable for the tort—unless there is a specific exemption for that tort in the FTCA. Hence, we need to know what the FTCA specifically excludes and covers. Figure 23–7 tells us.

There is an important distinction under the FTCA between torts committed at the *planning* level and those committed at the *operational* level. Sovereign immunity is not waived for torts at the planning level; it is waived for torts at the operational (or ministerial) level. Planning involves policy decisions and judgment (for which considerable discretion is used) on whether to perform a government task. (An example of a planning task would be the decision of the government to raise taxes.) Something is operational if it involves the carrying out of a plan for which very little discretion is needed. (An example of an operational task would be making a delivery in a government truck.) Even less discretion is involved in *ministerial* tasks. (An example would be sending out a standard government form in response to a citizen phone request.)

The federal government may try to avoid liability by claiming that a tort committed by one of its employees involved planning discretion. Suppose that the United States Coast Guard negligently maintains a lighthouse, causing a private ship to crash into rocks. Do we have planning or operational negligence? Surely the initial decision to install the lighthouse involves a great deal of planning discretion, for which the government will not be liable, even if the Coast Guard was negligent in that planning. But the maintenance of the lighthouse itself is an operational function. To be sure, discretion is needed in running the lighthouse, but this discretion is at the operational level. Negligence at this level *will* impose liability under the Act. The same would be true of negligent operation of government motor vehicles.

Before a citizen tries to bring a claim under the Federal Tort Claims Act, the administrative agency involved must be given the chance to settle the case on its own within certain dollar limits. If the citizen is still dissatisfied, he or she can sue under the Act in a federal court.

Federal employees themselves are generally excluded as claimants under the Federal Tort Claims Act. Injuries that they receive on the job are covered by other statutory schemes, such as the Federal Employees' Compensation Act.

State Government

The state government consists of the governor's office, state agencies such as the state police, state hospitals, and state commissions and boards. To what extent has a state government waived its own sovereign immunity so that citizens can sue the state for the torts of state employees? States differ in their answers to this question. Some states have come close to abolishing sovereign immunity. Other states have schemes modeled in whole or in part on the Federal Tort Claims Act. Finally, other states have retained most of the traditional immunity.

Special protection is always given to agencies and offices when they are carrying out policy deliberations involving considerable judgment and discretion. It is

---

[1]28 U.S.C. §§ 2671-80 (1994).

FIGURE 23–7 Federal Tort Claims Act.

Exclusions	Coverage
(Claims for which the United States will *not* be liable; sovereign immunity is *not* waived)	(Claims for which the United States *will* be liable; sovereign immunity *is* waived)

I. Explicitly Excluded Torts

Claims arising out of
1. assault
2. battery
3. false imprisonment
4. false arrest
5. malicious prosecution
6. abuse of process
7. libel
8. slander
9. misrepresentation
10. deceit
11. interference with contract rights

A limited exception to this list of exclusions is created for investigative or law enforcement officers. The United States government *will* be liable when such officers commit the torts of assault, battery, false imprisonment, false arrest, abuse of process, or malicious prosecution.

II. Discretion

Claims arising out of the non-negligent or negligent exercise of discretion by an employee at the *planning* level, involving policy decisions and judgment on whether to perform a government task. Also excluded are claims arising out of acts performed with due care in the execution of a statute or regulation, even if invalid.

III. Strict Liability

Claims based on liability without fault, such as acts or omissions involving ultrahazardous activities. To make the federal government liable for such activities, fault (i.e., negligence or intent) must be shown.

IV. Other Exclusions

1. Claims arising out of the following activities: war, mail delivery, admiralty, customs, tax collection. (Government liability for some of these activities may be covered under *other* waiver-of-immunity statutes.)
2. Claims by members of the armed forces in the course of their duties.

I. Covered Torts

1. Trespass to land, trespass to chattels, conversion, invasion of privacy, or other tort, as long as the claim does not also arise out of one of the eleven excluded torts or involve any of the other exclusions mentioned in the "Exclusions" column.
2. Assault, battery, false imprisonment, false arrest, abuse of process, or malicious prosecution committed by investigative or law enforcement officers.

II. Ministerial/Operational Level

Claims (usually negligence) arising out of acts or omissions of an employee at the *ministerial* level, where no discretion is involved, or at the *operational* level, where the discretion involved, if any, relates only to the carrying out of the planning decisions.

sometimes said that it is not a tort for a government to govern! Rarely, for example, will any government waive immunity for tortious injury caused a citizen by a judge, legislator, or high administrative officer. Negligence by a lower-level employee in the judicial, legislative, or executive branches, however, may constitute an act or omission for which the state will waive immunity, e.g., a court clerk negligently loses a pleading that was properly filed. Acts that do not involve much discretion and that

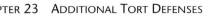

do not involve the formulation of policy will often subject the state to tort liability because the state has waived immunity for such acts.

Keep in mind that we are not talking about individual or personal liability of the government employee at this point. Personal liability will be discussed later. Our focus is on the government's liability via respondeat superior for the torts its employees commit within the scope of their employment.

Local Government

Local government units have a variety of names: cities, municipalities, municipal corporations, counties, towns, villages, etc. Also part of local government are the schools, transportation agencies, hospitals, recreational agencies, and some utilities. Whether any of these local units of government can be sued in tort is again a problem of sovereign immunity. A number of possibilities exist:

- Sovereign immunity has been completely or almost completely waived.
- The sovereign immunity of the units of local government is the same as that enjoyed by the state government.
- The sovereign immunity of the units of local government is different from that of the state government.
- Different units of local government have different sovereign immunity rules.

In short, extensive legal research must be done every time you sue a unit of local government. You must determine its category or status. What is it called? Who created it? Why was it created? What are its powers? Is it really part of the state government? Is it separate from the state government? Is it a hybrid combination of both state and local government? Many cities and counties receive substantial state aid. Does such aid entitle them to the same sovereign immunity protection as the state? You may find that for some purposes, the unit of government is considered part of the state, whereas for other purposes it is considered entirely separate and local. Over the years, a great deal of litigation has dealt with the problem of determining the nature of the unit of government in order to decide what sovereign immunity principles apply.

Units of local government perform many different kinds of functions. These functions are often grouped into two classifications: **governmental** and **proprietary.** The sovereign immunity rules may differ depending on what category of function the employee was carrying out when the tort was committed. The general rule is that sovereign immunity is *not* waived when the tort grows out of a *governmental* function, whereas it *is* waived when it grows out of a *proprietary* function. (An important exception is when the city, county, town, or other unit has created a public or a private nuisance. Even if this nuisance grows out of a governmental function, sovereign immunity will usually not prevent the suit.) Of course, there is always the possibility that a government will waive its sovereign immunity for torts arising out of both governmental and proprietary functions. The waiver, however, is usually limited to proprietary functions.

Unfortunately, there are few clear rules on the distinction between a governmental and a proprietary function.

Governmental Functions   A governmental function is one that can be performed adequately only by the government. The operation of local courts and local legislatures (e.g., a city council) is considered governmental. The same is true of the chief administrative offices of the local government (e.g., office of the mayor, office of the county commissioner) where basic policy is made. Police and fire departments, jails, schools, and sanitation also fall into the category of governmental functions where sovereign immunity will prevent suits for the torts that grow out of these functions.[2]

---

[2]W. Page Keeton et al., *Prosser and Keeton on the Law of Torts* 1053 (5th ed. 1984). See also *Restatement (Second) of Torts* § 895C (1965).

Proprietary Functions   These are functions that generally cannot be performed adequately *only* by the government. Examples include government-run airports, docks, garages, and utilities such as water and gas. For some of these functions, the local government often collects special fees or revenue. The test for a proprietary function, however, is not whether a "profit" is made. This is simply one factor that tends to indicate a proprietary function. Some functions are very difficult to classify, such as the operation of a city hospital. You will find courts going both ways for these and similar functions.

There are courts that do not rely totally on the distinction between governmental and proprietary functions to decide whether sovereign immunity prevents the suit against the local government. Some courts make the same distinction we saw earlier under the Federal Tort Claims Act between a claim arising out of planning decisions made by the government (for which sovereign immunity will not be waived), and claims arising out of the implementation of the planning decisions at the operational or ministerial level (for which sovereign immunity will be waived). For example, a city may be immune from liability for damages resulting from its negligent decision on where to construct sewers, but would be liable for damages resulting from the negligent construction or repair of a particular sewer.

Finally, some governments have purchased liability insurance and have waived sovereign immunity, but only to the extent of this coverage.

OFFICIAL IMMUNITY: THE PERSONAL LIABILITY OF GOVERNMENT EMPLOYEES

What about a suit against the *individual* government employee as opposed to one against the sovereign, or the government itself? If the employee is sued *personally,* any judgment is paid out of the employee's own pocket. Although there are circumstances in which **personal liability** is imposed on government employees, it should be pointed out that the law is reluctant to impose such liability. Public employees must be "free to exercise their duties unembarrassed by the fear of damage suits in respect of acts done in the course of those duties—suits which would consume time and energies which would otherwise be devoted to governmental service and the threat of which might appreciably inhibit the fearless, vigorous, and effective administration of policies of government."[3] On the other hand, critics argue that public employees should not be treated differently from employees in the private sector. When an employee of a business commits a tort, the employer is **vicariously liable** if the tort was committed within the scope of employment, but the employee may also be *personally liable.* The critics say that the same rule should apply to government employees. For the most part, however, it does not.

When government employees are *not* liable, it is because of *official immunity.* This is a defense under which government employees are not personally liable for torts they commit within the scope of their employment. Three questions need to be asked in this area of the law. First, was a tort committed? It may be that the government employee had a privilege to act so that there was no tort. For example, a police officer has the privilege to arrest someone. (See Figure 5–1 in Chapter 5.) The privilege prevents liability for torts such as battery and false imprisonment. If, however, a tort was committed, the second question is whether it was committed within the scope of employment. (See Figure 12–7 in Chapter 12 on the factors that determine scope of employment.) Judges may have official immunity for defamation they commit from the bench against attorneys or defendants, but not for defamation they commit against their neighbor in an argument over a football game. The latter is clearly outside the judge's scope of employment. A government employee is as liable for torts outside the scope of employment as any citi-

---

[3]*Barr v. Matteo,* 360 U.S. 564, 571, 79 S. Ct. 1335, 3 L. Ed. 2d 1434 (1959).

zen would be. If a tort was committed by the government employee and if it was within the scope of employment, we then ask a third question: is the official immune from personal liability under the doctrine of official immunity?

A citizen who has been the victim of a government tort may face one of several scenarios in looking for a defendant to sue:

- Sovereign immunity may prevent a suit against the government, and official immunity may prevent a suit against the employee; the citizen is without remedy.
- Sovereign immunity may have been waived so that the government can be sued, but official immunity may prevent a suit against the employee; the citizen can sue only the government.
- Sovereign immunity may have been waived so that the government can be sued, and official immunity may not apply so that the employee can also be sued; the citizen can sue either or both.

If the citizen can sue both the government and the employee, and successfully does so, the citizen does not receive double damages for the same injury. There is one recovery only. The plaintiff can usually collect from either defendant until there has been a satisfaction of the judgment.

Official immunity must be examined under two main categories: the employee's personal liability for a traditional common law tort (e.g., negligence, battery, defamation), and the employee's personal liability for a civil rights violation. First, let us examine civil rights violations.

Section 1983 of the **Civil Rights Act** of 1871 provides as follows:

"Every person who, under color of any statute, ordinance, regulation, custom, or usage, of any State . . . subjects . . . any citizen . . . to the deprivation of any rights, privileges, or immunities secured by the Constitution and laws, shall be liable to the party injured in an action at law,. . ." 42 U.S.C. § 1983.

Under this statute, a person who acts or pretends to act as a state official in a governmental capacity is said to be acting under **color of law,** or, to be specific, under color of *state* law. If that person deprives someone of a federal civil right, a special cause of action arises.

> **EXAMPLE:**   Fred Jamison is a state police officer. He sees Loretta Walker driving down the street. Jamison decides to give Walker a speeding ticket solely because she is Black. Jamison knows that she was not speeding at the time.

Such racial discrimination is forbidden by the Equal Protection Clause of the United States Constitution. Since Jamison was charging Walker with violating the speeding law (a state law), the police officer was acting under color of law when he deprived Walker of the constitutional right not to be subjected to racial discrimination. Walker can sue Jamison under § 1983 of the Civil Rights Act. A civil rights suit seeking damages under this Act is called a **1983 action,** which asserts a federal cause of action called a **1983 tort.** The phrase **constitutional tort** refers to a special cause of action that arises when someone is deprived of federal civil rights.

Liability for a traditional common law tort such as battery is separate from liability for a constitutional tort. It is possible for a government employee to commit a constitutional tort that is not, in addition, a common law tort. An example is the Jamison/Walker case just discussed. There is no indication that the police officer committed a common law tort when he wrote the ticket, but he did commit a constitutional tort for which he might be liable in a 1983 action. Sometimes, however, the wrong committed by the employee is both a common law tort and a constitutional tort as in the following examples:

- A police officer punches a citizen (battery) to prevent him or her from voting.
- A government tax auditor destroys the flag of a citizen (conversion) in order to stop him or her from participating in a lawful demonstration.

A plaintiff can assert the common law tort and the constitutional tort in the same lawsuit. A major benefit of winning a constitutional tort is that attorney fees can be awarded, whereas for common law torts, the parties pay their own attorneys.

When will a government employee be personally liable for common law torts and for civil rights violations (constitutional torts)? As Figure 23–8 demonstrates, the answer often depends on whether the employee has an **absolute official immunity,** a **qualified official immunity,** or no immunity at all. An immunity is qualified if it can be lost because of malice; it is absolute if malice will not defeat it. Whether the government employee can claim the protection of one of these immunities depends in large measure on the nature of his or her job. The more ministerial or operational the job, the less protection the employee is given. Of course, it is difficult to think of any job that does not involve at least some measure of discretion. The difference between

FIGURE 23–8 Official immunity of government employees for common law torts and for violations of the Civil Rights Act.

The Government Employees	Official Immunity for Common Law Torts	How the Official Immunity for Common Law Torts Can Be Lost	Official Immunity for Violations of the Civil Rights Act (Constitutional Torts)
Judges and legislators	Absolute official immunity for torts committed in the course of their employment even if they acted maliciously.	a. They did not commit the tort while performing their judicial or legislative role. b. They acted totally outside their authority or jurisdiction. **Note:** The immunity is not lost if they acted merely in excess of their authority.	Absolute official immunity for violations of the Act committed under color of law even if they acted maliciously. (The immunity is lost, however, for the same two reasons listed in the third column: *a* and *b*.)
High administrative officials	Same as for judges and legislators.	Same as for judges and legislators. In some states, however, they have a qualified immunity that is defeated by malice.	Qualified official immunity, which is lost if a reasonable official would have believed that the conduct violated a "clearly established" constitutional or statutory right.
Lower administrative officials who exercise considerable discretion in their job	Qualified official immunity for torts committed in the course of their employment.	a. They did not commit the tort in the course of their employment. b. They acted totally outside their authority. c. They acted maliciously or not in good faith.	Qualified official immunity. Same as for high administrative officials.
Lower administrative officials who function at the ministerial level with little or no discretion	No immunity in many states. They are personally liable for their torts, whether or not they acted in good faith or without malice. Statutes may have been passed, however, that provide absolute or qualified immunity for such employees.		Qualified official immunity. Same as for high administrative officials.

Note: As indicated earlier, the words "immunity" and "privilege" are sometimes used interchangeably in this area of the law. Absolute immunity, for example, is often referred to as absolute privilege, and qualified immunity as qualified privilege. In this chapter, we use the word "immunity" as a doctrine that prevents liability for a tort that was committed, and the word "privilege" as a doctrine that prevents the defendant's conduct from being a tort. The practical effect of either word, however, is the same with respect to the ultimate question of whether the government official will be personally liable.

a job that is primarily judgmental and discretionary, on the one hand, and a job that is primarily ministerial or operational, on the other, is often a matter of degree. Some jobs clearly involve a great deal of discretion, e.g., a high administrative officer, judge, or legislator. Jobs such as repairing roads, driving trucks, and collecting taxes also pose little difficulty; they are clearly ministerial jobs. The gray area between these two extremes has produced a good deal of litigation.

Congress and the state legislatures are always free to pass special legislation that changes the basic rules outlined in Figure 23–8, on the official's immunity for common law torts. For example, a statute might be passed to extend the qualified immunity to employees who act at the ministerial or operational level. The Federal Employees Liability Reform and Tort Compensation Act of 1988 is an important federal statute that grants extensive official immunity to federal employees who commit common law torts within the scope of employment.

CHARITABLE IMMUNITY

There was a time when a charitable, educational, religious, or other benevolent organization enjoyed an immunity for the torts it committed in the course of its work. The law was reluctant to allow the resources of such organizations to be depleted in a suit brought against the organization because of a tort committed by one of its employees or volunteers. **Charitable immunity,** however, was never complete. An organization, for example, was liable for its negligence in selecting personnel and in raising money. Most states, however, have abolished the immunity altogether, and other states have severely restricted its applicability.

INTRAFAMILY TORT IMMUNITY

Suppose that one family member wrongfully injures another. Can they sue each other in tort? If they are not allowed to do so, it is because of the **intrafamily tort immunity.** This topic is covered in Figure 18–1 at the end of Chapter 18 on Torts Against and Within the Family.

SUMMARY

A defense is the response of a party to a claim of another party, setting forth the reason(s) the claim should not be granted. The defense of immunity is that there should be no liability for the tort that was committed. The defense of privilege is that there should be no liability since there was no tort committed.

Consent is a defense to most torts. The plaintiff must have the capacity to consent and must voluntarily manifest the consent. The test is the reasonableness of the defendant's belief that the plaintiff consented, not the plaintiff's subjective state of mind. For the consent to be valid, the plaintiff must know the nature and consequences of what the defendant wants to do; gaining consent by misrepresentation renders the consent invalid.

There are several self-help privileges. The defendant can use reasonable force to protect him- or herself in the reasonable belief that the plaintiff will immediately inflict harmful or offensive contact on the defendant (self-defense). The defendant can use reasonable force to prevent the plaintiff from immediately inflicting on a third person harmful or offensive contact which the plaintiff does not have the privilege to inflict (defense of others). If the defendant reasonably believes that persons or property will be immediately injured or damaged, he or she can make reasonable use of the plaintiff's chattels or land to prevent it (necessity). If the defendant possesses land or chattels and this right of possession is superior to the plaintiff's claim of possession, the defendant can use reasonable force to prevent the plaintiff's immediately threatened or continued interference with the defendant's possession (defense of property). If the plaintiff wrongfully acquires possession of a chattel and the defendant has the immediate right to possession, the defendant can use reasonable force to recapture it promptly after the plaintiff takes possession or promptly after discovering that the plaintiff has taken possession. There must be a request that it be returned before force is used, unless this would be unrealistic or unsafe (recapture of chattels).

Under the Federal Tort Claims Act, the federal government has waived sovereign immunity for designated torts. Examples include negligence at the ministerial or operational level, trespass to land or invasion of privacy committed by any federal employee, and battery or false arrest committed by a federal law enforcement officer.

State governments differ on the extent to which sovereign immunity is waived. The state often retains its immunity to cover the conduct of its judges, legislators, and high administrative officers. The less discretion and policy involvement a state employee has, the more likely the state will waive its sovereign immunity for harm caused by that employee. Local governments often waive their sovereign immunity for the proprietary functions they perform, but not for their governmental functions.

Government employees with official immunity cannot be personally liable for the common law or constitutional torts they commit within the scope of their employment. (A constitutional tort is a special cause of action, such as a 1983 action, that arises when someone is deprived of federal civil rights.) Generally, judges, legislators, and high administrative officers have an absolute official immunity; lower officials who exercise considerable discretion in their jobs have a qualified official immunity; lower officials who exercise little or no discretion in their jobs have no official immunity unless changed by statute.

Most states have eliminated the charitable immunity that once relieved charities and similar organizations of liability for their torts.

KEY TERMS

defense   303

privilege   303

immunity   303

volenti non fit injuria   304

consent   304

implied consent   305

coercion   305

informed consent   306

self-help   308

self-defense   308

defense of others   309

necessity   310

chattels   310

private necessity   310

public necessity   310

abate a nuisance   311

defense of property   312

recapture of chattels   314

fresh pursuit   315

shopkeeper privilege   315

in loco parentis   316

arrest   316

sovereign immunity   316

respondeat superior   316

official immunity   316

just compensation   316

taking of property   316

Federal Tort Claims Act   317

governmental   319

proprietary   319

personal liability   320

vicariously liable   320

Civil Rights Act   321

color of law   321

1983 action   321

1983 tort   321

constitutional tort   321

absolute official immunity   322

qualified official immunity   322

charitable immunity   323

intrafamily tort immunity   323

Workers' Compensation

Chapter Outline

- Introduction
- On-the-Job Injuries at Common Law
- Workers' Compensation Statutes
- Injuries and Diseases Covered
- Filing a Claim
- Benefits Available
- Tort Claims Against Third Parties

INTRODUCTION

The estimated cost of on-the-job injuries and illnesses is between $70 billion and $170 billion a year. According to the United States Bureau of Labor Statistics, in 1997:

- 6.1 million injuries and illnesses were reported in private industry workplaces.
- This consisted of 7.1 cases per 100 full-time workers.
- Over 93 percent of the reported cases resulted in lost work time, medical treatment, loss of consciousness, or transfer to another job.[1]

Under the common law, the major remedy of the worker was to sue the employer for negligence. This was not a satisfactory option. Not only was negligence difficult to prove, but also, as we will see, the employer could use some powerful defenses that effectively defeated the vast majority of such negligence suits. After 1910, however, a strict liability system was created under which the cost of worker injuries was spread over an entire industry or enterprise regardless of who was negligent or at fault. This no-fault system of enterprise responsibility was called **workers' compensation.**[2] Before examining its scope, we need to take a closer look at the common law fault system that workers' compensation was designed to replace for most workers.

---

[1] *Workplace in Brief,* San Francisco Chronicle, December 18, 1998, at B3; *Report: Job-Related Injury, Illness Costly,* San Diego Union-Tribune, July 28, 1997, at A6.

[2] For legal materials on workers' compensation on the Internet, see http://www.law.cornell.edu/topics/workers_compensation.html. See also Tort Law Online at the end of Chapter 1.

ON-THE-JOB INJURIES AT COMMON LAW

When an employee was injured on the job, his or her traditional remedy was a negligence suit, brought on the theory that the employer unreasonably failed to provide a safe work environment. This was, of course, a common law tort remedy (on negligence, see Chapters 10 to 15). For years, there was widespread criticism of this remedy, primarily because it was difficult for an employee to win a negligence case.

The difficulty was due to the employer's ability to establish one or more of the following three defenses:

Contributory negligence: The employee acted unreasonably, which contributed to his or her own injury, along with the negligence of the employer. The contributory negligence of the employee prevented recovery against the employer (unless the latter's negligence was willful or wanton, or unless the employer failed to take the last clear chance (see Chapter 15) to avoid the injury).

Assumption of the risk: The employee knew about the hazards of the job and voluntarily took the job or voluntarily remained on the job, even though the employee understood the dangers involved. Assumption of the risk defeated the employee's recovery for the employer's negligence.

Fellow-employee rule: The employer was not liable for the injuries received by an employee if the injury was caused by the negligence of a fellow employee. An exception existed when the fellow employee was a **vice principal,** i.e., an employee with supervisory authority over other employees or an employee of any rank who has been given some responsibility for the safety of the work environment; the employer *will* be liable if the employee is injured because of the negligence of a fellow employee who is a vice principal.

WORKERS' COMPENSATION STATUTES

Throughout the country, workers' compensation statutes have been passed by the legislatures as an alternative to the common law negligence system. Under these statutes, an employee will receive compensation for an industrial accident without having to prove that the employer was negligent. Hence, the liability of the employer under such a statute is a form of **strict liability.** This means there is no need to prove that the employer caused the injury negligently. It is a **no-fault system.** The defenses of contributory negligence, assumption of the risk, and the fellow-servant rule are abolished. See Figure 24–1 for an overview of the advantages and disadvantages of workers' compensation.

Not all employers and employees are covered under workers' compensation. When employees are not covered, they are left with a traditional negligence action in which they must face the "unholy trinity" of defenses: contributory negligence,[3] assumption of risk, and the fellow-servant rule.

The primary way in which the workers' compensation system is financed is through insurance. An employer must either purchase insurance or prove that it is financially able to cover any risks on its own. The latter is called **self-insurance.** When insurance is purchased, it comes either from a state-operated insurance fund or from a private insurer or carrier.

Every state has an agency or commission that administers the workers' compensation law for employees in the private sector. It may be an independent entity or be part of the state's department of labor. Government employees have a separate workers' compensation system to cover their employment. Workers' compensation for non-military employees of the federal government, for example, is administered by the Office of Workers' Compensation Programs within the United States Department of Labor.[4] In this chapter, our focus is workers' compensation for employees in the private sector.

---

[3] Or comparative negligence if the state has abolished contributory negligence. See Chapter 15.
[4] See Federal Employees' Compensation Act, 5 U.S.C. §§ 8101 et seq.

ADVANTAGES	
To Employee	**To Employer**
• In a WC case, there is no need to prove the employer was negligent. • Contributory negligence, assumption of risk, and fellow-servant rule cannot defeat a WC case—they are not defenses in a WC case. • The WC administrative procedure is quicker and less costly than a suit for negligence in court. • Recovery of benefits in a WC case is usually quicker than filing an action for negligence in court.	• Limited liability: the cash benefits awarded an employee under WC are limited to set amounts specified by statute, whereas a negligence judgment in court against the employer could be much higher. • The WC administrative procedure is quicker and less costly than a negligence suit in court.
DISADVANTAGES	
To Employee	**To Employer**
• Recovery of cash benefits in a WC case is usually smaller than damages awarded in a successful negligence case in court.	• Critics charge that the WC system is riddled with fraud. The temptation to fabricate a WC claim is large. Consequently, WC insurance premiums paid by employers are very high.

FIGURE 24–1 Benefits/disadvantages of workers' compensation (WC).

The statutory code of your state will list the categories of employers and employees covered by workers' compensation in the private sector. It is important to note the definitions of employer, employee, employment, and any other word that will tell you who is and who is not covered. Some codes may say that everyone is covered except those specifically excluded, such as domestic workers, farm workers, casual workers, independent contractors, or people who work for employers with fewer than a certain number of employees.

INJURIES AND DISEASES COVERED

Not every on-the-job misfortune is covered under workers' compensation. A few states, for example, do not cover certain diseases that occur as a result of long-term exposure to conditions or hazards at a job. In most states, however, diseases as well as accidents are covered.

The basic requirement is that the employee's injury must **arise out of** and occur **in the course of** employment. "Arising out of" refers to the causal connection between the injury and the employment; "in the course of" refers to the time, place, and circumstances of the injury in connection with the employment. We will explore both issues through the following themes:

In the Course of Employment
1. while clearly at work
2. while going to or coming from work
3. during trips
4. during horseplay and misconduct
5. while engaged in personal comfort

Arising Out of Employment
1. causal connection tests
2. acts of nature
3. street risks
4. assault and battery
5. personal risks

In the Course of Employment

1. While Clearly at Work The vast majority of injuries pose little or no difficulty, e.g., a hand is injured while operating a printing press, or death results from an explosion while the worker is in a mine. Liability under the workers' compensation statute is clear for most cases of this kind.

2. While Going to and Coming from Work A **going-and-coming rule** exists in most states: workers' compensation is denied if the employee is injured "off the premises" while going to or coming back from work or while going to or coming back from lunch. The company parking lot is usually considered part of the employer's premises, so that there *is* coverage if the employee is injured while on the lot. A number of exceptions have been created to the going-and-coming rule. For example, if the route to work exposes the worker to special dangers or risks (e.g., passing through a "rough" neighborhood to get to the plant), the injury will be considered within the "course of employment" even though it technically occurred beyond the premises owned or leased by the employer. Such risks are said to be **incident to the job.** The court will conclude that there is a close association between the access route and the premises of the employer.[5] Some courts also make an exception if the injury occurs when the employee is on a public sidewalk or street that is close to the premises of the employer.

3. During Trips Of course, any trip made by the employee that is part of a job responsibility is within the course of employment, and an injury that occurs on such a trip will be covered by workers' compensation, e.g., injury while making a sales trip or a delivery. Even if the employee is going to or from work, the trip will be considered part of the employment if the trip is a special assignment from or service to the employer, e.g., an employee is injured when asked to return to the shop after work hours to check on an alarm or to let someone in. It is not always necessary to show that the employee is paid extra compensation for such a trip, but when such compensation is paid, the argument is strengthened that the trip is within the course of employment.

Suppose, however, that the trip serves a *personal* purpose of the employee as well as a business purpose of the employer. This is a **mixed-purpose trip**, also called a **dual-purpose trip.**

> **EXAMPLE:** Helen is asked to deliver a package to a certain city. She rents a car for the purpose at company expense. She takes along two of her friends so that the three of them can attend a party after Helen makes the delivery. While on her way to the city, Helen is injured in a traffic accident.

Helen had a business purpose for the trip (make the delivery) and a personal purpose (go to a party with her friends). The criteria a court will use to determine whether the trip is business (and hence covered by workers' compensation) or personal (and not covered) are as follows:

- The trip is considered a business trip if it would have been made even if the personal objective did not exist.
- The trip is considered a personal trip if it would have been made even if the business objective did not exist.

Therefore, the characterization of the trip depends on what would have happened if one of the purposes failed or did not materialize. The business nature of the trip is established once it can be said that the trip must be made at some time by someone, whether or not the person making the trip will also attend to some personal matters.

Suppose that an employee is on a purely business trip. While on the trip, however, the employee decides to take a detour for personal reasons, e.g., to visit a rela-

---

[5]Arthur Larson, *Workmen's Compensation Law* § 15.13, p. 4–22 (1978).

tive or to inquire into another job. The general rule is that the employee is not covered by workers' compensation if injured while on a personal detour. Once the personal detour has been completed and the employee is once more attending to the business purpose of the trip, coverage under the compensation statute resumes.

4. During Horseplay and Misconduct

It is not uncommon for workers on the job to be playful with each other or to engage in horseplay. What happens if an employee is injured during such horseplay? If the employee is the innocent victim of the horseplay, he or she will be covered by workers' compensation, e.g., the employee is hit on the head by a hard aluminum-foil ball that other employees were using to "play catch," in which the injured employee was not participating.

Suppose, however, that one of the employees participating in or instigating the horseplay is injured. Such injuries are often not covered by workers' compensation unless it can be shown that the horseplay was a very minor departure from normal work responsibilities, or that the horseplay had been occurring over a long period of time and had, in effect, become customary.

The employee's injury may be caused by his or her own misconduct on the job. Recall what was said earlier about the defense of contributory negligence: the employee's own negligence is not a defense to recovery under workers' compensation. Some workers' compensation statutes, however, provide that if the employee is injured while engaged in **willful** misconduct, such as the willful failure to use a safety device, workers' compensation benefits *will* be denied or reduced.

It is important to distinguish between the following:

- what the employee has been asked to do—the **objective** of the job, and
- the **method** that the employee uses to carry out the objective

The general rule is that employee misconduct related to the objective of a job leads to no coverage under workers' compensation, but misconduct related to method is still covered.

> **Objective:** A bus ticket clerk violates specific instructions never to drive a bus, and is injured. The injury is not covered under workers' compensation.

> **Method:** A bus driver is injured because of careless operation of the bus. The injury is covered by workers' compensation.

Other examples of injuries that grow out of the method of doing the job and hence are covered under workers' compensation include reaching into a machine before stopping it, climbing over a fence rather than walking around it, repairing a machine while it is still operating, and using a machine with its safety guard removed.[6] Even if these methods of doing the job were specifically prohibited by the employer, workers' compensation will still be allowed unless the statute has an exception for certain willful violations, as already mentioned.

5. While Engaged in Personal Comfort

Simply because an employee is injured while taking care of a personal need on the job does not mean that coverage is denied under workers' compensation. Here is how one court described this aspect of the law:

> For the purposes of the [workers'] compensation act the concept of course of employment is more comprehensive than the assigned work at the lathe. It includes an employee's ministrations to his own human needs: he must eat; concessions to his own human frailties: he must rest, must now and then have a break, and he sometimes, even on the job, plays practical jokes on his fellows. Course of employment is not scope of employment. The former, as the cases so clearly reveal, is a way of life in a working environment. If the injury results from the work itself, or from the stresses, the tensions, the associations of the working environments, human as well

---

[6]Arthur Larson, *Workmen's Compensation Law* § 31.22, p. 6–20 (1978).

as material, it is compensable [under workers' compensation]. Why? because those are the ingredients of the product itself. It carries to the market with it, on its price tag stained and scarred, its human as well as its material costs.[7]

When an injury occurs while a worker is taking a lunch break, going to the restroom, or stepping out for a moment of fresh air, workers' compensation usually applies. Factors that will be considered in reaching this result include whether the accident occurred on the premises and within an authorized area for the activity, whether it occurred within working hours, whether the hazard that led to the accident is considered normal for that work environment, and whether the employer prohibited the activity that led to the accident.

Suppose that the employee is injured while engaged in a sports contest at a picnic or other social event involving coworkers. Workers' compensation is applicable if the activity is sponsored by the employer or if the workers are otherwise encouraged to participate by the employer. The more benefit the employer is likely to derive from the activity, the more inclined an agency or a court will be to conclude that the activity was within the course of employment and hence covered by workers' compensation.

ASSIGNMENT
24.1

Examine the following situations to determine whether the injury was within the "course of employment."

a. An employee is killed while crossing a public street immediately in front of her office. She is on her way home when hit by the car of another employee on the way to work.

b. The street in front of the company building is over 50 feet wide and is heavily traveled. An employee, walking to a restaurant during a lunch break, is hit by a car on this street. Another route to the restaurant is available through the rear of the company building. If the employee had used this other route, the trip would have taken an extra twelve minutes.

c. An employee is injured in a public parking lot 800 feet from his place of work. The company parking lot has spaces for only 200 of its 500 employees. The public parking lot is the closest alternative parking lot available.

d. During the work day, the employee is given an old company radio and allowed to take it home on company time. While putting the radio in her car in the company parking lot, she drops the radio and injures her foot.

e. An employee is a company salesperson who travels extensively throughout the city. At 6:00 P.M., the employee makes the last call and is on the way home. The employee is killed in an automobile collision one mile from home.

f. A teacher attends an evening PTA meeting and is on the way home. The teacher stops for a few minutes at a tavern and has half a glass of beer. After leaving the tavern, the teacher is injured in an automobile collision one mile from home.

g. An employee is a lawyer who works for a title insurance company. She usually takes a bus to work. On Tuesday, her employer asks her to come to work as soon as possible. The lawyer takes her car and has a collision on the way to work.

h. A real estate appraiser leaves home to inspect property listed by his employer. On the way, he stops at a jewelry store to buy a present for his wife. He slips in the store and injures his back.

---

[7]*Crilly v. Ballou*, 353 Mich. 303, 326, 91 N.W.2d 493, 505 (1958). See also Malone, Plant, & Little, *Workers' Compensation and Employment Rights* 126 (2d. ed. 1980).

i. An employee is a salesperson. While on a sales trip, she stops at a store to buy some groceries for that evening. The stop takes her ten miles out of the way. While in the store buying her groceries, she meets a prospective customer. After a brief discussion about a possible sale, she injures herself in a fall just outside the store.

j. An employee injures his back while putting out a cigarette in the lunchroom during his lunch break. The employee was leaning down to extinguish the cigarette in a bucket that had sand in it.

k. An employee has a heart attack while dancing at a Christmas party in the company hall.

l. An employee is injured while playing handball in the rear of the plant during a break. Employees have been playing handball there for months in spite of a company sign forbidding play in that area.

m. The elevator door in a company building is broken. All employees are forbidden to use it until it is repaired. Two employees use this elevator and are both injured during a friendly wrestling match while the elevator is in motion.

Arising Out of Employment

1. Causal Connection Tests   "Arising out of employment" refers to the workers' compensation requirement that the injury must be caused by the employment. Various tests have been used by the courts to determine whether the requisite causal connection exists between the conditions under which the employee works and the injury sustained.[8]

Peculiar-risk test: The source of the harm is peculiar to the employment. The danger must be incidental to the character of the business and dependent on the existence of an employer-employee relationship. The risk must not be one that the employee shares with every citizen, e.g., injury due to cold weather. The risk must differ in quality.

Increased-risk test: The risk of injury to the employee is quantitatively greater than the risk of injury to nonemployees. The employment must increase the risk of an injury, even if others are also exposed to the risk of the injury.

Positional-risk test: The injury of the employee would not have occurred but for the fact that the job placed the employee in a position where the employee could be injured.

Proximate-cause test: The injury is foreseeable, and no intervening factor breaks the chain of causation between the conditions of employment and the injury.

Actual-risk test: The injury is a risk of this particular employment. Whether or not the employment increases the risk, there is causation if the injury comes from a risk that is actually present in this employment.

Most states use the increased-risk test to determine whether the injury arises out of the employment. You must be aware of the other tests, however, because they are used by some states as sole tests, and they are sometimes used along with the increased-risk test.

2. Acts of Nature   There is usually no problem showing that an injury arose out of (was caused by) the employment when it was due to an **act of God** such as a storm or freezing weather that occurred during work. The increased-risk test is most often applied to reach this result. An injury received by an employee by lightning, for

---

[8]Arthur Larson, *Workmen's Compensation Law* § 6, p. 3–1 (1978).

example, arises out of the employment if the job places the employee on an elevation, near metal, or in any place where there is an increased risk of this injury's occurring.

Suppose, however, that the act of nature delivers the same harm to everyone, e.g., a tornado levels an entire town. In such a case, it cannot be said that the employee was subjected to any increased risk by being on the job as opposed to being at home. Workers' compensation will be denied, because the injury did not arise out of the employment. Many courts make an exception to this rule if there is contact with the premises: if the act of God produces a force that makes actual contact with the employment premises, e.g., the hurricane blows down a company pole that hits the employee.

Exposure to the elements may bring on diseases such as Rocky Mountain spotted fever, which many people in an area may contract. If the employment increases the employee's chances of getting the disease, causation is established.

3. Street Risks Traveling salespersons and employees making deliveries or soliciting sales are sometimes injured by falls or traffic accidents. Even though everyone is exposed to the risk of such injuries, most states will say that if the job increases the risk of their occurring, compensation will be allowed. Other courts will go even further and say that workers' compensation will be awarded simply by the plaintiff's showing that the job requires that public streets be used.

4. Assault and Battery What happens if the employee is injured because of an assault or a battery? If the employee is the aggressor and the quarrel is personal, having nothing to do with the job, the injury does not arise out of the employment and workers' compensation is denied. It does not take much, however, for the assault or battery to be connected with the employment. The following are examples of injuries due to assault or battery that are sufficiently connected with the employment so that it can be said that the injury arises out of the employment:

- A police officer is hit by someone under arrest.
- A cashier is killed in a robbery attempt.
- A lawyer is raped in an office located in a dangerous area.
- A supervisor is struck by a subordinate being disciplined.
- A worker is struck by a coworker in an argument over who is supposed to perform a certain task.
- A union member and a nonunion member have a fight over whether the latter should join the union.

Fights on the job pose some difficulty. It is not always easy to determine whether a fight is due solely to personal animosity or vengeance (not compensable under workers' compensation) or whether the fight has its origin in the employment, so that it can be said that the employment is a contributing factor to the fight (compensable under workers' compensation). In most states, the fact that the injured employee is the aggressor in the fight does not mean that compensation will be denied to him or her, as long as the employment itself contributed to the fight.

5. Personal Risks Some employees are more susceptible to injury or disease than others, e.g., someone with a heart condition or epilepsy. An on-the-job injury or disease suffered by such an employee will be said to arise out of the employment only if it can be shown that the employment increased the risk of the injury or disease occurring, or if the employment **aggravated** the extent of the harm resulting from the injury or disease. Workers' compensation, of course, cannot be awarded for any **pre-existing injuries or diseases** that the employee brings to the job, because the job did not cause them. Such injuries or diseases are personal to the employee, unrelated to the occupation. Workers' compensation will be granted, however, when the job contributes to the risk or aggravates the resulting injury or disease. For example, if an employee falls on a machine after blacking out due to a pre-existing condition, the dangerous consequences of a blackout have been increased by the employer because the employee was stationed next to such a machine. Since the employer increased the risk of serious injury, workers' compensation will be awarded. Most courts, however, would reach a different result if the injury resulted from a fall onto the floor (without hitting any objects) while the employee was standing on a level surface. The injury following the blackout was not increased by the employment; it is the same injury that would have occurred if the employee had blacked out at home.

An employer cannot insist that all employees be fully healthy or normal at the time of employment. The employer takes employees as he or she finds them. If the employment produces stress, exertion, or strain that activates or aggravates a preexisting condition, the resulting injury or disease is said to arise out of the employment. Workers' compensation will be awarded.

ASSIGNMENT

24.2

Examine the following situations to determine whether the injury "arises out of the employment."

a. A caddie is struck by lightning while under a tree on a golf course during a sudden storm.

b. An employee is a door-to-door salesperson. While at a home trying to make a sale, he asks the prospective customer if she would go out with him to a dance that evening. She breaks his arm.

c. Two employees have an intense argument on the job over which employee is entitled to go to lunch first. Thirty minutes after the argument, one of the employees walks up behind the other and hits him over the head.

d. An employee has a weak leg due to an injury sustained before she began her present employment. As part of her job, she is required to use a ladder to store supplies on shelves. While on the second rung of the ladder, she falls due to the weak condition of her bad leg.

FILING A CLAIM

States differ on the steps involved in making a workers' compensation claim. The basic procedure is often as follows:

1. The worker reports the injury or disease to the supervisor and/or to the insurance carrier.
2. The worker receives medical attention.
3. The doctor, worker, and employer fill out forms provided by the workers' compensation agency and/or insurance carrier.
4. The worker receives disability benefits after a waiting period following the injury, e.g., seven days.

Each state has a statute of limitations within which the worker must make a claim, e.g., two years from the date of the injury or accident.

Most claims for workers' compensation are uncontested. No questions of liability for compensation arise. The employer or insurance carrier and the employee sign an agreement on the benefits to be received consistent with any state laws on the extent of such benefits. The state workers' compensation agency will usually approve such agreements as a matter of course. Some states do not use this agreement system. In such states, the employer or insurance carrier simply begins to make direct payments to the employee or to the dependents of the employee.

If there is a dispute, it will be resolved by the agency responsible for the workers' compensation program, often a board or commission. The procedure is frequently as follows:

- A hearing is held before a hearing officer, arbitrator, or referee of the agency. The proceeding is usually informal, unlike a court trial. Paralegals are often allowed to represent claimants at these hearings.
- A decision is made by the hearing officer, arbitrator, or referee. A party disagreeing with the decision can appeal it to the agency's commission or board.
- The commission or board makes the final decision of the agency. This decision can then be appealed to a court.

BENEFITS AVAILABLE

Most statutes are very specific on the number of weeks of disability benefits that are available to an employee who establishes a workers' compensation claim. For an example, see Figure 24–2.

The weekly disability benefit is usually based on a percentage of the employee's weekly pay over a designated period of time. The percentage is often 66⅔ percent. This benefit is in addition to the cost of medical services. Different benefit periods, percentages, and amounts are provided depending on which of the following the employee has suffered:

- permanent total disability
- temporary total disability
- permanent partial disability
- temporary partial disability
- disfigurement
- death

TORT CLAIMS AGAINST THIRD PARTIES

As we have seen, a covered injured worker cannot sue his or her employer for negligence when the benefits of workers' compensation are available. Tort litigation between employer and employee is barred in such cases. This does not mean, however,

FIGURE 24–2 Example of a schedule of weeks of benefits.

Injury	Weeks of Compensation Benefits
Loss of thumb	60
Loss of hand	190
Loss of arm	250
Loss of foot	150
Loss of leg	220
Loss of eye	140
Loss of hearing in both ears	175
Permanent disfigurement, face or head	150

Note: The schedule of weeks is based on a 100 percent loss of the body member indicated. If the disability rating is less than 100 percent, the percentage rated should be multiplied by the number of weeks shown. For example, a 20 percent loss of function of a thumb would be computed as 20 percent of sixty weeks, or twelve weeks of compensation benefits.

that all tort cases are eliminated. It still may be possible to bring a tort action against a third party involved in the worker's injury. For example:

- A worker is injured on defective machinery. Although a suit against the employer is not possible, a products liability suit (see Chapter 16) against the machinery's manufacturer is possible.
- An injured worker files a workers' compensation claim. The workers' compensation insurance carrier fails to process the worker's claim in a reasonable and timely manner. A bad faith action (see Chapter 22) against the carrier is possible.

Attorney fees in workers' compensation are often not large enough to entice attorneys to take workers' compensation cases. Yet, an attorney may become very interested in handling a workers' compensation case if the attorney sees the possibility of suing a deep pocket third party in a related tort case that is not barred by the workers' compensation statute.

SUMMARY

Traditional negligence actions brought by employees injured on the job were often won by employers who used the defenses of contributory negligence, assumption of the risk, or the fellow-employee rule. An alternative remedy is workers' compensation, which is a form of strict liability, because recovery is not dependent on establishing the negligence of the employer. To be covered, the injury or disease must arise out of and occur in the course of employment.

Generally, injuries off the premises while going to or coming back from work or lunch are not within the course of employment and hence are not covered. Injuries that occur while on a mixed-purpose trip are covered if the trip is primarily business, because the trip would have been made even if the employee did not also have a personal purpose in making the trip. But an injury that occurs during a personal detour while on a business trip is not covered.

An employee who is the innocent victim of horseplay is covered, but not the employee who participated in or instigated the horseplay, unless the horseplay was a very minor departure from normal work responsibility or had become customary. The employee's own misconduct is usually not a bar to recovery unless it amounted to a willful failure to use a safety device. An injury that results from misconduct in the method of doing a job is covered, whereas one that results from misconduct in what the employee has been asked to do, or the objective of the job, is not. Whether there is coverage for an injury that occurs while an employee is engaged in personal comfort on the job, e.g., during a break, depends on factors such as whether the injury occurred on the premises, within an authorized area for the activity, and within working hours.

Courts use different tests to determine whether the injury arose out of, and hence was caused by, the employment. The most common is the increased-risk test, whereby the risk of injury to the employee is quantitatively greater than the risk of that injury to nonemployees. An injury that results from an act of nature is covered if the job increased the risk of that injury occurring. The same is true of injuries incurred from street risks. An employee who is injured from an assault and battery or a fight is covered if the event was connected with the employment. Workers' compensation does not cover pre-existing injury or disease, but does cover their aggravation due to the job.

Claims are made to the employer, to the insurance carrier, or both. If the claim is disputed, the workers' compensation agency will attempt to resolve it. If this is unsuccessful, the claim can be appealed in court.

When workers' compensation applies, tort actions between employer and employee are barred. There may, however, be tort actions that can still be brought against third parties such as a products liability suit against the manufacturer of a machine that caused the worker's on-the-job injury.

KEY TERMS

workers' compensation   325

contributory negligence   326

assumption of the risk   326

fellow-employee rule   326

vice principal   326

strict liability   326

no-fault system   326

self-insurance   326

arise out of   327

in the course of   327

going-and-coming rule   328

incident to the job   328

mixed-purpose trip   328

dual-purpose trip   328

willful   329

objective   329

method   329

peculiar-risk test   331

increased-risk test   331

positional-risk test   331

proximate-cause test   331

actual-risk test   331

act of God   331

aggravated   332

pre-existing injuries or
   diseases   332

Automobile Insurance

*L*iability insurance protects others who are injured by your vehicle.[1] Every state requires motorists to demonstrate "financial responsibility" by carrying a minimum level of liability insurance or proving an ability to pay a tort judgment at this level without insurance. For example, the minimum level might be $25,000/$50,000/$10,000. (This means that for a single bodily injury in one accident, the coverage is $25,000; for multiple bodily injuries in one accident, the coverage is $50,000; and for property damage in one accident, the coverage is $10,000.) Motorists must apply for liability insurance on their own. The cost depends on factors such as the applicant's driving record, where the applicant lives, the sex and age of the applicant, and anticipated use of the vehicle. If no company agrees on its own to sell liability insurance to a particular motorist in the voluntary market (e.g., because of the applicant's bad driving record), he or she becomes an *assigned risk* in the involuntary market. Insurance companies are required to write liability insurance for assigned risks (at higher rates) in proportion to the amount of business they do in the state.

Under our tort system, an injured party sues a defendant in court in order to prove that the defendant was at fault in causing the accident. Most liability insurance, on the other hand, is based on a *no-fault* system. Under no-fault, each person's own insurance company pays for covered injury or damage up to policy limits, regardless of who was at fault in causing the accident.[2]

Liability insurance has not replaced the tort system. No state has a no-fault scheme that eliminates the option of bringing a tort suit in court for all automobile injury cases. Some states have what is called *add-on no-fault*. Here, liability insurance is simply added onto, but does not replace, the tort system. The injured party can recover under his or her liability insurance policy and can bring a tort suit in court against the person who caused the accident. If, however, the plaintiff wins anything in court, his or her insurance company is reimbursed for whatever benefits it paid the plaintiff. Other states have a *modified no-fault*. There are several versions of modified no-fault among the states. In general, the right of a victim to collect certain kinds of

---

[1]*Collision insurance* covers damage to your vehicle from a collision with an object. *Comprehensive insurance* covers a variety of other risks to your vehicle such as theft, vandalism, and fire. *Medical-payments insurance* covers medical costs for each person injured in your vehicle. *Uninsured/underinsured motorist insurance* protects you and the occupants of your car for bodily injury and property damage caused by someone who is uninsured or underinsured. These forms of insurances (unlike liability insurance) can be subject to deductibles.

[2]Liability insurance is *third-party insurance* in the sense that the insurance company pays a third party—someone other than the insured—who has been wrongfully injured by the insured. Fire insurance and collision insurance are examples of *first-party insurance* because the insurance company pays the insured for a covered loss; third parties are not directly involved.

tort damages in court depends on whether a threshold has been met. There are two kinds of thresholds: a *dollar threshold* covering medical costs and a *verbal threshold* covering the kind of injury involved such as death, serious disfigurement, or dismemberment. Meeting a threshold means that the medical expenses of the victim exceed a designated amount (in a dollar threshold state) or that the victim's injury was of a designated severity (in a verbal threshold state). If the threshold has been met, the injured party can sue the other party in court for a tort. If, however, the threshold has not been met, the courts cannot be used; the parties are limited to the insurance coverage.

A

abate a nuisance. To use the privilege of taking reasonable steps to correct a nuisance that is interfering with the use and enjoyment of your land.

abduction or enticement of a child. A tort involving serious interference with a parent's custody over his or her child.

abnormally dangerous conditions or activities. Unusual or non-natural conditions or activities that create a substantial likelihood of causing great harm that cannot be eliminated by the use of reasonable care.

absolute liability. *See* strict liability.

absolute official immunity. A defense to tort liability available to high government officials; the immunity cannot be lost even if the official acts with malice.

absolute privilege. *See* privilege.

abuse of process. The proper initiation of legal proceedings for an improper purpose.

act. A voluntary movement of the body.

actionable. Furnishing a legal basis for a cause of action.

act of God. A natural occurrence that is independent of human interference; a force of nature.

actual malice. *See* constitutional malice.

actual-risk test. The injury is a risk of this particular employment (a causal connection test for workers' compensation).

adequate remedy at law. Money damages will be sufficient to make the plaintiff whole. There is no need for an equitable remedy such as an injunction.

adhesion contract. A standardized contract for goods or services offered on a take-it-or-leave-it basis without any realistic opportunity for bargaining.

adjudication. The process by which a court or administrative agency resolves a legal dispute through litigation.

admissible. Allowed by a trial judge to be considered by a jury.

adverse possession. A method of acquiring title to land without buying it or receiving it as a gift through a will or other traditional means: a trespasser obtains title to the land by occupying it in a hostile and visible manner for a designated number of continuous years.

adverse possessor. Someone who obtained title to land by adverse possession.

affirmative conduct. Activity, action, or conduct; the opposite of inaction or nonfeasance.

affirmative defense. A plaintiff's response to a claim of the defendant, setting forth new factual allegations by the defendant that were not contained in the complaint of the plaintiff.

agent. Someone who agrees to do something on behalf of another.

aggravated. Made worse.

aggravation. An increase in the severity of the original injury, usually because of a failure to take reasonable steps to prevent the increase.

alienation of affections. The tort of causing a person to become alienated from his or her spouse.

alternative dispute resolution (ADR). A formal method of resolving a legal dispute without litigation in administrative agencies or courts.

American rule. Each party pays its own attorney fees and other legal expenses. There are exceptions to this such as when a judge has special statutory authority to award attorney fees to the winning party. *See also* English rule.

Andrews test. A duty is owed to anyone in the world at large if the plaintiff was injured as a result of unreasonable conduct toward anyone, whether or not the plaintiff who sues was in the zone of danger (from the *Palsgraff* case).

annotation. The notes and commentary on issues in selected opinions. The annotations and opinions are published in *A.L.R., A.L.R.2d, A.L.R.3d, A.L.R.4th, A.L.R.5th,* and *A.L.R. Fed.*

apparent present ability. Appearing reasonably able to do something now or very shortly.

application. An explanation of the extent to which a rule governs (applies to) the facts. Connecting facts to the elements of a rule in order to determine whether the rule applies to the facts.

apprehension. An understanding, awareness, anticipation, belief, or knowledge of something.

appropriation. The unauthorized use of a person's name, likeness, or personality for the benefit of someone other than that person.

arbitration. A method of alternative dispute resolution in which the parties submit their dispute to a neutral third person who renders a decision that resolves the dispute. *See also* alternative dispute resolution.

arise out of. A causal connection between an injury or disease and the employment. *See also* workers' compensation.

arrest. Take another into custody or bring before the proper authorities.

assault. An act that intentionally causes an apprehension of a harmful or offensive contact.

assignment. The transfer of rights.

assumption of risk. The knowing and voluntary acceptance of the risk of being injured by someone's negligence. There are different categories of assumption of risk: *express assumption of risk:* the plaintiff knowingly and voluntarily accepts a risk by express agreement; *implied assumption of risk:* the plaintiff

---

Note: See also William Statsky, *Legal Thesaurus/Dictionary* (West 1985); "Glossary of Insurance Terms," *No Fault Press Release Manual* (State Farm Insurance Companies, 1977–   ).

knowingly and voluntarily accepts a risk by reason of his or her knowledge and conduct; *primary assumption of risk:* the plaintiff knowingly and voluntarily accepts a particular risk that the defendant did not have a duty to protect the plaintiff against; and *secondary assumption of risk:* the plaintiff knowingly and voluntarily accepts a particular risk that the defendant had a duty to protect the plaintiff against.

attractive nuisance doctrine. A duty of reasonable care is owed to a trespassing child unable to appreciate the danger from an artificial condition or activity on land to which the child can be expected to be drawn or attracted.

at will employment. *See* employment at will.

authority. Any written material a court could rely on to reach its decision. *Primary* authority is any law and *secondary* authority is any nonlaw that a court could rely on to reach its decision. *See also* legal authority.

avoidable consequences. Harm or injury that could have been avoided by taking reasonable steps. *See also* aggravation.

B

bad faith. (1) The opposite of good faith and fair dealing. (2) The absence of a reasonable basis for denying or delaying the payment of an insurance policy claim. A frivolous or unfounded refusal to pay the proceeds of a policy.

bad faith liability. Wrongfully acting on an insurance claim. *See also* bad faith.

bailee. *See* bailment.

bailment. The delivery of personal property to someone under an express or implied agreement to accept and later redeliver the property. The *bailor* delivers the property; the *bailee* receives it.

bailor. *See* bailment.

battery. A harmful or offensive contact with a person resulting from the defendant's intent to cause this contact or to cause an imminent apprehension of this contact.

benefit of the bargain. A measure of damages that gives the plaintiff the benefit of what he or she was promised.

bona fide purchaser. One who purchases property for value without notice of defects in the title of the seller.

breach of duty. Unreasonable conduct endangering someone to whom you owe a duty of care. The *breach-of-duty equation* is as follows: the foreseeability of an accident causing injury outweighed the burden or inconvenience on the defendant to take precautions against the injury, and the defendant failed to take those precautions.

breach of the peace. An offense committed by violence or by acts likely to cause immediate disturbance of the public order.

breach of warranty. *See* the entries under *warranty.*

business guest. Someone who has been expressly or impliedly invited to be present, primarily for a business purpose.

but-for test. One of the tests to determine causation: Without (i.e., "but for") the act or omissions, the event in question would not have occurred. Also referred to as the *sine qua non test.*

bystander. One who stands near; one present but not taking part; one injured by a product but who was not a seller, buyer, user, or consumer of the product.

C

CALR. computer-assisted legal research.

caps. Limitations; ceilings. *See also* damage caps; fee caps.

Cardozo test. A duty is owed a specific person who is in the zone of danger as determined by the test of foreseeability (from the *Palsgraff* case).

case. (1) A court opinion. *See also* opinion. (2) A client matter.

causation. Bringing something about. *See also* causation in fact; but-for test; proximate cause; substantial factor test.

causation in fact. "But for" the act or omission, the event in question would not have occurred. The act or omission was a substantial factor in bringing about the event in question.

cause. (1) Justifiable reason. (2) Bring something about; causation.

cause in fact. *See* causation in fact.

cause of action. A legally acceptable reason for bringing a suit. When you *state a cause of action,* you list the facts that give you a right to judicial relief against the wrongdoer. When you *state a tort cause of action,* you list the facts that give you a right to judicial relief against the tortfeasor.

caveat emptor. Buyer beware. Protect yourself. If you make a mistake, the courts will not be sympathetic.

chain of distribution. All persons or businesses who had a role in making or selling a product that reached the person injured by that product.

charitable immunity. A tort victim's loss of the right to bring a tort suit against the charitable organization that committed the tort.

chattel. Personal property; property other than land or things attached to land.

child. (1) Someone too young to appreciate the dangers that could be involved in a given situation. (2) Someone below a designated age.

civil arrest. Arrest for the purpose of treatment or protection, not because of the alleged commission of a crime.

civil law. (1) The law that governs rights and duties between private persons or between private persons and the government concerning matters other than the commission of a crime. (2) The law that applies in many Western European countries other than England.

Civil Rights Act. A federal statute that gives a citizen a right to sue a government employee who deprives the citizen of a federal right under color of state law.

class action. A lawsuit in which one or more members of a class sue (or are sued) as representative parties on behalf of everyone in the class, all of whom do not have to be joined in the lawsuit. If a prospective class member can decide not to join the class (i.e., can opt out), it is a *permissive class action*; if he or she cannot opt out, it is a *mandatory class action.*

coercion. The use of strength or pressure to secure compliance. If strong enough, the coercion can invalidate certain acts.

collateral source. Financial help to the victim of a tort that comes from a source that is independent of the trial of the tortfeasor. Examples include a health insurance policy of the victim and an employer who continues to pay the victim's salary.

The collateral source rule is that the amount of the damages caused by the tortfeasor is not reduced by any injury-related funds received by the plaintiff from collateral sources.

colloquium. The part of the complaint in which the plaintiff alleges that the defamatory statement was of and concerning the plaintiff.

color of law. Acting or pretending to act in an official, governmental capacity.

commercial speech. Communications made in the pursuit of business, e.g., product advertising.

common area. An area controlled by the landlord that is used by more than one tenant.

common law. Judge-made law created to cover a dispute before the court that is not governed by statute or other controlling law. *See also* at common law.

comparative negligence. In a negligence action against the defendant, if the injury was caused in part by the plaintiff's own negligence, the damages will be reduced in proportion to the plaintiff's negligence.

compensatory damages. Money compensation designed to make plaintiffs whole, to compensate them for actual loss or injury. They are designed to restore an injured party to his or her position prior to the injury or wrong.

complete. Total; confinement is complete if the victim knows of no safe or inoffensive means of escape from the boundaries set by the defendant.

component part. A part of a consumer product that is often manufactured by a company other than the assembler of the final product.

concert. An activity undertaken by mutual agreement.

conditional privilege. *See* privilege.

conditional threat. A threat to do something in the future if a specified event occurs.

confidential relationship. *See* fiduciary relationship.

confinement. The restraint of the plaintiff's physical movement.

consent. Express or implied agreement that something should happen or not happen.

consequential damages. See special damages.

consideration. Something of value that is exchanged between parties, e.g., an exchange of money for accounting services; an exchange of promises to do something or to refrain from doing something.

consortium. Love, affection, sexual relationship, and services that one spouse provides another.

conspiracy of silence. The reluctance or refusal of one member of a group to testify against another member.

constitutional malice. Knowledge that a defamatory statement is false, or recklessness as to its truth or falsity. Also called *actual malice.*

constitutional tort. A special cause of action that arises when someone is deprived of federal civil rights. Also called a *§ 1983 tort.*

contingent fee. A plaintiff's attorney fee that is dependent on the outcome of the case.

contract at will. *See* terminable at will.

contribution. The right of one tortfeasor who has paid a judgment to be proportionately reimbursed by other tortfeasors who have not paid their share of the damages caused by all the tortfeasors.

contributory negligence. The failure of the plaintiff to take reasonable precautions for his or her safety, helping to cause his or her own injury.

conversion. An intentional interference with personal property that is serious enough to force the wrongdoer to pay its full value.

cost of restoration. The amount of money damages that will restore property to its condition before the defendant's tort.

covenant not to sue. An agreement not to sue one of the joint tortfeasors, provided in lieu of a release.

crashworthiness. The design of the interior of a motor vehicle so that it can avoid or minimize injury after the vehicle has been hit from outside.

course of. *See* in the course of.

criminal conversation. The tort that occurs when the defendant has sexual relations with the plaintiff's spouse.

criminal law. The law that governs crimes alleged by the government.

cut-off test. A policy test to determine whether a person should be liable for what he or she has caused in fact. *See also* proximate cause.

culpability. Fault, blameworthiness, wrongfulness.

custom. What is commonly done. Also called *custom and usage.*

custom and usage. *See* custom.

cyberspace. The Internet and World Wide Web.

D

damage caps. Limitations on the amount of damages that can be awarded in tort cases.

damages. (1) Monetary payments awarded for a legally recognized wrong. (2) Actual harm or loss. *See also* compensatory damages, general damages, hedonic damages, nominal damages, punitive damages, and special damages.

dangerous propensities. A tendency to cause damage or harm because of prior acts or omissions causing damage or harm.

deceit. *See* misrepresentation.

deep pocket. An individual who has resources with which to pay a judgment. *See also* shallow pockets.

defamacast. Defamation communicated on the radio or TV.

defamation. The publication of a written defamatory statement (libel) or an oral defamatory statement (slander) of and concerning the plaintiff that causes damages. *See also* defamatory statement, disparagement.

defamatory statement. A statement of fact that would tend to harm the reputation of the plaintiff in the eyes of at least a substantial and respectable minority of people by lowering the plaintiff in the estimation of those people or by deterring them from associating with the plaintiff.

defective. Lacking in some essential; not meeting standards.

defense. The response of a party to a claim of another party, setting forth the reason(s) the claim should be denied.

defense of others. The use of reasonable force to prevent an immediate harmful or offensive contact against a third person by someone who is making an apparent threat of this contact.

defense of property. The right to use reasonable force to prevent an immediate interference or to end an interference with the possession of your personal property or land.

defensive medicine. Ordering precautionary tests and procedures intended primarily to shield doctors (or others in the medical field) from possible lawsuits.

derivative action. A plaintiff's action against a defendant to recover for a loss that is dependent on an underlying tort committed by that defendant against another plaintiff.

design defect. The product is dangerous because of the way in which it was conceived and planned.

disclaimer. Words or conduct that negate or limit a warranty. Repudiation of a claim.

disparagement. The intentional discrediting of a plaintiff's business (sometimes called *trade libel*) or title to property (sometimes called *slander of title*).

dispossession. Taking physical control of a chattel without the consent of the person who has possession but without exercising dominion over the chattel.

domestic animal. An animal that has been domesticated or habituated to live among humans.

dram shop liability. Civil liability imposed on the seller of intoxicating liquor to a buyer who then injures a third person. Sometimes applied also to a social host who gives intoxicating liquor.

dual-purpose trip. *See* mixed-purpose trip.

duress. Coercion; acting under the pressure of an unlawful act or threat.

duty. An obligation to conform to a standard of conduct prescribed by law. In most negligence cases, duty is the obligation to use reasonable care to avoid risks of injuring the person or property of others.

E

economic loss. An objectively verifiable monetary loss such as medical expense, burial expense, loss of earnings, and cost of repair. *See also* non-economic loss.

eggshell skull. An unusually high vulnerability to injury.

element. A portion of a rule that is one of the preconditions of the applicability of the entire rule. A cause of action is also a rule. Hence, a cause of action has elements. *See also* factor.

emancipated. Married or otherwise living independently from a parent or former legal guardian.

emotional distress. Mental anguish such as fright, worry, and humiliation.

employer/employee relationship. Employment. A work relationship between a person who hires someone and controls the goals and manner of his or her work. The person hiring is the employer; the person hired is the employee. A master/servant relationship.

employment. A work relationship in which the person hiring (the employer) controls the goals and manner of work of the person hired (the employee). *See also* scope of employment.

employment at will. An employment relationship that either the employee or the employer can terminate at any time for any reason without liability. An exception is that an employer cannot fire an employee at will for a reason that violates public policy such as a retaliatory discharge.

English rule. The party who loses the trial must pay the other side's attorney fees and other legal expenses. *See also* American rule.

enterprise liability. A system of spreading the costs of injuries over an entire industry or enterprise.

enticement of child. A tort involving serious interference with a parent's custody over his or her child.

enticement of spouse. A tort in which the defendant encourages the plaintiff's spouse to leave or to stay away from the plaintiff.

entrustment. The transfer of possession to someone's care. *See also* negligent entrustment.

estate. All the assets and debts left by a decedent.

exculpatory agreement. An agreement releasing a person from liability for wrongdoing.

exemplary damages. *See* punitive damages.

exempt. Not reachable to satisfy a debt or other obligation.

express assumption of risk. *See* assumption of risk.

express warranty. *See* warranty, breach of express.

extreme or outrageous conduct. Atrocious, totally intolerable, shocking behavior.

extrinsic fact. A fact not evident on the face of a statement that is needed to establish the defamatory meaning of the statement.

F

FACE. Free Access to Clinic Entrances Act. A federal statute that provides a remedy for victims of assault or other attack while trying to obtain reproductive health services.

fact. A concrete statement that can be objectively established as true or false. An express or implied communication containing concrete information that can be objectively shown to be true or false.

factor. One of the circumstances or considerations that will be weighed in making a decision, no one of which is usually conclusive. One of the considerations a court will examine to help it make a decision on whether a rule applies. Unlike elements, factors are not preconditions to the applicability of a rule.

fair comment. An observation or opinion on a matter of public interest. Fair comment is a qualified privilege to a defamation action.

fair competition. Honest, nonfraudulent rivalry in trade and commerce.

fair market value. What something would probably sell for in the ordinary course of a voluntary sale by a willing seller and a willing buyer.

fair on its face. No obvious or blatant flaws or irregularities.

fair report privilege. A newspaper or other media entity is not liable for defamation when it publishes fair and accurate stories on government reports and proceedings even if the stories contain defamatory statements made in the government reports or proceedings.

false arrest. An arrest for which the person taking someone into custody has no privilege.

false imprisonment. An intentional confinement within fixed boundaries set by the defendant.

false light. An inaccurate impression made by publicity about a person. It is highly offensive to a reasonable person.

family purpose doctrine. The owner of a car or person controlling the use of a car is liable for the negligence committed by a family member using the car for a family purpose.

fault. Wrongfulness, blameworthiness.

Federal Tort Claims Act. The federal statute that specifies the torts for which the federal government waives sovereign immunity.

fee caps. Limitations on the fees that attorneys can be paid in designated categories of cases.

fellow-employee rule. An employer is not liable for injuries caused by the negligence of one employee against another employee (unless the negligent employee was a vice principal).

felony. A crime that is punishable by incarceration for a term exceeding a year.

fiduciary relationship. The relationship that exists when one party (called the fiduciary) owes another loyalty, candor, and fair treatment. Also called a *confidential relationship*.

filial consortium. The right of a parent to the normal companionship and affection of a child.

financial responsibility law. Law requiring an operator or owner of a motor vehicle to give evidence of financial ability to meet claims for damages when he or she is involved in an accident.

first-party coverage. An insurance coverage under which policyholders collect compensation for their losses from their own insurer rather than from the insurer of the person who caused the accident.

fitness for a particular purpose. *See* warranty of fitness for a particular purpose.

foreseeable. Having the quality of being seen or known beforehand.

foreseeable use. *See* use.

foreseeable users. Those persons who a manufacturer or retailer can reasonably anticipate will use the product.

foreseeable plaintiff. Someone who the defendant can anticipate will be within the zone of danger.

fraud. *See* misrepresentation.

fresh pursuit. Going after someone or something promptly, without undue delay.

frolic and detour. Acts of an employee performed for the employee's personal objectives rather than primarily for the employer's business.

G

general damages. Compensatory damages that usually result from the kind of harm caused by the conduct of the defendant. Damages that usually and naturally flow from this wrong, e.g., pain and suffering. The law implies or presumes that such damages result from the wrong complained of. General damages differ from special damages, which are awarded for actual economic loss, such as medical costs and loss of income.

general rule on duty. Whenever your conduct creates a foreseeable risk of injury or damage to someone else's person or property, you owe a duty to take reasonable precautions to prevent that injury or damage.

going-and-coming rule. Workers' compensation is denied if the employee is injured "off the premises" while going to or coming back from work or lunch.

Good Samaritan. A person who comes to the aid of another without a legal obligation to do so.

governmental function. A function that can be performed adequately *only* by the government. Unlike a proprietary function.

gratuitous. Not involving payment or consideration; free.

gross negligence. The failure to use even a small amount of care to avoid foreseeable harm.

guest. Someone invited or allowed to be present for a non-business reason.

H

harmful. Involving physical or actual damage, impairment, pain, or illness in the body.

heart-balm statute. A statute that has abolished actions for breach of promise to marry, alienation of affections, criminal conversation, enticement, and seduction of a person under the age of consent.

hedonic damages. Damages that cover the victim's loss of pleasure or enjoyment.

helpless peril. A predicament created by the plaintiff's contributory negligence that he or she cannot get him- or herself out of.

highly extraordinary. Unusually rare.

highly offensive. Extremely distasteful or unpleasant to a reasonable person.

hypothesis. An assumption that is subject to be verified or proven.

I

imminent. Immediate in the sense of no significant or undue delay.

immunity. A defense that renders otherwise tortious conduct nontortious. The right to be free from civil or criminal prosecution.

impeach. Discredit or attack.

implied assumption of risk. *See* assumption of risk.

implied warranty. *See* entries under *Warranty*.

imputed. Attributed to or imposed on someone or something.

imputed contributory negligence. The contributory negligence of a person involved in an accident is attributed to and imposed on the plaintiff.

imputed negligence. Negligence liability attributed or imposed solely because of the wrongdoing of others.

inattentive peril. A predicament created by the plaintiff's contributory negligence that he or she could get him- or herself out of by the use of reasonable care but the plaintiff is negligently unaware of this peril.

incident to the job. Sufficiently connected to employment.

increased-risk test. The risk of injury to the employee is quantitatively greater than the risk of injury to nonemployees (a causal connection test for workers' compensation).

indemnity. The right to have another person pay you the full amount you were forced to pay. In the law of insurance, indemnity is the transfer of loss from an insured to an insurer to the extent of the agreed-upon insurance proceeds to cover the loss.

independent contractor. Someone who is hired or retained to produce a certain product or result. This person has considerable discretion in the methods used to achieve that product or result. The person is not an employee.

independent liability. Personal liability based on what an individual did or failed to do him- or herself. The opposite of vicarious liability.

indivisible. Not separable into parts; pertaining to that which cannot be divided.

inducement. The part of the complaint alleging extrinsic facts in a defamation action.

informed consent. Sufficient information provided so that the person can weigh the benefits and liabilities of taking certain action.

inherently dangerous. Being susceptible to harm or injury in the nature of the product, service, or activity itself.

initiate. To instigate, urge on, or incite.

injunction. A court order requiring a person to do or to refrain from doing a particular thing.

injurious falsehood. The publication of a false statement that causes special damages.

injury. *See* physical injury.

in loco parentis. "In the place of the parent"; assuming some or all the duties of a parent.

innocently. Done without negligence, intent, recklessness, malice, or other wrongful state of mind.

innuendo. The explanation of the defamatory meaning of words alleged by inducement in the complaint.

instigation. Insisting, directing, or encouraging.

insurance. A contract (called an insurance policy) under which a company agrees to compensate a person (up to a specific amount) for a loss caused by designated perils. *See also* liability insurance.

insured. The person designated as being protected against specified loss under an insurance policy.

intangible. *See* tangible.

intended use. *See* use.

intent. The desire to bring about the consequences of an act (or omission), or the substantially certain knowledge that the consequences will follow from the act (or omission).

intentional infliction of emotional distress. Intentionally causing severe emotional distress by an act of extreme or outrageous conduct. This tort is also called the tort of *outrage*.

intentional tort. A tort in which a person either desired to bring about the result or knew with substantial certainty that the result would follow from what the person did or failed to do.

interest. (1) A right, claim, or legal share of or in something. (2) The object of any human desire.

interference with contract relations. The tort of inducing a breach of contract.

interference with prospective advantage. The tort of interfering with a reasonable expectation of an economic advantage.

intermeddling. Making physical contact with a chattel.

Internet. A self-governing network of networks to which millions of computer users all over the world have access.

interspousal immunity. Spouses cannot sue each other for designated categories of torts.

intervening cause. A force that produces harm after the defendant's act or omission. An *intervening force of nature* is a subsequent natural occurrence that is independent of human interference; it is an act of God. An *intervening innocent human force* is a subsequent occurrence caused by a human being who was not careless or wrongful. An *intervening intentional or criminal force* is a subsequent occurrence caused intentionally or criminally by a human being. An *intervening negligent human force* is a subsequent occurrence negligently caused by a human being.

intervening force of nature. *See* intervening cause.

intervening innocent human force. *See* intervening cause.

intervening intentional or criminal human force. *See* intervening cause.

intervening negligent human force. *See* intervening cause.

intestacy. Dying without leaving a valid will.

in the course of. Occurring while at work or in the service of the employer; pertaining to the time, place, and circumstances of the injury or disease in connection with the employment. *See also* workers' compensation.

intrafamily tort. A tort committed by one family member against another.

intrafamily tort immunity. Family members cannot sue each other for designated categories of torts.

intrusion. (a) An unreasonable encroachment into an individual's private affairs or concerns. One of the invasion of privacy torts. Also called *intrusion on seclusion*. (b) Physically going on land, remaining on the land, going to a prohibited portion of the land, or failing to remove goods from the land. One of the elements of trespass to land.

invasion of privacy. *See* appropriation, false light, intrusion, and public disclosure of private fact.

invitee. One who enters the land upon the express or implied invitation of the occupier of the land, in order to use the land for the purposes for which it is held open to the public or to pursue the business of the occupier.

J

joint and several liability. Each wrongdoer (defendant) is liable for all the damages suffered by the plaintiff, who can sue any or all of the defendants until 100 percent of his or her damages are recovered.

joint enterprise. An express or implied agreement to participate in a common enterprise (usually of a financial or business nature) in which the participants have a mutual right of control. A joint venture.

joint tortfeasors. Persons who together produce a tortious wrong.

joint venture. A mutually undertaken activity in which each person participates. *See* joint enterprise.

judgment creditor. The person to whom a money judgment is owed.

judgment debtor. The person who owes a money judgment to another.

judgment proof. Having few or no assets from which a money judgment can be satisfied.

jurisdiction. The power of a court. Its *personal* jurisdiction is its power to order a particular defendant to do or to refrain from doing something. Its *subject matter* jurisdiction is its power to hear certain kinds of cases.

just compensation. The fair payment for property "taken" by the government for a public purpose.

justifiable reliance. Being reasonable in taking action (or in refraining from taking action) because of what someone has said or done.

K

knowledge with substantial certainty. A high degree of knowledge; having no more than very minimal doubt about a result that will flow from what you do or fail to do.

L

last clear chance. The opportunity to avoid the accident at the last moment in spite of the contributory negligence of the plaintiff.

latent. Not readily visible; hidden.

legal authority. (1) The power of the government; the right to do something. (2) Any law (primary authority) or nonlaw (secondary authority) on which a tribunal can rely to help it resolve a legal dispute before it.

legal cause. *See* proximate cause.

legal malpractice. Professional misconduct or wrongdoing by attorneys. *See also* malpractice.

legal remedy. A method of enforcing a legal right or redressing the violation of a legal right. *See also* adequate remedy at law; remedy.

legislative intent. The purpose of the legislature in enacting a particular statute.

legitimate public interest. Newsworthy; information the general public would like to have.

lessee. Person renting property from another.

lessor. Person renting property to another.

liability. The imposition of legal responsibility for something.

liability insurance. Insurance in which the insurer agrees to pay, on behalf of an insured, damages the latter is obligated to pay to a third party because of his or her legal liability to the third person for committing a tort or other wrong. *See also* insurance.

liability without fault. *See* strict liability.

liable. Legally responsible; under an obligation to pay for a wrong committed.

libel. Defamation that is written or embodied in a physical form. *See also* defamation.

libel per quod. A written statement that requires extrinsic facts to understand its defamatory meaning.

libel per se. A written defamatory statement that is actionable without proof that the plaintiff suffered special damages.

licensee. One who enters the land for his or her own purposes, but with the express or implied consent of the occupier.

limitation of liability. A modification of responsibility that would otherwise apply to harm that is caused.

local standard. (1) A doctor is required to have and use the equipment, knowledge, and experience that doctors have and use locally or in localities similar to the community where the defendant-doctor practices. (2) Evaluation based on what is acceptable locally rather than nationally.

Lord Campbell's Act. A statute that allowed a separate cause of action for a tort that caused the death of the victim.

loss of consortium. See consortium; derivative action.

loss of services. An action by a parent for interference with an unemancipated child's ability to perform household chores and other tasks for the parent. *See also* derivative action.

lump sum judgment. One payment at the end of the trial to cover all past and future damages.

M

made whole. Restored to the condition before the wrong was committed against the victim insofar as this is possible.

malfeasance. Wrongful or illegal actions by a public official.

malice. (1) Ill will, hatred, or a desire to harm. (2) Recklessness. (3) Knowledge of consequences. (4) Improper motive.

malicious. Acting with malice. *See also* malice.

malicious prosecution. The initiation or procurement of legal proceedings without probable cause and with an improper motive. The proceedings terminate in favor of the accused.

malpractice. Professional misconduct or wrongdoing consisting of ethical violations, criminal conduct, negligence, battery, or other tort. *See also* legal malpractice, medical malpractice.

mandatory offset. A required reduction of damages by a designated amount. A *permissive offset* is a reduction of damages that is allowed but not required.

manner. A method or way of performing a task.

manufacturer. A business that makes a product.

manufacturing defect. The product is dangerous because of the way in which it was assembled; the product does not conform to its design.

market share. The proportion of the market attributable to the sales of a particular company.

market share liability. Legal responsibility according to the proportion of the market attributable to the sales of a particular company.

mass tort. A tort cause of action asserted by a large number of persons who have been harmed by the same or similar conduct or product of a relatively small number of defendants.

master/servant relationship. A work association in which one person (the master or principal) hires another (the servant or agent) to perform work, the master controls the goals and manner of the servant's work. An employer/employee relationship.

material. Important to a transaction or event.

med-arb. A method of alternative dispute resolution in which the parties first try mediation, and if it does not work, they try arbitration. *See also* alternative dispute resolution; arbitration; mediation.

mediation. A method of alternative dispute resolution in which the parties submit their dispute to a neutral third person who helps the parties reach their own decision to resolve the dispute. *See also* alternative dispute resolution.

medical malpractice. Professional misconduct or wrongdoing by doctors. *See also* malpractice.

merchant. Someone in the business of selling.

merchantable. Fit for the ordinary purposes for which the goods are used. *See also* warranty of merchantability.

merits. *See* on the merits.

method. The means used to accomplish something; the manner of performing a task.

misdemeanor. A crime that is punishable by incarceration for a term of a year or less.

misfeasance. Improper or unreasonable action.

misrepresentation. A false statement of fact made with the intent to mislead and to have the plaintiff rely on the statement. The plaintiff suffers actual damage due to justifiable reliance on the statement. Also called deceit and fraud.

mistake. An error; an unintentional act or omission.

misuse. The improper use of a product. Misuse is not a defense if the product was being used for its intended or foreseeable use.

mitigate the consequences. Take steps to lessen the damages or other impact of an injury.

mixed-purpose trip. A trip taken by an employee that has both a business and a personal purpose. Also called a *dual-purpose trip*.

motive. The emotion, feeling, or need that induces a particular action or inaction.

N

National Practitioner Data Bank. A collection of information about doctors who have been defendants in malpractice cases and have paid claimants through settlement or litigation.

national standard. (1) A doctor is required to have and use the equipment, knowledge, and experience that doctors have and use nationally. (2) Evaluation based on what is acceptable nationally rather than locally.

necessity. The privilege to make a reasonable use of someone's property to prevent immediate threat of harm or damage to persons or property. If the threat is to private interests, the privileged use is a *private necessity*. If the threat is to the public, the privileged use is a *public necessity*.

negligence. Harm caused by the failure to use reasonable care. *Ordinary negligence* consists of unreasonable conduct that is not egregious or reckless. *Wilful, wanton, or reckless negligence* consists of unreasonable conduct that creates a very great risk that harm will result; acting with the knowledge that the harm will probably result. *See also* gross negligence.

negligent entrustment. Carelessly allowing someone to use a vehicle, tool, or other object that poses an unreasonable risk of harm to others.

negligent hiring. Carelessly (rather than intentionally) hiring an incompetent person who poses an unreasonable risk of harm to others.

negligent infliction of emotional distress (NIED). Carelessly causing someone to suffer emotional distress.

negligently. Taking unreasonable risks. *See also* negligence.

negligent misrepresentation. An action for the careless communication of a false statement of fact brought by someone to whom the statement was intended to reach.

negligent per se. Negligent as a matter of law. There is no need to present evidence that the acts and omissions were unreasonable.

newsworthy. Pertaining to information the general public would like to have; pertaining to matters of legitimate public interest.

NIED. *See* negligent infliction of emotional distress.

1983 action. A suit based on § 1983 of the Civil Rights Act of 1871 against a government employee who deprives someone of federal rights under color of state law. The deprivation is called a 1983 tort.

1983 tort. *See* 1983 action.

no-fault insurance. A motor vehicle insurance plan in which each person's own insurance company pays for injury or damage up to a certain limit, regardless of whether its insured was at fault.

no-fault system. A method of providing compensation for damage or injury that is not based on which side carelessly or wrongfully caused the damage or injury. Compensation is based on proving causation and the loss being within prescribed limits.

nolle prosequi. A statement by the district attorney that he or she is unwilling to prosecute an individual for the commission of a crime.

nominal damages. A small monetary payment (often $1) awarded when the defendant has committed a tort that has resulted in little or no harm so that no compensatory damages are due.

non-delegable duty. A task considered so important or critical that you are liable for injury or damage caused by performing the task even if you hire an independent contractor to perform it.

non-economic loss. A non-monetary harm such as emotional pain, suffering, inconvenience, mental anguish, loss of enjoyment of life, loss of companionship, damage to reputation, and humiliation. A nonpecuniary loss.

nonfeasance. The failure to act; an omission.

nonpecuniary losses. Mental suffering and grief. *See also* non-economic loss.

notice. (1) Formal notification sent or otherwise communicated. (2) Information or knowledge obtained by observation.

nuisance. A *private nuisance* is a substantial interference with the reasonable use and enjoyment of private land. A *public nuisance* is an unreasonable interference with a right common to the general public.

O

objective. Goal or purpose. *See also* objective standard.

objective standard. Measuring something by comparing it to something else. Assessing the behavior of a person by comparing what he or she did with what another person or persons would have done. In negligence, comparing what the defendant did or failed to do with what a reasonable person would have done under the same or similar circumstances. A *subjective standard* measures something solely by what one individual (e.g., the defendant) actually did, knew, believed, or understood.

occupier. Anyone in possession of land claiming a right to possession.

of and concerning the plaintiff. One of the elements of defamation that requires the defamatory communication to be reasonably understood by the recipient to refer to the plaintiff.

offensive. Offending the personal dignity of an ordinary person who is not unduly sensitive.

official immunity. Government employees are not personally liable for torts or other wrongdoing they commit within the scope of their employment.

on its face. Without reference to extrinsic facts. *See also* extrinsic fact.

online. Being connected to a host computer or information service—usually through telephone lines.

on the merits. Based on a substantive decision of who is in the right as opposed to being based on a preliminary, technical, or procedural matter.

opinion. (1) An express or implied communication containing a relatively vague or indefinite value judgment that is not objectively verifiable. (2) A court's written explanation of its decision. Also called a *case*.

ordinary negligence. *See* negligence.

out-of-pocket. Pertaining to amounts actually paid or to be paid to cover losses.

out-of-pocket rule. A measure of damages that gives the plaintiff the difference between the value of what he or she parted with and the value of what was received.

outrage, tort of. *See* intentional infliction of emotional distress.

outrageous and extreme conduct. Atrocious, totally intolerable, shocking behavior.

P

pain and suffering. Emotional distress; disagreeable mental or emotional experience. Part of general damages.

parasitic. Attached to something else, e.g., another tort.

parasitic damages. Damages for mental anguish (pain and suffering) that attach to a physical injury.

parental consortium. The right of a child to the normal companionship and affection of a parent.

passenger. Someone riding in a car who confers a benefit on the driver, other than the benefit of social company.

peace officer. A person appointed by the government to keep the peace.

peace of mind. The lack of anguish due to serious interference.

peculiar-risk test. The source of the harm is peculiar to the employment (a causal connection test for workers' compensation).

pecuniary loss. A money loss. Examples include cost of repair and the amount needed to replace the loss of support and services that would have been received.

percentage fee. Payment in the form of a percentage of the amount involved in the award, settlement, or transaction.

per diem argument. A certain amount is requested as damages for every day that pain and suffering has been endured and is expected to continue. Also called the *unit-of-time argument*.

permissive offset. *See* mandatory offset.

person. (1) A human being or a business. (2) For purposes of battery, one's body, something attached to the body, or something so closely associated with the body as to be identified with it.

personal liability. Damages paid by the wrongdoer out of his or her own pocket.

personal property. *See* property.

personal property tort. *See* tort.

personal tort. *See* tort.

physical impact. Actual contact.

physical injury. A wound, cut, or other detrimental change to the body. *See also* emotional distress.

physician-patient relationship. The relationship that arises when a doctor undertakes to render medical services in response to an express or implied request for services by the patient or by the patient's guardian.

PI. Personal injury.

pleading. A pretrial paper or document filed in court stating the position of one of the parties on the cause(s) of action or on the defense(s).

plenary trial. A complete trial.

points and authorities memorandum. *See* memorandum of law.

polling. Asking each juror if he or she agrees with the verdict read.

positional-risk test. The injury of the employee would not have occurred but for the fact that the job placed the employee in a position where the employee could be injured (a causal connection test for workers' compensation).

possessory interest. Anyone who has a present or future right to possess land.

preempt. Be controlling over.

pre-existing injuries or diseases. The injuries or diseases that existed prior to the time in question, e.g., prior to the employment of someone claiming workers' compensation benefits.

premises liability. The liability of landowners and others with possessory interests in land for injuries suffered in connection with the land.

preponderance of the evidence. The standard of proof according to which a party must prove that its version of a fact is more likely true than not.

present cash value. *See* present value.

present value. The amount of money an individual would have to be given now in order to produce or generate, through prudent investment, a certain amount of money within a designated period of time. Also called present cash value.

presumed damages. Damages that a jury is allowed to assume were suffered by the plaintiff, who does not have to introduce specific evidence that these damages were in fact suffered.

presumption. An assumption of fact that can be drawn when another fact (or set of facts) is established. The presumption is *rebuttable* if a party is allowed to introduce evidence that the assumption is false.

prima facie case. Enough factual allegations by a party to cover every element of a cause of action.

prima facie tort. Intentionally inflicting harm that causes special damages.

primary assumption of risk. *See* assumption of risk.

primary insurance. Insurance that pays compensation for a loss ahead of any other insurance coverage the policyholder may have.

principal/agent. The principal is the person on whose behalf an agent is acting; the principal has authority or control over the agent while the agent is acting for the principal.

private affairs. Information that is not of legitimate public concern. Non-newsworthy facts.

private citizen. Someone who is not employed by, an agent of, or acting for the government.

private necessity. *See* necessity.

private nuisance. *See* nuisance.

private person. Someone who is not a public official or a public figure.

privilege. (1) The right of an individual to act contrary to the right of another individual without being subject to tort or other liability. A defense to a tort. An *absolute privilege* is a privilege that cannot be lost because of the bad motives of the party asserting the privilege. A *qualified privilege* (also called a *conditional privilege*) is a privilege that can be lost if it is improperly asserted. (2) The right to exclude otherwise admissible evidence.

privileged competition. Business competition that uses no unfair or illegal methods.

privilege to recapture. The right to use reasonable force to obtain the return of personal property (chattels) shortly after someone obtained them wrongfully.

privity. The relationship that exists between two parties who directly enter a contract with each other.

probable cause. (a) A suspicion based upon the appearance of circumstances that are strong enough to allow a reasonable person to believe that a criminal charge against a person is true. (b) Reasonable cause to believe that good grounds exist to initiate a civil proceeding.

pro bono. Free.

products liability. A general term that covers different causes of action based on products that cause harm: negligence, breach of express warranty, misrepresentation, breach of implied warranty of fitness for a particular purpose, breach of implied warranty of merchantability, and strict liability in tort.

promise. A declaration asserting that something will or will not be done.

property. *Real property* is land and anything attached to the land. *Personal property* is every other kind of property. *See also* tangible.

proprietary. Concerning a function that cannot be performed adequately *only* by the government—unlike a governmental function.

prosecution. (1) Bringing any court action, civil or criminal. (2) Bringing a criminal action. (3) The government attorney bringing a criminal action.

proximate cause. The defendant is the cause in fact of the plaintiff's injury, the injury was the foreseeable consequence of the original risk, and there is no policy reason why the defendant should not be liable for what he or she caused in fact. Proximate cause is also referred to as the *legal cause*.

proximate-cause test. The injury is foreseeable and no intervening factor breaks the chain of causation between the conditions of employment and the injury (a causal connection test for workers' compensation).

publication. Communication of a statement to someone other than the plaintiff.

public disclosure of private fact. Unreasonable disclosure of private facts about an individual's life that are not matters of legitimate public concern.

public figure. A non-government employee who has assumed special prominence in the affairs of society. A public figure for all purposes is a person of general power, influence, or notoriety. A public figure for a limited purpose is a person who has voluntarily become involved in a controversy of interest to the general public.

public necessity. *See* necessity.

public nuisance. *See* nuisance.

public official. A government employee who has significant authority.

public policy. The principle inherent in the customs, morals, and notions of justice in a state. Principles that are naturally right and just.

publicity. Communication to the public at large, to more than a few people.

puffing. An expected exaggeration of quality.

punitive damages. Non-compensatory damages designed to punish the defendant and deter similar conduct by others. Also called *exemplary damages*.

Q

qualified official immunity. A government employee will not be personally liable for his or her torts or other wrongdoing committed within the scope of employment so long as he or she does not act with malice. Also called conditional official immunity.

qualified privilege. *See* privilege.

R

real property. *See* property.

real property tort. *See* tort.

reasonable. Pertaining to what a reasonable person would or would not do. *See also* reasonable person. Pertaining to someone who is not unduly sensitive.

reasonable alternative design. An available design that a manufacturer could have reasonably used that would have been less dangerous than the design that caused the injury.

reasonable beneficial use. Space above and below the surface of land to which reasonable use can be made.

reasonable care. Conduct that a reasonable person would follow to avoid injury or harm to others.

reasonable doctor standard. A doctor must follow the standards of the profession as to how much information about the risks and benefits of a proposed treatment would be disclosed to a patient with the plaintiff's condition.

reasonable patient standard. A doctor must disclose information about the risks and benefits of a proposed treatment that a reasonable patient with the plaintiff's condition would wish to know.

reasonable person. An ordinary, prudent person who uses reasonable care to avoid injuring others. An ordinary person who is not unduly sensitive.

reasonably safe. As free from danger as is reasonably possible.

recapture. To obtain the return of possession. *See also* privilege to recapture.

recapture of chattels. *See* privilege to recapture.

reckless. Creating a very great risk that something will happen. Acting with the knowledge that harm will probably result. Totally outside the range of the ordinary activity.

reckless disregard. Consciously ignoring something such as whether a fact is true or false.

recklessly. Acting in conscious disregard of something.

recklessness. A very high degree of carelessness.

release. The giving up or relinquishing of a claim.

reliance. (1) Placing faith or confidence in someone or something. (2) Forming a belief, taking action, or refraining from action in part due to confidence in someone or something. *See also* justifiable reliance.

remedy. (1) A means by which the enforcement of a right is sought or the violation of a right is compensated for or otherwise redressed. (2) Relief; a solution.

remedy at law. A remedy available in a court of law (e.g., damages) as opposed to one available in a court of equity (e.g., injunction).

republication. Repetition of a defamatory statement originally made by someone else. *See also* publication.

respondeat superior. "Let the master answer." Rule by which an employer is liable for the torts of the employee committed within the scope of employment.

retaliatory discharge. Dismissing someone from a job for a reason that violates public policy, e.g., for reporting a fire hazard at work.

reversionary interest. The right to the future enjoyment of land that is presently occupied by another.

risk-benefit analysis. Do the risks outweigh the benefits? The determination of whether the foreseeability of serious harm outweighs the burden or inconvenience of avoiding that harm in light of the value or social utility of the product. Also called *risk-utility analysis*.

risk-utility analysis. *See* risk-benefit analysis.

Rylands v. Fletcher. The case holding that if the defendant knows he or she is engaging in a non-natural or abnormal use of land that creates an increased danger to persons or property, the defendant will be strictly liable for harm caused by this use.

S

sale. The passing of title to property from a seller to a buyer for a price.

satisfaction. Full payment or compensation.

scienter. The intent to mislead. Making a statement while knowing it is false, or without a belief in its truth, or in reckless disregard of its truth or falsity—with the desire that the statement be believed and relied upon.

scope of employment. That which is foreseeably done by an employee for the employer under the employer's specific or general control.

screening panel. A group of individuals who will examine a case before it can be litigated in court. The panel can often make recommendations and encourage the parties to settle.

secondary assumption of risk. *See* assumption of risk.

secondary authority. *See* authority.

§ 402A. The main section on strict liability in tort from *Restatement (Second) of Torts*.

seduction. The tort of engaging in sexual relations with the plaintiff's daughter.

self-defense. The use of reasonable force to prevent an immediate harmful or offensive contact against you by someone who is making an apparent threat of this contact.

self-help. Preventive or corrective steps taken by the victim of a tort or other wrong on his or her own without resort to the courts.

self-insurance. The ability to pay workers' compensation benefits out of one's own funds rather than through an insurance policy.

seller. (1) Anyone in the business of selling. *See also* merchant. (2) A person who sells something. *See also* sale.

servant. *See* master/servant relationship.

services. (1) Activities performed or benefits provided as part of one's line of work. (2) Household chores and other tasks an unemancipated child owes his or her parent. *See also* loss of services.

shallow pockets. Individuals without resources from which a judgment can be collected. *See also* deep pockets.

shopkeeper's privilege. The right of a merchant to detain someone temporarily for the sole purpose of investigating whether the person has committed any theft against the merchant.

sine qua non test. *See* but-for test.

slander. Defamation that is spoken or gestured. *See also* defamation.

slander of title. *See* disparagement.

slander per quod. (1) An oral defamatory statement that does not fit into one of the four categories that constitute slander per se. (2) An oral defamatory statement that requires extrinsic facts to understand its defamatory meaning.

SLAPP suit. Strategic Lawsuit Against Public Participation. A meritless suit brought primarily for the purpose of chilling the defendant's exercise of the right to free speech and to petition the government for a redress of grievances.

social guest. Someone who has express or implied permission to be present, primarily for a nonbusiness purpose.

social value. Quality as measured by the general public good.

sovereign immunity. The government cannot be sued without its permission.

special damages. Actual economic or pecuniary losses, such as medical expenses and lost wages. Also called *consequential damages*.

special relationship. A relationship that the law considers sufficiently important to impose a duty of reasonable care even in the absence of affirmative conduct.

spectrum of foreseeability. The extent to which something can be anticipated.

speech. *See* commercial speech.

standing. The right to bring a court action because of the sufficiency of one's personal interest in the outcome of the proposed court action or because of a special statute that gives this right.

standard of care. The degree of care that the law requires in a particular case. In most cases, the standard is what a reasonably prudent person would exercise under the same or similar circumstances. *See also* local standard, national standard.

standard of proof. The degree to which evidence of something must be convincing before a fact finder can accept it as true.

statute of limitations. A law that designates a time period within which a lawsuit must be commenced or it can never be brought.

strict liability. Liability or responsibility for harm whether or not the person causing the harm displayed any fault or moral impropriety. Also called *absolute liability* and *liability without fault*.

strict liability for abnormally dangerous conditions or activities. Liability for harm caused by abnormally dangerous conditions or activities whether the person causing the harm acted intentionally, negligently, or innocently.

strict liability in tort. Physical harm caused by a defective product that is unreasonably dangerous.

structured settlement. An agreement in which the defendant pays for damages he or she caused by making periodic payments for a designated period of time such as during the life of the victim. The payments are often funded through an annuity.

subjective standard. *See* objective standard.

subrogation. The process by which one insurance company seeks reimbursement from another company or person for a claim it has already paid.

substantial factor. A significant role.

substantial factor test. A person has caused something if his or her act or omission had a significant role in bringing it about.

substantially certain knowledge. *See* knowledge with substantial certainty.

summary judgment. A decision based on the pleadings, facts revealed through discovery, and other facts placed in the record, without going through a trial, because there is no genuine dispute on any material facts.

superseding cause. An intervening cause that is beyond the foreseeable risk originally created by the defendant's unreasonable acts or omissions. An intervening cause that creates a highly extraordinary harm.

survival. The continuation of a cause of action such as a tort after the death of either the victim or the alleged wrongdoer.

T

taking of property. The forced acquisition of private property by the government for a public purpose for which the government must pay just compensation.

tangible. Pertaining to that with which we can make contact with our senses such as touch. Having a physical form that can be seen or touched. Intangible refers to what cannot be perceived by the senses; property without physical form. Rights are intangible.

terminable at will. Something (e.g., a contract) that can be ended at any time for any reason without liability.

testate. Die leaving a valid will.

tolled. Suspended or stopped temporarily.

tort. A civil wrong (other than a breach of contract) that causes injury or other damage for which our legal system deems it just to provide a remedy such as compensation. A *personal tort* injures the person. A *personal property tort* damages movable property not attached to the land. A *real property tort* damages land and anything attached to the land.

tortfeasor. A person who has committed a tort.

tortious. Involving the commission of a tort.

tortious interference with employment. A wrongful discharge. Terminating employment for a reason that violates public policy.

toxic tort. Personal injury or property damage wrongfully caused by chronic or repeated exposure to toxic substances such as chemicals, biological agents, or radiation.

trade libel. *See* disparagement.

transferred intent. The defendant's intent to commit a tortious act against one person is transferred to the person who was in fact the object of this intent. Also, if the defendant intends to commit one tort but in fact commits another, the law may transfer the intent to cover the tort that was committed.

trespasser. One who enters land without the consent of the occupier and without any privilege to do so.

trespass to chattels. An intentional interference with personal property resulting in dispossession or intermeddling.

trespass to land. An intentional intrusion on land in possession of another.

trial within a trial. To win a legal malpractice case against an attorney, the plaintiff must establish that he or she would have won the case that the attorney lost if the attorney had not acted negligently.

U

unavoidably unsafe product. A product that cannot be made safe by using current technology and science.

unconscionable. Substantially unfair because of highly unequal bargaining positions of the parties.

undertaking. Doing something; a task.

unemancipated. Still under the control of a parent.

unfair competition. Dishonest or fraudulent rivalry in trade and commerce.

unforeseeable plaintiff. A plaintiff who was not in the zone of danger. A plaintiff whose presence could not have been reasonably anticipated.

Uniform Commercial Code. The statute that governs commercial transactions in most states.

unit-of-time argument. *See* per diem argument.

unreasonable. *See* unreasonableness.

unreasonable conduct. *See* unreasonableness.

unreasonableness. The failure to act as a reasonable person would have acted under the same or similar circumstances. A breach of the duty of care.

unreasonable risks. Those risks that a reasonable person would not undertake because of the danger of harm.

unreasonably dangerous. Containing a risk of injury that a reasonable person would take reasonable precautions against.

use. The *intended* use of a product is what the manufacturer wanted the product used for; its *foreseeable* use is what the manufacturer anticipates or should anticipate the product will be used for.

V

veggie libel. A cause of action created by statute that allows producers of perishable food products to sue when they lose business because of false statements that disparage the safety of their products.

vendee. Buyer.

vendor. Seller.

viable. Capable of surviving indefinitely outside the womb of the mother by natural or artificial support systems.

vicariously liable. Being responsible for a tort solely because of what someone else has done.

vice principal. An employee with supervisory authority over other employees.

voidable. Terminable and unenforceable at the option of someone.

volenti non fit injuria. "No wrong is done to one who consents."

W

waiver. The loss of a right or privilege because of an explicit rejection of it or because of a failure to claim it at the appropriate time.

wanton. Extreme recklessness.

warning defect. The product is dangerous because its instructions or warnings are ineffective.

warrant. A written order issued by an authorized government body directing the arrest of a person.

warranty. A guarantee; a commitment imposed by contract or by law that a product or service will meet a specified standard.

warranty, breach of express. Damage caused by a false statement of fact relied on by the plaintiff and made with the intention or expectation that the statement will reach the plaintiff.

warranty of fitness for a particular purpose, breach of implied. Damage caused by a sale of goods by a seller who had reason to know the buyer was relying on the expertise of the seller in selecting the goods for a particular purpose. The goods were not fit for that purpose.

warranty of merchantability, breach of implied. Damage caused by a sale of goods by a merchant of goods of that kind. The goods were not fit for the ordinary purposes for which they are used.

weight of the evidence. The amount and believability of the evidence.

whole. *See* made whole.

wild animal. An animal in the state of nature.

willful. (1) Knowing. (2) Acting with the knowledge that the harm will probably result. (3) Malicious.

willful, wanton, and reckless conduct. Actions or omissions of a person who knowingly creates a great risk of harm, or consciously ignores obvious risks of harm, or who is being malicious.

windfall. An extra amount to which you are not entitled under the original understanding of the parties.

workers' compensation. A no-fault system of covering the cost of medical care and weekly income payments of an insured employee if he or she is injured or killed on the job, regardless of blame for the accident.

world at large. The Andrews test of duty. *See* Andrews test.

World Wide Web. A tool that allows you to navigate locations on the Internet that are often linked by hypertext.

wrongful adoption. Wrongfully stating or failing to disclose to prospective adoptive parents any available facts on the health or other condition of a child that would be relevant to their decision to adopt the child.

wrongful birth. An action by parents of an unwanted deformed or impaired child for their own damages in the birth of the child.

wrongful civil proceedings. The initiation or procurement of civil legal proceedings without a reasonable belief that good grounds exist for the proceedings, which ultimately terminate in favor of the person against whom they were brought.

wrongful death. A death caused by a tort. *See also* Lord Campbell's Act.

wrongful discharge. Terminating employment for a reason that violates public policy. Tortious interference with employment.

wrongful life. An action by or on behalf of an unwanted deformed or impaired child for its own damages in being born.

wrongful pregnancy. An action by parents of a healthy child they did not want. Also called *wrongful conception.*

Z

zone of danger. The area within which it is foreseeable that someone may be injured.